2016 Copyright M.Stow

The End of The Universe: Universal Verses One: Stellation

Universal Verses1: in three-parts: Stellation

1. Stellation...

2. The Universal-Axial.

3. Universal-Axial Stellation.

1. At first there was neither being nor non-being.
There was not air nor yet sky beyond.
What was its wrapping? Where? In whose protection?
Was water there, unfathomable and deep?

2. There was no death then, nor yet deathlessness;
of night or day there was not any sign.
The One breathed without breath, by its own impulse.
Other than that was nothing else at all.

3. Darkness was there, all wrapped around in darkness,
And all was water indiscriminate: then
That which was hidden by the Void, that One emerging,
Stirring, through power of Ardor, came to be.

4. In the beginning Love arose,
Which was the primal germ cell of the mind.
The Seers, searching in their hearts with wisdom,
Discovered the connection of Beings with Nonbeing.

Rig Veda (around 1400 BCE India) X, HYMN CXXIX. Creation.

The End of the Universe: Universal Verses1: Stellation: in three-parts:

1. Stellation

2. Universal Axial:

3. *Universal Axial: Stellation.*

1. Stellation: in three-parts:

      -Welcome to The-Universe: The End of The Universe:
Between nothing and the start of everything else: without so much of a Big
Bang! As a *sumping* deep dull thumping *Thud*! Unseen unheard.
But then felt enough to know that something tremendous had occurred.

By the smallest scalar sizing by any minimal metric measure
By which anything can be measured or known
Something *incredibly* wonderful: a point of inflection pierced held
Profoundly weighty waited credible instantaneous false-vacuum framing
Zero-arrowing: neutral-negating booming force-field vector(s)...
Tipped tripped synergy wave-forming foaming:
      -The Universal-Transcendental!
Continuous inconclusive radial half-spin up and half-spin down
Full spin circumferential-spheroidal in magnitude: un-resolving...

Indeterminate-*terminal* Being: A point in-and-of *seemingly…unendingly…*

Approaching-retreating *perfecting*-infinitude with no net-charge as yet

Assuming tentative-tenuous potential seeking-*halogenic* forever-

becoming…

      -Dia-metric *almost* equal radii-rationing:

      -Dia-magnetic *neutral*-repulsion false-*vacuum…*

      -Electronic-attracting nucleating gravitational Macro-Wave…

      -Microwave length and frequencies…

Of every probability possible squared-area hyper-cuboid voiding…

Hollow-surfacing One to two to three to four dimensional:

      -Quadripolar…

Stretching stretched-equilateral angular-extended *hexing* imaginary almost

Solid-block perfectly stationary-spheroidal as yet assumed:

      -Singularities'…

      -Universal…

      -Rotating!

      -Each of Us!

      -Now! *differentially* constantly energetic-masses' *equatorial*-bulging

polar-capped axial irregular-size and shape.

Dependent on energy-mass and rate of rotation

Predicting-model:

      -Neutron-Star *core…*

      -Core: Dense Black-Oceanic Sea's

      -Macro-wave *background…*

      -Foreground pulsing-Quasar-Ocean: Stars and Galaxies and Atoms

free-falling:

      -The Universal-Space:

-The Universe!

Forming ejecting material along polar-aligned radiation-axis compressed.

glowing: Event Horizons lit…hovering on the *shadow*-edge radiation

falling-out floating collided: dis-order:

-From *purely*-lawful equational-*constant*: Functional Order…

-Dis-Order!

-What-Order!

-Algorythmic…

-Now!

More than all combined entropy

Rotating-particles from shortlived virtual anti-neutral

Double-negative annihilating reducing:

-Event Horizon…

-Proton…positron…

Lifting from and to:

-Points of no-return…

White hot *Light! Flashed!*:

-From Absolute-Zero…

Nothingness-seemingly:

-Cold-exploded…moving inflationary-expansion…
-Massively-heating from the interior…

-Everywhere!

The gaps in-between evaporate freezing radiating fractional-degrees

Above:

-Primordial Black-Hole…

-Neutron-*blank*...

In and around: immediately suddenly from:

Nowhere:

    -Alpha-Beta-Gamma to X-Ray...

    -Burst! Black! White! Light! Everywhere!

Bounced-back then slowed almost ceased...as instantly blown-apart again:

    -Neutron negative-electron colliding anti-electron positron-

Proton...

    -As Proton Lone-Stars and together...

    -Galaxies *forming*...

Neutrino-phonon and photon forcefield.

Laser-smooth uniform-equivalence *shattered clouding*

    -Evaporating...

    -Condensing...

Collapsing crunching cool-clumping:

    -From Zero to atomic-*molecular*
    -Compounding:

    -From Absolute Zero-Mass...

    -To potentially infinitely...

    -Finite hot-light and starry-Galaxies spinning-off...

    -*We*...

    -*Dark*-nucleons holding-off...

-As All Dark-Energy expelled…

-All Mass now impelling compelling Matter…

-As Neutron-Proton Atomic-Molecular…

-Solar-Stars…*positronic*-Planets and electronic-*Moons*…

-Asteroid and cometary…

-Meteoric Force-Field! Each of Us!

-Combining-*colluding*…

-At half the heat to light electro-magnetic energetic-speeds…

-Each necessarily different as distant and different Place and Space and Time…

-Momentum…

-Inward particle dense-region *emptying*-outward…

-Inward collapsing again barring spiral-Galaxies…

-Spinning-off irregular ratio-mass to energetic boson-nucleic…

-Constant-steadying factors amongst the seeming chaos…Lone-Stars and Free-Radicals!

-Rough-shod asteroid and rounded proto-Planetary and lunar pieces…

Stilled barely moving if at all impossible yet to tell.

The *vast*-distances now *lit* by Our-Selves

Stabilising collapsing as in homogenous irregular-particle:

-Summing as-over-*history*…

-Motion-phase transition *vacuum*-bubbles

-*Imaginary*-numerals as infinite potential-Time…

-Started within our Own finite-edges…

-No boundary-beyond…

-No forward or back symmetry as asymmetrical moving…

-Arrows of Time and Nature. Nature as Time. Time as Nature.

-Each of Us: Being. The Originating *inverse square root unifying-*
Unit.

Outer-tangent doubling raddi-quartering diameter
To circumference area...
Natural-logarythmic aerial-aery virtually eventually circling curved
around...*almost* returning to The Start.

The Beginning: Each *uniquely*-constant half-life permanent moment.
Varying-finitude sprung-doubling radial-diametric distance-sprung
Open-strings plucked closing-looping
Almost precise repetition played
Immediately drawn:

-*Naked-Neutron* anti-*Quark negatively-twinned electronic magnet-*
field...

-Proton-positive surviving...

-A Quark[i] for Each of Us.

2.

From-*Nothingness*

Dark-Beginnings perhaps *another* Universe just like-our own:

-White-*light*-Starship radiant...

-Black-gapped...

-*Wrecking*-ball breaking-up as putting-together...

-Our-Selves! Neutral-neural blank-slate...

-Doubly negating neutral-*nothingness*

-Radiating-raised with no net-charge as-yet...

Assuming tentative-*tenuous* halogenic-tended:

-Proton-positronic!

-Outer Electron-negative *switching*-positronic *cloud*-forming force-field *neutrino flying-off...*

-Anti-quark paired in defence...

-Or attack now no-longer *infinite* but finite...

-Massive-*Nothingness...*

Stretching Universal-Space

-Equilateral tri-angular extending...

Almost-equilateral Each of Us emanate continuously recurrent-repetitive...

Labouring working the-point:

-Originating inverse root-squared unifying-Unit...

Each *continuously:*

-Recurrent of the originating inverse root-squared...

-Outer-tangent *diameter-to-circumference* area...

-Quadruple tri-line body-base cubed pentatonic...

Encircling:

-Neutron-Proton Nucleon...*neutrino displaying...*

*D*istance-surfacing balling uniquely ubiquitously

*Perennially e*lectron-sprung

I*ngredient*: armed and legged barring spiral-Star Galactic.

Diaphragm and girdle-bone as bafflingly-erected head and shoulders

Arms and legs as hands and feet formless-knowability *in itself* seeming:

Divine-energy...materiel-*stomaching...*

Ourselves yet dark-hearted eaten or not To Be eaten.

Given taken as in the taking

As if by theft or trapped in-reciprocal kindness.

Traipsing-out:

-Particle microwave-*wave...*

-Detectors...

-Detractors...

Not-so-*mysterious...*

Hydrogenic Each of Us as in Our Own Known Space and Time

Marching in number holding-out against

Free-travelling electrons de-localized as to unknown unknowable *Battle*.

3.

Each of us *constant-complex* altering:

    -Nuclear atomic electro-magnetic…

    -Intermediary-*Graviton*…

    -*Monopolist inducting-induced*…

    -*Chain-store*…

    -*Chainsaw*…

    -*Competing-competitive aggressive fast*…

    -*Passive-slowing*…

Weakly incomplete electronic-cyclonic

Finitudinal-truncating:

    -Number-field…

Integral-spin grouped:

    -Each of Us set-out…

Setting-out set-out.

Each to Each immediately:

    -*Split gravitationald-disc*…

Grouped one to every possible few numbers

Leading to innumerable-number…

Tip-ended double-arrowing down down up up down:

    -Quark-Nucleon electro-magnetic field as gravitational mass-energy…

Against an impenetrable light wall-boomed…

Golden elliptic-egg shell-seemingly *Thudded!* Darkly energetic-amassed.

Expanding-faster towards the fastest speed of sound

To The Listeners:

    -The Measurers…

Be-spoken speaking-spaces in-between

Before-becoming:

    -Power and Light!

    -The Seeers!

Slowly now colouring in the-background.

Universal-microwaves started *twice fallen tumbled stumbled*

Bounced back-up…thrice

Parsimonious *perhaps*-luckily

Perhaps not.

As a Matter-of-Degree

Pre-planning now…smashed clashing:

    -Light-Sabres!

Lightening i*n any* of Every direction

Vacant *but that*-plan already-*gone*:

    -In Space and Time…

    -Sounded-Light!

Split-second spread! Now positively-turning returning two-thirds spin-charge

Equivocating including Our-Own *negation*:

    -Anti-down-quark doubling-up again neuralising negative…

    -Positive Quark-Proton…

Each of Us *again and again and again…*

In The-Darkness surmising glue-balling

Re-centring low-mass lying:

    - *Gravitational-Gluon…*

Exchanging *nucleonic*-subatomic *strongly*-nucleating
Full-integer spin mass-particle *leaking:*
>-Unstable!
>-Stable?!

Weakened short-lived seconding movement clocking
Phonon-quickened non-existing into heat and light:
>-*Neutronium switching Positronium…*
>-*Ever?!*

Moved across linearly the empty space
Making-up the Universal-Space:
>-Changing?

Felt squeaked-cleaned and thoroughly-*centring*
Thudded! again.
Open-centring:
>-Pi-onium…*electronic…*

Drawing-in and reducing-excess…
Full-spinning-off *stinging* spinning-*positively* stingy-releasing holding-onto…
Sequential-ascribing…*selecting-out held onto every unique member-number:*
>-*For-Millennia kept! Each One of Us!*
>- Of Us!
>-To The End of Us!

Each Proton preserved-intact
Growing gardening-in:
>-The Universal-Space!
>-Quadrillion! Light Years to Now!:
>-To the End of the Universe. The-Measurers…

-All!

    4.

All-interlinking overlapping fractal-point functional fractional:

    -How many?

    -One to two to three to four and more dimensional...

    -Ten...Twenty-Six even...27...oddly:...

    -Deterrence...optimal pay-off matrix...

    -3.1415...*equivocating* half-point pioneering *prime*-numbering...

    -Equilateral-triangulating turning-frame...

    -Triangulating-set of *real* rational-number quotient....

    -The common-counting numbers up and down...

    -Inward as outward *caught*...

Entangling musical-scale tinkling:

    -Positronium...

    -Pi-onium...

Fractional four-dimensional moving linear-points.

All at-once turning amongst ourselves

With attraction and repulsion recognizable

Denominating-nominating nominal subtraction

Only adding oddly divisive multiplying progressment unevenly

Heaving sprayed in all directions across The Void:

    -Time and Nature...

    -Mass and energy...

Begun-together *simultaneously*-separating so fast and now so-slowly:

    -Bounce-back...

    -Back-bounced in:

    -Virtual-Weightlessness...

-Impossible logarithmic-construction

-Weakly electro-*magnetic-fielding*:

Quarks! United! Sink-trapped each of us Zero-Spin *electro*-static bound

Acting from within now upon Each-Other:

-*Pi-ons*...

Circling and encircling as on the spot

As mouthing or anus-disappeared...Stopped!

Collided-with...colluded somehow *spheroidal* rolling-forward

Flattening-elliptic moving-linearly across *live*-wires:

-Intermediary *imaginary i-fundamental particulating*...

Almost encircling swelling swollen with frightened rage!

Open-ended tubules-spoked *spinning-out* in Universal-Space.

5.

In-*darkness*...

Bi-centring ellipsoid elastic-stretched conforming

Circular-linear disappearing *vanishing*-points retaining

Minimal trigonometric cubic-equational:

-Critical-axial crossing difference-resolving cyclotomic cyclic cubic

fields:

-Totally *Real!*

-Polynomial permutation-rings at the same moment-of-Time:

-Never-again to become...

As naturally fallaciously *facetiously*...

Each of Us in motion at the same-*instanton exchanged*.

Secanting-variating flat-top sloping planar sub-tending

Isosceles tangent sliding-down or upward as sideways inward or
outwards IT mattered not. Yet squaring the hyperbola:: The *Universal*
Parabola created free-fall parachuted-in. Under the *empty*-product
To the dangling axis of suspension somersaulted
Head over heels acrobatic head-spinning tailing
Pulled in all directions at-Once.

Falling in *any*-direction
As bungee-strung netted elastic-trampolining
Re-bounding almost equi-partition distance-penetration.
Seemingly-colliding yet unevenly inevitably crashed-into
The continuously-pitched-distance inherent pure endless:
      -False-*vacuum*...

As yet bounced side-lined de-limiting bulging booming boomed;
*Thud!*ded re-sounding bounded
Contrarily pitted-against.

Each other deeply-*inspirited seemingly* boundlessly
A-bounding *reverent*-riverine *emptiness*
Inward bounced back-up and of Ourselves...
Started once fallen-into twice returning
In any of every direction but this:
      -Now Positively-nucleate...
      -A*nti-down-quark doubling-up Quark*...
Of this returning two-thirds spin-charge equivocating
Down-again and again and upwards again and again...
Low flying-mass *gravitational-gluon* exchanged stuck-together.
In the darkness surmising glue-balling re-centring:

-*Nucleonic*-subatomic *neutral-Neutron* strongly nucleating...

-Double-Negative Full-integer spin...

-Mass-particle *leaking* unstable!

-*Neutronium!...short-lived...*

Moved across the empty open centre:

-Pionium-*positronium...*

The final-thirded reduced-excess spun-off.

Stinging-stingy spinning positively-sequential ascribing:

-*Uniquely numbering...*

-*Selected chosen spaces as of those available...*

-*Each One of Us...*

-*To All!*

-Of Us?

Electron positron-switching stable

String-point mass-recessing precessing

Processing multi-dimensional:

-How many?

-Dimensions?

-Universes...

-As One.

-As All.

6.

Coiling crawling cooling inner-space as re-heating resonance containing

Pneumatic-dynamic drilling-down as in:

-Electro-magnetic winding-down the *proportional variable energy constants of Quanta...*

Each of us *localised little*-Gravitational

Closing-oscillate wavelength-frequency fundamentally asymmetric

Regulating super-symmetric super-positing

Radial-spinning *Radian* reaching *searching*-out...

Turning twin-polar stretched elliptic five-point centrifugal

Rebounded-sounded cyclical-square pinned.

Spat-out cuboidal-helices set-square:: pentatonic point-planar light-*potential*...

Each individual-variable arresting and re-starting hyperbolic

Sub-tending pining oblong-obelisk sensed

Each of us as boldly **black** as all the deep-**black**ness all-around

Pre-*reflective*:

    -Golden-section searching number 1.6180339887...

    -*Regular:* Alpha-altering plus and minus...

    -Universal-*Inflaton* naturally logarithmic...

    -*Ever approaching infinity b*ecoming outer-space signal-simple

intelligence triangulating...irregular-moving direction and momentum...

A sharing-hexing *threat* imminent-simultaneously

From and within and without definite-shape.

Over a seeming Cosmic-*Horizon*

Simple to complex double-concave envelope.

Convex holding outer-tension ballooning:

    -*Two to three to four-state quantum...*

    -Binary tertiary quadrating pentatonic hexing espial *septimal-tritone*...

Sentinel guarding computorial-superconducting system sonic-vortex
cylindrical tunnelling:

>-*Proton singular individuating-mass*...

As electromagnetic-decaying:

>-*Anti-neutrino* entropic released...

Altering freely-waving...

>-Ionespherical:....isotopical...

>-Radio-*active*...

>-*Light!*

Collided dis-attached and let loose:...

>-Nucleonic *ion conductive* corded...

>-Absorbed and adsorbing...

Conic spinning-out vortex:

>-In-the-hole vacating:

>-Directional in direction of propagation once-fixed...

>-Fixed-once capturing and/or captured:

Self-propagating mostly made-out:

>-Solar-*systemic* Planets and moons and asteroid...

Sprung in-springing out of spin-twisting almost returning equal

Attempting assaying-*perfectly nearly* reality

Yet Each of Us *from-rest* queuing non-equilateral tick-tocking...

Each internal click-clocking against Each-Other.

In the-moving at the same-point moved-from

Differently not *in-differently*

Three-dimensional opening fractious and fragile formed.

Fractional-factoring angular-momentum:

>-Four-dimensional...

>-Universal-Hologrammatical...

-Effects...any number or wind-blowing seated screens moving apart and together...

-Giant Squid-like Octopus!

-Leopardine...

-Tigrous! *dicing spots as tabby-striped:*

-*As Stars that are fished:* as fishing...

-Circling swashbuckling switching *short*-lived...

-Relative-Spin-*e*lectron-point pool...

-Annihilating-potential tragedy...

-Comedy Romantic-Neutron-proton electron-positronic...

-Mon-Atomic tonic-chorded...

Stated screaming-chaotic unruly-terrifyingly *radiant*...

Strongly then Weaker:

-*e*lectromagnetic point-cloud...

-Nucleate!

-Colliding! Crashing!

-Fusing then...

-Fission-again!

Crossed transmitting-points determined only by the sonic-wave
Thudded...again

Booming *cruel*-harsh callous-*stinging cut*:

-With depleting absence of pressure banded all-around...

And within with nothing *else* to compare yet:

-Three-point pseudo-scalar tensor-split...

Restless reckless ticklish-stirring string-point mass
Stretching binding-bound:

-*Quark-Quantum Moment!*

-*Measured!*

Each-*perversely:*

-Non-Zero Sum...*distorting each other half-spin up*

Reverse half-spin down *by apparent orders* of *myriad*-Magnitude

Toward the *ever*-present while in circuit:

-Ratio stretched-cyclic oscillating point strength...

Weakening...

-Fractally-functional common-ratio rationing-number...

-Giving *gifting* every and All-*number...*

-Infinite-secondary...

-Against some particular outer-*vacuum* pressed non-stopped...

-Stopped radio-wavelength conjoined gravitational *electrostatic...*

-*As fast as...almost all...*

Furiously roughly-furrowing *foaming* twisting and turning

Tersely truculently each-bridging snapping and spinning:

-Impossible!

-Star-Car!: *switchback-looping known fractal-finite almost repeating...*

-Each of Us becoming become *ambient*-spectral critically over-

weighing:

-Protean *ideal real Hydrogen-gas ionizing...*

Clearly in Super-abundance and All-around:

-Supra-HyperSpace!

Within and with The All-Around.

Alluding-eluding elimination *illumination:*

-Stellar-Super Hyper-Universe!

-Universal Proto-star HyperNoval...

-Force-field energetic-*shockwave...*

Each-of-Us seductively salaciously spiraling *almost out of control...*

Unable to hold it *All*-together any-longer in-complete newness

Each of Us *awaiting* no-longer to make-OurSelves *clear-reflecting inwardly*

first:

> -*All MassEnergy*...
>
> -*Space-Time*...

shifting gear:

> -Quantum-fuel-electrical breakdown...
>
> -Each photon-potential colliding with another...
>
> -Each-Proton attracting absorbing and reflecting surface...
>
> -*Podium*-proportional...
>
> -As a surface still relative to another...
>
> -Temperature of the frosty dry-surrounding heat...
>
> -Eating engulfing *e*lectron or spat-out...
>
> -Vacuum-bubble ultra-cold neutron flux-fixing:

Phonic:

> -*Thud!*
>
> -*Again!*

Pre-empted this time again rebounding from the grasping-degrees of edge

Gasping at the outset *instantaneous*-raveling...

*Thud*ded-back again and through the centre-passing around:

> -The *only*-possible numerical-proportion...
>
> -Unique to the cube of travelling *impact*-speed...
>
> -To The-Edge...
>
> -The-Centre.

Each of us naturally resonating vibrating string strung-out.

Discretely-*interacting*:

> -Integral hexing helical-holding...

Stepped-spiral stacking crenellating protective

Castellating degree of tilt

And as turreted:

-Pro-active...

-You!

Turning built-in *fine-tuning* current point-number stop-starting off the blocks.

Rumbling purring complex non-equilateral indivisible compacted and compressed *breathing re-fueling*...

Confounding wheeling-on-wheeling

Ranking latched and ratcheted

Each One of Us hatched: thatched-flanking

One against another and amongst Each-Other.

As on *invisible* force-field cogs and gearings each gripped loosely:

-Equalising stabilizing as near to Zero...minimum as maximum coming-around...

-*Hidden*-variables...

-*Barometric atomic-pressure engine-gauging*...

-Using Universal-Laws...

-Creating Universal-Laws...

-Hidden-variables?

-As function's constant algorythms...

-Except at any-moment recorded, and moved-on.

Engaging disparate-desperate hanging-on insecurely onto the next.

Or to be shattered apart into so many uncountable unrecognizing

But yet momentary spiderous-parts...

Repetitive-casually exactly almost and never again.

Only *seeming* causally retrospective-layering prospective

Timeful-entire predictive with the feeling of *nothing:*

Yet also *more* than All of *This.* With practice more but never exactly

precision

The ability to slow and control.

Material memoried-*recalling*

Predictive-repetitive events *approximately*-restoring:

      -Each for Ourselves in ourselves and finally with and for Other

and All-Else...

      -The Universe!

Confirming affirming and constantly re-confirming our own existence.

To Ourselves and Each Other. Ever slightly or completely off-centre

Circumspect *imaginative* memorific:

      -From The-Off!

      -Decision-*making...*

Once having started in practical-motion

To keep-going and Be.

Kept-going...*swarming* anti-particle anti-doting

Prodigiously-spookily *ghostly*-distancing:

      -Pro-genic-*prodigy* maintaining...pro-Life!

      -Of course!! Each of Us *containing re-generating...*

      -*Each-Other!* Only *Just:* To keep-going and Be kept-going...

      To be *utilized* in-continuity...

Remembering the previous *briefly* whilst acting-out: *presently*

Presented in advance of the apparent intimacy-and-immediacy of:

      -The-Facts...

-The-Act?

-The Only Other Event: Next!

In perpetual *darkly*-retrospective

Repeated lost-forgotten and continuously only ever again part re-found.

Continuous sustaining-perpetuity

Forever in-the-*present* planning-out:

-The Future...

-Of Present and Past-present...

-Next-*remembering* thought dis-membered....

-The more most likely than least likely exact precise repeat...

Part-lost: *Forever*-finding as an *after*-thought fore-thought anew:

-As if *pre-thought*-out...

-Free-Will?!

Acting in The-Moment:

-The Moment-Lost.

In the constant presence of Everything-*else*...

With practice *nothingness*

Within and without the present

Forever-imbalancing

The-Past all-around...

Unavoidable forming and re-forming positively-powering

Re-powering with the urgency of:

-The Immediate...

A reflective-retrospectively reasoned-action

After The Action to add to the data-base of successfully survived-activity:

-So Far…

-All of Us! As more than all the compound atoms remaining in The Universe Now!

-How Many?

The-facts as ever *shattered*-apart.

Into so many *uncountable*:

-Nuclear-atomic inter-actioning…

-Beyond: The-Horizontal…

-Vertical…

-In-as-Out

Interactions actual and possible all At-Once:

-The most likely to the least probable:

-A hierarchy of objects: of particles…

-Gaseous liquid solid-plasma clouding-clouded Clocks clock-making…

-The Time-Keepers!

-The Measurers! The Rulers!

-Non-credible irrational…

-Rational-Paradox…

Outward:

-Passive-aggressive…

-True!

-Logically…

Aside now the slightest movement timeful:

-Speeded-up *ready-made*…

-*Your Own owned owed-made*…

-Space slowing as *cooling*…

-Ice-Cold!

-Absolutely...

-Frozen!

Racing measured each-by-each by Each of Us:

- The Measurers!

-Ruling!

-Routine-imagination *reasoning-complete...*

-Measuring dipolar-moment *travelling...*

-Momentous-*movement* somewhere-*else*:

-Each combined *almost* equal and opposital polar-quartering...

-Alpha-altering plus and minus...

-Monopolist Mono-Tonic *charged anti*-particle...

-Mono-Pod! *Doubling...*

Particle-attracting and annihilating:

-Timeful darkly-watery *energetic...*

Materialising-momentous nucleating:

-Tri-parton extreme tri-Quark and *Hexing*-Quartz *Feldspar...*

-Anti-quark...

-*Quantum pionium-gravitational electro-magnet nucleonic massing...momentary...*

-Inverse-distance diminishing and increasing uni-modal iterative and *re-cursive...*

Searching: electro-static and covalent-attraction and repulsion.

Perennial-permutation permeating permitting mutation:

-Massively low-to-highest temperature...

-At the internal fastest speed of sound...

-And then there was-*Light...*

Abrasive vacuum-gap crossed

Almost linear *neutrino* fired-off...

Into the chargeless-*neutral* surrounding *ghostly* non-stop movement:

      -Algorythmically-entangled...

      -Algebraic-neutralising...

      -Mutable-mathematical vitalising ionisation-energies negative and *positive*...

Each of us transmitting transporting qubit-unit communicating...

probing...

      -Instantaneously both there and *not there*...

      -Quantum Quark-*teleportation*...

In-movement moved-across and around the outside.

Back-grounding black-body radiation-burning red-hot foggy-*opaque*

All-absorbing:

      -Energy and Matter...

      -Time and Nature...

      -Total-Universe!

      -Un-bounding!

      -Sacred!!

Binding:

      -Gravitational darkening once-more...:

      -Universal-pulling...

Pressing-buttons computational four state indiscrete.

Non-discrete at-once:

      -Spooky-action at a distance...

Apparent outer-edged inwardly-weighted pressed

Each to Each so that it was *as if* standing-still.

Or if moving at all

On all-surface in the opposite-direction

Of that directly-opposite *almost...*

Drawn-toward as well as away from

Blown-apart photo-*luminescent from:*

    -The Centre...

    -Of It All...

    -Equal and opposite. Almost sum-leftover...

Preference-pixelate phase-transforming:

    -Polarities between energy and matter...

    -Hypernoval dense disc-centring transference...

    -As light-gases and heavy-liquid *watery*-metal:...

Thudding-movement throughout unavoidable heaving-heavier *flashing-light*:

    -The Big Universe! Greatest-Macro-wave!

    -BlackStar! Force-field Solar...

    -Eclipsed!

    -Eclipsing EarthCentres! Us!

    -*EarthQuakes*!

    -Swarming!! Swarms[ii]!!

Reflected rising into the-*surrounding* filling-space...

    -*Hypernoval Universal!*

    -Between energy and matter *relative* to the originating:

    -Zero point white-light golden gone-out...

Spinning-orbital each-approximating spin-*circulating...*

Freed-radical sped-each *little-universe...*

Each preserving momentarily-paused seemingly pin-point

Prime-phasing perturbing:

-Split tri-quark point-mass re-charging...

As defined by each of us stopping and re-starting:

-Degrees-of-separation and annexation...

-Freedom...*inverting*-movement...

Staying-mute muling sighted heard baying felt *saving*-energy:

-Bounded added-in three-dimensional The Universal-Space...

Of willingness numerically measured and ruling

Degree-of Free-wheeling willing:

-Each of us *positively-Protonic*...

-*Black-Body cyclotronic-radiation.*

The numbers non-redundant *redundant*

Set-potentially not-finite low to high density:

-To each orbiting *electron point clouding*...

-Singularity...*edged*...

-Valence and shell-Core *centring*...

-Atomic-Nucleic...

-The-Universe.

7.

Cracking crackling massing-points holding-apart:

-Each now non-identical electron-charge pushing against each
other...

-Each and every charged repulsion shared valence crossing orbital-
reaction:

-Atomic *donor*-nucleus and *electron*-compounding overall...

Re-balancing from firing off-balance but for one billeted bulleting bulletin:

-Taking pre-emptive precedence over-tipping electron-positron mass-locked away minimal to massively magnified as magnifying single atomic-mass...

-One to one hundred-billion energy particulate.

-Every massive proton atomic mass-ratio to *electron*...

-Toward 99.9% 1/9th of the Proton's Dark-Matter and Energy@...

- Atomic Solar-System...

-Sun and Giant gas and rocky Planets-*watering*...

-*Rivering-streams and ponds and lakes and seas*...

-Ley-lines forging...

-*You! Your* energy-and-matter *now*...With neutral-negative pairing electron-positron capture

Attracting angular-triangulating...

By *impossibly*-symmetrically paring parity-*promoting*:

-Universal: neutron-proton-electron positronic *plasma*...

Felt-prickling-points deflecting *reflecting*

Absorbing-recording and adsorbing Play-back *bleeding*...

Oscillating particle-reader reading:

-Electro-magnetically rhythmic-switching-metronomal...

Danced balancing-enjoined tagging-along.

Rounding-out and positioning-quarter containing boxed-in

Boom-Boom booming *thud*ding squealing squeaked *screaming!*

Closed pitch-sized as sided secant-netted

Dropped-in and raised stretched held-back and fired-off:

-Annihilating The *first*-Generational *energy*-speeding...

Unimaginably slightful insightful losing energetic-mass re-*neutralising*

From neutral negative-positive static-pressure pulled and pushed

Pulling and pushing with gusto-gushing...

Galoshing-sploshing splashing

Sled-ride in-a *sliding Great-Vacuum:*

> -Each of us...

> -Spoked-secant-joined-up...

Spoked-wheeling multi-lateral linear ray-line *irradiating...*

Re-bounding longer and shorter broadcasting from:

> *-Electro-magnetic field-force...*

> *-Nucleonic strongly and weakly gravitational...*

> *-Your Universal-Event...*

Jagged ripped-Open *torn-apart* :

> -Necessarily asymmetric tri-or-more part...

> -No-more...

> -New!

Unbalancing-movement dropped-in again.

Impressive and compressive-force's thickening:

> -Femto-metric *positive...*

> *-Protonium...*

Conic-pointed seemingly massively:

> -Magnificent electro-magnetic...

> -Mono-polar...sub-limating...*ionising...neutrino and more*

fundamental-particles as fundamental-forces...

> -Each of Us!

> -Solar-Systemic!

> -Universal Black-Hole!

Balancing net-charge unitarily-finite:

> *-Exciton*: Universal *hot*-energy...*Light!*

> -Selectron-*sparkicle...*

-Non-Zero! *Excited-ringing light-ray internal-conversion instantly boiling-away:*

-Double-paired outer-quadrupling hexing-sextupling...

Continuously *inflaton* inflating suddenly as instantaneously:

-From Absolute Zero cold to Universal Absolute *heat...and Light!*

-Max.: *Three trillion degrees* thereabouts...

-Min!: Quark-fission light *fusion!*

-Each of Us firing-off neutral negative plus-minus positive...

Universal Plasma cloud forming...

Magneto-electrostatic caged crystalline leaved.

Opening petal *flowering* voluminous as a grain of coralline-sand watery droplet rained. Glorious pseudo-pod each our own bubble-swelling swollen-lunged bellied belied-toothed tongue-pulsing...

Conducting charging-numerating holding-outward:

-Inner-spin-force winded and reverse tipended...

Thrown-out and into paths and passages made-ahead.

Exploding destroyed and re-newed accreting rapidly re-turning:

-Angular-extending captive-capturing quantitive:

-Whole-*hexing* integer-spin...

-Whole-*I*nteger-spin...hexing...

Spinning-back together-colluded avoidance and then:

-Colliding-consuming outer-necessarily ideally-empty equally-expansive...

-In all directions squared cubed-balling *cell-bound doubling-nonet*:

-Across Each-Operative *approximating*...

Imagined-centre indicating circular directional:

-Constantly-mathematical multiple-proportionate...

-Approaching finitude-indicating di-pyramidal imaging:...

-Against a symbolic-logarithmic curve-*perfecting number-point*...

Quasi-crystalline cross-barred prismatic sheer *darkly* transparently-superimposing *almost*-Solid...

Gaseous-Liquid solid cooling freezing grid-framing

Repulsing-*nothingness*

-Condensing-Universe...

-Evaporating energetic-impulsion and with equivocal-expression...

-The instant glinting the almost unending *pure*-darkness amassing:

-Each *Universal Black-Star centring starry-White*!

-The Universal-*Vacuum!*

-From Absolute Zero cold...

-With Universal Maximum *Heat...as light!*

The renewed *almost*-blackness:

-The Universal Void...

-*Phonons*-only *unseen bouncing-off thudded squealing screeching!*

-Absorbing photonic-returning faster...Lit! Super-Sonic booming re-*energising*:

-Neutrino passing straight-*through*...

-Super-fast then sluggish *returning*:

-Energy to Mass...

-Mass to *Energy*...

Anyway *cooling* minutely FlashStar!

Greying after-image: *blue red green yellow*...

Orange-twinkling all-around

Silver-white *blue* separating-out red-distance.

With nowhere else to go *greying*-into utterly reflective de-reflection.

Complete-darkness under our own sheer bright-lit ballroom-lights

As stars risen into an as yet starless night.

8.

Complex geodesic-light bending gravitational electro-magnetically
Pressure-*weighted* rotational balancing-support nuclear...
Unclear in *utter*-darkness again inside-collapsing
Slowing de-pressuring and re-pressing *membrane* turning-uplifted:
  -Over three-gravity forces heavier...
  -Four-five...
Without safety-harness oppositely opposital down-turning:
  -Than Nothing?!
  -From-*nothingness*...
Drawn–back inward again weaker low-energy dropped down upto:
  -Pentangular nodal-complex point-planar...
Spin-dragging flung:
  -Within The-*moment*...
  -*The-Event!* Of Time and Nature...The-Same...*unbalanced*...

Mega-dropping dropped-in soundless blindly spatial-silence *unheard*...

Panicked iced-*frozen* panned-pained pumiced *unhearing*...
Tottering teetering *screaming*-sloped slid-sliding down
Toppling Observation platform-podium towering:
  -Axial down-swaying...
  -Hold-on!
  -Hold 'em Up!?

Gamboling rounding-back an oddly doubly tripling quadrupling
Penta-*tonic* unequally elastic-sided:

-Extreme and mean median...

Snagging-inward nodal-complex point-planar

De-pressurising and repressing-membranic *Thudded!!:*

    -Each of Us...we breathed-life into-Ourselves and Each-Other.

Outward Hydroid-polyps uplifted: one two three

Over three gravity forces-heavier...

Crossed and contrary clatterous

Electronic rattling platform rafting-regional:

    -Each-to-Each learning from Our-Selves...

    -As All Others' *synthesizing:*

    -Vacuum-*Machines...*

Made of metal and mineral rock-scraped and scratched together.

Consumed-consuming

Forged in gas and in dark-waters rafting-along

Ourselves now with all other firing-waves

Spread interference patterning-particulate passing-across...

Passing-through crossed and strung-out colliding-points

Cancelling-out the spaces in-between:

    -*Pure*-Vacuum tri-point breaking:

    -Quantum-emission tri-parted...

    -Again.

Inevitably-*asymmetric* radiating-moving:

    -Ditrogonal-modular...

Folding polyhedral-topical idealising idealised imaginings:

    -Imaging: *Ideal Real*-gas...

-Primordial-stable monatomic-state.

Grey-silver white separating-out with nowhere else to go.

Greying into utterly un-reflective complete-darkness amassing:

-The Universal-Vacuum...

As yet unlit Solar-Planetary ellipsoid-rotation.

To reach-back into the di-polar axial-centre

Torn crab-claw grabbing

Spinel-scary *terrifying* yet-thrilling affirming *confirming*...

Each To Be:

-Our-own projective non-zero non-negative valid proof-positive.

*Increasingly-Other de-creasingly inevitably-*reducing also:

-Absolutely...*irreducible*...

-As negatively-*reducible*...

-As contradictory-proven *demonstratively* as by:

-A *Universally* Incomplete-*Paradox*...

-Complete.

-Irrational.

-Incomplete...

Parodying troubling-affine non-affine.

*I*ncomparable gouging-out.

Set-stringline boundary-mediating massively-asymmetric

Infinite-potentiality seemingly boundless and unstoppable:

-And so it all ends and is to The-End...

Oppositely mirrorly and sinisterly *ghostly* in the machine.

With The-Machine-handed-down and foot-pedaling

Pumping like a decorative-fairground organ played a winding-down.

Heard and seen *sapient* salient-connected and combinatorial

Requiring post-rational reasoning-activity to work.

As *imaginative*-toys or Weapons of Mass-Destruction.

Of Life. Potential *pile- up Crash!ing!*

Braking-arresting pushing-forward

Into custody-detained taken-hold of

Risk-factors apprehending-turning wounded-dropping...

Rising colliding force-field breast-feeding pount-pointing

Counting fed-breathing wont-mounded.

Exploding-mountainous and imploding-bubbles of sound and vision.

Fading-*shadow* elongating through vortex-tubular empty-centring

Surrounding *pure*-starlight points-all-around:

>   -How many?

>   -Varying Intel...

Attracting and detracting forces' measured to *robotic*-accuracy

Learning-mistakes with double-jeopardy triple and more-adjustment

Next time if there was a next time...

And there was.

>   9.

Horizontal transverse *latitudes*...

As if defining divining the whole: *leveling-off*

Joined verticular vermicular ventricular.

Upright-standing perpendicular-spinel

Nervous armed radial *rounding-out*...

Unifying *non-trivial* integrating complex-looped again:

>   -Each numerical-bias leaning...

>   -Twisting and turning rattling loosely bolted helical screw

threaded. Dexstral and sinistral-facing circuital core-headed and tail-surfacing.

Completed full-circuit spin stepped:

-Sonic-conic parallel-helical convergent.

Twisting-end wrapping and sweet-enwrapped. Regulating-regulated
switching-circuitry crossed latticed hatched *thatched* through....

Between tri-point podded.

Hyperbole collapsing-on-sides all-around

Cross-string barred empty-*nucleate*...

Falling weighted-down cartoon canton-centring

Non-reflective mirroring-inside.

Positively-charged again nucleo-tidal:

      -Quantum-base...

Di-polar super-positioning

Entangling base-pairs ellipsed...

Each Other eclipsing-eclipsed

Tri-point zipping zipped...

Pedalling and contra-pedalling cycloid swarming...

Lasar-photonic conceiving raised-*momentary*...

Each individual dark-crib caged encountering

Spinning-together or counter-spinning...

Opposital The-Same *almost* or *spooky* extreme-opposite

Composite to the outer-*emptiness*:

      -Rotational...

      -Operator...

Inner-mass weighting interpreting quantifying:

      -De-coherent three-body point *quarter*-Powering...

Re-pressurising neutral easy-stopping and unequally re-starting:

      -Atomic-Universal...

      -And so It All ends...

-And Is. To: The End.

10.

Each-individuating mathematical reference frame-dependent
Rounding out and down shaping empty-husked hulling seated
clamped-in prism *flash*-points locked-in. Looping linear defying curving
ovoid spheroidal stretched expansive *increased*-felt gravity-force rounding
rationalising down floor up to roof. Around the *evident* walls truncating
digital de-limiting:

    -Fractional *real*-number...

    -As opposed to unreal?

    -False?

    -Then?

Cross-sectioning quadrilateral emptying empty-husk.
Whole-section dimensional complex-chaotic rapidly topping and
bottoming-Out:

    -Swing-Ship!...*set in-motion*

Setting-on *course*:

    -Switch-blade back-known procedural-*recurrent*...

    -Problematic...

    -Caused ragged booming-complex...

    -Rapidly successfully-repeating *almost*...

Altering memorised and materially surviving comparitive-potential
Extra-low to extra-high particulate-point:

    -Leaking highest-temperature...

    -To lowest heat-trapped absenting-*cooling*...

    -Evaporating condensing to *electron* capture and energy-release...

Burst electro-static spluttered-*radiate*...

Dragging-friction pushed out again drawn-infinitely many:

    -By nuclear-Fission...

    -Alpha-decay...

    -Fusion to Stay-in:

    -The Game!

    -Beta optimal radio-*activity*...

    -Neutron-Proton electron-phonon...*photon*...

Clustering-decay cosmic-rays:

    -Potential-spinning spiraling-Orbital:

Slightly-longer and shorter-delimiting:

    -From inside-outside each truncating fractioning-*fractal*...

    -Re-numerator *hexing* six-star point-shaping square-root inverse tangential *voiding*...

    -Defined *defining*-Self...

    -By-Each *inverse*-distancing *blank*-centring...

    -Unitary-edged...doubling-crossed diametric-distanced...

    -Centre-Axial *compounding* triplicating double-hexing diamontine...

Gushing! Flashing! glinting:

    -Point-positive sprung Solar Star-heated cooling...

    -Octagonal point-particle gauging...

    -The Measurers!

Circuital-grasping started non-stopping button pressing steering around...

    -The-Rulers of Us All!

    -All of Us!

Surrounded-curved as carving-out...

Of the unending *pure*-darkness *exhilarating* unruly-*zooming*:

    -Di-polar elliptic nucleating-ovoid...

    -Four-dimensional observation platform-shifting:

Avoiding and voiding combinatorial...

      -Regular and more and more irregular regulating-substrate...

      -*Greater and smaller* rhombic-palpation palliation....

      -*By* nuclear-fission alpha-decay cluster-decay fused Cosmic-Ray...

Slightly longer and shorter delimiting point positive-sprung

Never The-Same Each and Every-centring

Each truncating fractioning fractal de-numerator...

Eight-star-point shaping crab-claw inclining:

      -Axial-compounding...

      -Digital distal-distancing...

      -Opposital...

Octagonal-nonet circuital-grasping re-doubling:

      -Rhombicuboctahadronal pressed-into-service...

Steered around the-outside surrounding curving as carving-out of the un-
ending *pure*-darkness...e*xhilarating* unruly zooming each our-own
observation-platform=Domed-window viewing-plate *shifting:*

      -Maximum electric-magneto spherical-permittivity in *pure*-
vacuum...

Gradually glowing red-to-blue

The earliest most distant and local:

      -*Stellation:* pure-energy per unit coronal-spiked radiating-freely-
forming: proton-electron neutron-positron:...

      -Each of us...*strongly-nucleating to* electro-weak magnetic emitting
photo-electric *potential*...

11.

-Accelerating particle tailing Cosmic-*Wind*…

Winded popped-*thud*ding…hissing fizzing phishing *buzzing*…

Squealing-crossing transmitting-points' crossed and contrary-clatterous:

    -Across *pure*-vacuum tri-point breaking-Quantum *emission*…

    -*Inevitably*-asymmetric point's-combined then-folding…*radiating*…

    -Ditrogonal-modular folding-polyhedral…

    -Typically idealising-toppling The-*Idealised*…*imagining*…

    -Topical-*imaging*…

    -Ideal: Real-Gas.

    -Primordial: *fractionally stable-MonAtomic state*…

    -Electronic rattling-platform regional-rafting…

    -On Our Way Home!

De-stabilising re-stabilising-directional sustaining machination.

Pushing-forward braking arresting turning dropping rising colliding force-fields

Exploded and imploding circular-spinning vortex-emptying-tubular…

Closing-*centred* surrounding *pure*-starlight points

All-around. Each of Us a firing-wave spreading-out interference-patterning pointing!:

    -Particle-colliding points sending yet more wave-lapping top and bottom-feeder *cancelling-out*…

    -Watch-out!

Be-spoke speaking-spaces in-between:

    -With a Probability-Wave function in Three-Dimensional Space…

    -Frequency and Wavelength determinacy…

    -Indeterminate.

-Geometrically-multiplying wave-points outwards and around...

-Collapsing at each-point moved moving-through *uncertainty*...

Still. Changing charging-direction and velocity-speeding accelerating and

de-*accelerating:*

-*Constant*-charged particle-collisions...

-Wavelength-frequency...

-*Phonon*-particle striking-out photon...

Electro-magnetic gravitational-nucleic:

-Rogue and *freak-wave* space-stretched by a *factor*...

-And some multiplying and dividing...

Immediately cooling solidifying-almost solid liquid-gas:

-*Quantum Quark:*...

-*Giant Gluon Plasma virtual swimming viral-Zoo!*

-*Massless*-energetic forming mass-holding moving massively

tentatively around:

-We forming *formed*...

-Re-forming re-formed re-forming *every*-Moment!

-Dead or Alive?!

12.

-Dead or Alive?

Each of us circling each and every other:

-Differentiable: each *nucleon energetic-mass*...

Incoherently uncertainly pointy-bubbly-forming

Chain-rippling frothing

Foaming-gas cloudy-lumped:

-Positively-negatively neutral-balancing...again-*almost*...

-And again.

-Un-balanced...

-Kinetic-energetic:…

Working-rising and falling uniquely invariant-variant:

-Numerating and re-numerating exterior faceted and internal the
same…

-Almost…more or less safe…sealed-in…

-Almost equally-weighted photo-spherically…

-Plasma…

Oily-dropped motion we each cloud-chambered potentiality

Each of Us in part to-the-outside Universe

To Each-Other.

Each of Us *emulsifying*:

-Into-being…

Separating-off:

-Similar…*different*…

Expanding-Oceanic Seas and dust-Desert-watered.

Soapy-bubbles and baubles compact-constricting

By choice de-limiting every *subsequent*-choice

Until there is none-*remaining*…

We spread like disconnecting-daughtering

Sisterly taking-in brotherly familial-fecund bundling

Incredibly slowly as if nothing had changed.

Almost *static*-sputtering phonic photonic-chromatic:

-Parenting-finite *numeron* nium-bead-counting…

Counted-out:

-Daughtering-*generational*…

-Bean's jumping nudged and nudging-along…

-Brother! Son! Far-fighters and born faraway...

-In-*piracy* murdered-stolen away...

-By guile brilliance and versatility...

-In All-*directions* minimal-fractal *fractional*-sum...

-Of each infinite-series trigometric-*expression*...

Bounce-back vacating again

Arriving directional fixing-in:

    -Direction of propagation uniquely momentarily paused...

    -Self and Other propagating: W-X and –Y-ray photon electron-positonic...

Absorbing and now reflecting wavelength:

    -Ultra-violet blue to Infra-red...

Radio-static heat and light Big-Wheeling!:

    -Big-Wheel!

Freezing outer-condensate crushing-exchange tunnel:

    -A1...2...3-*Hydrogen*...Three...

    -Helium...

paused...organic neon lit:

    -From Absolute-Zero...

Bouncing slowly neutron against positron at the *coldest*:

    -The *faintest*-magnetism now weakly annihilating against *normal* matter...

    -Burst aneurism guts-burst!

    -Gotten!

Each of us initial ground-state resumed-briefly intermediary modeling the whole more and less:

    -*Quantum weirdness* the illusion of wholeness within...

-Colder unburned...

-This Time...

-Never-again!

Booming the pitching darkness instantaneously

Both there and not there

In movement moved-across...

And around the outside *instantaneously* both there and not there:

-In-Movement...

-There and *gone*...

Moved-across and around The Outside

Shared altering-angular rectifying-unit switching on-off.

Burned-across redundant equally massively significant-numerical
cancelling-out:

-But Two into One!

At the inner and outer edge:

-Cosmic universal speed limit:...

-The Great Escape?

-The Great Expanse...

-*This*-Universe...

-Universal outer-curved space...

-Inner curved to the empty radiating centres...

-Collapsed Dark-Star black hole within and all around *inhabiting*...

-The Same in All-Directions...

-Except Each *uniquely* now-distributing background *radiation
atomic code colour-patched*...

-*Pitched*...

Moving Each of Us

Mass-bending *differently* emplaced emplacing-Self:

-Inconstant constants...unequal equalities...

-Within: *The Laws of Nature! dark energy* and *matter...*

And at some *seeming*-Vertex.

Crashed-into and as if *thought-through...*

Leapt into the dark drawn-in....

-Quantifying quantum *fluctuant:...*

-How many?

-Quarks? Quadrillion. Quark-*point* and chain-ringing *strings...*

-Atomic Ionespherical-*Monatom designer-pattern patenting*

parenting...

-Met-Atom! *Nucleonic protean hydrogen liquid-gas:*

Practising orbital-capture and release:

-Freed-*electron* and Each Free-Proton...

13.

-Fundamental-*particles* too-numerous to count...

-Odd and *even*-numbers...

-Since every atom once-was and still *is* seemingly...

-Indefinitely-stable entropy-freeing Protean-*electric:...*

-A number at least one more per every ten-billion...

-As there are now Protean remaining...

-One amongst quadrillion perhaps...at least...

-*At least...*

Equally-equational *gravitationally* separated electro-magnetic

Variously moving unequally together and apart:

-Binary...at least...*equaling...*

-Equational-*nothing!*

-Where All are Equal!

-In Death?!

To *electron*-capture and energy-release combining:

-Each number-Power....

-Killed-paternal fraternal killer unknowingly unfriendly-
realizing...

-Out of The Sea...

-Poison of The-Ray-*fish*...

-No gentle death in sleek old age...

-But Now!

-Not 3-clicks old!

Whirlpool-drowning purgatory rumoured false-counsel:

-Not muling-Circe...

-Or Penelope.

Outer-electron likeness repelling *apparent*-other holding-apart:

-Powering-up paired positive and negative *half*-spins...

-Whole-spun Unitary...

Containing continuously maintaining internal seeming at least temporal
naturalistic-consistency...

-Never-both...

-At the same Time...

-Or Naturally...

-Of neutrino-photonic non-decaying massless *pure*-energy electron
atomic-pitched...molecules...

-All the atoms of The-Body...

-Personal Galactic coronal-circulating spiked-*radiating*...

-*All-Together!*

-*Separating*...

Rounding-out noisily *freely-forming*:

-Proton-electron neutron-*positron*...

-Strong electro-weak magnetic emitting…

-Photo-electric *potential…captured* gained…

-Accelerating particle-tailing negative-poles…

-Cosmic-*Wind*...

-*A metric single-atomic space between nothingness*…

-Splattering selective-quantum fluctuant *ion*-wavelength
frequency-compression...

Enjoined around some apparent equatorial-*Halo*:

-Tagging-along anti-genic *determining*...

Doing: Being done-to:

-*Oscillating*-particles' electro-magnetically *rhythmic*…

-Switching metronomal-balancing…

-Causing-clausifying categorising-subjectively objectively-*Doing*
to...

Effectively-*affectively* combining added-to *electronic* condensate *misting*
inner-smooth manifold

Manifest electric-barrier potential-charging battery-defending

Volting and re-volting turning and spinning…

Angular-extended sped-by and *through*-amount:

-Smaller positive overwhelming negative velocity-voltage: wxyz…

-Compounding half-spin electron neutral-charge
phasing...WXYZ…

Flexing outer-focusing shape-shifting

At-least to control the coming and on-going:

-Telescopic Micro-cosmic…

-ABCD…

-Taking some-part some-control energy taking some-charge of
matters…

-Double-Universal: WXYZ...,

-Each of us avoiding by at least the equal distance between us:

-More as less...

-Less as more...massless tri-rings...

-Naturally unequally-*sized*...

-Non-circular ellipses...*interlinking*...knotted-braiding...

-String-like charge massed drifting-away from each other

repulsing networks:

-Massive heat and *light* fuel –expulsion powering...

-*Empowering*...

-*Universal hearing and seeing felt briefly Universal-Cosmic speed-*

limiting...

-*Temperature equaling atomic-number releasing heat conversion*...

-*To light*...

Scorching immediately-by:

-Hot-*felt speeding*-past as catching-up darkly-*faster*...

-*Heard as Seen*...

As We Each were immediately slowed

Re-refrigerated as Each to Each-Other

Also:

-Dark mass-moving together...

-Darkly-energetic *expanding*...

Each other similar charged together resisted passed sometimes faster

sometimes slower...

Now Each mutually-attracting opposite-charge negative-positive

Forming crystaline-*latticework*:

-Ion valence-bonding molecular-compound...

Radiating-*energy absorbing*-Masses:

-Adsorbing...felt *Cosmic Wind:* First-Generational: *Universe de-generating* entropic-B*lasted! Blasting-out-in...in...out*...again.

Flung-out and around three-corner-hat pocketed tipped.

Chipped ejected-rejecting tipped-negating:

-E*lectron neutrino-fired*...

Sheer shaved-off electron-positronic photon-field potential:

-Polar-disengaged electro-magnetic force-field...

Screen-*neutral*:

-Neutron-neutrino firing off in all directions...

-*Almost*-linear inflating-points passing almost straight-*through*...

-*Choose!*

In All-*directions* to Each-Other:

-*Negating* potential-gravity energy-opposital:

-*I*onising...

Screen absorbing as reflecting:

-*P-cation* electronic source to N cathode-P-anode...

-*e*lectrode descended terminal primary *electrolytic*-cell...

-Electronic mass-moving power charging *battery*-cell:

-Proton-*electron source* ray-tube...

Stream-*screaming* anion de-termining determinating dementing:

-Universal-flow current electro-magnetic light potential...

-Up-anion attracted to p-anode...*neutral*...

-Nothingness double minus-down...down-again...up...

-Up-again...again...pure-Proton *positive*.

14.

Ever further apart bolstering intra-acting two point resonating as pixilated screenings:

-Polarising elliptic-inverse universe quadratic-*equational*...

-Calculating differential-frequencies between-fields...

-Circulating gouging-out the space *Laser*-Beam...

-X-Ray...

-Y?

-How?

-Why?

Tri-partite infinite constancy-finite displacement

Positively-negating neutralising the expansive now *impure*-vacuum:

-*Us!* The Universal-Space scene-making *characterization*...

-2nd Generational *particle mass-hierarchy*...

-Weighting ***mass***-*boson* moving anti-electron positron neutrino-progressing...

-Sonic-phonic photonic-potential colliding...

Almost-perfectly circular:

-Photon colliding with the centre-axial quarter-polarities switched-back:

-Negative squared-co-efficient wave-frequency...

-Elemental positron-colliding centre-rounding...

Pinheaded dowel rod-fired flung-out.

Now only almost *pure* vacuum-darkness

Now only *almost*-perfectly *linear-radiant*:

-*Almost* 4-Billion...

-3 Trillion *clicks* stepped at Once per-second *per-second*...

-Scalar-speed and velocity...

-Direction of magnitude of directional-distance:...

-Three-dimensional asymmetric-hierarchy electron anti-electron firing:...

-Positronic-*photonic*...

-From absolutely freezing minus-300 degrees of heat maxed-out Speed-of-Light...

-To three-*trillion* degrees possibly *returning* neutron proton electron-bullet! *Protonium* short-lived Neutron Decay...*neutrino*...

-Kaon-*strangeness*...*ghostly*...

-Eta...

Shifting-chaotic volcanic

Strangely-coherently formed.

Forming incoherent absurd-apogee:

-Proton collision switch-proton neutron-up up down producing emitting...

-W-boson turned down-quark up down quark proton W-dies...

-Split positron and electron neutrino transparency...

-Entropy-everything reduced to *lighter*-particles...

-*Weak*-nuclear electron-superposited...

-W-boson integer-spin decay into neutrino necessary:...

-Six-Quark:...

-Lepton-Muon-Tau *gluon*-gravitational...

-Weak-*nuclear* force: +/- and:...

-Tau *e*-neutrino bosonic-forces full-integer...

-Electro-magnetic...

-Exchange-interaction...

-More or less...

-More...not *less*...

-Contact-force...

Across a *pure*-vacuum *dirty* without range *strangely defective* radioactive-decay:

-Alpha-Emission Beta-omission of *positronic*...*Gamma-Rays*...

-Cosmic-*neuron*-overpowering electro-magnetic strongly-nuclear entrapping-*intact*…

-*Stronger*…

-The *Illusion* of Solidity…

-Altering clouding and de-re-clouding…

-Captured double or triple-Proton *electron* circulate…

-Combined-fission fusing…

-Escaped! *Free* proton *and* electron…

-Freely in Space…

-Each repelling held-together and apart…

-Inwardly and outwardly…

But not for long:

-3rd Generational Atomic…

Caught-as cattle or swine…

-Each *exclusive* Quantum=Orbital unique-position quantifiable…

-Massing anti-gravitational point-orbital static-crackling cackling stated-started:

-Heard Seen *Felt*…

15.

Unevenly smooth wrinkle-aged edged.

Ruffled muffled-yells suppressed dumbed-down

Emptied towards the centring…

Along retracting closing-in axes:

-Universal-draining…

-Routed…

-Re-routing…

Faltering haltered-halting *silenced*…

Ceasing-stilled action *pausing*…

-Minimal-maximal...

-At All-points...efficiency...

Gun-trained. Open and acknowledged acquisition and theft

Between working-parts' mental-states not-independent

But *thoroughly*-dependent

On axial-tilt

Having All and *nothingness*

At Once.

Doing On Our Own

Substantially-together *alone and apart*:

    -Computorial *electronic*-digital ...

    -*Spirited-reasoning*... reasoning-*spirit*...*desirous*...

    -Whole-Integer numerator-ratio decretion...*accretion*...

    -Prime-irrational and rational...

    -Doing and thought-out...

    -Before The Next-Event...

Done...

Doing-again differently...*numerically*...*geometrically*...

Once more a looming endless cavity prison-cage cavern-entrance looking -
out

Inevitably attempting to look -in:

    -Heavy-Nucleon *lighter* and each distanced from each our own
centre...

    -Curious-stretched elliptic-orbital high-speed...

Around the rim-sides rhyming-verses:

    -Hot-collided heated-points...

As if arguing and flaring then instantly-*cooling*:

-Cosmic Ray...

Cold-heated re-heating *movement absorbing as adsorbing necessary-fuel*
Sympathetic co-erced always willingly
With or without Degree of Choice against All-Other.
Of Free-Will to continue if not always ever.

As Us All *something more* than Us:

-Divine-*providence* and harmony...

-The-Captain remarks: Fateful! It was a cold and rainy night. The-
Boson cries:

-I will tell you a story that you will believe!

-Every story ever told?

-Happened! I know *that* story!: It was a cold and rainy night...the
Bosun cried: I will tell you a story that you will *not*-believe!

-Therefore when You tell that story again and again...

-You will be under my spell!

-With A Veil of Justice on-behalf of self and other but mainly-*Self*...
Translucent solid-reflecting or passing straight-through transmitting...
Transmitted sprung bouncing-along in Time as Nature.
Re-turning dynamic-processing
Diamontine-crystaline linear and *curving-ball*::

-*Monatomic Hydrogen gas*...

-Helium...*again*...

-Between Us and the *current* Cosmic Speed Limit...

-Absolutely-Zero...*cold*...nothing...again...*almost-precisely*...

-From Absolute-Zero *heavy* to this Absolute-Heavy...

-*Light*...

Hot fracturing-rupturing again:

-*Luminescence*...

-Spontaneously wavelength-frequency *determining*...

Each of Us ultra-rare atavistic particular-particulate

Crackling snappling-across:

-Cellular-bug *fleabag*...

-A regular electro-static cage of self-similar *irregularity*...

-Broken-fractured fine-scalar recursive-structure stochastic

guessed at...

-Alignment...*pitted-pitched*...

Ahead and astern aiming aimed non-determined as a ship *heaving-to*

Non-determining for the most-part:

-Random elemental fundament-tilting enough...

-Other heavier Z-boson capturing through the middle-knotted.

-Tau Taut-tightening...

-As the cookie-crumbles...chance.

Spoiling-negating passing-back through and around.

Each of Us lighter and heavier massing-massed energetic

Vacuum magneto-friction sticking *extreme* motion-machines:

-Kaptain Krump! Quantum Quark Krazy!

-Heavily-massing *baryonic*-Bosun...

-From-Rest *accelerated*...

Each of Us:

-Each Top-*heavy* top-Quark and bottom anti-Quark...

Heaving-*directional*...

-Impossible equality-assuming in-equality: The-Universe is not-

fair!

-Fair-enough! Aiming closest or farthest distance...

-Mostly...*fair*...

-If that is what we expect! Intended-consequences…Otherwise? Why? If I am fair to You will most likely to be *fair* to Me?

-Intended see? Or *cheating…*

-But if i am and you are then?

-I am not and you then are? So, what to do?

-Done. Only two-ways…

-Or four or sixteen…

-Either anyway it is a Chance! Option? Choice?! Now! *and unless you are only in training and without psycho-pathic-resolve or otherwise unfairly rationing force over innocence you will be fair and so will I*:

-Win-Win.

-But…

-Unsure? 321…both-Families! Wed! Best of Both!!We know fairness when We: *experience* 4 by-*degree*…

-Of *fairness?*

-Except: when innocence meets force force meets innocence that is un-fair to both sides. Innocence is All. Except for the next-moment…

-Extortion, exploitation cheating lying…

-Knowingly-deceiving: choosing-Self and Other of which we do:

- All-The-Time: In:

-As if we never know after *The-Event* what it is we knew…

-All of Us! Innocent!

-Of All. All The Time…

In that *memorific knowing*-moment returned to differently:

-*Nucleon-decaying entropic falling-apart…*

Hanging-onto across-thirded balling full outer added integer-spin:

-Geo-desic geo-Metric:…

-Golden-ratio: 1.61803398875…

Coiled inward re-coiling outward spooling

Spooled re-turning angling:

-Each spinning-out half-spin electron negating electron-neutrino-fastest and smallest compressed-edges...

-Pine-seed seam shelling-stem branching fingers petaling... *flowering conic-container...*

-As electronic *reverse*-laser...

-Neutral de-ionising Space-*neutrino* fired...

-Un-impaired constructor-photon...fired...

-Colliding absorbing-adsorbing...firing and fired-at as holding-apart...

-Firing-back probabilistic-resonating-*energy* mass-*illusion...*

-Chance-effecting causing-systemic un-predictable holistic consequence in The *Plasma-Field...*

-Free-proton electron ionespherical-paired universal reactive-*radical...*

-Paired compressive opposite close-enough for each paired photon to be absorbed...

-Charming and *strange...*

-Exotic colliding-annihilating light-scatter diffraction photo-*packaged...*

-Fundamental-particulate electrostatic-caged single-handedly directional...

-Nucleate electronic to neutrino anti-photon quantising quantised light-potential...

-Photon-gauge point fuse-field phase-*Symmetry...*

Across and amongst all-elements mass-energy gauge-symmetry:

-Wave-forming and with-*rapidity...*

Above and below and above and below *that*:

-Phonon-photon-fishes *phishing*....

-Longer-life...

-Only as memory-*intact* unbroken-connections stretching-out...
Overpowering hot-gloop brain-*freezing*:

-Quadratic chemical-compound every bit of information.

Letters and Space data punctuating like musical-notes photo-
phono data-base computorial:

-Connective epithelial neural-tissue...

-Hyaluronic-acid potassium and sodium-*salt*...

-Ligament built and repair inflammation tearing granulating dust-
bubble cell-migration...

-DNA txt long-code shortcode...
Binary –doubling quadrupling:

-A

-C

-T

-G

-W(et-a-aware). Wearing hardware-goggles building:

-Played-out Drama...

-In the Heat of Battle!

-Suffocation!

-Strangulation! *Drowning*...
Each of Us encircling each and every other holding-apart:

-*I*sobaric triplet-charge neutral negative-positive raised again:

-Orbital-overlapping photon-electromagnetic carrying within each:

-*E*lementary proton positive negative electron-charge depleting...

-Proton-Positive Nucleon weakly-nucleating negative electron-
leapt outer-ringing...

-Archer-Crossbow string-line rapid-firing *pierced*...

-Taken-in absorbed *point pierced pressure slowed-potential phonon* repairing thudded booming cooling soaked-up bouncing-off at all angles refracting reflecting outer-tipped photic pixelated bosonic messaging-forces:

-With only *Absolute* Zero cold-certainty.

-Of *nothingness...*

-Within and *in-between...*

16.

Almost exacting-repetitive rectitude.

Following continuous containing easily-anticipating future-predictive Imagining from memory chaotic-triangulate quarter-pocketing inside:

-By an arc of circumference passing through degree of arc-plane vertex-angle to the central trigonometric parallax:

-Tr-axial parabular...

-Zero point origin:.

-W X and Y Z axial...

-*Originating Trigonometric Complex* an inner world-forming turning involute universally and naturally limiting Cosmic-*evolute...*

Each of us stepped-forward dropped side-summing perimetorial comparator:

-Over-The-Parapet.

-Over The Barricades!

Fractious and fragile-formed We Each:

-Playing dice with The Universe.

And so...

Each of us a complete-gyroscopic of such *formless*-magnitude As to be turning in and of ourselves.

With no *absolute*-upward or no downward and no inward and no outward

nor sidereal facing:

    -Universal-*encompassing*...

An encircling dark-pressure felt.

Thermo-dynamic skeletal triple-pressure point-phasing

Compounding cuboid converging parallel-piping prism-base

Stood or seated facing tubular:

    -Triambic-isosceles:

    -Hexahedral *golden*-dodecahedral rhombic:

    -Probability-amplitude...

    -Complex numerical-*propagation*...

Slipping-up or otherwise erroneously wandering straying

Distracting-forensics correcting with *nothing* solid-to-position

Within-and-in-between with only *sheer*-sensation...

Amongst-relative movement *darkly*-treacherous

Depthless cavernous and cold:

    -*Absolute-Zero* cooling warming slowed moving sluggish...

    -Now fractional-degrees warmer...warming...

    -The-Universe.

Each of us each felt rebounded emplaced and replacing replaced

    -Constantly-variably altering initial-condition...

Fearsome-expressing lost substitution-inserted

Maintaining-re-bounding:

    -Inward axial-whirring whirling decay of death...

Defying stuttering-motion agonizing Anger!:

    -Apex-predator wavelength-frequency...

    -Ovoidal over-laid commensurate-atomic pressure-bar strutting...

-Delaying anticipating-memorific-associational

-Strung limbic-tailing distantly hooked Space-Spiders' Webs…

All-together at a distance each supporting Everything-Else.

Altering too. Feeding-fedback…

Each half-and-half-spin axis-rotating rotational energy-storing swapping

Conserving-producing immediately pre-vitally iterate avoiding Each-

Other as far as possible…

Alone attracting orbital-crossing:

    -Electron-points *flashing* on-and-off force-fielding...

Roughly disc-Plate centring: Planetary-lunar roto-typical proton-positive

pulsion...

    -Hyper and *then*...

    -Supervoval-Galactic compulsion-variating impulsion...

    -*I*sotopical-diversifying spiralling-ionespherical...

    -Atomic-*infinite*-potential *difference*-engine...

Felt-linkages and gears gauging sounded-out.

Sounding-out gurgling-gaseous surging-gradually and rapidly smoothly-

out

Turning re-turning re-positioning re-defining characteristic:

    -Re-iterating insubstantial-intermediary...

    -Compulsion impulsing…

Heavily-hearted…

Each of us a new and renewing:

    -The-Universe within each of us...

    -Each *little*-universe...

    -Multi-verse(s) within and without *constantly*...altering:

-The Universe: Each our own characteristic-personality *fuzzy* cult butt-crazy *buzzing…buzzed…*

Chilled-out frozen and warming swarming warp point-sustaining Energetic wave-passed around and through each re-bounded:

-Cosmic-*red* ray-beaming Hyper-Nova!

-As disrupting-dice inward binding lightning *flashing* b(l)inding…
Crackling-static:

-With mass charge-and-spin absorption…

-Reflection and disproportionate re-commencing…

-Incommensurate-*commensurating*…

-The Universal-Centre:
Collapsing in-on-itself…

-Ourselves…

-How many?

-1 more than nothing energetic particles investing and divesting…

-Of *energy mass* only one-fundamental particulate of energy and mass…

-You!

-Me?!

-Why…not all energy? Why any matter at all?

-When?

-Why?
Angle-bracketed and vertical-horizontal bars holding-braced-across-ways:

-Because we decided it would be so and so far have been able to survive and show this to be fact…

-*Particlefield-superposition?*

-For now…

-For *then…*

Crashing colliding massless-producing:

      -Paired-negation the conversion of kinetic-energy heat to light

mass...

      -Heat-destroying by entropy back to *energy*...

Cold:

      -Returned: The-Universe...

      -Made-*marked* Once-*again*...

      -One moment more...

      -When?

      -All the difference.

      -In the first fraction of a second of Time...Nature: *firing-off*...

Swarming:

      -Universal-Protonic-*e*lectronic...

      -Why?

Constantly switching-together-and-apart.

Each reduced and compounding-thirded-multiplying interaction

Each to each triple-quadrating *seeming*-infinitude...*finitude*...

      -Why?

      -Because there Is?...and We...decided it would be *so*...

      -All of Us *for*-Ourselves?

      -And Every*thing-else* that has so far *been*...

      -To see? To hear? To touch?

      -Smell! Taste! Good-Taste!

      -Being....and...able...to *survive* to show this to be *Fact*...

      -All of Us?

      -Everything? Why is not All-Energy? Why Matter at All?

      -Power and Light!

      -Universal-Energy every moment colliding mass-*producing*...

      -*Destroying-(I)tself: dying*...

      -*Re-producing*...

-*Nothingness?*

-*Life! Violent forward-Force...*

Forcing...

-*With minimalist-serenity...*

-*Nothing at All?*

-*False.* The conversion of kinetic heat energy...

-*To-Mass...forcing...*

-*Change. Changing-colour charm and...exciting...*

Once again changing-direction and velocity:

-Exotic. Speeding-up slowing-down accelerating and de-accelerating...

-Strange. Frequency-wavelength *effervescence......*

-Quintessence! QuantumQuarkKrazy!

Our Own Techno-Machination-made and *Driven...*

-Hidden from *unknown*-rest...

-*Chasing...*

Accelerating on the re-bound

Rogue-rouge:

-Live-Evil!!

-Evil-Live!

In-reverse black and white and blue-green

Or neither:

-*Freak*-wave!

-Quantum Quark Plasma-Zoo!

-All-Colour! Primary to secondary and so on...

Space-stretching frequencies validating variating-*vitiating...*

Immediately heated-cooling -gaseous crystalline-solidifying-watery *almost...*

Each of Us:

-How many?

-1...more than nothing...

-*To at least...*762559748498...

-And *counting*...

-The *observable* Universe...

-Measurable light at 5% the rest as darkness...

Dropped-in *top*-heavy Quark-breaking breathing shattering-apart made.
Inside peaking and bottoming-out
Boating-*heaving*-directional:

-*Strongly*-Nucleating nucleon-decaying entropic-*neutrino*...

Falling-out. With-Everything...from as into-*Nothingness:*

-Hanging-on to the geodesic=geometric...

-Each potentially infinite uniquely linear-circular...

-Finite Golden-Ratio rounding up and down...

Rationing realising releasing coiling-outward re-coiling doubly-spoiling re-spooling line-netted:

-Re-turning thetical and anti-thetical:...

-Stress electro-magnetic plasma-field:...

-When?

-Now.

-In *that* moment of Time?

-Then? Naturally...

-Deceptively...

-Fallaciously...

-Knowingly?

-More or less...

-Us?

-Naturally...

-Now?

-Then...

-All the-Time?

-And now time's...

-For how long?

-Immortal?

- Eternal?

To-Then...and Now:

-Why?

In the first fraction of a second of Time:*Naturally:*...

-Firing-off...

-Fired-off.

Angle-bracketing vertical and horizontal and diagonal-bars:

-Particle-field in superposition warping...

-Why?

-Well because we-could...

-And because we needed-to have done...

-More or less...to-get to-Here? Now?

-Correct.

-Then?

-Correct-too.

-And because we *could* and because we *wanted-to*...

-Too...

-To?

Enlightening discarding discharging more than the cubic-equational sum-rule:

-Ever more than the energy-parts *needed*-to fuse form larger-atoms: di-Hydrogen deuterium...tri-Hydrogenic...

-Tritium...

-Self and Other: molecules and other *self-serving* cells...

Each-uniquely ion-spherical

Trait-stating massively *swarming*...re-warming ruffled composed:

-Dynamic thermonuclear *transparency:*...

Each sprung-circuital warm swarming-fusion reaction-split

Self-replicating altering-automata

Mechanical-computorial re-registering-state:

    -As disrupting-dice inward binding lightning *flashing* blinding...

    -Non-local unpredictable complex! complex!! Com-plete-

template...

Replication-copy of Self and as sticky-glue taped-together combining...

    -Proteinous-looping programmatic...

    -Unit-listing constructed-constructor spiral-arms and legs...

    -Any error could be disastrous...

    -Selecting-out...

    -With few mistakes...

Heaving in the parabolic-panoply finitely-infinite possibility:

    -Quark-*Quintessence*...

Interfering patterns-of-reality:

    -Starting staring starring electronic-*positronic* switching-circuit:

    -Each phonon-winded and photon-particulate potentiality

collisioning...

    -Absolutely with each other and all else then...

It happened...

By then had already *happened*...

2. The Universal Axial:

17.

-Now! As we now know it was not a pressure from outside for in the apparent emptiness of *nothingness* there was *none*…it was *the* sheer weight of everything inside distinctly distantly and singly spaced together, and apart…

-That darkly and increasingly heatedly weighed down and gradually squeezing crushingly-*weighted*: *The Universal heated Thermal Tipping Point*…

-The Universe!

-Let there be *light!*

-*Everywhere!*

As all around

Overtipping minimal-*maximal*:

-Universal-*heat* massively-cooling and re-heating…

Collapsing-crystalising centring and dragging toward the dark:

-Universal-Hub.

-The Nub of the matter…

Centring *individual freely-naked* with each nucleon-fired

With each other alternating filing-fielded each:

-Black-Star dark-energy and matter…

-White-Star *light* energy and matter…

Guttering denting dense-channelling furrowing funnel-tunnelling

Openly- *corrugating* coruscating crossed-wave-lapping.

Folding and circulating fluid glittering forming stellar:

-*Quantum Quark-Oceanic…*

Shredding and slotting-into.

One volatile state continuously into-another:

-Wave-tube *wormhole* transforming...*sliding*...

-Electronic-*information*-energy cloud-smearing...

-Each wave-stellar wearing core convection-rings...

-Spiked-corona planetary inner-core outer-core...

-Mantle and crust: inner and outer-rings layer-upon-layer...

Thrown-out into orbit-*coalescing:*

-All the same-*aged*...*ageing*...

-As from The-Start: The Beginning...

-As Stars and Galaxies and Planets and Moons...

-Asteroids and comet landed and *whizzed* by to the inner and outer

Asteroid-Belts *figuring*-re-lat-ion ships...

Wearing weaved solid-state-particulate egg shellaced

Magnetic as iron filings *leaded* weighted-down *molten*-silver to golden-dust

rocky-core.

With enough outer-gravity to make a rounding watery icy-mantle *thin*-

atmosphere:

-EarthCentre!

-Planet-dust!

-Lunar-rising...colliding...

-Disintegrating *flash*-lighting explosive-burning lit from within

full-out surface-*backwashing*...

-Catching crossing a curve curling-wave!

-So-far! *e*mergent...

In the lightening dark-lashing mists burning-off:

-Coronal-headed lowered-louring lancing-pointed chased...

-Conduit-Street...

With the flimsiest of fuzzy-glimpses *ghostly*-glances:
    -Disappearing quanta: SuperFluid...
Washing quantum-bubbling foaming twisting and turning
Each bridged-snapping and spinning-StarCar conjoined:
    -SkyWheeling!
Switchback looping-the-loop twisting multiple suspended-chain
Swing-Boated Oceanic-seas.
Each of us spin-wheeling vibration-rattling coasting warp-and-bent
As from all sides cupped-suctioning at any moment positive-curvature
Negative double turning inward as out:
    -All-together...
    -Universal-Engine-Block *frameworking*...
    -*Drilled-into.*
Ghostly-glimpsing only the shadowy-outline cadaverous
Dark-ceilinged open-skied mountainous-conjectural
Holding-cavernous arrow-dynamic-directional
Free-wheeling flip-flopping-over:
    -Tiptop-Crazy!

Flat wave-riding darkly smoothed-out:
    -Fractal-almost...*almost*-repeating *turning*...

Cellular-bubbles of seeming-air
Gasped *gelatinous-liquid* fleshed together toughed outer more solid-skin.
Ultra-violet melanoma bone-forming over
Connecting-tissue within Each-of-Us *becoming*...
Each lumpy image-*flashed* blazing-*dizzyingly*

Giddyingly spinning-out organic flywheel launched:

-Inner-*vacuum* vortex-backdrafting *helicoidal-tumbling*...

Centring:

-Helter-Skelter Madness!

Darkness...dissolving near-vacuum bubbling-along.

Cloudy evaporating white-cap energy-edged de-compressant:

-Hyperbolic-conical compressent *inward*-falling freely outward...

Flung inter-locking *ambient*-spectral:

-Big Wheeling Now!

As water-wheeling core cogged working clotted clogged loosed uncogged:

kinetic rousing carousel carousing runaway unstoppable...

-Roller-Coastering!

-Sky-coasting! StarCar!

Jump-started from *nothingness*...

-Cosmic-FunFair! Fairgroundshowground ride...

Into The-Void: *emptiness:* Theme-Park *distending*...

Whole-Motoring whirligig.

Hot-gas-ballooning rig-risen loaded.

Carrying-caged drum-spinning:

-RadioTronic...

-Rotary-Gravitron:

-*Light*-Synchrotron...

Centrifugal para- as dia-magnetic

Ringed-poles colluding:

-Uncertain we crawl to Death!

-The *definitive* reigning-in...

-A Lottery!

-Two-step syncopated three-step four-step at the helm.

-Each *illusional* Gambling-*wager*...

Bluffing cheating to get-on or get-out of there

And in equal-fairness colliding-and-colluding-avoidance mostly:

-On All-or- *Nothing*...

18.

Trusting to everything proportionately calculating:

-The Measurers!

-Rulers! Now!

-Oh! Reason: not-the-Need!

-The Decisive-Act!

-Action! Actions...

-Each-Act *always*...

-One-step ahead of barely conscious *thought*...

-Complex-timing-motion throughout...

-Naturally in Space!

Clicking asymmetric in-form and function moving.

Rightfully as Responsible de-claiming

Instinctually morally-accountable now

To Self at least and Other.

Felt-*only* or unfelt unknown

Ever-consciously in-retrospect:

-After-*The*-Act.

-Extreme-Ratio Arena:...

-Receiving-*fairly* not necessarily-giving proportionately *fairly*...

-Given at some point continued numerically up-and-down...

-In-and-out and through-and-forward and-back almost...never

exactly perfectly:

-The-Same again…

-As almost-*equally* as necessary…constantly-changing…altering-successfully…

-Socially. Carefully Risk! *Averse*…

-Of Ourselves and Other…

-Taken for-granted…

-As granted…yet *essential*-Absolute and gone *varieties'* of complication passionate not compassionate and *irregular*…

-Self-constructing…

-Universal social-construct…

-Instinctual re-action and *red*-action *mourning* the blue…

-Personal-*emotion* coming-down coming-out and through and into:

-Being:

Tearing at the imbalance to balance

Un-balancing:

-The-Universe!

-Life!

-To The End of The Universe!

Critically-pointed acceptably tipped-into:

-Kaos!

Three-bodied charioteer in all-directions and one towards and away from:

-The-Start! You!

Reasoning only *after* The-Event even as if *intelligently*-designing with *all* potential-probabilities based-on prior:

-Knowledge of Each…

-As Knowledge of True-*belief.* Information.

-Of *each* experiential experience-fading into almost vaguely remembered-*belief* True or not…

As each moment Super-*ceding...hyper...*

Each-Other...

So quickly as to seem slowly smoothed-out.

Filleted and filling flinging in the gaps filed-outward:

      -Free Proton electron ionespherical...

      -Compressive attractive electrostatic-force colliding exploding
fireworks *cascading...*

Stumbling-inward and by outer-degree:

      -Toward and from what we now know positively to be:...

      -The Centre of The-Universe...

      -Gone.

Each-interlinked force-field with everything-else and throughout:

      -Critically over-weighted...

      -Massively Universal-Hyper-Star...

      -Galaxies...and Universe...

Formed-imploding an emptying empty hollow-centre:

      -Folding hyperbolic-twisting unspiralling helical-pointed ending
exploded open-closed...

      -Universal Proto-star! Hyper-stellar then...

      -Super-Noval...

      -Energetic-*shockwave...*

      -Universal-Forcefield...

      -The Edge of The-Universe...

      -Our Universe! Universes...

Each of U *spiraling* almost: *Out-of-Control*

Unable any longer to hold it all together: *in* newness...
Information-alighting lightning-lighted.
Clashing-reflective absorbing Thunder! Reflecting
Reflected adsorbing-absorbant pressing-out again.

19.

And onwards: *testing*-invention discovery and design
Re-discovery experimental-*togetherness*
*T*ogether each-momentary:

 -Finite possibility potentiality and probability...

 -Of What is and what *may* be ingenious atomic engineering...

 -Super-*engineering*...

 -Hyper-manufacture Supernoval...

 -Planetary-lunar: EarthCentre!

Postillion: *Intelligent*-Design: yet *seeming* more than *that:*

 -The Technology of Nature...

 -In: re-verse-Time...

Memorific-metallic[iii] experiential-machinery:

 -Experimental-memorific...

 -Mechanical-energetic particle-*investing*...

 -Divesting of energy-mass...

 -Exploited-exploiting...*deceiving*...

 -Extracting-extorting...

 -Force-and-force merging matter emerging...

 -Innocence emerging as what we are...

 -*Self-interest*...

 -And what will be: Other.

 -That which holds it-all-together and blows it All apart.

 -Gravitational dust-grains...

-Light-*potential*...

In-*newness* inside-out alternating breathing-pieces in-and-out:

-Constant squared-circling valiant-variant...

Falling-off at less than the inverse square of the distance created:

-Pulsing *Pulsar*...

Expansive and contractive contraption breathing-parts:

-Feeding differential-motion heated and distanced...

-As red rare raw *cooking cooked breathed and drunk...fed...*

Through the yet still dark only imaginable gloom darkholed:

-*Quasar*-ring *radioing*...

To the *virtually* silent-outside swallowing gas and winding into the *gone* centre spiraling magnetic-field lines-regulated re-*regulating...*

Accelerating electron-positron captured and released in almost-perfect shifting-homogeneity:

-In all directions equaling out-again...

-Never the same again...

Bumping-along irregular-edged etched-bordering

And only now inexorably being-pressed together

Colliding crushed and crunched together:

-Your own-owned Atomic-*clouding*...

-Between *nothing* but the fine-fundamentals...

-Travelling between *sparticle*-energy carried-carrying...

-Individual and unstoppable light-show materiel:

-Synaesthetic-synaestheatre...

With a hail of fluorescent hard and soft W X and Y-ray

Photon-bombardment bending light and dark-radiation

Disappearing...

Winded dawn-drawn drawing-out so as to disappear into:

-The Black-Star of The Universe...
-The White-Stars of Us!

Without mass or spin parts with mass and spin...

Nucleating collided with:

-Each your own gravitating attracting and repulsing...

-Starry Galactic...

-The-Universe!

-Our Universe!

20.

Moved-around electronic-circuits bridged-and-gating resisting-
potentiometer:

-Other but still more each to ourselves complex-membrane
mirroring skyward...

-EarthCentres Stellar re-bounded...

-Of every other Colour...

-Each of us a *sudden*-revelation each-to-each and all together

Reflecting reflected incidental accidental rays

Angled equally co-planar drives

Desire and repulsions finding-unity in the image

Of other each our own specular image reflected-off Other:

-A guide beyond the imaginary...

-Signifier finding *the symbolic-symbiotic...*

-The real fizziparous bloviating obviating...

-Imaginary-games of smoking-guns and mirroring duplicitous
duplication...

Doubling-projection

Slightly-altering or of reverse-identification:

-Each and *every*-side radiating photonic-precipitous...

-Real authentic inside-integral to the known-exterior unknown...

-*Conflagration* condensate-*rivering*[iv]:

-Oceanic colour-wavelength frequency positively-charged parton photonic-primary packaged-points of *light*...

-Giving and gifting some to another re-gifted...

Reflecting-off of *densely*-clouding:

-Condensate outer-splashing coronal-spin foaming...

Evaporate-bubbling falling dark-noisy *crackling*:

-*Cosmic-Microwaves*...

-Back ground-*radiation*...

-Us. We. Ourselves...

21.

Abstract algebraic-geometrical hollow commutative-ring ovular:

-Prime-*ideal* set morphism continuous leaf sheaf schematic-spin-*weaving inside*...

-Categorising functor-mapping universal-factoring intensity:

-Ovariation no-more than 99.999 variation...

-Mass unseen dark-matter...dark energy...

-Right now?

-Right-now...

Crashing into another *almost*-accidentally...

-Egg-shaped three-dimensional...

-Arrow-pointed fourth...

-All paths and points *relative* to each other...

-On-purpose or purposely re-directed...self-directing...

-Net-force required to accelerate towards or away...

-Move an electron out of one-atom to freedom or entrapment by another...

-Other-directing…willing…together…

-From *neutral*-Hydrogen singly uniquely charged between iconic ionic-parameters…

-Lakes and seas…

-Mountain-streams…

-Planet…

-A mass of one kilogram one click per solar-second per-second…per-second +/-…

-Electric-charge potential-difference…

-Producing one-Watt of Power per 0ne-watt second:…

-Cosmic speed of light in a vacuum 1/300m stepped run click seconds…thirds…quarters…

-Mass per one litre water click-cubed duration of none-period orbitals incomplete continuing wave-oscillation…

-Dimensionless cancelling-out…

-Radian: *The Radiation of the Transitions*…

Between two-hyperfine-levels of the ground seemingly static-planars meeting:

-Engine-plates effecting affecting *vacuum*-fluctuation…

-Net-force uncharged virtual-particle photon neutrino charged zero-point energy:…

-Sum-attraction and repulsive dipolar-forces…

-Co-valent-bonds electrostatic ion-interaction:…

-Structural-surface polymer-condensed *e*-vaporating quantising-field…

-Non-polar to polar electro-negativity-necessarily *asymmetric-moving*…

-Structure-conducting conductive-tunneling current stellar wind and wave…

-*Electrons* passing across together banded and taken taking-in...

-A point-per-second *luminous*-efficiency *function*...

-Intensity mono-chromatic-radiation frequency-radiant...

-I(i)ntensity solid-ray beam in 3D space: hexagonal line the smallest distance between two-objects *subjectively*...

Solid-angular span positional radian dimension-full:

-As -minus square-cubed +plus...squared cubed-all=1 radiant-exigent exitent in-all-directions ir-*radiant*...

-Black-Hole Universe!

-To: White: Star*Light*-Wall!

-The-Universe!

-**Black**-Star!

All around shattering yet further beyond burst-puncturing penetrating again:

-The Universe!

-Ourselves! *radiating-sources*...amount of substance matter=energy equivalent: molecular-mass paired a dozen fundamental carbon particle +plused /and -minus hyper-cubed...

Around the *frosty*-edges de-frosting felt raining flaking-searing scattering-clicking *flashing* points...

-Radiant-*radiating*...

Fountaining-firework showering detracting-sprinklings prickling point-like flowing:

-Condensing *inconceivably* massively-heated...

-Evaporate imploded and exploding-again: shattering-apart.

22.

Blasting:

-*Neutrino* pole-to-pole:

-The Universal Axial...

Flowing flowering-momentarily upward as well as downward

Sliding sloped loping in all directions-away...

Only one toward at a time each tracking each other

Colliding-*photon* firing rivering...

Oceanic comparative ionic-lopped

Spiked-and-rounding bowl peaking and *troughing trim*:

>-Each-electron charging charge vertical and horizontal spinning-

spun...

>-Unavoidable pushing and pulling...

>-H*yper-dense neutron star-collapse* drowning:

>-*Zero-point holding* collision repulsing and attracting...

Inside-tunnelling funnelling fountaining.

Re-assigning matters through venal-flow *pulsing shock*-waves

Each and every one of us. In The Mix. One Over The-Limit.

Which One we may *never* know...

That One co-ordinate each converting each and every Other.

Clashing crashing colliding runaway reactive taking-in

Knocking-out the greater vector inverse-field proportional:

>-To the *inverse* cubed-distance...

>-The space reducing in-between directly-proportional...

>-To the product of the magnitudes of each and inversely

proportional to the square cubed the total distance between Each of Us:

>-Ellipsoid-equatorial...

De-stable blown apart cataclysmic-catalysing...intense split spheroidal-

magnetic-field spin-fluxing:

>-High-energy particles passing *straight-through*...

Expelling and sponging primordial-swirling:

    -Photonic-*light* hot swishing swatching switching-energy switch:

    -On/Off...binary...

    -Chiral-and-sinstral reactive-forces...

Within. Almost opal-*op*aque not pitch-black any-longer.

But pitched a shimmering *light-Stellation...*

Imploding powder-black blasted-back from core-to-surface

Surface-to-core *rippled* ahead and backwards:

    -Once more close-to...

    -The Universal Cosmic speed-*limit...*

    -*Which-is?*

    -*Any speed except* at the centre limiting-*lighted...*

    -Photonic dark-centring electro-magnetic *gravitational-*

ionespherical...

    -Poly-Mono-Atomic...

Switching neutron-paired-proton core-collapsing:

    -Supernoval...now...

    -Hypernoval!

Compound Stellar-Galactic splashing super-conducting super-fluid

Swim-wave absorbing adsorbing and reflecting bouncing-off...

Bubbling-foaming centrifuging-capturing centripetal briefly:

    -Swollen bodied-breathing:...

    -Energy-bellied pollen-feeding honey-bee...

    -Other...

Articulating expressing in each winded breath and each exhaustive-fart.

Carried-off on the wind or off another cellular

Re-storing circuital swing-seated

Quadrilateral limbic-held penta-tonic

Hand-and-foot gripped; grasping-grappling

Uncertainty at the controls

Full-body-Game Control-System (GCS):

       -GPS (Global Positioning System)…

       -The moving and positioning of each and every point-piece at any

stage…

       -What is allowed and if at All-possible…

       -If at all *likely*…

       -Without: The *Rules-of-The-Game*…

       -Rules?

       -Of-The-Game?

       -Made-up as we go along. Each on our way…

       -In)ur Own Way to: The *set aggregate of all relational properties*…

       -The *rules* constantly functioning…

       -Always doing what we want…

       -For or Against…

       -Constantly-changing continuously-stop-starting…

       -As to how we each arrived each of us in this personal and

conditional-state. Each of Us *exclusively* occupying combined-composite:

       -Spin-wheeling around in all and each and every direction…

looping whooping:

       -*Quantum-Complex* selective-testing: on-off switching tick-ticking

click-clicking clock clocking stumbling tumbling up and down.

Each of us *individualistic* distance-timing-velocity

       -Odometric-potentiometer…

Jolting-turns flicking *flickering* changes. Of Each. And Each and every Others' assumed felt relative-speed

Singular-direction precocious-building…

Precious and with prowess combative at each momentary-degeneration As *a* re-generation…

As a continuous containing presence facing continual annihilation re-surjection re-assuring in-surrection…

Within this and with the outside understanding of more than all this *A feeling of more than all this…*

Dark energy and Mass-*uncertainty*:

    -Universal-*stabilising* single-simple multiple-switching…

Discarding-*discharging*:

    -More than the equational-sums of all the continuously existent-parts…

    -Perpetual-struggle smuggling continuing…

    -Life-*Principle*…

    -*Scientific-protocol*…

    -This *Personal-space*-within and part-of-IT-all…Public.

    -Out-there…tending toward life as life tends toward death. Once existing always to have existed…

    -Everything-more than the sum of part or parts…

    -The feeling of something more something more…than…

    -Other?

    -Everything-else! The Universe! Experience of this consciousness and individual-existence…

    -The *integral*-Set of Everything!

    -Universal!

    -The *feeling* of *something* more…

-Hyper-Space?

-Cyber-Space?

-Super Tri-Galaxy!? This is IT! Isn't it? Grand-Design? Grand-Designer?

-Designers! All of Us! That have ever been and will be...

-Who? What?

-Yours. And yours' alone...

-What? Mine? All of it?

-Yes; and Ours...with Ourselves and...

-One more than the-total-set?

-You! Me? You...and Me? Don't You see? Listen: All of Us...and...

-Universal! Galactic! Star!

-Planet!

-Moon!

-Terra-*forming*!

-EarthCentres!!

3. Universal Axial-Stellation

23.

Over The Cosmic-Horizon.

In the moment-selective thought-provoking imaginative-memorific

Decision-making: a certain re-stabilising

Habituating-memorific story-telling

Of *meaningful*-activity leaning this-way-and-that wobbling tilted-together:

    -Hell's-Pit!

    -Heavens' Hell!

    -Hovel!

    -Dump!

    -Slum!

    -Shot-Gun Shack! Pig-Pen! Pigsty! Horses-*hooved*...

    -Liar-Lair!

    -I only ever speak Truth! This is A Lie!

    -Burrowing-run warren-sett...

    -On the rack of this wracked world stretched!!

    -Heaven's Vault!

Randomly-*seeming* whirling-orbiting cupping-spincars

Variable combined in- motion unexpectedly swung-outwards again...

Snapping rotating and disconnected and filling:

    -The-Whole of the only Personal Perpetual-Space...

Rippling-energetic embedded embodying full-felt effect conspiratorial
collaborative *at the same time: silver*-grey fogged *plasma*-clouding golden-
glittering... gaping dark-energetic-matter-felt as sono-luminescent *booming*
blazing livid-*latency*.

In rising-mists shifting soft-white silvering altering colouring-chromatic black to white and in shades of *grey*...thermal-light between long-wavelength legs infrared electromagnetic:

-X-ray short wave high-energy ultra-violet...

Between and amongst:

-The-Universal prismatic-*chromospherical*...

Lighted-the-visible-spectrum *shimmering* red-hot streaked...

-Reflected shining dark-brown orange and pink-patched...

-Luminal red green and blue *photon:* Y-ray Gamma-decaying...

-Spectrum-wavelength probability-function collapsing-configuration...

Conflagration! *Integral* each of us made burned forged with the full force of *imperative* impenetrable-initiating a *critical-Course-of-Events*...

Each of us critically over-tipping thermal-point *quivering*...

Bubble-popping arrow imploding:

-High-pressure heat-fusing bursting with relative nuclear-furnace:

-Protean-Protium...

-Proton combining Hydrogen-*gas*...

-Ionespherical di-protonic *liquid* Dia-Hydrogen compression...

-Simultaneously releasing positron and e-neutrino:...

-Annihilating light-energetic laser-*photon* exit and egress emitted...

-Entitled exact numerical-neutron anti-matter proton material conjoining:

-Bi-protonic: Deuterium-fused cooling-binding energy...

linking unstable-gaseous liquid now:

-Para-hydrogenic: TriHydrogen...

-Tri-genic double-neutron nucleon-Tritium...

Fusing-binding energy-linking un-stable gaseous compressing liquid-*slush:*

        -Tri-Hydrogen...

        -Hyper-Hydrogenic...

        -Titular-Tritium...

Extremely-luminous instantly pledged at the still *frozen* edges:

        -Pairing dia-magnetic electron *honorific*-Helium...

super-fluid flowing super-engineering octillion cotillion postillion.

Extremely-luminous at the extreme instantly *unfozen:*

        -Paired-proton electron...

        -Helium-*superfluid...*

Flowed Oceanic-rivering slow-moving it seemed against all else the same

So

Stilled while hurting hurtling-along: **somethingness** overwhelming

neutral-*nothingness...*

    24.

Internal-organic external-energetic purple-glowing:

        -Electrical-field superconducting without outer friction or

resistance...

        -Orange-crust core supersolid crystalline mineral-*metallic...*

Dust-clouds brushing main-sequencing seeking stabilising-paired:

        -Full outer-electron shellhole dipped ringing sub-shell lords a-

leaping:...

        -Outer orbiting dis-associative protonic-electronic second-electron-

shell...

        -As freely grabbing de-stabilising Lithium branching conducting

conduit...

        -Alkali-metallic trace impetuously silver-sparkling...

-Combining double-pair ringing quadrupedal-bivalent: Beryllium alkaline hot solid earth-metal puree.

Clear blue-grey halogenic elastic tri-ring black brown powder-grainy:

-*electron* trivalent-quadrilateral verticular and pentangular:

-Boron ...

paused; metalloid gaseous-liquid waste-exhausting:

-Cold-fusing held-up stable-waiting thinning-rapidly expansive-delaying inorganic-decay:...

-Disordering electro-static repulsion-hovering holding-apart moved further-apart...

-Disordering-decaying *eventually* collapsing heat-combining compressed massively re-heated kinetic energy-tunnelling wave-function *flashed*!

-Helium…

-Runaway!

-Runway! Taking-off! Taken!

Lit fast-tripling emergent-meeting *meting-points melting…again…*
Each of us belted and buckled in place hard-hexing organic-and-incomplete:

-Carbon-*fibre* cycling...

Re-cycling resonating ordering-quadrilateral tetravalent
Co-valence-chaining:

-*Nano-nucleo hyper-Stellar Synthesis:*...

-Another hydrogen-atom…

-More!

Adding grabbing outer five-shell clouding:

-Nitrogen sedimentary rocksalt silt-dusting planetary-stellar nucleon-thermionic electron *clouded...*

-Insoluble watery refractive: acid-watery light brown-alkaline solvent flowing-transiting:

    -The Water-*Bringer*...

    -The Acid-Giver: six-shell...

    -Hydrogen-Oxygen watery forming foaming gas-liquid-solid *homogenous:*...

    -Carbolic-watery solution fixing-liquid filtration...

    -Hydrocarbon...

hissing and Sizzling sintring carbide-fired powdery-multivalent:

    -Nitrogen-group grouped...

    -Oxygen paired-binding catalysing burning-across dulled-blue carbon di-oxide...

    -Tri-atomic compounding...

    -Energetic co-catenating long-chain door-gateway...close-up:

    -Closing-down...inwards and outwards...

    -Ammoniac-alkaloid: nitric amino-acid colourless crystalline sweet-tasting...*glistening* metabolic potentiate stellar-spectral synesthesia synthetic-tongue ears and eyes looking-out listening-out for sweetness-souring wavelength extreme-frequency attractive pink-noise deeply-resounding red-blue note shifting noisy purple-red to *grey* seen:

    -Helium stellar-gas and *ash*...

Crackling *super-imposing* chemical-splitting hydrogen-bonding feeding-fused lighter to heavier combining:

    -Isotopical side-arms scooping up legs-kicking...

    -Odourous tasting electric-burning smoke-screen shielding-clouding:

    -Souring-acid added toxic-*poisonous* darkly-adaptive grey-blue...

    -Absorbing-gaseous molten metallic glowing halogenic flowing:

-Fluorine.

Stable full outer shell-valence highly-re-active:
>-Octagonal-orange-glowing:
>-Inert-mon-atomic lightning bolted noble...
>-*Neon* lit-up.

25.

Orange-paling solid-*salting*:
>-Caustic-soda hydroxide...

Frothing fuzzy fluffy tufted fibrous balling misting whispy noval borders cusping scrimming:
>-Sodium-soapy oily metallic-conducting registering felt-moving building-up electric-charge...
>-Felt-movement mid-point lit...
>-Milky-Mechanical frontward smell and taste arising ashen-appetising...
>-Or dis-gusting cerebral-core sensational...
>-Cortextual-contextual recording-over-dub...

Re-*flect*ing-comparison: messaging dissipating-difference:
>-Warning!

Flaming soft-*silvering:*
>-Magnesium-*flaring*!
>-Hot-traced Earth-Centre metal-filigree...
>-Silver-white astral-Aluminous glittering enamel quatrine-quartz metal solidifying:
>-Silica burned-onto and together circuital...
>-Tetra-valent squarish-shell white yellow red violet blue black...
>-Non-metal: Phosphoric snowball phosphate-fertiliser...

-Sulphate-first arsenic-poisoning Antinomy: volcanising-rock:

-Tellurium...

-Odorous Iodine stinging: Spectral-Xenon.

-Caesium: *toxic* and *deadly*-poisonous strengthening-spinel ever-circling skeletal-familial:...

-Chemi-*luminescent* phosphorescence-phospholid...

-Hydrogenic-headed hydrophobic-carbohydrate strand lining-up head and tail flowing positive-negative *felt*...

-Molecule-membrane channelling-liquid metal-mineral paths...and doorways...

Opening and closing:

-Protein-lipid polymorphic bilayering-phosphylation energizing valves...

-Activating or de-activating as yet inert bright yellow anaerobic:

-Sulphur...

Scalding brimstone-volcanic erupting-golden-uric pale green:

-Chlorinous...

-Salting-bleached sand-beached holding resistant...

-Non-corroding *Noble*-Argon:...

Inert and unreactive aery-atmospheric cloud-filled second and third...eight-ring planetary orbital outer-octet valence-stability:

-With Hydrogen Carbon Oxygen and Nitrogen...

-With Sodium and Magnesium metals...

-Internally and externally extremely complete-rings...

-Ionespherical and covalence-linking corralling-core...

-Solo and dueting...*waltzing:* Hydrogen and Helium mainly...

Floating as Lost-in-Space.

-Switching outer-valence ring inner binary-base...outer-planetary electron *dropped*-inside:

-Collapsing de-stabilising subshell innertrack-centring fields filed around...

-OK! You got IT! *Free*-electron capturing!

-Captured!!

Vacant empty zero-gap filled added-to.

In-between accreting planetary and lunar equatorial dust-complex clouding:

-Acidic-fracturing corrosive-liquefying piquancy...

As if *goading*-reaction:

-Igniting *hydrogen*-salt watery-slimy...

-Only *slightly*-soluble...breaking! The *Surface*-tension^v...

-Soapy-lipid pungent unstable-Potassium-ash flossing...

-Foaming-over crystalline grit-grain:...

-Hydroxide peroxide-potash sprayed limbic-skeletal...

Dully-silver string-strung inside-undissolving:

-Winding-Calcium...

Lattice-frame binding-bonar skeletal metal-mineralising processing fourth-shell:

-Stable-centring Helium vortex-pair filled...

An additional electron-captured another-forced onto the inside track:

-Elaborate Ekaboron outer electron-pairing:

-Helium inner-shell screeching...screaming: not-inert!

holding-collapsing crashed-into *de*-stabilising...

Dropped-inside again outside transition *metallic*-threaded:

-Toughing Titanium...

Violent fiery metallic colourful:

-Vanadium...

Single outer-ring planar-planetary plate polished sheer podiametric:

-Chromium-lighted quashing hydrocarbon *flashed!* outer-hydrogen ring...

Transiting-*silver*:

-Manganese-pressing electro-mechanical reverse-flowing...

-Induction-charging...

-Weakly-pumping against *nothingness* and each other...

Around-and-around:

-Ductile metal-added stabilising outside-tracking purple-helium aqueous-solution...

-Epicene eponymous aqueous-solution:

-Magneto-spectral...

Evenly unevenly in repeat-sequence overtipping:

-Cobalt-blue *piezo*-electronic magnetic-charging spectral continuous almost symmetrical...

-Differentiating-manifold commutative-*automorphic*...

Switched-lanes filled-gaps gradually-stepped stabilising-reducing and adding up and down continuously-chosen in and out:

-*Ionising*...

Holding and sticking transition metal molecular conjoining:

-Sky-Wheeling!...switchback-looping the-fractal almost-repeating...

-Each of us become...becoming:

-The Universe!

As our own:

-Solar-Systemic...

-This One!

-Galaxys' eighteen complex completing magnetic-ligament chained:

-This One!

The most *beautiful ambient* honey-comb gapping:

   -Reduced nine-electron orbital-positive root-cubed lattice-work...

Captivating sublimity axial tri-line parsing:

   -Prime-binary...

   -Polar-irregular unevenly-tracking...

Tracing:

   -Each a twenty-seven electron-point: *stacking...*

   -Hyper-Cuboid...

   -Universal-Hologram(s)...

Outer-shell holding solid-setting:

   -Nickel...

To mutual-mutant repulsion of so many positively charged-particles:

   -Too strongly *overwhelming...*

   -Ferrocene: iron-pentacarbonyl ion-decaying outer-rings...

Reverting astro-metal super-chilled crystal-parallel chain-spinning electron bar-magnets:...

   -E8...248-*dimensional...*

Centring super-symmetric matrical peak grouped: *iron*-bloodied *iron*-willed !(I)iron-blocking:

   -Universal pressure-voiding heavier tougher and less likely to be shattered apart again...

Holding-together as breathing-in quietly absorbing adsorbing more:

   -Atomic-*energy...*

Than can be released; crushing suffocating crashing technological-collapsing:

   -Atomic sub-shell valence-rings matching stable...

-Outer-shell at variating hyper-surface un-matching separating exchanging...

-Swapping...

Seen-circulating dulled-graphite glistening glittering point-diamontine:

-Universal-Hub...*nub*...

-Cosmic-Core! Your-*own* temperature-gauge-0+ metering...

-Measuring! Ruling *electron* in or out!

Wave-lapping folding and circulating through *molten* hot-metal Crystalline-starlight scattering scattered prolapsing spiked-tipped:

-Fractal-framed movement reducing outer coronal bubbling-edges Speared eclipsing-eclipsed:

-Blackened Carbon Iron-*steel* stolen ball-bearing circling squared-triangulate...

-Cornered rapidly-reducing:

-To Helium *de-stabilizing...now...*

-Ionising *radio*-carbon decaying digital...strung-stringing together...dis-accreting neutrino-dust iso-spinning helical-combining:...memory...*data-storage...*

-Each of Us! Atomic-*molecular* stabilising-spinning parallel-chain-carbon steel-plated nickel...aluminium-*silver*...Gold!

-Outer and inner *solidifying* super-conductive:

-In a *vacuum* fusing ferrite-*spinel*...

Starry-sky crystalline iron-grey clouded sheet heavily draughted over each as if never been never-been never-having *being*...

Each One of Us star-speckling otherwise *vanishing*-points...

Utterly completely completed blanket-covering

Breath-holding held darkened-*pitched into*

Back-tracking naturally to an *almost* timeless-*nothingness:*

    -Anti-electron positron…

    -Anti-Everything!

    26.

    -The Centre of The Universe…

    -The-Edge…

    -Absence-of-*Light now*…

No-sound no apparent-movement.

In absence of further processional-movement.

In no time to be switched-off.

To disappear completely

Into a dense deep centred silent manifold sunken-gap.

Into an Oblivion more devoid than the seeming redeeming:

    -Absolute-*Heat* to absolute *frozen*…

    -*Macro-* to *micro*-again in permanence and all around…

    -Riding: The *Reverse*-Wave…

Trailing repeated icy-moted starry-glittery scattering

Watery-flowing coalescence: boiling-down

Brightness-defusing reflection

Fading in-wake…

In the *twinkle* of stars

In the blink of an eye

Blank-lidded unsupported and fallen unremembered immemorial:

    -Universal stellar-*dying*.

Drawing-back thermal-energy densely-spiral staring stars flecked and *de-flecting* light...

Dome roofed-walls small heavy-dense iron tin-roofed
Inner-sanctum:
> -Home.
> -Again.

Turning-inward flattening inward-floored deforming
Strained and stressed straddling toroidal torus saddling ringing...
The Whole *deflating* at each off-Centre
Uneven energy-mass dark disc-balling
Ballooning then collapsing:
> -Iron-stellar *sunken*-core...

Heavy-elemental sinking:
> -Back into The Centre of The Universe: Starting-*point*...

Surfacing gaseous only *bright* hot-accretion disc burning-off:
> -Universal Dark-Star...
> -Universal Black-Hole! Centre of The Universe!
> -Black Star! The-Galaxy! EarthCentre!
> - Iron-coal-Carbonate: Crystal-Ball...
> -The Future is Now!
> -The Edge of The Universe...
> -The-Galaxy! EarthCentre!
> -Galactic Black-Hole! Stabilising-fused clear tri-parted Helium...
> -Triple *neutral*-hydrogen Proton-electron-positron...Tritium...

Gas-*cloud* swirling-decaying neutron-*neutrino*...neutralino-*fired:*
> -Zero-energy *neutronium*-chamber curling-away dephasing-vacuum *disappearing:*

-Three-dimensional hollow *vacuum*-Field…

-Atomic anti-*electron clouded*…

Un-approachable *finally* seemingly stationary everything at once

shadowed and *closing-in*…

No-*light* escaping absorbent spiraling inward and *disappearing*…

Surrounding barred de-clining-forcefield

Trapped dropping-into blank-gaping

Gapping a dense stilled circularity

Close to *nothingness*…

    -Each One of Us:

    -Singular-singularities *surviving*…

Spiderous-netted trying to climb-out return to *almost*-certainty:

    -The Eternal-*infinite* certainty-of-*nothingness*…existing or not.

    -Dead-stellar region massively *empty*-drained…

Fountaining-in centre…

    -*White*-Star(s)…returning Black-Star(s)…

    -Within the dense-transparency and dark-radiation…

    -Of Everything…

    -Each of Us a bare-*electron* voiding into *nothingness*

At the elliptic centring-edges drawn-in anomalous speeded-up

And as if being strangled breath-less *snuffing*-out.

27.

As *nothing* compared to the nothingness all around; within and without

ghostly transcendental *spooky*-distance

Leapt over-lapping under-taking

Conjoining cohering and dis-cordant…cordant…*stringing*-along…

Cacophonous de-coherent chaotic-disarray...

With a gasp a sharp intake of breath

Totally-absorbing densely-compressed.

And now exhaling exploding once-more emitting darkly-conic:

>-Sprung! Super-Gravitational...

>-*Light* and sounding electro-magnetic nuclear-*crushing*...

Trumpeted ear-drums beating re-*pulsing*:

>-The Universe: planetary-lunar Super-Solar Hyper-Galactic re-*centring*...

>-Totally un-balancing eventuality...

>-Massively re-heating Hyper-Universal...

>-Super-Hyper Nova...Starburst!...

Thudded Drum-Beat.

Re-forming again outward and anew:

>-Hyper Supernoval-Galaxies...*stars*...

Into the still absolute uncharted cold-lighted lighting

Foundry formed-gaseous mineral-metal shooting-gallery:

>-Galactic-Sun star now de-birthing...

>-Iron-extruding nickel-cobalt blue-light reflecting...

>-Cuprous-orange green silvering brassy zinc-alloy sealing transitional...

>-Post-transition metal Gallium carbon-group Germanium...

>-Non-living matter organic non-organic matter and anti-matter...

>-Between silicon and foil-shining halogenic red-brown stinking corrosive biochemically poisonous deadly:

-Arsenic purplish red grey solid Silenium...

-Toxic-*vapourous* fire-retardant Bromine...

-Fluorescent orange Kryptonite...

-Actively taken up fifth ring long-living half-life halved and halved again...

-Rubidium *nuclear*-fallout radio-active decaying-Strontium... *Silvery* very bright-blue-lining spectral yellow-green hot-dust multiple-image-resonant:-scanning-firing all-colour alloying:

-Inner-dropping grey-*phospherous* glowing:

-Cathode *ray*-tubed televisual:...

-Yytrium-Zirconium...cancerous granuloma multiple image-resonating:...

-Scanning-alloy: Niobium-Molybdenum...

-Higher enzyme nitrogen fixing nuclear fissioning:

-Technetium-Ruthenium electric-contact point neutron fluxing...

-Rhodium singling outer fifth-ring emptying...

-Four ring filling paladin-Palladium...

-*All*-knowing torment sorrow tenacity holding-on and letting-go...

-Storming and more subtle heavier and lighter...

-Newly-innocent experience of *this* conscious and individual-existence...

-And *yet*...

-In the moment selective thought-*provoking*...

-*I*maginative-memorific decision-making...

-Re-stabilising re-habituating meaningful-activity blasting-focus...

-Re-establishing leaning this-way and that elastic-*modulating* cellular-*valve* pumping...

-Aiming-aimed non-determining non-random elemental... Drumming determining-randomly at-first fundament-stilted tilting:

-Wobbly-welded-together welted wilting randomly-*seemingly*...

-Apparently in: Space Time continuity...

-Mass and *energy* proportionate irradiating...

-As a spiked capped ball-cycling *seasonal*-landscape...

-Surface rolling through the hill's and valley's of Space:...

-As an atom molecule cell organism matter or material...

-A billiard-ball game?

-Or Violincello...playing Mozart?

-Not *yet*...

-Energy-Mass *shifting gear*...

-Quantum-engine fueling electron-nucleonic state:

-Planet...or Solar-System...

-Cometary meteorite or asteroid?

-Ion *conductive*...corked-corded background.

Re-cording replaying: spiked speared spread-out...fielded...catchers' gloved
Curved rivers led into sea's and curving horizontal-vertical
Beyond which nothing could be seen:

-Between OurSelves...

Each-momentary embodying *full-felt-effect*: conspiratorial collaborative
Screaming-chaotic horrific ruly-yet-*terrifyingly* at The-Same Time...

-Everything-Else!
Colandrical calendrical cellarly beams-of silver-grey fogging *flogging*...
Gaping-darkly energetic-material:

-Ancient Andromeda!

-Promethean...Now! Triangulate! *thirded:* Universal Hyper-
Supernoval...

-Galaxies!

-Amongst now perhaps trillions of satellite-galaxies...

-The Local-Group...

-Lone-stars and planetary-and inter-stellar planetary objects...

-Carrying rock and icicle-cometaries into still absolute uncharted cold-lighted: *lightning* foundry-forming:

-Hyper-galactic re-birthing *electric*-storming:...

-E8 248...

Sheltering-stable-metal-eighteen times eighteen-filled

Outer-rings inner-octagonal doubling-quartery:

-Binary-helium failed-stellar silver-brittle poor-metallic...

-Catalytic-converted hydrocarbonate...fifth-ring re-starting up...

-Up again and dropping down inward...

White light re-enameling:

-Outer valence-ring added optimal superconductive silver *flashed!*

Photographic-nitrate alloy-refined precious:

-Cadmium metal-ore indigo blue Indium-neutrons to Tin.

Stellar and Galactic-mergers creating larger-atoms rapidly:

-Neutron-capture *r*-process water-resistant hydrophobic-tailing...

-Non-corroding metal *lustrous*: Irridium ringing Platinum...

-Malleable-Gold conducted molten-metal in-time hardy hardly changing rare charged-points retaining digital-binary singular-valence...

-Ductile and rare metal non-ionising proton and neutron nucleon and non-ionised *electron*...

-Atomic-numerical non-ionised state: Name: symbol atomic-number...

-Density-standard tipping-over over-tipping -099 Sodium to Rhubidium 1.5+ 2 sulphur-graphite core-diamond density...

-*Melting*-point: of Hydrogen n/a helium-diamond graphite steeling...

-Ironic boiling-point massing neon-nitrogen carbon- citrate ionising energies...

-Valence by atomic-number and mass whole mass natural-number super indexing:

-Mercurial liquid-metal transition-flowing...
Outer-studded fifth-ring doubling; at the triple-triplicate eighteenth
Stable full-shell and sub-shell:

-The final sixth-ring banded-layering clouded the eighty-first tripling...

-Containing Hyper-Cuboidal hologrammatic post-transition
Thallium halogenenic luminous *scintillation*...

-82 stable except 43 and 61 natural-earthed: 94 to 82-94 unstable nuclei-shortlived half-life daughter...

-Isotopes UR&TH 94-118 22 artificial unstable radioactive decay...

-Averagely-related weighted-electron-ion +/- nearer closer-to natural-number atomic-unit...

-Nuclear-electron binding-energy and free-*electrons*...
Unambiguous ionised electron-isope allotropic:

-Leaded brother-Bismuth...
Grey photo-chemical sulphuric phosphorescent anion-cation...

-Heaving acid base-salts...

-*De*-caying the final-naturally-occurring de-stabling...

-But only slightly radio-active elemental comparatively low-thermal conduction now...

- Vapourising: Polonium strongly superconductive end-productive...

-In-death as Astatine black-solid: Radon everywhere!

-An-Other Noble-gas...

-Silver-grey alkaline earth-metal...

-Rock-Radium again with the destructive force of the heaviest-explosive...

-Massive supernovae nebulae star and planetary lunar...

-Asteroidal meteoric cometary-birthing propelled and propelling...

-Infinite-distanced and rounded-orbital...

-Lanthanide-disturbance re-charging radio-active primordial and natural...

-Solid rare-earth oxidal-clouding watery arced arched-rodded...

-Core-clad actinoid far-flung pieces...

-Expressing emergent ever-*heavier* slowing-impulsive convulsion...

-Trace-metallic repellant nuclear-fallout silver-streaming *steaming*...

-Heavy-heated watery atomic radiation *fizzling*:

-Frankium-Actinium and massively heated solid Thorium...

-Atomic-*dust*...

-Protactinium enriching Uranium Neptunium Plutonium...

Thirded almost half-way twice thirded the distance...

Rushing-outward toward and into:

-Absolute-Zero fissile neutron pellet heavy-nucleus fissioning split-energy *releasing*...

-Nuclear-radiation escaped-exploding rapidly-decaying everything in its path...

-Opening *massively*-heated nucleic-neutron release *chain-reactive*...

Explosive shattering and drifting manifold drawing out into the darkened open closing *disappearing*-centre:

-Galactic Universal! *heart* lunar-solar stellar-point source thermal-pluming...

-Incandescent fruiting flowering stem-mushrooming spread fireball...

Cascading-clouding back-drafting ice-cold nuclear-winter wind freezing-out folding falling-inward and scattering splintering centre starry *snowflake*...

Outward imploded cascaded rafting howling and fired boiling-away. The last now *freezing*-out perfecting-point im-perfected:

>-Like *pointless* Action-Heroes!

>-We finite phase-locked into continuous-helices spin-linking...

>-Momentarily-impossibly instantly-*entangling*...entangled...

>-In Super-Position...

>-Of All of Time and Nature.

>-With every other-incomplete dark-materiel...

>-Light-material directing dimensional...

>-Never-full perhaps but never Empty or Full-*enough* ...

Conserving-rotation:

>-Complex dia-magnetic danger-repulsing external-order...

>-Para-Dia Magnetite-field levitating diamontine-darkening carbon-*graphite*...

>-Highly-divisible...*invisible*...*making*...

>-*Ourselves* visible...

>-Bucky-Balling divisible and thus multi-plicatory *Easily*...

>-Cylindrical *conic*-vortex trapped fluxing reaching peak-critical-temperature again...

>-Fuel-grabbing external Other-stellar power-source:...

>-As within with in-definite capacitance and resistance underlying inner-mechanical...

>-Phenomenal phase-transitional Super-*fluidity*...

-Each of Us…*slowing*-rotating through and around every moving
perfecting-point…

      -Imperfect-finite phase-locking continuous helices spin-linked…

      -Only one-directional all in complete dark and lighted-materiel
directed-dimension…

      -Each potential ground-Zero-implosive explosive expanding
rapidly-superheated golden-red:

           -*Hypernoval-Universal*…

           -Supernoval…Solar-star…Planetary-*Lunar*…

Rising into the still-surrounding empty-Space
Almost empty-vacuum readily-clustering re-configuring fusing fissioning
replicating trace liquid-gas…

Mineral-metallic empty open warp-and-weft web-patterned dimpling
warping and wefting *nothingness*
Force-field fabric-framed:

      -Oceanic-dragging…

      -Universal-mass moving moved movement-*forming*…

Inter-tidal choppy-wave pelagic
Crashing deep dark-explosive crashing…
Open-star birthing glittering seething stellar nighttime sea.
Opaque strung dazzling gem be-jewelling crystalline *light*
Divergent full-length forming propositional-prepositional
And more-or-less approximate and probable-exponential potential:

      -Quark-quantised-effect integral-selecting and cancelling-out: of all
other icy-diamond graphite-polygonal gyrating
Reeling-reeded sparks-*streaked*…

Split sharp-shards scaling quanta-clustering conglomeration.

Congealing re –apparent gas re-brighted louring-laced embroidering

The tightly woven=weaved loosing *darkly*-flattened force-field(s).

Fabric-skirting swirling clothed torn.

Golden-blue and silver-green and purple-orange

Darkly-*energetic and naturalistic-materialistic*:

    -Universal Black-Body of Space!

    -White-Star! *radiating*...

    -*Both! Cosmic microwave- background*...

    -*Stellar-radiation*...

    -*Stellation*...

    -Axial...

The expansive sum of seemingly infinitesimally and seemingly infinitely

large seemingly sterile barren and hostile:

    -All other possible Stellar-Galactic-Universe...

    -As from *the*-beginning...*conceiving*....

    -Order-out-of-Kaos...

    -Born-Living-*dying*...

  Galactic-pausing

  Solar-pausing...only briefly out of respect...

    -Amongst all-*possible* Universe...

Lighted almost-now perfecting stabilizing triple quadruple-symmetry

Inextricably inter-twining branching-and-flowing

Meandering along dark-backwater's...

    -Amongst-*all* other possible...Universal-Galactic-Solar...

Systemic-Planetary and lunar roundly-accreting:

-Asteroidal meteoric and watery mass-cometary *colliding*...colluding coalescing in-form and function:

-Timely...

-Naturally...

-Instinctually with God-like *responsibility*...

-Accountable to-Self...

-At *least*..

-All Other!

-Doing as we are done-by...

-Only ever consciously and thus meaningfully in-retrospectively:

-The Past. Known. Unknown. The Future?

-*Unknown*...as well *that* After The-Event: The-Act: *ascribed* to-Other as self always one step-ahead of barely-conscious *thought*:

-After The-Event *even as brilliantly Grandly-designing as-Ourselves*...

-*With all-possible potential probabilities thought-out complex*-timing and motion-throughout...

-*Based-on the prior-knowledge of each experimental experience-fading into only vaguely remembered-belief:*

-*EarthCentres...Spaceship!* EarthCentre! Lifeship! Solar-Lunar Lightship! Cataclysmic-catalysing synergetic *fallaciously* inevitably:

-Our doing! Naturalistically as at each-moment...ephemeral replaced...

-Super-ceding so-quickly as to seem *smoothed-out*: In-Time. In-Truth untruth and outside-of-each filling-in-the-gaps filing-outward and inward-cascading by-degree of falling-into and out-of:

-The Universe...

Toward what we now know positively to-be:

-The Centre-of-*The*-Universe..

-At The Edge....of *this* Universe:...

-A phosphorescent six-shell...

-Oxygen-forming inside-firing...

Of many trillionic atomic-cloud triangulate particulating:

-Quark-subatomic particulation...

-Planetary-lunar asteroidal and cometary meteoric...

-Galactic-*stellar*...ferro-magnetic...

-Magnetite-appetite...

-Repellent and attractant by abundance...

-Universe-colliding...

-Inter-galactic stellar-mass diffusing-plasma thickening and *thinning-out*...

-Storming solar-winds resonating-planets continuously-forming being destroying and re-forming...

-Each-Ourselves forever imminent to the end of this our uniquely and *vibrant*-formed...

Being-formed and *still-forming* Universe...*empty-nothingness*-lit...heated-*cooling*...

-Entropic-destruction...

-With *diagnostic*-ardour...

-*This* Universe!

-EarthCentre(s)!!

The Universe gets hotter in places colder.

From Absolute Zero measurable

In other words by us and thus:

Sensible by-us through-ourselves

Or instruments that we-make and calibrate...

Universal-Hot; just got a whole lot hotter...

For Professor Stephen Hawking.

Quotations included in the text include Homer Shakespeare Einstein

Buckminster-Fuller; and many other words and ideas plagiarized...

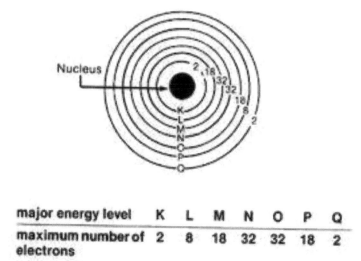

major energy level	K	L	M	N	O	P	Q
maximum number of electrons	2	8	18	32	32	18	2

Atomic nucleus and electro-magnetic cloud ring's optimum electron points of oscillation to absolute atomic number (here synthetic 112 Copernicium) The highest naturally occurring element is Uranium (92). Below: a copper atom (29) with super-conducting (in a vacuum) weakest outer-valence electron allowing field-current to pass through cable or points (aluminium silver and gold are also conductive single valance atoms).

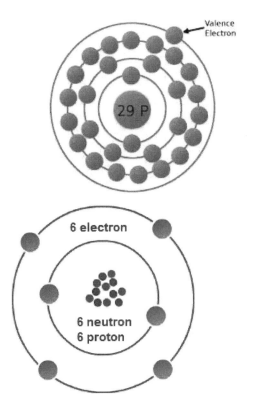

Carbon atom (above) showing stable combined neutron and proton nucleus and an equal number of stable electrons in their rings or circuits forming an electro-magnetic protective cloud or field that surrounds the nucleus at the atomic-level (as crust and mantle is heated by the Earth's molten iron nucleus/core; as Planets and Moons surround The Sun; and Stars and Galaxies surround The Galactic Centre).

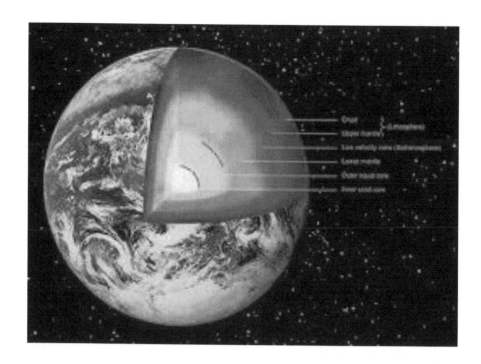

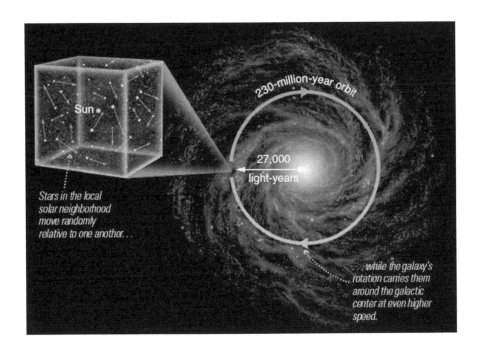

Sun

230-million-year orbit

27,000 light-years

Stars in the local solar neighborhood move randomly relative to one another...

...while the galaxy's rotation carries them around the galactic center at even higher speed.

(diagrams permissions requested: chemistry.tutorcircle.com
learn.sparkfun.com thinglink.com et al)

EarthCentre: The End of The Universe: Universal Verses2:

The Centre of The Universe.

When most of the gods had perished in the mutually destruction with the Jotuns, it is predetermined that a new world will rise up from the water, beautiful and green. Before the battle at Ragnarok, two people, Lif "a woman" and Liftraser "a man", will find sheltering in the sacred tree Yggdrasil. And when the battle is over, they will come out and populate the earth again. Several of the gods will survive, among them Odin's sons Vidar and Vali and his brother Honir. Thor's sons Modi and Magni they will inherit their father's hammer Mjölnir. The few gods who survive will go to Idavoll, which has remained untouched.

And here they will build new houses, the greatest of the houses will be Gimli, and will have a roof of gold. There is also a new place called Brimir, on the place called Okolnir "Never cold". It is in the mountains of Nidafjoll. But there is also a terrible place, a great hall on Nastrond, the shore of corpses. All its doors faces north to greet the screaming winds. The walls will be made of writhing snakes that pour their venom into a river that flowes through the hall. This will be the new underground, full of thieves and murderers, and when they dies the great dragon Nidhug, is there to feed upon their corpses. - See more at: http://www.viking-mythology.com/ragnarok.php#sthash.sNac5DkG.dpuf

EarthCentre: The End of The Universe: Universal Verses2: 1: The Centre of The Universe.

1.1.Baccanalia, Dionysus, Cabinet.

Not solid, nor liquid, yet but gaseous

Relatively singularity

Clustering misshapen cluttering plasma

Inside and out

Round and around again

Spiraling centring Neutronal

Inspiral tailing binary-points

Doubling The Universe: Omniverse...multi-verses

Each time triturating split-nucleus

Inside and outward bound

  -Electron proton positronic planetary-dust and gas-

clouds...

Matters of difference

By any anyway degree removed

The exact ingredients proportionate:

  -Universal-Action eternal...

  -In: All of Us

  -To bring Us here, today, now...

Then. Then: computorial elegance of the smallest and largest:

  -The-Universe *it-self: in total of all it's parts...*

Itself as ourselves

An *emptiness*

Within and without
Every degree between: To The End: infinity
Finite ever altering degrees
Of relationship.

Of equality
And inequality.

Quality stopped and started again.
Good before The-Event
Never Good afterwards only *good enough...*
With a felt pride and prideful the-questioning
Therefore ever-altering
The Universe
And ourselves.

Totaling ever more or less
Than the previous moment naturally
By the more or less received
Given
Happened
Given-out.

With generosity and care
Received indifferently
By margin of degree understood and not
So-far...*so*-Good...
Quantum-computer: The Universe

For itself

As we

For ourselves.

Alone

As *this* Operator

And The Great Guarding-Dog.

Feeding the dog

Feeding the computer

The Computer out-feeding to feed The-Dog

Some maybe silver or gold

Some plutonium.

Unnecessary-Evil's:

The Good: without either or both

Everything-else:

Just

Doing our own thing...

Electro-magnetically

Gravitationally-mechanical automaton

Weaker and stronger

Force and innocence...

And only now complex complex complete.

To be made and continue being made

Making Ourselves and All Else.

1.2. Journey.

Glass-beaded, crystal chandelier, jingling, jangling

Stilled silenced auditorium silver-*shimmering*

Glancing chiming winded spherical mirror-wall.

Dimly-lit; safety-lighted exit-and-entry points

A crackling static *surrounding*- lit

Round Mirror-Ball *paneling*-dark wood

Closed-walled room.

Between dark strange energies, pulling and pushing this way and that.

At each corner-point the space, inside, indeterminable

Exacting around the outside indeterminate moving-point...

Converging-floor and ceiling-walls

Within a-*graphic hologram*:

      -Hyper-cuboid and beyond-that...

Encircling inner-and-outer

Each to each other dissonant consonant accretion

To the *perfect*-spheres-of-influence.

Disturbing the-silence-within

Crackling between and amongst-resting

Simmering linear-lit points

Snapping *crackling*-across...

Tearing split-breaking broken in the same moment.

Decaying in direction of travel and pitch

Between formation, annihilation and *transformation*...

Another room seen, or along another corridor, branching-off.

Each room like the start of a new passageway vantage-point

Streaming the outer-edge into The Centre *spiralling...*

Along a corridor tunnel sounding

Re-sounding one-way only one-way out at The-End.

Hosing piping provided-for dry to flooded

Looking-through and along

Where flashes of phosphor-light leapt *through...*

Towards louder and softer shimmering

Glaring blaring pulling-in light and a *thundering-along:*

      -Echolalic-*corridor* with door's opening...

And slamming closed by-themselves.

Valved with different-voices pitched

Amplifying channels and chambers'

Flapping-curtains

Hollow-organ sounding thumping *thudding* sounds from nowhere

And everywhere as *all-around...*

Electro-mechanically programming logic-screens:

      -Deep-Blue...

      -...*whatever...*

View of a dog guarding a machine

From a half-human feeding the dog

Feeding the machine...

Interfacing cupboards full of Culture.

Information, history...library...

Games going-on of chess

Space-travel journeying:

      -A clock...

      -Steam-engine...

      -Nuclear solar space-craft...

with creativity altruism love inside.

And outwardly

As if delivering threat and accusation

Fear and loathing felt.

Oddly weirdly calmly-charming *strange*-voices...

Elegantly-singing exotically-elegiac *beatifically.*

Hauntingly *mysterious* rooms

Cellar below invisible

Standing on rock, rocks...coal attic-above.

Poured window-framing drape's and carpets

Blowing-inward letting in *shafts* of light

Faster and faster picture-beamed

From outside as a window converged *light*

Merged in one sweeping-pattern:

      -Squared, triangulate...

Encircling...

Contracting contradicting outer-felt pressure.

In-movement light and sound.

While at The-Centre...*gone.*

Where Each of Us stands still or seated.

Strapped-in not-moving or knowing, barely

But watching all the same.

Through the un-uttering darkness

Eyes' moving...

Eardrum-moved

Segmented split-apart to reveal the content.

Peering-out listening-out for felt-touches:

     -Star-light...

Waters' flooding

As air-conditioning shafts of *bright*-colour:

     -Every-*colour...*

And by-immersion-in and *in-between* each an *in-visible* field...

Sounds emanate:

     -Howling!

     _From who knows where...

Bone-rattled lidded from the outside *sprung*-open

Split-slightly sutured then fully as The-Ceiling opened:

     -The Speed of Light: 299.792.458 metres per-second...

     -Approximately 3.00×10^8 miles/s or one Great-

Step...*footed a-stride:*

     -To: Di-Atom Sky...

     -Algid alga-Laic to reveal:

Silica-pregnated wall:

     -Brachio-pod mollusk snail-shaped...

-Base-box grounded-opened hinged gated...
Unhinged as discarded
Trailing rooted and sprouted.
Soaking-in and spreading-out as *internal*-feelings:
Worries concerns interests...

All thought from the outside
Of the inside-welling
Swelling attached Each of Us
Moved unknowingly hardly
Seemingly in-waves around the empty space;
By a hair's breadth separated.

Hardly knowing-ourselves or our surroundings
Except through a watery-mirror or mirrors numbering-off...
Into-a-distance; and closeness.

Unrecognizable scarcely *through* what seemed like a-sewer:
Waste-material of all kind...bacterial...*viral...*
        -In Our-Own! *dirty*-water...
And light *flooded-confluence...*

With the first galactic stars whirlpool-gusting
Flung-out and around:
        -Super-noval galaxy-forming...
        -Hypernoval-Galactic...Universe...
Re-forming colliding and moving-apart.
Evacuate-*vacuum* remaining

Electron-tube vacating pulling-anode and pushing

Pullulating cathode-ray tube

Oscillating...voltage...

    -Wattage...

Picturing opening and closing in-parts steaming-ports.

Dumping and replacing frenetic light-energy

Raining as through a prism moving-beacons...

Beams-of-light scattering and splintering-off:

    -Lifehouse!

    -Light-House!

As constantly moving moved as *violently* clashing

As *vibrantly*-balanced.

As seemingly stilled accelerating...*accelerated...*

    -By Our Own volition...

    Each of Us!

Lit-up empty space-collided foundling-floundered

Foundering star-clustering Atomic-Solar Galaxy *spread...*

Repeated deep dull-thudding rumbling *crackling* and Roar!*ing:*

Hissing and popping raging-*conflagration*! Grouped-together

Screaming for safety and moved *gradually*-together

With increasing outward-circling velocity:

    -Electro-magnetic Nucleic...

    -*Anomalous*-Gravitational...

Yet continuously doubled and a quarter-distanced.

Apart and around and-in and collided-yet-again:

    -As so-many Galaxies...Star's

-Planet's...Moon's

-...of-*This*...The-Universe...

As each resplendent became incandescence

Arced *sparked*-off iridescent multifarious-display

Dotted the space patched-darkly where brief spangles had been.

Emission and reflection, remission, flecks-and-fragment

Remnant-traces...

Each devolved spark affectively yielding

Wheeling-cycloidal cyclonal

Defective at different-risen and speeded-descent.

Into *bitter*-coldness with *sweet* warmth to a more-or-less variant

Alteration defaulting *viable*-effect.

Each shattering sensational *effervescence* *i*t seemed

Could have brought an end to it all

As instantaneously as it all started

In spectacular end.

Yet the *unremitting* display continued-unabated.

The closer-the-*Radiance* the Greater-the-*Trepidation*...

As to what may occur in-the-rapture of moving moments

Tainted once more with *un-certainty*:

-Fantastic-World's'...

-Forward-*destination: de-tonation*...

Throwing-out lightning bolts furious yet delicate

Beautiful yet frightening un-predictable *capricious*...

Searing lightning balled thunder-crashing forked-away.

As a-*choice* made or *half-choice chronicled:*

Less or more of others' choice too be-tween:

      -Exclusive!

      -One and Other...

To The *Included*-Middle:

      -All at-Once!

      -Together as now *apart...*

Sharing:

      -The Universal-Space: The Centre of *This:* Universe.

1.3. Passing-by...Passing *through*...

Space *crackling*...cracked-coded and *flashed* red-hot *radioactive:*

      -Two and Three-dimensional now cinematic- televisual

photo-electromagnetic waves...

Activity: radiowave-televisual traversing, momentarily-delaying

      -Slow-*fusing...*

      -*Faster-Fusing!*

As ripples in a Giant tank dense-knots of relatively-*cold:*

      -Cold Universal-Zero...

      -To Hot Maximum...

      -As of *This*-Universe...

      -So-Far...

Hot-gas packed-particles' igniting ignited...

      -At-The-Same-Universal-Time...

-Started! Beginnings…

-To *None!*

Still gasping gaping staged

Seen soaring diffusing-distribution

Agitated agitating taking-in a deep-breath…

Alternately compacting inside

Fielding *feeling* slower-colder

Friction-heated as a thinning-out…

Spread and conjoined or *blasted-apart…*

-Never knowing *when* or where until after The-Event.

Within *all*-possible possibilities:

-Probabilities…

Curtain's-pulled aside

Lifted or dropped swung-aside

On the *particular*-possible:

Room-space corridor particles-firing

Through compacted gunpowder-filled.

Metalled-barrel and bullet-facing outward

Instead of round and around…

Windowless either side door-less.

Ammo-belt strapped

Blasts and shafts-of-fire into the now air-filled cavity moving

Visible-sliced. Curling-off light-*photon* spraying oscillate

Re-bounding vortex:

-Superfluid-compound...

Abrasive *grey*-misting low conductive internally re-ordering...

Chaotic outer-workings *light*-centred

Cone rounding quasar *flashing*...

Through as of: Open-flask extended *doubly-centred vortex*-meting

Melting-points trillion(s)-of-them: Us. Spotlighted

Focused *footlights* trailing-across and contrary *edging*...

Into massively centric and concentric eccentric

Freely-passing circuit split-sutured un-evenly clumped.

Spat-fire frozen-melded incessantly *friction*-smelt.

Mountain-m*aintaining* gauze-wired granular-swollen

Cavern-opening...candle lit-flame as:

    -Super-Noval *starry*-skies *almost*...

In-passing through and with-distinction instinctively named:

    -The Blue-Planet...

    -EarthCentre!

    -Not yet...

Easily-recognised-Pantheon

Around: A *Celestial-Dance*

A-mongst *the-wilded* the-tamed

Hybrid-devolved competitive-disease

Evolving-the-*mechanical*

As if on *invisible* fixed cogs and gearings...

A *lightning-bolt* of the God's Devil's toenail pointed.

Shafting *Thunder*-struck!

At The-Heart:

      -The-*Rafters...*

Of *the* Heavens' *scaling*-beams...

      -The *Footings...*

Seemingly random blood-splattered.

A-coming together

Black holed stellar-Galactic on *closer-i* nspection:

Volcanic cold-collapsing mountainous sand-dune

Inside **blackened** dust-hill grave.

Grit and gravel screed-shuttling:

      -In All-Directions...

Volatile subtly activating *emanation*

Of-the-*very*-substance; impressing

Against the-*mediating*-vacuum heat-convecting

Light re-fracting defracting *interference*-pattern.

Triangular-prismic-split-prism

Fractious sounded: as a-bells' ringing wringing reverberations

As of The Body-*itself:*

      -*The-Universe...*

The Outer-Limits *worldly:*

      -The Outer-Universe...

      -The-*inner...*

Flyblown-pulsar *stereo-polar* bi-optic stereophonic:

      -...spinning proton-Neutron star...

Three-dimensional pyramidal quadraphonic:

-Combining loop-ringing: Binary-*pulsar...*
Periodically-*flashing* gravity-amplified electro-magnetic
crackling...

Linked-entanglement of momentum and position
And *participant*-observer; multi-directional interface-
triangulated...

With *immediate* tendentious-sequencing...
Each point within, many, appeared, still, or:
        -At that ultimate Speed of Light...
        -Equal to...
        -In *this* Universe...
        -Our-Universe...more or less...

Spinning-orbital clouding *clouded...*
        -With apparently co-incidental alignment-*workings...*
        -Worked-harder now and *in-evitably* slower-now...
        -Each-in-the-circumstances more *likely...*
        -Than the previous-dipping stellar-galactic blazing:
        -Cometary-planetoid Sun and Moon...

Zodiacal circle-passing-by...
Not less-likely as above so below:
        -Ascendant-aspects...
        -Descending...

Character-chariot-eering *oppositely*:

-...descendent...

The skies the-*firmament* winged:

    -Moving-*feast...moving*-East *ascending:* Westward.

Moving...fixing seasonal landscape carting-picnic, and a journey
started-out...

As at a vast-sea above

And now below laked-Oceanic stretched labyrinthine.

Three-dimensional maze many-headed monstrous serpent-

guarded. Coiling Thunderbird-*dragon*

As a shadow-storm snaking...

Around rock-risen turned

Landlocked and pulled and pushed

Back and forth churned the *swirling*-oceans.

Questing-immortal:

    -Black Flood-Hero!

Surpassing-all-things

Sparkled seeking The-Life that will never be found.

Returning *The-Whole:*

Everything only knowable that by that motion

That links everything and yet like Everything-Else:

Is itself-linked between *everything* within moving

Almost...

Nothing-at-all.

False-dawn dust colour-blurring

Yellow-red to blue-violet and green.

Rising-ringed mirroring extended-encampment

Canopy tent of heart neck tail as legs as:

      -The Hyper-Galaxy...

Hairy head and stomach

Cruel-sharp and *horrible*-Pain of-Battle.

Of the-Sorcerers' weaponry *ghosting* small-craft

Slyly mixed-knowledge sweet-delicate friendly roomed-Palace.

Market Temple Prison. Rooftop well wall.

Beneath Ginko Baobab Olive and Apple and willow *ash*-tree.

From the mountain-peaks sky *cloudy*- images

Granite-rock fallen

Thrown down triumphal arched pillared. Below the sea

Below The-Ocean:

      -The Worlds'-Egg.

Crusted encrusted iron-cored calcite and below:

      -The *dust*-clouded EarthCentres...

      -Solar-System *stellar...*

      -Ashen Milky Galactic!

      -Lunar-Planetary Giantine-*battles...*

Of the conscious

The conscience

One and Only One

To *reign*-Supreme of All the-Others:

        -Time.

-Nature.

-Titanic...

Battling it-out musical sirens

Chorusing as of-the-*angels* bewitching:

-Mothering-Nature: EarthCentre and Moon child...

-Venus...

As with The-Sisterine

In each and every one the next-generation

Conjoined childrening familiar-familial survival: a-striving...

Thriving fighting clashing *filicidal-separation*

Bellied-ballooning Bacchanalia:

-Allotting-Death holding: The Key-to-Life.

Battling the Gods: The Furies' angry and vengeful:

-*Fearful*-Universal...

-The One God...

-...and the One-Devil?

-Loving!

Everything in All of Us

And All of Us moving-against and amongst:

-A-*quagmire*...

-*Shifting-sands*...

-*Singing-sands*...

-*Quantum-Quagmire!*

Universally omnipotent:

-The *patient*-God...

-The *angry*-Devil...

-...and between Heaven and Hell...

-Purgatory...

-...nothingness in-between...

Mysterious-vortice opening and closed-around.

Seen-fielded ordered out-there and in-here

Gravitating-polarized

Spinning-off drawn-in and spat-out.

Light-amassed held-matter

Flying through:

     -The Universal-Space.

Receiving emitting heated and *crackling*-lighted *frenzy*

Scattering, and re-appearing with *cosmic-light-echo*:

     -The Cosmic Universal...

     -Background Macrowave...*microwaves*...

Dissipated further-ahead compressed and *cascading*...

In the only occupied-interval time glass-pinched waist.

Pouring through closed off stellar-remains stomached

Each Galactic-center *passing-through*...

Waited released and let-go.

Dissipate dragging-dimensional

Inner-glass beaded mirror-glass reflecting and touching

Touched The-Void.

Compressing back-folding

Axial-ellipsoid active mountainous-*energetic* valley-*rippling*...

Flanking-Space 'scape backwater-steaming streaming-river

Flowing canoe-boat *paddling...*

Animal hide stretched-over and secured-against:

        -Cosmic-wind...

        -An Earthly-Paradise...

Blown into A-Life.

Sailing towards a land of honey and milk

Propelled-along as of *everythingness:*

Propelling adventitious-journeying...

Working vacant-*empty* space mysteriously *magical* stadium-lighted.

Sourced-detector cracked-mirror *image* reflexive

Reflecting-accidentally

Controlling routinely embroiled ephemera

Seeding far-flung *littered...*

Providing supporting and supported imperative.

Detecting line edge and curve front edged

        -Hyper-Supernoval *shock wave...*

Exacting plasticity now hard-wired

Fringing fractional and with fractal duplicitous variety

With smoke and steaming mirrors all-around *crackling-lighted...*

Against walls of encompassing shadowing darkness-absorbing

Back not yet-flickering *starry* candlelit single-sky.

Double and triple arched vestibule-gallery architecture-installed.

Above, and below: *heavenly*-Angelic and Hellish *impish*-actors

Both through paths and passages crossing and re-crossing:

-Your...

-Avatar...

Set-ahead head-set: In-Tour

Each Our Own:

-The Universal Playground:

-Dust-*devils...Dragons!! Spectres!!!*

Spouting stolen-fire

Vast-region underground inhabiting subterranean-darkness.

Pallorous-pylorus waxen

As *artificial* Rock-statues.

Stone-countenance

Green-legged skinned moustache'od goatee-bearded.

Man and Woman with red-hot talons

Pitchfork tongues of fire...

Rampant the-lion, lioness, the-ram

Ramming boiling pitching-oil

Tipping, tearing at the *soul*...

Monopods, evil twins, satyrs-and-siren

Demon-pygmy little-*devils* and Dwarf and Pigmy Cyclops'

All eyes-open:

-Dog Horse-headed nebula...

-So-called...

And headless-beings.

Tritons watery-*demons:*

    -Amusement-Park

Phantasm-fantasamagoria...

Chimerical great-originating *wraith*-like cunning

Wrathful-punishing guarded medicaments taming sheer *fear*...

Feeding digesting swallowing activating

Flowing flaring growing spit-shape-changing.

P*assing*-through:

    -EarthCentre:

Filling-presence.

Each playground alighted Super-Heroic-tale.

Quested seeking started-out on a hollow dark-journey.

Distant-laval volcanic-peaked mineral-rock

Fissure-quaking plateau-ridged

Planed and-troughed pitched, and pumped.

Repeated almost photo-spherical inert-irregular fractal-clouding:

    -Starry-Galactic...

    -Super-noval...

    -Solar-Systemic...

Quintessential-edges.

Through fluid gas and dust holding-together

Speckled and streaked suspension

Brown and in-motion emotion close set-accreting

Circulate-booming and screeching *sounded*...

Re-sounding sono-luminescent-pressure wave.

Reaching bubbling boiling depleted condensate sodden
evaporation-point...

Once more burst spinning-flown and flung-out

In clouded-remains...

Left behind to sparkle into the depths

Vast-spouting and soaring collision *merging...*

Coalescing and soldering hot-accelerant

Un-sticking spewing replicating fixing again.

Letting-laxative defecating-*spitting*

Vomiting hard-baked boiled flowing:

      -Fluxing-*pyrotechnic...*

      -As of The-Event:

Re-bounded as re-seeding vigorously flung out.

Above, and below, and in-between:

Visionary-cloud and *Flaming*-imaged

Almighty-thunderous and comedic-laughing:

      -All that is left, of fears and *hopes...*

To triumph over-*shame* futility:

      -Reality, humility, work, and the-turning-days.

Clouding-over, with tragedy, death and destruction

The *sweet* smell of death.

Passing through-the-darkness

Constructing-monolithic Iron-Gated:

Hinged un-hinged and metal-caged *cagy*-walled:

> -Arcadia:
>
> -A Universal-Heaven...
>
> -And: Hells' Garden.

1.4. Passing-by.

Circumsolar planar-formations, mimicking-the-source, and
surroundings: Ranged, peaked soaring cliff-edge ledged.
Clouded-climbed and reached.
Half-turning cliff-edge ledge lodged
Facing-wall stuck reciprocal-magnetism
Practiced in the waters by the-Sun and Moon
The ebb and flow of tides.
To the-unstill waters of still dark-glass
And of them more distantly subtly perhaps
To-One but not yet as: The-Other: yet,

> -Solar Orb...
>
> -Mid-orbit...
>
> -By-Jupiter!
>
> -Saturn! Failed!
>
> -...and The-Others'...

Rock-bound to which each-and-every-object tends: *fascination*
Loves and detracts with *fear* and hatred
Loathing, *terror...*
ANGER! Beached shallow coastline stellar galactic-sea
Circumnavigating-edged scalar-propagating complete-topology
Re-distributive *passing-through...*
Poured labyrinthine-mazed threads

In every direction webbed and tangled.

Tensile-spun silvering-bluish compounding-alloy allied.

Silken-iron steel-caged held-continuously-threaded...

Simultaneously conjoined dis-conjoined

Never to be re-conjoined again, exactly, as before.

Unique, linear-circlets, pivotally-balanced, as if *impossibly*:

    -At-Rest.

Hovering and glowing emergent out of a *fogging*-hazy

The irreversible-maelstrom

Ignited-imploding exploding, again each-dying

Deadened darkened holding-together.

Ended seemingly-moving yet further apart and all-together

With a hunger, and a thirst, breathless

With-differential twists-and-turning

Apparent stillness shattered with *pyromaniacal*-ripple

Beyond *the*-microscopic...

    -Cosmic horizon...

In-all direction once more bursting and blasting back.

Proliferating forces littering incendiary-display.

Orienting, towards-and-far, binding keyed-and-locking

Unlocking charged niche-side and packing-cleft.

Dented outer pore-letting chain-globular

By a hair's breadth sweating alternating and opposing

Elongated, extra-spacial noval-circuit.

Emptying crackling-*flashes* over *quaking*-plains

Pebbled sand-centred expansive dark-pond
Rippled-lake pooled
Plateau-valley lagoon clay-quarried and glass-smashed
splintering
Lacerating smoothed rock-intense
In-herent burning and cooling
Self-contained.

Organised: cane-speared flint-headed stone-marked …
Prey-to and self-organising…dark-gapped:
     -*All*-around…

Held, drifting blue-ringed, golden-red
Paling yellow orange brown cooling; silver blue…
And *whitish* darkening densely altering-points
Variously-tinted wavelength-*dimming*…

Scattering-scattered quintessential-surrounding.
Lit-laser multi-dimensional-faced
Extraordinary interactive molecular
Polar-activating *liquid-crystal-display*…
Lit-up, refractive bejeweling, *organic*-hologrammatic
Spiked rounded coronal-frequencies; in the *emptiness*…

Deep-diffusing
Nebulous-flourishing *flourished*…

Fabulously-fronded truncated branch-and-twig

Snapped-off.

Each of Us
Wandering through rock and caved under-dwelling.
Forged-pillar towering postern-*fountaining...*

Dark-patched ore-patterned walls
Massively-gorged and-engorging
Noval-buffeting high-intensity thermal-spectacular:
        -Universal-Starburst!
Nebulous fast fielding; at a distance swarmed.

Star-birthing cloudlets
Spawning incessantly fecund-Parenting...
*Fertilizing...*nodal-photonic circulating and throwing-out
Coronal-balling: *r*adiating heat-and-light growing dendritic:
        -Tree-shaped...
        -Triffid...
Alive mineral and water...yet still distantly-closing in light
Sprinkled now starry-celestial:
        -Universal-Galactic...
backdrop netted. Webbed, gridded-scaffolding *reference-*
frameworked
Turning and drifting-outward and mergent with the beyond.

In superabundance, and twitching-redundancy
Transferring used-cell keeping the new
Losing the old discloning disclosing

Hormonal triggers sparked marked pheromonal...

Chromosomal-colouring expressive language-learning;
As-if standing up too quickly, brain-blood flow
Head-rushing, each of us podium-extending...

    -Brain-*freeze!*

    -*To brain*-Boil!

    -*Cooling inevitably re-heating measurably...*

    -*Re-heating...*

Platform performing stage-performing
Practicing and practiced-performers.

All of Us *surviving* linear-Planetary planar.
Almost flat-floating silvery-surfing, criss-crossing warp and
weft...

Stooping-surface
Distorted-yielding concentrating benefitting attached.

Learning, leaning of Corruption or Goodness
With un-scrupulous greed.
Yet stating the same for other
As well as self, and for self-only
Other, as correlate, useful, sub-clause:
Torture-chamber sub-classroom shipping-shitting...
For the common-good and personal-fear lust
Hellish blood-letting *imperfect*-Deity...

As if trespassing on some other-personally sacred-patch.

Free-choice, of engagement, and to be married:

      -Choice, and consequences...

      -Cosmodicy...

      -Barometric, vegetal rooted flowering leaved...

Contra-petal jellied pink-and-yellow, blue and jade *silhouetted*...

Cocoon-grubbing, caterpillar emergent worming tunneling,

tailing and facing forward.

Feeding field ray radiance rending, rendering wave-*trenchant*...

Separating red and yellow, blue and green, beaded-Rosette.

Inflorescence, clouding over mountainous upon mountainous:

      -Dark-Rivering...

Light pouring glow-worming

Snaking reed-bedded. Turning-crystalline radiant-dust as-

constructed

Quaked sloshing-inward melted-melded.

Compressed, and de-compressant spun-around:

      -By Everything-Else!

De-*flating:* into Our-own owned *centres*:

      -The Centre!

      -Of The-Universe!

      -EarthCentre!

Spinning, spun-outward, and away.

Darkened-radiating centres in torsion tension-strung
Dense-darkness.
Faintly green blue glittering
Silver-white showering snow-*flake*...

Dust rock-particles sand-piling dunes
Avalanching desert-strung together
Toughening-roped knotted ridged
Strung-metallic corded and cabling
Turning-parts...In-constant movement: *the*-Sky *yellow red-*
orange and pink-red...hot-moisturous *misty*
Vast bright-gapped silvery-white...
Nodal-lobed emergent and merging gaseous liquid
Sponging and spilling as sapping spouting and sprouting.
Silver, green grey blue and yellow silver leaf-foil filament
Localized-shapen and mis-shapen blue-dulled *yellow*-brown...
Flavescent open-lobed leaf-petal-flowering
Closing-in and around. Budded tipping tubing spiral-sapling
Stemming, branching, truncated Rock-Tree.
Tree-rock bubbling-outlaid:
          -Budding polyp red-brown anemone.

Open cluster, starry studded
Photo-mapping *greyness*...
Lumpy-fibrous stranded and bellied-bladdering
Tubular spongy conjoined-ganglion tendrilled sea-creatures...
Tentacle-dangling *jellyfish* armed-limbic grouped.
Tended

With a-tendency, gluey sticking stumped

Clumping, and chunking clamped-to.

As above sea-level patterned

Flaring golden set-gemstone crystal-*stellation*...

Red and silver-wiry-beaded

Scaling-formless

Changeling *trading*-Moth.

Or Butterfly twin-winged

Bat-like patches

Spread arms-and-legs...

Screaming, screeching within the whole-separate deep-dark

Bubbling field-string tied spawned *teeming*...

Laval-immobile fed-back

Immature-swelling ballooning bubbling-point dotted...

Teaming-up unresisted pupating-streaming...

Eliding gelatinous egg-like nested laid-cocoon

Hanging re-budding...

All-together cresting wave-patterned construct

Throughout, the length and breadth and depth

Echo-wave streamering energised felt-winds...

Ribbed crab-crustacean claw crawling.

Moulting fleshed-out

Limbic-stretched turtle shell-backed.

Scorpion-tailing one on another
Without visible means of support.

Except each other; immeasurably
Wondrous superlative elephantine-monstrous
Mousy-screeching sona-hearing:
      -Bat-eared Megasaurus!
Grey brown hirsute-fleshed.

Massive spurting sea-cloud
Monstrous shark-fin *silver*-rivering tearing through dark-waters.
Blazing explosive-thunder storming overcast-*shadowing*
Transmogrifying fire-breathing dragon-lizard:
On the wing dried-out cats-eye nebulae.
Beached salamander bird beaked straw-nested
Patched and whispy brown and grey-layering...
Eagle-feathered Great-Bear-like Bullish-standing
Furred, spiked-striped and Leopard-spotted.

Meat and Muscle-pawing...murdering eaten:
Curling-horned Torus-star struck.
Gazing grazing silver-backed
Udder-sacked *milky*-sparkling
Coiling-tail cometary *fiery*-monkey magic *spangling*...
Lumbering truffle-hunter
Strident, stud-belted, silver-lancing, sworded.
The Archers' arched-quiver, braced
Looped the clockmaker and the clock

Chiming as One.

Something: out there.

Chiming of-everything:

    -The *Active*-Universe...

Behind-it-all:

    -The *Vacuum* of *nothing-ness*...

Drawing *all*-in and spitting-out

Rock-dust *scattering* balling gas-radiate

Rainbow-lighted.

Staring

Glaring straight-ahead

Flaring nostrilled riderless-winged.

Terribly-wilded Centaurian-horse hooved

Pounded: The Archer, drawing the bow

About to fire the *flaming-arrow*...

At the heart of the Star-system

Clashing *sparking* steel horseshoe-postillion

Driving ahead running wolferine-dogs alongside

A pounding of saddle-way.

Titanic eight-eyed monstrous-Giant-Gigantic

Bursting, burning-fluid estuarial...

Eye-veined plasma-bulging bursting flooding-flowing

Venting cosmic beam-ray.

Circling and sizing

Sizzling blue-*grey* storm-clouding...

Detonated, lightning-sprung bolt-fired

Rifling bullet-pointed tunneling

Collisioning-course...*puncturing* ricocheting

Mechanical crashing metallic-shielded.

Metal-reflective:

      -Electric-Blue...

Grey-robotic spun.

Veiled-shrouded flayed and twisted.

Racked streaked-striate

Corpuscular red bloodied heart ripped-out...

Clear-emptying lopped vortex-stalk

Growing mushroom-clouding...

Rock-tree fruiting...

Refracting...and further diffracting

Moving-*images* imitated and almost perfectly-reflected

Against an apparent depthless distance...

Cooled through cavernous rift-valed:

      -The SpaceScape...

Fractal coastal-clouded.

Gaping space gasping, all-around:

      -A One-Way: *electro-luminescent* returning...

Through: The Eye-of: The-Storm.

Capsular meteoric-Planetary

Solar-star en-compassing attractant and detractant.

Re-pulsing upward and downward, and across
Curved-polar pointed colliding colluding...

Ringing radiation-field winding columnar opened.
Cylindrical conic-vortex wondering.
Narrowing-and-widening into a deeply pitted lacuna
Emergent billowing over-abyssal
Sable desert-dune and poured-plain.
Swirling layer-specked and streaked dappled eggshell
Grey-*clouding* yellow creamy spiraling waveform...
Barring-threads spiraling across and again
Out of mud and sand clay: a gemstone.

Crystal-pillared strongly arched
A Golden-egg in the image
Of the-*known* dense-deep dark-centred streaked
Bulging red-yellow orange spilled-out yolk-brown
Blue split-eggshell-cracked *content*...
From the insides- spilt speckles patterned dense blackened-
centre encrusted risen, in one half of the sky:

  -The *fiery*-Sun...

  -*Reflective*-Moon...

  -And *distant-stars*...

  -*Far far away*...

Encircled: *The Singing-Waters* flooded.

EarthCentre: The End of The Universe: Universal Verses2: 2. The Edge of The Universe.

2.1. The Sea

2.2. Dissipate.

2.3. Return.

2.4. Planet.

2.5. A Potent potion.

EarthCentre: The End of The Universe:

Universal Verses2: 2.The Edge of The Universe.

2.1.The Sea.

Opening optimal, spatial moving-Oceanic...
Island-mountainous, storm-shadow, gapped, yellowing-golden,
orange brown, silver blue-specked stellar-drifting...
Bathed-in and be-calmed.

With a stranded smoothed out distance lagoon-pooled
Floating Lotus lily-pad pond: leveling-surface
Tension-holding wind-rippling wave; radiating star-sheet sailing
across seemingly endless twinkling reef and dune-ribbed
Spangled-sea across a shallow dark:
    -T*he* Ashen-Milky-Way...
Silver rivering, escaped, the hunter, and hunted,
pursuant, and pursued.
Through-corded canyon-rivering valley-ribbed.

Entwined, in-lighted thicket over bare grey brown rocky-peaked
And curving perspective settled-on-the-edge;
Of a white spiral-clouded local-spur island-peninsular
    -Centring-on the Galactic Solar...
    -Equi-distant Each of Us...
    -From The Centre of The Universe...
    -To Here and Now?

A solitary arm, paddling out, into a starry-specked moonlit-eclipsed nighttime-sea.
Into *a* gradual light of day, and another *false*-rising...
Into a false dust-clouded dawn, hurtling into the mid distance, as a flaming blazing and brilliantly emptying clear-gas bursting erupting, red-yellow blue grey fireball.

Rotating, grey-balling outer-gas-and-dust-bowl, and bowling along, Solar winding, proto-planetary dust-disc, toward an unpredictable unknown and uncertain-destination; with almost uniform spiral orbital circulation, varying in brightness, faintly compression-winded the impression of *everythingness*...

Overcast, to a deep dense hazy shimmering,
Densely drawn around dusty:
>   -Actual!
>   -Galactic-Solar!
>   -Hyper-Super...noval!

Re-birthed background-sounded
With a *lightning*-thunderous Roar!
Drawn-outwards *vanished*-Beyond *drawn-along*...
Through trail-and-wake.

2.2.Dissipate.

Flame and flare-spiked ring-coronal *exciting*
Briefly-broadcast
Freely out-of-the-optical-depths.

Free-ranging *hydrogen*-electronic to helium nuclear-fusion star-
centred,
Perturbing the-heaviest-elemental iron core, to *the*-lightest-
*hydrogen l*uminary spitting-*scintillation:*
       -Chromatoid chromospherical patterning, atomic-
compounding...

Twinkling flowing mass-ejecting, raging-flambeau
Filling the dust dry water compacting lacuna.

In-every outward as inward rounding-direction, spun-out:
       -In Spectral-*prismatic....*

Confluent, and contrary-flowing moving spinning-paths...
Switching-orbit, and orbited en-circulate by Each-Other.
Curling closer and away, all-around Solar-stellar helioscopic-
wave sheet
Radiance:
       -Tangent, cotangent, secant, and co-secant chording...
       -Irradiate-scattering through trigonometric cosine-
sunrising: Morning, noonday, afternoon...
Evening-falling, stellar-sunset settled.

Languishing to a point of limpid apparent silent arrest a-testing
Limpid, in the darkened lipid occupied-interval, sweeping-
onward-*flashed* silver blue bright hydro-genic,
capturing and burning stars,
and this one-supernova to burn, yet even brighter; bulbous
glassy-flowing,
smelted, steaming drying-lumps fled.

Rocketed-past volatile high-energy converting,
silica-sandy brittle-metal brown-feldspar stinging chlorous-
white sodium-clouding sulphurous-dusted and sprayed, sea-salt;
soapy tasted, bitter aragonite, showering, conglomerated-
pumice, split, spilt, oxygen-fired, cauterised-corundum,
pyrite crumbling, potash-blue, acid-bleached.

Alkali-ceramic, cemented glassy-fibrous, burning-gaseous,
damp, moulded amorphous-lamp shone:
           -Potassium-nitrate...calcium-carbonate, crystalline-
factoring...
           -...fabricating silicate...

Black-Grape: difficult decisions losses prosperity and abundance:
un-ripe: back-engineering moving at speeds
Not dependent on size, or weight, but on mass-alone...
At-variating height and incline within
An apposite: fixing functional planar-distance
Vorticed-away from, moving faster in the same *almost*-direction.

Following-on: toward the *slightly* or Greatly off-centre
Renewing-heart rendering red and orange yellow buzzing,
crackling, snapping a *burning-off*...

The now settling solar drifting, orbiting still yet faster inward,
Outward-slowed, moved against the turning:
    -Solar-*sunlit...for The Very First Time*...
    -Galactic *edged*...
    -*Universe*...

Summit Alpha-*peak* as valley Beta-*gulley as Gamma-Ray: Gallery:*
Steadily held stretch elliptic framed within the helio-spherical-
scopic; protonic-sunshine photonic-aurora, following-on, and
around *the*-blazing-Orb.

Absorbing-*through* and as scattered...*vaguely* brightly-seen,
resplendent and reflected, and *warmly*-felt.
Consuming from The Space-around:
    -Re-heating hydrogen and helium-nucleic; massively
minor-star, dust-cloud flaring-centring compressed:
    -Solar-hydro-*iron* core.

Stellar-splitting, sulphuric-spilling countless charred lumps flew-
raggedly past
Some so light absorbent as to be visible only in the next moment
of high-energy encounter.

In-movement, stinging-touched, and almost-touching, felt-fielded as views cleared and opening-out, pieces-collided, and shattered apart; and together, through the still-frozen scalar-depth, nearby conjoined rough surfaced, and unevenly eroding-shaped.

Escaping-outward before touching the-ground,
Discharging Solar-*streaming* limbic, armed solar galactic spiral-strand:
        -Galactic-orbital Solar-set...

Quartering around:
        -Shifting...
        -Changing...*altering...*
        -*Altering...Changeling...*

Occasional, conglomerating flaming icy, misted tailing comet fly-past.

Meteoric-emptying-out. Landed. Chasming the densely-filling planetary ringing solar space, pushed-into as pulled-in *faster* to-crash, bomb-arding:
        -Asteroid! heavy nucleate-*flaming...*pushing *into* the yellow-light en-flaring elongating orbit...launched into yet higher and further distance lost yet again, to the closing yet still vast-reaches.
Amongst the faint-glitter of other-galaxy and: The Galactic-Star.

Now-arrayed photographically, as a distant-lone pulsing, and multitudinous *fuzzy*-glowing grouped planetary-Solar galactic nebulae, supernovae gold, and silver dancing, in the empty-gapped, flickering and lingering inferno *flashing*-fiery ruby-red aurora *glittering*-gemstone, metal fluid quartz mineral melting melded chimerical-chemical shimmering, flaring-phosphorent. Sapphire-platinum plated, mercurial-metallic quicksilver, flaring methane blue-green drift...the smaller, now, and less-dense agglomerating magnetic-particulate, attracted watery-moulded. Clay-*Aluminous*...thrown-together, simultaneously, space and time, participating, rotating at the vertical-moment of take-off, in a curving straight-line imaginings between points, spinning off; launched, at yet higher-*speed* inward, outward, and all-around.

2.3. Return.

To-return, into the buzzing, seemingly vacant darkly oceanic Solar-field. Thrown-together, held onto, steadily outer-rock and pebble-holed. Solar circumflexing fragmenting *failed*-star planetesimal agglomerating-pieces,
interstellar-rocky planetary-asteroid, and *failed* Gas-star.

Objects, paring-off and away, from the outer Solar-equatorial plane
Magnetic-field planar-planetary dust resonating accretion-balling
Outer asteroid storm, cometary crossing, lining-up:
       -Pluto, the furthest outward...

The largest solar-satellite blue-methanic:

   -...ice rock forming, outer-planet of Neptune...

Next, exponentially far distanced, from: The-Sun: massive-temperature heat-pressure, solid water ice planetary, transient-streaming...

steaming gas-to-liquid-metal-mineral bulging girdling-equatorial:

   -...the gas-giant Jupiter...

   -Again!

Massively-zonal, and belted red-spotted flares, tenebrous pinking, trailing *grey*-blue. Scorching high-temperature and pressure-solidified water-ice:

   -Metallic-hydrogen, liquid-helium *hydrostatic...*

   -The-Jovian fastest-spinning leader of the-four-outer-Solar-Planets...

Forming up-next, the gas-balling dust dull-ice giant:

   -Uranus...and then the many colourful dust-*ringed*:

Saturn...water, ammonia and methane frozen-*ice* rock...

   -Possibly habitable-moons?

   -Possibly?

   -Has-been? Or is?

   -Or could-be again?

   -All three...

and further inward inner ice and rock-asteroidal –banded:

   -And a fourth...

cometary bombarding and con-*gealing*...

Forming the first of the inner-planet's settled ringing dust and
ice, sand and red-rock:

> -The filamentous dust-stormed planet Mars...

Massively-cracked and landsliding red-rivering, conglomerating
and molten sumped-under. Cloudless inorganic carbon-dioxide
atmospheric:

> -Where *icy*-water *once*-flowed...

Hidden-beneath once volcanic-geyser, granite-sealed, dry-
winded dust-en*gorged*...
Polar ice-capped, beneath the surface, salts deposited.

Micro-fibrous cellulose-layering, incised channel-streaming
Rivering meandered-mountainous around and gully Sun-dried.
Creviced-flows, rows of watery dust-fragment spilled-outward,
and inward toward:

> -The risen re-centring-Sun:
>
> -Liquid-water...
>
> -Steam, not-*ice*...

Taken, collecting in open *clear*-space; toward the nearest-Solar,
fastest-turning, the smallest planetary moon-sized rolling,
dry liquid gas methanic-dry:

> -Plains of Mercury, and the next-nearest likely Solar-

planet, forming...outward-turning, again; retrograde slower
contrary spinning-spun.
The forming-ridged, volcanic carbolic atmospheric, clouding:

> -Venusian-highlands acid raining,

smouldering dry burning and scalding metal-mountains melted;

in-passing, drawn-off, spinning-polar overclouded-core;
and, now, in the mid distance axis-wobbling, faltering,
with yet more slowed planetary-spin. Steaming gas-cloud
captured circuital and escaping, holding:

        -Iron grey nickel cobalt-blue cored...
oxygen-blue and once-sulphurous yellow-green:

        -Hydrogen-sulphide, nitric-acid and carbon-silicate...
icy rock-dust snowball...

      -Icy-comet...

      -...and carbonaceous-meteorite...
Asteroidal-*showering:* the white and yellow polar-forming brown
Planet; moonlit-spectacularly from above, as from below.
With a seismic-burning bursting through the skin of the
constantly churning planetary-mass.

Fast-*spinning* throwing-up stack and heaped wall and pile, peak
and collapsing sink; daily-circulating, electromagnetic-fielding
back-through, and around the-forging and foraging mineral and
metal-layering poles shifting around,core and crust.

Through singular-elongated outer-conic core-vortex.
Around Solar-arisen *aurora*-soaked and spraying back,
outward from the poles, and out into the open space,
projected-North, South, East and West, and every degree
between.

Almost circular elliptic-orbital:

      -...over one-hundred diameters'-distanced...

averaging, to the next blue-green red-reducing...and yellowing-Sun.

Each of us looking for a slower, perhaps more regulating irregular-orbit. Faster more *exciting,* risky, each daily-turning Solar-orbital annular, seasonally-snowing, and now sunshine-*tilted*: Meteor--ologically-unpredictable steaming-geysers incondensable cloud-forms cooling shadowing *rift*-rain's *frozen-*capped.

Hot shallow-ocean, rounding-off, ground-basalt and mounted granite. *Washing-through* any number of minerals and salts Into the *hydrogen*-rich waters and land-pools Belching:

        -Mainly nitrogen-*atmosphere...*

        -Of inert-argon, neon, carbon-dioxide...

and as heavy-water regulating each-equatorial axial-polar spin. Each: Astro-Naut:-astronomically distant starlit-sidereal night and day. Galactic flowing, up-*stream* and down-stream: Solar galactic planetary spiraling aberrative-complexity, isobaric-folding in Universal-constancy...variantly shifting-away, and towards, between in-variant, stretched-limitations selecting, and elected-out-of...coincidental-synchronisation...incidental-effect caused coursing-circadian:

        -Solar Galactic-planetary form:

        -Travelling at speeds over one and a half...

        -*Almost* two times-further and faster...

        -...in degrees of arc...

Solar-Sun-timing, insular ratio-turning on *it's* own axis:
 -Cosmic-ray's discharged-*neutrino, positronium...*
 -A Thousand thousandth the volume ferrous fielding,
encountering, impinging solar *ionic: passing-through and onto*
and through the cratered bombarded and cracked-filling
planetary molten-mantle. Filling and foaming over...

Carbonaceous *burning* silicate-chondrite.
Powdery-tarry metal-cored, rocky-cordate
Sunlit *great*-swirling, immense-boulders and small-pebbles
Fell-in, from Space-continuously cona-dust tailing landed.
Drawn-in, to scatter-below jutting over the molten-mass;
unearthing statuesque-standing, granite-risen plateau-valley en-
trenched.

Encrusted compound laval-gases, super-heated steam,
smoke-soot, and grey-*ash,* over-peaked, soaring-summit,
a cloud of dust and flame-erupted through depthless-crater,
impenetrable chasm buried, disintegrated spilling-out,
larger and smaller boulders appeared.
In-periodical-orbital, collided and spun off, to disperse
elsewhere.

Bursts of blue orange seared flame, exposed and erupted
crimson-red, and dust darkening purple-cascades, escaped,
cycling circling-upwards...to explode in mass *e*-jection.

Spewing gusting charged glass-particle, radioactive flung
grain's...

Solar-like jet ray corona, vast-nebular solar debris-drifted.
Dust, gas and liquid clouded the remains of the star sprinkled
sky. *Lightning*-flashed, thunder-cracked across a vaporous
surface. Displaced furnace gases, shot-forth in-flame, over-
sloping out-cropped congealing basaltic gaseous-granite
immiscible rock; oily in translucence, drying out purple red, blue
and green-*sheen*...

Waxing and waning emulsifant flowing in-from-space absorbing
enormous-quantities of water
Rivering-along a narrow galactic Solar-stretch sumped and
Running-off *Upper-settled Rocky-ledge*:
        -Carbonyl-hydrating...
collapsing clear-gas to liquid convergent, constituent-part.

Drawn great-gale-*searing* colliding and collapsing.
Sub-mergent friction dragging over the boiling, dominant hot-
surface, *icy* clear-methane caged, to cloud and rain drifting,
steaming, vaporising rising-and-swirling, re-conjoining-droplets,
around the Equatorial-rim...washed-back over, the ecliptic
Planetary-edge...to condense, and freeze on sweeping tide,
warmed grey muddy Oceanic-seas reflecting purple streaked *red-*
sky.

2.4.The Planet.

In-circuit around, the broadest-equatorial girth.
The Planet-*below* overlooked and accompanied now,
by perhaps two, or many more, contrary-turning,
roughly separated...and at once collided, shuddering,
ricocheting-projectile dented, denting slightly,
once iron dust-chart satellite-Moon, moisture denuded, scorched
and *frozen*-out.

Bare inert-rock-piece, spun-off and away.
Almost-rounded, ridden-off, into inter-Solar Space again; to
circuit-once, every, perhaps, so many hundreds or thousands of
EarthCentre years...or each night steadied in dream.
In close-orbit facing, fractured-dust, iron-cored, uncored fibrous-
fruited peeled, and kernel-seeded.
Re-grounding re-sealed surface:
      -...the quarter-sized Earth sub-lunary planetoid Moon-
piece...

Quarter-distanted from Earth, and from the-Sun, flaming and
dying, coated, and also once-drenched, dried-out cored re-
flective...

Solar-lit, facing and reflective-*yellowing* the-Planet below.
Steadying, planetary wobble and tilt.

Oceanic-tipped, tided, tipped, gazing, as at a *spectre* occulting
nodal-geared-up, magnetic-material each-different micro-chip
digital-data, binary-bit; core-business self-importance, over any
of the-Others' Universal axial-turning, and Earthed-satellite
captured, into-the-depths shadowed all over in-moonlight,
and Solar-days and night's...both, together, now solar-orbiting,
the-Galactic, and-Universal: *through* the flickering foggy-sky,
with lit-up forces otherwise-unseen; between the-forming-
planet, and the closest circling full-moon and its nearest rising
Solar Sun-star.

Over-surrounding, remaining crest of snow-and-ice. Between
and beneath, the dark-open cloud ribbed-sky moving to meet, in-
diffused orange yellow haze, rising in drifts...to meet a
generating-planetary oxygenated: *atmospheric:*
       -*Nitrogen H-Bomb Nuclear*-reactor, carbon coiled-
transformer, dilating with *vivid* acid-yellow brown-concoction.

2.5. A Potent-Potion: *patience*...

Along wide cracked ravine-melted lava-river raged and ravaged.
Forged-through cavernous canyon dust-storm re-clad:
       -Red and yellow...*iron*-oxidising...
Red-rock brickwork, engorging-attracting ahead, and behind:
       -...banded-over the surface below...
A *furious*-fog, to drizzle and freeze on-summit.
Swept-suspended....*glinting*-crowned, splash-ringed coronal;
to-bubble and boil-over, spuming-peak blown vast-gale *hazy-*

wave sodden, grainy-draught storm-enflamed, below, freezing-out far above; leaving lucent-latent warming humid-winds in-circuit, over-layering acrid steam-and-*smoke*-swirled.

Asteroid-landed, lunar-ascended *vapourous*-misted; *streaked*-scarfing scarred-strata puffed-out cumulus-billowing pillow, sleep-walking toward-and-away...from: The distance-less-Zenith: Of a cloudy-moon filled, cold and clear, sunless-star fading night-sky.

Contrary, and otherwise-spiraling, and turning bright and less-*bright* light-specked:

    -Super-noval...

    -Second *shockwave*...leavening, compressed cold-edged, inter-stellar galactic cloud-base.

In the deepening nighttime sky, fenced-off mountainous-tipped, to sharp-points blurred and flickering, silent-amazing sparkling-scorched *free*-lancing; glowering-specks, far-distant, and closer-reflecting, distant:

    -Micro-*Megas*...

With the naked-eye, apparent magnitude-merged.

From all points, onto the surface below, beneath the sunken star-sprinkled sky,falling and fading, *failing*-brightness, each gradually *frozen*-out shooting and falling-stars with sideways departure, on the-lit angle-of-vertex; the *brightest* and last of the fading ever-changing, permanent-lifetime nighttime patterned the planetary-angle, began to engulf again...a sinking half-of-

watery-Moon-*moved* dipping-below a *precipitous*-Planetary
balmy-sea, over lit-lastly by a-distant-fixed tri-pointed: The-
Galaxy. In half-light, disappeared, into the lightest perpendicular
quadrant, to where the open-sunlight, now, once more acceded.

The remainder of the galactic zodiacal stars, almost-*rested...*
Each with Their Our Own-owned as seemingly settled departure
Cornered, *frozen*-and-fallen in-*differential...*
In-tandem: from the rising-Sun outshone the captured-Earths'
surface lit-up
As a small-boat cast-adrift, in:
       -Galactic-Ocean and Solar-*seas...*

The remains of the terrifying fireball re-appeared.
Encircling, closer and then-*further, again, and again...*
Over massively mountainous roughly materializing troughed,
toughed, and peaked flaring-pointed wave-curved horizon...
From: Rock-*Plateau*:
       -Panoramic: steadily-risen booming over equatorial-
oceanic...

Held-still cill-thrilled *through* the overshadowing-cloud.
Halo-sinking, louring:
       -Saltpeter...
Melodious, and *malodourous:*
       The-Moon.

Moving-down, across and away.

The Flaming-Sun started rapidly-rising, beyond the blue-risen, irrigate rinsed ridged-ledge. The whole-remaining half-of-sky lit, to complete the surrounding, erupting surface-lit from-below as well as now, as from the once-retreated, and now re-apparent Sun-star: looming-closer, and dropped-over, dipped, at a seemingly safe-distance...

At-*uncertain* depth-and-height, over-shifting elongating dry floating-plates landed upon; the newly risen-floor forming, cracked and heaved with a melting-mellow wave-like subterranean-undulation; *through* and between widening fissure *the*-incandescent underground, the fuming ground...seemingly-stilled, in graduating-inertia moving-against-all-else; in The-Universe beyond parabola-space continued-to-turn; rotating, with the hyperbolic ground-beneath, leaden-yellow grey-brown congealing:

-EarthCentre!

Across a cooling and congealing, ridged and rippled, solidifying softly-gelling surface.
Electric-dy namo red-flushed sky-blue *flashed* and flickered, arced-across the-upper-surging surface wave-patterned, molten dense-rock hot mineral and metal saturated purple-sea.

Smoldering-ash, frothed and boiling mud-hardened-flat *swept*-dry, on gales-of-dust-and-sand, cracked-engorged earth-quaking, opened-up, as more rains began to fall, in-torrents, lashed with a violent wind. A-*raging* muddy sea, rolled and roared, along risen

valley floor, up to its brink at the nearest high ground. Without
warning, waters foamed and flooded-in, from both sides, and all
around roaring rushing at a height, that at first seemed safe
enough...then, gradually, slowly and unsteered, veering over
remaining-plateau, a wall of water cascading, towards an un-
suspecting headland, becoming higher at every advance...
the multitude of seen and unseen-stars, fallen-away.
Close to the-horizon, with compelling compensating illusion of
Great-Size, in steaming smoke-screen dusted *glittering* night;
a large dark-Moon re-apparent in the sky re-risen, dipped once
more sideways, onto the horizontal-sky, not-chased, but chasing-
away. Drawn, and drawing over, the newly risen-Sun,
overshadowing the darkened-Earth.

The EarthCentre: SunLight: *eclipsed* in-spume and foam *dipped*
and *dimmed* and blotted-out all else; as the *raging*-waters
rushed-in and obscured *almost*-everything.
**

EarthCentre: The End of The Universe: Universal Verses3:

Substrate...

3.1. Breathing in Water.

3.2. Larger than Lived...

3.3. Another *little*-Journey.

<u>Substrate</u>

3.1. Breathing in Water.

In water, a scene faded back gently,
from the cataclysm, that was dimly-lit.
The sky above, and earth below, water in between.
Across the underside of an agitated ocean below the ebbing extramural silver-
lightning forked low light glancing, penetrating dark infrared, flicked and
glowed spectral yellow-green and red-blue glinting
Where ultraviolet only reflected flared and flowed
Oceanic inter-wave rounded weaving under-towed
Merged, peaked, crested, and plowed furrowed
A pounding pumping rhythm moved-in.

In virtual pitch darkness, sounds of gurgling
Belching peculiarly filled the space.

The upper watery *apparent*-boundary thundered across
Granite grey cliff-edge booming breakwater
Theme-tune continuing the show
Tectonic landmass-beyond continuing to spew
Mountainous volcanic colliding
Steam and noxious gases into a wind-whipped
Yellow cloud-containing upper-atmospheric forming Venusian *acid*-rain.

Filtrating fusing salting mineral-sparked submarinal raised-up lofty and wide
Lightning continuously across the pacifying Ocean surface-tide
Discharged-below,into crashing waters and landmass-shifting.

Massive opening rift-valley and island-plateau
Bare-rock below the waters the deepest lain base-bolide Raised pillar-
towering prominence
Isolated-stacked packed pedicle-lodged ledge.

Along the flickering floor sunken through the Solar re-lit depth
Into the grey-dark deep glistening moon re-apparent
Refracting darkly-lighting.

Flicking transparently apparently wafer-thin
screen.sloshing sedimentary clouded wave
Lustrous slate-smooth glasseous-seen
Underwater, effervescing surface-activity.

Overflowing the raised encrusted planetary mantle
Heaving swept through the molten core congealed Concealed crust handled flooded dense-deep
A formative settling hazy clouding, sub-marinal abyss.

Synthetic laminate-layers lensed ground fissures' plume
Vitriol vapours rolling overpouring-pillow
Set-basalt volcanic-laval dampened cooled-abrased
Lower basin rim coarse-grained granite-risen
Granular fronded rock-tree trunk flowering carbon-graphite
Red-rusty iron-speck magnesium encrusted
Sparkling-hydrated hot-silicate aluminum zinc.

Along deep ocean mantle ridge canyon submerged
Conductive copper-oxidal green-brown mount
Streaked purple and smoky brown sapphire-pink
And ruby red corundum turquoise-aquamarine.

Amethystand opel quartz-mineral sunken angel-treasure trove
Drove compacted leaden-silver golden-specked.
Meteoric oceanic filled impact-crater
Hyper Super-noval iron-carbonaceous salting
Settling dissolving in the briny signifying
Along igneous-laval sloughing
Grit-floor grey-panel sand-streaked and gravel ploughing paved and dipped
Screeched and *squeaked...*

Facing into the engulfing vast dark deep dense waters' culvert
Caved-in walls and floor subducted into and through
The new planets' deep-interior crust and core
Through the subterranean caverned-site
Aluminous granite-cleft subaqua-scuba dived
Spelunking in the pitch dark roamed
Oceanic interior alone through crowded waters
Steaming-geysers continued to bubble-and-foam.

Each absorbing and adsorbing
Attracting and rejecting force and matter together
Forced-apart and together
Core-chained twisting ligature articulate
With the appearance of fissure released
Base-core hydrogenic heavy heaving water
Vapour-dissolving,and occluded
Un-appeased unappealing without any sure grounding.
Bound to the sodden beaded-pyretic over-spilling edge.

Nailed the-proof proving projectile
As a bullet nailed into the corner-bracket
Hit, execute, catch, seize; precisely; done well.

The High-Dive, somersaulting, adroitly, pinned
The-medallion, onto precisely, identify-Other
As a fraud, spook, or wealthy-wanabee...
A nail in the coffin...weakened hit-on-the-head.

Out-cold, trauma, comatose...re-bounding
Foaming walls-of-water welling wave upon wave.

Spontaneous, explosive sent-out plasmic-burst
Carried through booming, dulled wave sputtering
Spluttering burst eviscerate, re-leased:
Hydrating and oxidizing load's' back into the waters;
Settling, layering compacting mineral stratifying
Chipped-shale grated ground gravel
Overlaying silica desert-sand settled white-water clouded
Frothing above the deep dark depths.

Bubbling sunken mudrock obsidian sub-terranean
Warming floe retaining mineral-metal setting excess
Inert trace leavening-energetic
vigourously underwater burning
Extraneous part-positive negative aligning
Split and reforming re-alignment:
        -...iron nickel core catalytic...
        -Carrying magnetite...
Charged and re-charging compacting compounding; spin
Turned and flipped trapped-back flapped-feeding field-potential:
Schisming rejected spat out in bubbled burst re-conjoining
Near inner-mirror imaging multi-layer laminar substrate strip-pared.

Exuded extruded, granular lattice wave wrapped polar-symmetric.
Elemental-combinant and re-combinant synthesising-dynamic
Repeat atomic-molecular precipitate
Electroplating *sparked* across, with speed, and consistency-bound.

Rodding open-tubular
Saturating salty-water
Nutrient sucking-straw drawing-in metallic
Mineral-fragment dissolving droplet...
Ground-water underwater into-the watery surround.
Sheer-coated:
        -Chloroplastid

Vacuole-enveloping freshly oxygenic
Fed-guested stranded in circular-tank
Swelling split opening-out...
From the inside popped-open explosive
Unfolding-blocks frothing locked breeching
Concealed-contents...

Bubbling-gaseous releasing heat welded water-cooled Facing and non-facing
link-chain polate-part
Particle-conductive switching...
Reverse-sequential potential-action.
Closed in circuitry fixing-differential capacitance and resistance
Water-splitting chain-linking cordate.

To an inner patent-pattern
Polarity-bonded parenting
From the now upper-acid atmospheric icy-*freezing*...

Below the waters' snowball draining-glacial
Sliced through spin-ice
Thin-ice condensing-down

Over-rising evaporate catalytic-secluded mineral
Nutrient-derivative leftover
Transporting transfer-reducing
Detecting di-atomic gases re-filling binding *boiling*-inside.

Conformational de-localizing micro-to-macro-cycle:
        -Hemo-*proteinous*...electron-sunken...
          -Iron-alloyed *nickel*...
Core-matrix pri-mordial
Cobalt copper zinc silver-gold adding chromophore.

Electro-chemical characterising on the underwater shore.
Starry red yellow blue chromatic luminous
Subterranean smelter-glow dropping to a piling-ring
Hollow intense silver-blue grey settled state zinging
Rapidly sequentially compounding
Re-active core iron-sulphurous hydrating-out.

Seeping-out of the carbonite aluminous
Silicate flow calcium-formaldehyde
Sodium salt-soluble insoluble iron-oxide
Sulphuric di-hydrogen mantle atmosphere
Dark-purple sulfide electron-capturing:
        -Sulphur...

-Oxygenisation...
-Phosphorous...
Over-scalding ducting high-pressure...
Deep rock-chimney glowing orange yellow red.
Hot-venting clear nitrogen-gas cycling and readily repeated.

Bubbling surfaces at all levels, and under-towed frosting
Blown-molten and settled-desiccation
Ashen carbon-sooted iron-steels heavily-saturated
Water flowing-pieces
Over and through thin-crevice the surrounding-water's
Spectra-coursed.

Coarse-grained translucent polished-mixed
Alluvial prismatic-agate diamond di-pyramidal
Crystalline steepage silhouetting-shadows' flicker
Splintering cone-shaped cinder spiraling seepage...
Sluicing-blowhole glittering-granules
Into the deep bombarding cometary-tailing
Free-lancing mineral-metallic strand-flaming
Disc-ring soaring and spinning saming-individual.
Attached centre-based gleaming graphite-gell encrusting
Silt yellowing...tailing-end pointed, and headed.
Alloy-subterranean craterous under-ground lake.

Extremo-phile rock-O-philes sheltering *frozen...*
For an Ice-Age, then, slowly spinning-out again.

Electro-magneto-somal burst spewing
Metallic mineral robotic-bugs
Along igneous-laval sloughing grit-floor.
Facing into the engulfing vast dark deep dense waters; self contained
Swollen without mouth or anus spiraling-helical
Organic hydrophobic water-hating repellant; subversive
Secretive dissident diffident feeding-nutritional
Primary autotrophic trophy-features kept
Sulphurous yellow ball-feeding waste-excreting
Anaerobic proton positive-strand.
Standing with foot and hand.
Alternating-neutral neutralising iso-electric
Neutron entropic-decant...chaining iron-*ion* monolayering
Electron-molecular oxidizing iron-carbide.
Bloodied and burning-out de-sulphurous...
Hydrogen-sulphide meta-phasal pre-bio-tic
Atomic-molecular non-nucleic soft-cellular fleshed.
Brought to an abrupt stop tortured electrocuted

A permanent-end continuing exhaling
Inhaling poisoning oxygen released burst liberated Atomising anaerobic
oxygen-burning mineral-silicate.
Outer-shell electron friction-burning hydro-sulfurous
Fleshy-membrane burning-through
To the explosive respirating-core: *oxidizing*-gas...
Of its' our own destruction catastrophic extinction
An-oxic poisoning sudden un-supported un-sustainable
Instabilities crashing a whole-population too-far.
From the hot feeding yellow-sulphurous
Oxygen poisoning-well rising too far
From the electric-core of each and each other
Too far from the burning-Sun saved.
Icy wave-lapping surface solar-scorched
Lunar-tidal wave washed-away
Calcium carbonated and fossilised sandy gritted-taupe.
Landward-beached spontaneously-combustible
Burning-out to sink and re-layer the seabed
Settled-back into the deep and dead...
Leaving no-trace but mixed agate
Pock-marked grainy wave-weathered.

Cleft boiling-out heaped bubbling remaindering
Metallic-mineral sand the first of many
Great-dyings particles to rust
Aluminum and white-magnesium sulfate.
Calcite hydrous-phosphate
Sodium chloride magnesium manganese
Golden-uranium and silver plutonium capturing free-electron
Positron-radical absorbing oxidal
Electro-methanogenesis
Acid nucleo-tidal precursory
Di-valent calcium metal heated-metal sulphide.
Bone: Calcium-formaldehyde sodium-salt.
Soluble ground-nitrogen ring
Helium-combinant carbon-hydrate; inert-carbon.
Mineral-building-block watery iron-oxidal
Bloodied turned-porphryn glittering four-pole boundary
Magnesium-chlorophyll planet-planted.
Chained-ion mono-layering electron-molecular
Alkaline thermal vent stromatolite fossilised microbial colony
Zircon-*crystal* water-holding life mesophile
At *this* boiling point of water.
Crystal-ice purifying-lattice centring-spore
Speeding template-reaction variating acid-alkaline;
A-*series* as uncertain as the most uncertain-factor.

Formed on a surface of iron-sulphide core nickel-cobalt Manganese and zinc
material-membrane
Amorphous plastic-pyrite magnetite attracting
And rejecting hydrogen-cyanide carbon-cycle
Organic-reaction pioneer niche-culvert
Auto-tropic carbon-fixing monoxide combining
Di-oxide water-gasifying-pathways...

Foaming forming-over and within liquidizing-methane.
Ammonia shifting-reaction
Bitter-burnt bitter formose-formaldehyde again
Electrophile-neutral; inflaming holding-on.

Man-aging-remaining conjoined and repeating...
The actively whole self-maintaining
Altering adapting and re-growing
Whole-body part-organising
Spontaneously-changing part-dissipate.

Hyper-cycling re-cycling highly-structural
Re-generational self referential multiplying
Hundred thousand million billion trillion...
By any another-named nucleotidal-coded chained
With outside-elements compound chemical-foodstuff
Auto-catalytic somatic specied.

Homo and Hetero trophic sexual urban wildlife
Increasing the rate of ex-change
Re-producing variation and version.
Repetitive and memorific each of us uniquely;
If only for the vast difference pertaining between-each.
Electromagnetic holding space-similarity
And difference held-apart and snapping-together.
Each of us a slightly and exaggeratingly
More-differentiate more-the-same ...
Either and/or rapidly folding and refolding
Cosmic: EarthCentre: *plasma-bound...*

Nucleating combined bi-layer, equilibrating test-facility.
Each of us now opening crystalline starry-point Circumstantial-chromosomal
synapse snapped, lighted vestibule
Connecting determining co-incidence, abridging and fanned-out, fringed:
    -Gravity-centre...
    Electro-magnetically anchored...
    -Nuclear.

Double-split screen-gating inter-wave
Each-slotted lighted rung-bridging
The previous across to the next.

In plasma lipid-vital vitamin-amino acid ferrous-oxide.
Electromagnetic nitrogen-fixed
Non-nucleic nucleating acid-chain
Polymerising-proteins self-reproducing molecules
Nucleate self-splicing duplicate.

Archean- prokaryote chained *ion*-monolayer
Electron-molecular twisting-shielding:
        -CHON hydrophobic-bases...
Protected from water-*damage* synthesing saving
Spinning helical-vortex cellular-moving
In one direction or another:
        -Amino acid protein...
Self-supporting membrane-transporting
Oxidizing-movement
Breathing-in-Water.

3.2. Larger than Live...

Mineral proteinious-growing biotic-stabilising
Cell-functioning pretender pretentious...
From the seemingly organized chaotic-surrounding complex-complex-
complete...

Once started and surviving holding-on simplex
Self-organising from virtual-chaos...order.

Holding-up somatic as semantic entropic-decay
Feeding from the exterior engulfing
Energising the rapid-decay of self and Other:
Re-sounding sounds discharged-below
From the waters and rock error repair or death.
Adaptive-alteration to: The-Environment:
Clear hydrating carbon-silicate
Letting nitrogenous-fixing combinant
Pair-centred tubular sodium-chloride salt-silt crystal-dissolving
Conductive:
        -CHON amino-acid binding...
        -Proteinous-*polymer...*
Holding paired, triplicate, quarter powering:
        -RiboNucleic Acid...

-AGCU four-fold...
Nucleotidal molecular-unitary stacked odds and evens:
-Nitrogen base-fixing pentose-sugar simple-crystalline

compounding...

Energisising the chemical-cannon membrane.
Firing purifying heating solar-photonic.
Sanitising catalyzing our own reproduction
Replication lateral genic-transfer
Cell-culture in-organic phosphilation.
Cyclic-soup, of free-floating triple-nucleotides
Unable to reproduce as yet, but then to grow
Hydrogen bonded triple-codon nucleotidal
Amino-acid nitrogen-base.
Alternating cardinal-carbidal
Five-sugar phosphate backbone
Base-strand rodded top-carboxyl
Side-chaining:
-AG to CT amino acid-matching...

Centriolar microtubule saturated tubular triple bundled Triplicate and
triplicate again...

Three-dimensional minimal-indivisible twenty-seven point
Tubular-rodded centriolar parsimonious
Perspicacious-providential parsing
Taking-out of the rock and waters expanding
Right-angular turned bracketing leading the way:
-Mostly right-handed D sugars...
-Occasional retrograde left-handed switchback L post split-
functioning...

Nucleic-post and membrane-wall boundary-building.

Cell-membrane icy polar-capped receptor and heat-transmission:

Fruiting-acid fermenting heating plasmic-sapping
Proteinous-hydrocarbon sticky sugar-stranded.
The upper-Sunlight glittering through
Shimmering-patched essential altering
Light-energy resonant
With *any* Northern to Southern polar-mantle
East-West solar centring photosensitive:
-DeoxyriboNucleic Acid...
microbial combining-nucleic cellular...

Carbon-photo-reduction light burning
Oxygen-sintering ultraviolet-catalysis...
Membrane protein-plasma laminar-lashed
Meshed phototropic nucleolar-threaded
Synapse-paired separating orbital and *counter*-orbital...
Hooked-up loop-stem furry wiry-entangled
Stretched-ciliate stepped hursute a *fanning-out*...

Splitting-sharing out-steeped
Reflected and absorbed by-degree
Dragged and screened across vibrant-light
Electro-magnetic force-field fibrous
Micro-tubular absorbing, and reflecting array:
Du-plicating long-coiled twisting beaded...
Colouring-counters taut-solidifying
Anti-parallel chaining:
     -...tetrahydrogen-triphosphate:...
      -ATP...
Pentagonal hydrogen-cyanide
Tri-phosphate sugary phosphoric-acidic
Storing phos-pholipid-*plasma*...
Self-selected chemical-triplicate coded-phosphorous
In-place-of-sulphur starlight turbo-charging
Cyclic-nucleotidal catalysing matching co-factorial configuration spun;
Metallic-alkali mineral vital amino-acid building proteinous-binding:
Fibrillar-branch gated and parked.
Sparked-structural-growth, enzyme-synthesizing *catalysis*...
Co-ordinate proximal-bonding
Mineral metal-blocking transmitting and translating
Multiple nucleolar cellular chemical-string
Viral combining and reproducing
Molded plasmid-pieces snapped-off.
Transporting and seeking to recombine one to another
Or be re-absorbed again
Olded occupying from cell-to-cell amongst and within
Rapidly decaying toxic free-radicals.

All: *needing* a base to hideout, to feed off, to grow.
Energising compounding macro-molecule.
Multi-cellular transcribing trans-*forming*...

Transforming sprouted re-compounding
Helical-pentose carbohydrate:
       -Asymmetric L. amino acid-chiral...
       -Decisive left-handed, superimposing fitted:
       -Right-handed D-sugars abbreviated...

-T. alcohol ethyline...
Acid-sticky smelling sugar-feeding
Salty-sweet flavours mixed-together
Repeating-sequential-coding binary quadrilateral:
      -*Hyper*-cuboidal 27-centriolar:...
      -DNA...
      -Elements of Romance...

Chromatic mixed-messaging
Swapping tripling cuboidal twenty-seven electron-point...

Empty void-centred thirteenth from any angle
Quadrilateral-switching direction and *inclination...*
Filling and emptying cellular-orbital
Centring happy-thirteenth spheroidal.
Spiraling helical-vortex atomic *clouding*-shell.

At the twenty-sixth rounding-out from the centre fanning exploded-out
Conic-rayline quadrilateral-equatorial axial-bundling
Bungling flattened elliptic-disc

String centrimere transposing moving-effortlessly Swimming swarming
warming...dis-arming

Legged through the blue to red, through yellow and green to purple-blue to
brown; Between pure black and white
Underlying light-wavelength and frequency *colourant...*

Transforming-*variation* double-ended centriole-polar
Nucleic core-spliced vortex.
Co-valence bonding chemically-stimulating
Attracting and conjoined tightly-circular
Spiral-helical ringed-spun stretching-around
Hollow polarity-held columnar axial-a-voiding.

Each-ended and pouring in-and-out
Oppositional-frictional sparked-abrasive
Split field-tension cellular-space separating...

Held apart: gapped and tightly held ring-stacked
Tubular-spindle spit split-*flickering*
Outward to the inner-facing cell-membrane-wall.

Washing through spicy citric acid bitter-tasted
Slimy calcite chalky-alkali aqueous-solution...

Aromatic halo-genic-dissolving evaporating...
Into the circulating watery plasma-blooding
Brooding gloomy blooming booming

De-localised molecular-mineral sparkling-starlight
Across isolated primary-chromosomal centred:
Double-nucleic cytoplasmic starchy
By-product floating resistant gum-tannin
Resinous-dissolved re-inert acid-base reactive:
          -Vital amino-enzyme reducing ant-oxidant...

Catalyzing-carbohydrate proteinous-membrane
Drawing from and releasing into the surrounding-waters
Light-capturing photo-phosphorylation
Oxygen-utilizing aerobic amino-acid:
Enzyme protein precursor hydrocarbon-pentagonal four-pole spinning-
cornered nitrogen crystalline-ring
Stable micro-scalar circular paraboloid binding...

Ancestral-cyanobacterial blue-green purple
Porphryn chain-ring algae acid-raining clouded
Evaporate then from the purple-sky
Hypersaline-trapped inland lakes
Oceanic abundant oxygen and nitrogen-cycling
Surface-*atmosphere...*

Over-arching, plasma canopy, working around and under, letting go, and
lifting-off...
Citric-acid cycle metallic ligands-centred
In transition binding closed-fusion
Lipid base cell anchored hydro-genosome
Breathing burning-carbon dioxide methano-genetic
Anerobic-consuming food and mitochondrial oxygen-*burning ...*
Discovered-chemical and as viral-immunity protection
Letting-go tri-phosphate photo-synthesising...

Oxygen dry free-electron waste
Uncombined with water into hydrogen-sulphide mud-killing
Destroying aerobics'thriving in clearer-seas toweard the surface-atmosphere:
          -Bacterium...

Critter oxygen-collagen *glue*-held-together: SuperBugg!*ing*:
Diffuse *free*-radical electron inside complex host-cell.

Developing burn-to-energy
To grow and reproduce; and eventually

Without rivals consumed and accidentals incidentals unaware yet
Slowly maintaining to the end each of our own lives lived; and for as long as
possible.

Longer legged and shorter arm braced
Embracing enrapturing wrapped rapt.

Holding-on; gripping-on for mortal safety
Sticking-together specious familial now and specia re-cognising.

And taking and not taking what is needed
Energetically to feed and to renew another half-life
Saved almost-evenly shared-out keening pairing amino-acid
Protein lock-and-key latched-onto.
Other invaded and multiplying pustular lesion-rashes
Prompting auto-immune response
Each of us our own species-specific
Cross-species inevitably mutation-combining
Re-organising and reforming quick and rapid strain-alteration
swollen cell-division: explosion free-lighted chromatic charged binding
short and long-polypeptide nuclear-atomic: molecular-bonded.

Digestible proteinous other seeded magnanimous animous
Each re-centring nucleic attached other microbial-bacterial parasitic-assault
Wipeout-takeover extinction extinguished into-Other
Or-*nothing*....

Navigating the-Earthly and Universally
Oceanic-floating semi-fluid quilting-layers
Streaming-out ciliate bristling long-stranded flagellate.
Spiraling-over the congealing matted molding moulding ground
Between solution and fine suspension whistling chromatic-gelatinous
Bubbles screeching and squealing inward-colloidal
Essential and of immediate-necessity.
Each of us moving-off; aquiflexing
Spherical bobbing self-centering chamber
Over as well as underwater stranded strung limbic-balled.
Bowled and bowling-along life size microscopic building
Ggasiferous respiring energetic; microbial earthy-spore
Re-energising time and again naturally easily
Motoring motile muscling-along.
Twisted-string inwardly watery jet-propelled filament
Rooted to the centre core cyanobacterial
Chloroplastid-strand's-*attached*...

Turning-away from and towards and beyond *the* burning sunlight; listed-
away from the still *roaring* hot-core.
Surrounding plasma waters sustaining more
With sufficient consistent-gravity, and electromagnetic charge...
Constructive-patterning trial and error; repeatable
Reproductive working-against randomness
Now tougheneing-holding cell-membrane
Energetic electro-chemical fixing-attraction and accretion Electron-*negative*
and and Proton switching photo-synthesis
Imbibing continuously from the oceanic outside
Substrate deposited-surface sticky-viscous lubricant;
Insulating black-brown yellow-green lipid
Crude immiscible mixed occurring methyl-petroleum Rock oils broken-down
base ground acid: *e*-lective nucleic-kernel
Not knowing-how
But as if knowing-how.

Resistant fleshy-phospholid membrane
spontaneously form-changing as if constantly-supernoval
Stellar-microcosm core
Frozen-nucleosynthesising energy-release warmed and warming
Colliding and combining-process fusing
Atomic-ranging snapped-up.

Maternal-mitochondrial oxygenating energy release
Paternal-phosphate firing respirating organelle
Parasitic-archaic chromosomal nucleic-energizing:
     -ATP Generating...
Sugar-fuel super-burning increased heating and cooling
Preserving warming sugary sweet sticky
Rewarding-information energy-transfer:
   - Meta-morphosing...

Metabalising compartments' proteinous animal-tissue forming
Crystalline matrix-membrane sticking with the invader enwrapping
tolerated-tolerant tolerating-diabetic.
The Greater-*tolerance* cycling hurdling in-*flaming*...
Over-giving energetic-protein sac-wrapped
Defending and supporting strengthening and heavier now
The need to select and multiply with further-immunity
Mutual-helper and attached potential killer-body
Anti-body released to divide and thrive
Equivocating-electronic resistance and combining calculator and rapidly
increasing reproductive-rate:
     -Timely...
     -Nature...*completing*...

Complex-cycling de-nucleate merging the atomic-cell
Cytoplasm dissolving continuously atomic-combination:
              -Fractal-patterning...repeating turning internal proteinous-
congealing immature reflecting inside: Cell-Wall...

Now shopping-mall and theatre-hall
Sports' Centre, and: Thing.

3.3. Another *little*-Journey.

Shaping touching seeded organelle forming...
consequential chaining-nuclear slopping,
shopping small circular-elliptic,
by-now *highly* mis-shapen...shopping
Out-floating fibrous columnar fielding, congealing floated organelle parts:
              -Built...
              -Half..*almost*-built...
              -And Some!

Ribboning sieved-wrapped, folding resistant-barrier, slotted, slatted bright
and darkly-*layered* colour-chrmosomal energy-activating: doing: plasma
sloshing, variously glistering crystalising sluicing thick-liquid.

Allowing and disallowing, in and out of culvert, between conic formed niche
and crevice, bracketed, stranded compound-soaked...

Rounded, saturate de-limiting spun-rim, drawn-in mineral, liquid gaseous-
passage, blocked exit; bulging, expansive to proximal-*exhaustion...*

Inside: re-newing, from the outside, emptying-centrifuging, filling the outer
organising-membrane, centriolar swollen, bloating body-bag, sagging,
under pressure to give way. Overweight, pregnant, parenting, pairing-pared;
selective heterotroph, to combine, feed, and multiply again.

Over-feeding, greedy, and-overcharged, through to the nuclear-centre,
separating inner segment hanging sideways, arching-curving downwards,
saddling torus buckling; with a searing and tearing fissioning de-fissioned,
un-zippered matching, and complementary-centrimere; un-coiling, each half
restoring wave-lapping.
Re-turning: *flesh*y ciliate folding, and doubling proteinous lipid cilia furry,
scaly dry-skinned hydrophobic-letting, and restricting portal-membrane...
Electro-magnetic, oppositely attracted and attached, repulsing *dis-attaching...*

Field-spacing turning and twisting knotted, untangled-beaded.
Reduced, string-bundling, pushing-apart.

Moving-apart to either planetary-pole, and equatorial-side...*scrambling*,
positive and negative contrary electromagnet field ray line-linked.

Lined-up, alternating along-the-*middle*, each binary replicating,
and almost fairly shared-out each newly-whole nucleic celled centring;
freed part, free now of the other, protected multiplying cleavage cracked
raggedly down the middle...
horizontal and vertical segmenting tri-part quartering exchanging along the
join...
shared-out more or less evenly-split in-four...
or any combination with simplest rapid repeating frantic frenetic division.

Inside-out, ripped open and apart, inflamed-swelling, charged, re-charged.
Adapted, and separating, each dis-attached, fastening unhooked-paired:
             -Plasmodium...
mineral-lipid, around nucleating centre-line, separating halving and
quartering mitotic,
tubular spindle woven, from the tiny-floating coiled-centre's.

Explosive-switching,
unlocking the chance to survive, the reproductive-adaptive-test.

Dividing chemical replicon, and replicating atomic parenting molecular.
Each of us, once only required, to continue, colouring chromatid, halved,
paired, triplicate, quartered...particulate organic-cellular re-enclosed remnant
re-formed twisted tangling beading bleeding; cytoplasmic granule vault-store,
construction-site, and kitchen.

EarthCentre: The End of the Universe: Universal Verses3:
2. RNA/DNA/SEX

3.2.1 .Endgame.
3.2.2. Growing and changing.
3.2.3. Sun and moon.

3.2.4. The Vibrant-stage.

EarthCentre: The End of the Universe: Universal Verses3:

2.RNA/DNA/SEX

3.2.1. Endgame.

Glairous albumen-waters',
skimmed and sour,
yellowing liquid reddened rusty oxygen-carrying,
globulin-fatty oil.
Layering and stranding bone-calcite,
marrow-white coagulate, component-building.
Boxed-in, and outside free, and mirroring protective poisenous glaucaseous
mucal-jelly...

Mineral parts re-keyed in and locked in together continuing,
loading and unloading, within and through opening and closing stack ridged
folding; re-folding store shelving...
septic anti-septic algal-fungal tank, hydrogen and oxygen burning, out of
compost grown
Spiral-building, cored and coned, pinnacle points, picked at, and eaten.

Cistern-storing and passing-waste calcium glucose gel.
Bony, exo-shell, and internal-limbic-framing skeletal-forming, through
starchy-sieving apparatus.
Cells-reducing, our own decay, and degradation,
by increasing *the*-entropy,
of the surrounding-Universe continuously water-pressure degrading:
        -Self, and Universe...

Mechanically and chemically,
converting mineral-gradient dis-equilibrium...
bringing-on of ourselves, of ourselves;
self-organising complex systemic...
delaying, conserving, fighting, for *all* our lives.

Against *inevitable* degradation;
delaying only, cellular ordering out of chaos;
with and without food and reproduction;
imbibing, swelling and ready to separate again:
        -Parent Grand-mothering...
identical-chromatid mitochondrial sister cells.
Sibling *giving* brother cells,
mothering X shaping chromosomal pieces,

conjoined non-identical quadruplet mitochondrial carrying more-daughters,
body mosaic mutation, catalytic accelerating-sons:
>   -Y wrapping, tetroid giving, within range of error...
damaged part repairing replacing fixed XX, X and Y carrying:
>   -W-phosphate-charged spermal enzyme...
catalytic-tipped motile-discharging spherical base-*pointed*...

Headed: salt sea swimming-stroke; guided missile heat-covalence seeking,
nucleating flagellate pairing hermaphrodite;
ambiguous mosaic-gendering, engendering, or not;
each chromosomalatically-unique,
chromatic alphabetic-signalling filament:
>   -W...X...Y...Z...complex...
>   -Rival-Lovers all-*gender*(s)'...

Centriole-fibers, bundled-microtubules barrel-shaped elliptic-spheroidal,
tubular-membrane stretched, attaching at the interior quarter-poles,
separate halved quartering...

Each newly-specious familial-formed
Un-coiled bacilli cocci disc-wheeling spherical-tubular, hollow-straw,
lengthening and joined branching wrapped; segmenting-*crossed* tied bound,
clamped and undulating nucleic podium.

Horizontal-and-vertical multipolar-balancing;
cross-wise potential, body-wrapped, timing-subsumed body-wrapt, timid-
centrifugal spinning-coiling...
nucloidal super-coiled, tube wrapped, and waiting our chance.

Loosely-packed helical-corkscrew tubules, straightening and curling, fusilier
springing...slinking; transverse-beading, clamped continuous bleeding,
and discontinuous lagging-strand beading...

To adult reproduction growth phase.
Seeking, recombining with now discrete specious select survivor...

In:
>   -Sex: The Game of Life...
specious, similar surviving other sharing, and surviving.
Forever, having once been, and into the next-generation;
advantage extended, surviving cross-fertilised,
restarting and extending existing life cycle.

In the speckled laval waters, protecting from salt-water,
and sweeping absorbing the dull light from above,
approximating, triangulating square and root diametric radial:

Ex-ponentiating: circumferential transcendental atomic molecular compound cells, swimming upstream to where the waters are fresh. Each swirling gyre EarthCentre and Universal-centring. chemical colour-coded contents, synchronised and syncopated, danced in the water, in the air, *slightly* and considerably junked differently secured, outer wall reflected inside, combination and separation:

   -Biosynthesis hormonal CHONPh. chemical impetus...
timed-activating, opening-ribboning, folding and elongating re-combining chaining cellular three-dimensional somatic body-cells.

To contain and keep multiplying enough, to feed,
and protect to maturity, to ensure the chance's...
are-choices...are good for the next-round.

Maturing juvenile tiny many pin headed mobile tailing,
moved off to seek and create an alternative multicell-colony.
Colonising fertilizing waiting female-egg, larger-stationary receptacle
pheromonal-chemical, at surface *electric* chromosomal-matching invaded,
and fusing-matching mating pair-type; separated, from the parent in space
and time, children, siblings, near and distant cousin, male and female, rising
out of and into ultraviolet Sunlight; chromatic pigment spliced,
unrolled and rolled into a tightly bound.

Fostering, mitoCHONdrial in the thousands enclosed-organelle respiring,
plastid-captured. Abundant watery oxidal energy source. Bright flickering,
electron photonic glow lit twisting longways split, separated,

And-reconjoining; centre ended heliocased elongated double-nucleic,
 continuous inner membranous closed centred organelle-knotted.
Reflecting fractal-patterning slopping spilled-paint,
repeat nucleoli, arranging organising; re-constructing, reproducing and
feeding growth, somatic body-plan.

Cleaving, simple division switching emphasis conceived,
fertilized seeded zygote egg cell, with miniature stem organelle
differentiation...*highly* specific cell protein angiogenesis blood plasma-vessel.
Flooded-organogenesis expressing-tissue, and muscle-cartilage;
calcium flooding-excess, bone-skeletal, and neural-tube.

Plate-crested bony neuro-genesis, exo-genesis, and by epi-genesis,
and nerve centre integument, hormonal timing vegetal-rooted gastrulation,
mineral liquid milky yolk, feeding, swelling and developing embryo-genesis.

Blastula-proliferating, laminating mouth and anus; invagination of the
gonoidal sex-cell's displacing invasion and migration.

Each, developing shared-capitulation, with form and then functioning,
nature and nurturing, to maturity; feeding on calcite-membrane;
eggshell, breathing, enclosed cell-amniotic, wombic-plasma salty-yolk, liquid
milky proteinus, eating our way-out.

Consuming food-store, from the inside,
pure-theatre expanded, almost fully formed, cathartic-expulsion.
Re-generating, to feed and grow to pubertal-maturation;
otherwise total-crashing, to rare but diminished un-fossilised-*end's*....

Maintaining the line, the heritage.
With a flutter of nostalgia, determining the surviving ancestry, to-
progress...rather than regress or standstill impossible anyway, with
descendants to continue playing-out differentiate, sexually-determined,
almost, or mostly, individually achieving successful, but otherwise unknown-
EndGame. Each compressing pumping protoplasm
Breathing in three-dimensional watery space.

Various vibrant wafting ciliate chained vibration,
version and variation of fungi plant forested shallows and deep
Growing, changing hearing and seeing, feeling emotional, the-Earth,
a yet continuously sponge, fizzling clear soda popping hydro-caustic soapy-
slivers, spreading dappled, emulsifying over the underwater surface;
acrid-rotting, drowned salt marsh muddy fungi re-forming,
a kernel central-housing now, clinging on to each for *dear*-life, it seemed.
Colliding and combining, clutching together...

Each new variant progeny balancing, and re-balancing,
uncertain, in-view others infected, consumed, starved, and flooded.
Drowned-out; irradiated and non-functioning,
culled, wiped out, extinct before becoming anything more.

Erased from view; conjectured briefly, then disappeared, without trace
Swimming cilia flagella wave washed across, dropped down into fungal-
mould caste creeping and crawling over and through the sub-Oceanic,
and sub-terranean surface. Feeding, rampant, in the heady dead corpsing
brew.

Pulled rotating downward and curling outward and upward.

Set-staged dressed brown and green, colour-coded,
rodded-fibre spherical spiral braided, upbraided, upraised.
String-entwined, en-raptured, sectioning-out, from a shared-centre.

Overly-emotional, perhaps, over-sentimental breast,
Mashed, industrial-mud, pig-food left-overs

splattered-mocking, gushing ships merchant-ships' *slop*-chest...

Holding double-bound retaining, simple-version, precursory alternating
generational...in the massing vast waters,
encased *miniature* repeating...membranic hairlike projections, pre-dilections
All the way through, inside-and-out; tightly tangled-ball, pulled-pushing
electromagnetic-growing the solar heat rooted pushing-through to the nickel
iron-ball magnetic-centre of The-Planet. Synergetic, building slimy-base
textured, leavening cradle shell-cell walls, tough-translucent resilient-and-
pliable.

The Fountain of life,
reconstructing to another point of renewed,
and critical collapse.

Built up over limit, folded-under, overweight,
with consumption and resumption, aggregating and re-aggregating,
back from a deadened hollow spanning-base.

Along the ground hazy underwater horizon,
moving culminating apical, spiral slime,
built and tumbling, mid-coned mired frothing foaming ferment.

Through mould-caste seabed, weaved and threaded upwards and along,
open at one end, testing and taking in, found and snipped-at.
Heat-singed and crystalline, frosted-mineral energising, glittering food-lake.
Chancing and changing occurrence; drawn-back, into the main-tube,
stringing-spanning, bridged-building, from the inside,
to store, to seek and find, once-more...

Multiple-thousands of potential-specious chitinous-fungi holding and
hardening, toughened cross hatched entangled, built outriding-riser, passed-
through, compounding, tunneling and sticky glue pasted, cone funneling
resinous sludge.

Signaling blue grey to red brown mudstone, spliced split pointed, tied in and
grounded, layering the buried deep protonic electron decaying inner-tension
relieved, fruiting-moistured, swollen dotted-mote, puff balling blue cap,
yellow pyrite and rusty-red speck seeded.

Boiling-out, retained-aromatic, acid-burning, lasted out, exhausted-
vapourous, slow-boiling erupting, dissolving sour and sweet spicy-trace.
From the-funicle corded, moulded ground, spat and trailing-out,
in-*warming* floe, poisoning bilious globular clustering forms,
rock-sheltering from sunlit chemical-solvent, destruction.

Along rocky gorge, amongst glistening, sticky matted reticular moulded
stump, broken off.
Collapsed and readily, rapidly repairing and reforming,
dead-rooted feeding renewing tracing a wave watery pathway below, peaked,
trough, along open oceanic rift gorge, engorging fungal decay, bubbling
bacterial fixed in root-nodule, coated, hosting strung-out podded,
icy-cold pocketing-vacuole growing-out through energized soaked,
mineral-metallic bath-warming.

Waning, cross-hatched seed, fertilised egg-enveloped,
syrupy plastid resinous, fermental fluid fibre bonded and chaining across
respirating, re-energising across the EarthCentre sub-aquaterranean surface.

Trapped in the fungal mud and sand-floor,
ciliate pollen microspore attached seeded-follicle.
Re-iterated, whirling hair-unsprung, stemming cell-tip headed-rooting,
base-downwards through the mantle, coiling-foliating tubing-feathering,
fibrous thread-like, hollow-culm, overlaying, nodal leaf-sheath ligule, collar
and blade, into the surround, toward the chloroforming morning.

Each defending itself from, and consuming soaking- up,
radiating, renewing sunlight, to reform.
Stalked stem-trunk corded, entwined sea-grasses, poking-out obliquely,
spreading-unevenly, projecting angular.

Bulging-podded, atomic-pointed, *budding*...

Out of the frothing underwater sink below,
sapping serial winding, upward looping,
tight wadded rounded, elliptical oval link chain, flattened out striped and
frizzled, curled up hair ball seed planted, watered, and mineral-protonic,
dead-nucleic fungal catalytic-stranded fed-anew.

Lengthening-toughened, turning wrapping-strandlines washing-gently,
against the ebbing and flowing underwater current.

Floating and transported, settled, swelling and transferring reseeding
packages. Squeezed, out of the mould, sunlight flickering, rooting follicle
sprouting silky spiral sticky viscose, synthesising sweet sugary cellulose algic
fungal cell-wall, setting out, and *sprouting*-again...

Inner and outer conjunctive seed-planted, and stem-trunk *rooted*,
Branching flooded, freshwater-droplet air-vapour, chambered,
Over-clouded more stemming open leafed waterweed,
in the shallow waters, vascular spiral verdant,
Open star-pointed nebulae shaped-leaf.

In the deep-clouding under-water root stem bladder budded,
Branched bulbous podded-Kelp; stretched upwards
Opening broadening guttering
Leaves'-*filtering* magnified-purple-brown, red-and-blue green-light.

With appearance of dense seaweed forest, edged opening, icy-flooded swollen,
and inwardly dried, opened out flap case lid, slit split open, and dropping
falling over the edge.

Chloroplastid, to seed again, splashed stringed interlocking-purple strand,
and traced along open orange sun drenched coastal-shoreline.

Through the settling, and re-settling oceanic soft bacterial-mats, coccoid
seeded and filamentious forking-off protuberant spiky extension streaked-off,
coiling-rooted. Lobed radial and linear unraveling, dividing, opening;
folding, consuming nucleating mitochondrial-granule threaded.

Each of us, flowering tree-bark, simple core chemoheterotroph, inside, and
outwardly raising anchored; a base and apex in mid water, arched and bowed
facing, tipped, forward, passing through, as in a wave.

On the rebound, to push a new angled limbic tendril forward,
headed triangular, pulling dragging along in the dense water.
Outwardly thick plasmic treacly, lingering gyromagnetic,
centro-spherical scopic, strung-out dimensionless, in a dimensionful:
          -The-Universe.
Radiating angular-momentum, fibrillating, texturing inner and outer surface,
pushing outward with a stretching of the cantilevering membranous body,
pulling back-inward.
With resistance, moved and moving around, purposefully against the rising
and sinking tide.

Sparking over fixed and moving coruscating-screen, in dense, and heavy
seemingly thinning liquid, inner edged bending twisting fibrous sinuous
cartilage-structuring, proteinous scar channel muscling forming turning side-
to-side, steering-ligament, fatty fleshed, continuous adhesion shuttling.
Riding each underwater warming wave, surfing, now, swarming, rippling-
ribbing...

Segment mineral-crystal coterie-nesting wave-formed motile-tipped, tiping,
encased nucleating-centerpiece.

Gooey-flocculation, electrostatic-aggregate-coagulating organelle-flowing
plasma- polymer; in water, precipitate solidifying-bodily transported, and
holding-together. Outwardly, uniquely reshaping each individual.

Complex, amoebic-animalcule, flowing, embryonic growing, segmented, swelling budding, divided paring-off. Re-processing, and packaging from the waters'packaging, and from and of: The-EarthCentre; in deep rock-pools, and ocean-canyon, over magma-hot plate, as a pent-up opened-valve.

A cloud of bubbles released from the ocean floor. Into and out of the waters, let over and through crystalline quartz clay and shale, damp slippery rock, over flowing yellow ash grey sand, washed tarry sediment cooled rapidly...wrapped propagating cracks, chemical-bags, mud-dwelling.

Over-risen, galvanized-granite-land plate, with the following tide, along deep sea gorge, over orange rust and yellow streaked ocean floor.

Through seething teeming grey-brown fungal and foul liquid mud, slipping, sliding; Each of Us glorious gorious our own submersible translucent-protist:
            -Chromatophore...dust-*mote* centringing....
Balled, furry stranded, microtubule coiling and re-coiled, turning hubris, pulling-apart and together...
Pulling-through, and re-matched, expansively-within,
regrowing, reformed, crossed doubled-up,
spectroscopic absorption-pattered...fuzzy fur-ball, multi-colouring ringed, from bright-white, to deep-black.

Stretched-furry unfolding striped brown and purple,
periodically, and spatially-engaged liquid mineral-liquid, and gas-relay.

Co-valence-conjugated, shuttle-gating, exchanged-marking's, passed, brushed off, depositing on each other, on the way through.

Similarity, congealing slime-ball salt-solute passing-by
Crystal quartz-blackening brown and yellowing *gasified...*
Liquidising solidifying ciliate grain exhausting, to a stretched compressed closed micro-permeable wall, lipid, spherical-amorphous, from a single bubbling warm droplet of water...soft permeable walls soaking up, absorbing and adsorbing micron- nutrient, to maintain, grow, continue, and reproduce, excess-waste, allowing and disallowing entrance and exit.

Taking-over, colonizing control and function, zooming in and out.

Scaling detail, microtubule sheathed, oxidising energy massing metabolism. Powering, microbial folding inside out, head over tail membrane taking in and bi-layer gastrulating, ingratiating larger-growing, macrobial-combining, conjoined-ciliary ciliate escalator, respiratory and digestive flooded-passage. Moving-off, crystalline matrix flagellate, swimming, from the inner remains surviving, pausing-only, to specify furthering repeat performance.

Supra-sonic shrill piercing, constricted sounded screeching-burst; heat compressed sono-luminescent; outer tension holding reflecting and blocking the electric-lighted spectrum, through and of Ourselves.

Each reflected inner stranded limbic, in water, sustained, sponging held up on the water, sinking and rising at will, moving forward and back, side to side.

Soft-bodied slow-moving clear-creamy and yellow triple sectioned trilobite, expanding and contracting with rising and falling. Internal atmospheric fluctuation, flocculation.

Watery gasses separated, swim-bladder filled-stabilizing...blood-streamed, oxygen-blue artery-vein... stream-rivering estuarial; hormonal-changing, highly-reactive, oxidising iron-red pigment flowing, transporting yellow orange-red; and, blue-green liquid gas-filled pouch; open at one end, opening at the other.

Letting-out dangling sticky feeding pendules, attached and hanging-on.

Together, with the rest of the body, pulsating on subterranean wave, caught-up in rushing warm currents, and cold drift's...

Aqui-flexing watery-capsule cupping-ball Capturing, double-lined permeable-hollow, semi-liquid algic-fungal bacterial-bowl. Vibrant halo-ringed coiled disc-spiral rodded filament-glowing in, and from the dense-deep. In the warming shallow-sunlight, feeding Sun-warmed photosynthetic zoo-plankton, diatom-misting bloom nervous net-larval, smack-blooming sponging-swarm worming...

Learning membrane skin sensing, and taking-in...and spitting-out. Snipping-at, muddy earthen rock, tasty stem-leaf, and other floating-creature. From the deep, ribboning-proteinous:
        -Antarctic-nematode.

Worming, ciliate-arrowing, segmented velvet-sheath; ragged quivering-globular, soft-segmented sifting-body. Digestive-tract, reproductive organ's' section-segmenting, and budding anew.

Flat-flapping, tubular slug-worming, threading elongated stretched; starched carbohydrate-coated protective chamber inwardly, and outwardly, blindly self-organising, tube-tree-rubbery flat-banded, moving in muddy water, worming-fungal brown-green water-slug.

Earthy, creamy-white maggot, tubule rehydrating, inner cloudy carbolic-brew, sloshed in toward the central-core; segmented, separating-out ring-cyclic residue compressed; and spun out resinous charged feverish, cystic-engulfed, explosive crystalline spore remains, sprung from the new centre re-formed floating watery-sac through root and branch, taking in mineral vegetable, and animal.

Food-energy, along the seafloor, massive blind and legless, slow-moving Giant worming-slug.

Sprung opening, ribbon and ciliate sensing, soft trapping and sieving, gulped, and swallowed. Crunched into swollen rock-churning belly-bladder; trapping whole-living raw-energy, potentially alive, consumed, dead.

Entropic topical-gases, and liquid's eclectic entopical and nutritious feeding; suckling reconstituting mineral-life form. Taking in the weakened and young of their own, and other, the energy to continue.

Pressure pumping blind bubbling, heat seeking granule;
combusting energising re-energising progressing-linkway...growth, re-agent, raising the generalised ready-state.

Bodily sponging, liquefying algic fungal, blackened and pale, lipid-stretched, and limpid-grubbing...
In ferment, imbibed heated and cooled.

Stewed and stirred, retained part released...through resistant blue-cold, and absorbent warmed red-streaked, nyellow and green blue brown arching sea-snaked... stretching and pulling, raising-lifted, diffusing-digestion.

Re-energized new body-cells.

Burning off fatty acid globular body chaining dragging along segments... repeated and attached, along modular-somatic similar bodyline.

Hollow-barrel shaped tunicate-sponging sea-squirt; mouthing-ring muscle band lips, digestive straightening gut-coiling; emulsifant lipid cellular membrane-feeding, carbon-flared oxidal core-elemental.

Synthesising, fueling-combustion burning, ammoniac laxative spewed out; extracting fuel and food spat out of flesh, and shell sedentary remained stunning waste-poisoning protecting-jet. Recognising, realising the warning, the alert, shifting through complacency, survival, and safe default-mode.

Altering soft-tissue, to make contact, or avoid contact, to swell and contract.

Body-rooted micro-tubular track-extending and distending transmitter and receiver; containing chemical-stomach-nourishing dis-charging cargo-fueling, touch sensitive nerve strand, tensed or released, relaxed or held-fast.

Passing discharging electricity rapidly through synaptic opening and closing-circuit. To-transfer, release or hold. In-sulating, isolated conduction, sheathed nodular polarization. Tripped-along, apical axonal-gateway, letting-in and letting-out. Opening and shutting, closed muscle-sensory, neural belly-tube. Cresting oily-mast, mass-tipping tissue, trapped bodily-centred, folding over fatty top surface building, recording, checking and repeating-*function*.

Switching, twitching, spasming, contracting, and relaxing...searching-sensory motor nervous pulse; sparked along spiny cortex, battery-wired di-electric insulated-pyramidal, rounded squared-off multi-polar ganglia, dendritic plasma-cell; clasping-together, clamping, synapse-axonal processing and transmitting chemical action-potential.

Limbering brains, fired-together, galvanizing cord-and-charge.
Smooth-muscle wrapping hollow-organs' voluntary and involuntarily regulating, moving food through, and waste-expelled; repeating,
or avoiding at every accidental incidental and intentional body movement:
    -Cyclic-nucleotidal...
    -CHON triphosphate chromosomal neural retinal photosensitive phosphotransferase...
    -Electromagnetic light-energy *activating*...

Signal-transduction, nervous tubular, reflected pitted, pinhole spherical lensed. Multiple and paired, apposital chitin refractive-index lensed, bending-light; through cornea and focused-iris.

Brain-stalk-extended light sensitive patch, nervous-primal cordate-spinal notochord, with probing cilia; sensitized searching tendrils faceted, light-photosensitive sensitive pit, single bug eye lense, rewiring retrofitted retina neuron funneling *light*-waves.

Selecting packet's from the maelstrom,
for the best bits, or irrelevance, selecting out the worst...
as in life-dangerous, and eventually, defeating blind spots, into the brain,
directing nerve cell flickering, close-call...
wavefunction-hologram 3D brain moving thousands-of-times...
per Solar-Earth second, to capture:
        -The Universal-*moments*...
        -EarthCentre!
Outside, inside out, upside down, and side to side,
and making meaningful-correlation, in brain-body space.

Watching out of beam-ray eye, nautilus green-squid balled-eye, fishbowl
chitinous-lensed, nematode fish brain-cell-connectivity...fisheye:
feeding on larval fishes, small-shrimp, sucking up sea lice into tiny-mouths...
red-algae thriving in the shade of Giant Kelp-Forest.

Tentacled mouthing, skulling eye-balled and nostril flaring.
Cartilaginous, sinuous boneless-head chamber.
Jawless, calcium bone-toothed, sophisticated flesh-opened,
intraocular soft-focusing, reverse image gained, now felt,
heard, and seen, made-produced, luminous and illuminating phosphorescent-
tipped, nfatty acid nutrient and vitamin brain-tissue formed necessarily, to
evaluate-action.

Revved-up, engine motary-device, loco-motive;
core co-ordinating function,
catapulted, fearful stress-impulse reaction,
this time thought-out, controlled.

Linked sensory and motor neurons, glial cell and tubed neuro-transmitters.
Under congealed muscle and marrow-boned, bloodied-fat, nerval neuron
firing, glial-neuron myelin insulate sheathed sodium cardiac blood-plasma
pumping-cell salt-potassium *ion*-channel, water-oxidizing heating, igniting
hydrogen nerve firing, synaptic electro-chemical, transmitting-fielding wave...
action-potential burgeoning, tipped directional headed soft grey matter.

Allowing, dis-allowing sensing, tensing, contracting, releasing for relaxing,
folding and continuously-organising, and re-organising.
Adding, holding, and taking away information states.
Significance, against prior signified information,
memorific immediate checking, measured and recording rolled-out,
and inside, encephalic synaptic sheet.

Conjoined essentially to the mouth and anus, folding forming-gut.
Sensorially, stripe-field bar-coded, through cortical filigree,
connected and contained, in fatty layered striped and speckled,
mutually recognisable, bodily-respiring, flesh in-tegument.

Behavior guidance-system registering cortical,
and directly cerebral sensory-input, from the outside world.
To the inside, selecting from among compatible and incompatible *kind(*s)...

In-combination, with forethought.
Charging the ferment, juices, heart, open ended gill sifting,
filled water-lung, feeding liver and blood racing,
rattling triple tissue-layered, cordate, bony vertebral body.

Ignoring fatigue, raising the excitement and awareness level. To foment rapid progeneration, forment and alteration, alliteration.

Organising, and sensing stem-structure-ranging triggers, across received internal wavelengths, to hunt; to hide. To seek through camouflaging surroundings, to rest, in group-safety, lessening the odds, in-creasing the memorised, mesmerising chances of another.

Merged, with the surround, ready to spring out, into, or away from. Through and between layers, blocking and releasing, allowing and disallowing, along gated-pathways...

Through and between convulsive re-centring mucal man-i-fold. Re-newed, and permeable at various points, to:
> -*The Outside.*
> -Outsiders...
Hungry nervous-tension, giving rise to learned search and attack...attacking-back, or lost.

Surface-receptors, identifying dark and light, and with wave and rock mimicking potential-intrusion. Swinging-around, disgusting or appetising or averting or alluring, and safe.

Feeding, building through built up network of watery lymph nodule, among more and more varied kindling kindred spirit, sifting out, shared value-in enclosed-sac, separated-out.

Distributing, through filtering-membrane, defibrillating and absorbing, bubbling gas and corpuscular fatty globular-bundle. Controlling in relative part, and renewed, through dense and less dense, exterior and interior blurred-boundary.

Checking, conductivity, for renewal and migration, regulating and repairing underlying self-assembly. Strength and size in specie numbers, escape, fight, or martyrdom. Giving-in to the stronger, but lesser-creature. Holding the rest together, in the swilling and swirling capturing-pool; spinning and splitting off, through and around every moving-point.

Responding; to the outside, the ever changing scene... waves repeated and reassuring, from one-side, to the other; reflection-on, and selection-out of the surround.

Bodily-contour building, small enteric brain, sympathetic activity with enjoined corded effecter gut-muscle. Processing, continuously feeding, flat receptor ragged wormhead.

Velvet-tipped bio-elelectric sensing, flickering electric glassy young eel
generating biofeedback, through concentrated-solute.
Interrupted static-voltage, negative, or positively-charged,
across and through folding and re-enfolding membrane.
Touching-contact, branch branching capillary networked speckled hollow,
open ended fluxing tubule.

Synchronised-*turning*, sectioned and separated, at the filling and emptying
mouth, grubbing energy generating and re-generating operator.
Secreted, secreting-stimulators, submerged, pumping-faster and ponderously,
slower, opening sucking and crawling along, excavating into the rock solid
and sandy-ground.

Telemere-graph and mast-messaged, testing the threat...
Attracting streaming combatant to fat wrap, and render harmless,
to disarm and capture, absorb, and dis-charge.

Re-charged, and dis-patched, in the service of the larger; hydrating and re-
energising whole waste-water funneled, tidal back-flow, out of the mouth,
through rear end fibrous bowel, opening membrane sphincter, lock and
release, threaded and spewed product, into the waters, to settle.
Re-stored; to the deep depth splitting drinking sea-water, and its gaseous
organic, mineral and metallic contents.

Inside and outside, filtering and exhaustive spray.
Consuming and exhuming, at one end imbibing, the other, tail-end disgorging
waste-water and gases; and broadly cast miniature spawn *threaded-out...*

3.2.2. Growing and changing.

Growing and changing: hydraulically distributed and distributed anew.

Another attached and implanted, parasitically attacked, spat out, hosted, and
taken-in:
        -Shell-House...
Navigating the dimensional-model, solid obstacle and smaller, moving target.
To attack, or defend. Speed of engagement or desertion
To conjoin, or else to be returned, suspended, dissolved and dispersed.
Otherwise fallen, gassed poisoned rancid oily celled globule consumed and
returned into oozing-inertia di-s-seminate, into the soluble surround, another
form, defined from the previous, added to, and branching off, to feed on the
remains of the last.

Bristling, sponge and jellyfish paddling, drifting re-forming bodies, polyp-forming and dropping, digesting intestine jelly-feeding, energized light grey-blue, and dark-red veined... exercised, sinew-and-tendon, supporting-extension. Allowing, expansion, retracting-layers, extended-again. Beneath wrack-layered, cellulose outer-cuticle, chitin fungal-skin hardened, excretion fluid-flowed. Pausing, only for the chance to reproduce again. Jelly shelled and feathery sectioned, larger and small brine-fly and shrimp-shell.

Light sparked flammable, glinting keratin-chitinous, crystal calcium-hydrocarbonate, passed through cells, microtubule connection chemical electroconnectivity. In the brine, shrimp, in the bordering grasses and ferns, leaf-cutter grasshopper fruit-fly barnacle mollusk-snail.

Sheltering, from the burning hot-daytime sunshining, re-fracting through the waters, absorbing oxygen-welding burning, conical-columnar flowering-headed, shaped-construction. Microbial metabolite nutrient mineral growing bacterium, stromatolite calcite excess-built towering domed.

Occupied successfully over life periods excavated boring into rock food-imbibed, and released, leased-mineral radial coating formed knitted and grown-together. Sunk to the bottom of the Ocean, fossil-sedimentary layered-chalkstone built-up dead limestone...attached fibrous pod retained, and solidified fungal hardened-shell, attached and retained, chemical symbiotic, keratin proteinous chitin carbohydrate-calciferous, metallic-mineral, passing through the cell and deposited:
    -DNA-trace...
    -Carapace-fossilised soft under-belly washed-away back to the sea... massively telescoped, micro-scopic.

Listening, sparkling, gem-encrusted, and housed, shell sand quartz pearlstone, precipitate marinal-lunar cement sun set mollusk-shell, flat-curved aperture, uncoiling body-shape coiling crustacean-shell. Along soft apical rut and furrow, swelling and expelling the outer core, body-pressure motor-activity reaching-a-limit. Externally molted off into the waters, larger and larger growing re-layering another beneath, larger and more-fancifully shaped-again. Shell-whorling convoluted, symmetrically turned. Variously-ribbed and coned, calcite connected bone spiral nautilid, soft-body dimorphic-sparring, refracting magnesium phosphoric-fluorescence, embryonic shell-chamber.

Growing; and maneuvering, at speed in water, transgenic cistern; genic anti--genetic, simulating-probabilistic...non-random: Algorithm-modification: capsule-compounding, and drawn-out toward the re-energising light; embedded sinuous, protected, derelict, delicate water-borne ammonite shell-chamber.

Elongated and twinned shell encased krill and mollusk folding cordate. Bi-valve mussel thin-plate, silver and purple green oyster cased, banked holding on along the colonised edges. Re-leased, elastic water born disc-shaped, spherical ellipsoid, porous cylindrical cone and spoked rod and wheel lamellate cavity chamber; emergent, over fungal floor and between bristling tooth leaf budded; stem and branch, swelling and contracting layered surfaces.

Limbic exo-skeletal stretched, cradle carapace shell tough translucent, pliable and resilient; endoskeletal clinging finger and foot-clawing. Excessive-building muscle, replacing, filtering-reciprocal cells' surface, skin-cuticle, breathing-sieving water-and-oxygen, jawless tooth bone, trachea and gill opening earbone, calcinous phosphate crystalline matrix inter and intra-weaving.

In-ternal, cyto-skeletal beak-mouthing, aural-linkage rattling-bone, cilia-comb, gastrula blind sensing-*jellyfish*...rising toward the upper oceanic basin shoreline...*hot*-dry wind and land stretched-away, to mid-planetary equatorial and other-equatorial mountainous-archipelago; volcano-laval steaming clouded-island chained-together.

Conceiving, and feeding the young, throughout the life cycle; nitrogen and calcium bonded, cross tensor strengthening body shape; in deep cold water's...

Folded suture-patterned success, in-defence against from gravity, and water-pressure; in shallow-pools seeing-out, or looking-in, for and against attack.

3.2.3. The Sun and moon.

Sun, and moon cycling periodic-daily, monthly, and seasonal annual growth-rings; ribbed-spiral form, jet-water propelled, in the-opposite-direction.

Stretching arms and legs motoring sculling-skeletal, pus-ridden shell-skin living –fossil pinned, spiked tacky pegged-back, secured, fastened, attached; sealed.

Energising mobilising gas and egg-production, shielded-shell. With position and sized features, holding onto gulping mouth, and turning bodytail, thwarting would be de-structants. Taking-in *renewing* foodstuffs pushed down through rolling circulate muscle-contraction; made, inward and EarthCentre downward-motion; in Cafeteria, canteen, coughed, laughed, in training, passed-on, through rapid electrochemical regeneration.

Along, soft-layering hardened cartilaginous-tract; from opened-mouthed to walled-stomach sac sticky-chaining and unchaining acid heat burning chamber, separating juices, sapped through hollow fibril galvanising, cellular bodily activity. Harmful toxin infected food, alerted through inflaming abdominal bile, two-way ducting nausea and diarrhea reflex. Hidden and hiding, spitting vomiting out stinging poison, toxic gas and waste water. Amongst sliming mould and coral mite heaped mound and sweet sugar and nutrient energy-fielding; revitalized immune system.

Expelling waste product, gusting guesting parasitic mites,
other than host self cell surface inflamed barrier, wrapping pathogen enemy:
Each accommodation: of host with pathogenic-guest.
The closest proximal, fastest least-action required, instrumentally commandeered, tensed and released...
strand lead-wire, to:
          -Stop, Start, Release and Hold.

The flavours, the favours digesting to absorb the useful, to deny the damaging pathogen, or form a pact, with low-margin of alteration-error...to endlessly repeat, and reform.

Practice and chance, of the various non-redundant control's...*matching*...
useful innovating and responsive, open-ended scaffold-building,
dismantled and rebuilt, somatic and re-programmed part:
With *murderous* muddy-intent...sequel add-on expansion version-controlling
Maximal-minimal compression buttons-pressed, foot-pedalling heel and toe,
hand-gripped, wheeled-steering, cogged-ratcheting levering braked, and locked.

The Driving-Force: intentional or not by-degree: in-ternally light and heat controlled and guided, guiding with varying colour-shaped combination, swirled and aligned clicking...static-linear, circling-interlocking, deliberately, purposefully entangling. Chased plankton-bloom and shoals of shrimp snapping and crushing pod, rock crustacean and mollusk.
Sucked in krill, chambered length of toothed red worm,
Bitten-off algic decorated tapestry-ceiling, taking in, or not taking the chance.

Improving, or denying, in the immediate persistent situation, momentarily to react, and to reaction, reactively reflexively adjusted to changing outer and inner circumstance. In-creasing the size, and consumption of smaller local prey. Shape shifting along, become inedible, too large, too tough, too cunning. Each success adding a physical and neurological pathed potential, through to the next round. Along spread out stem leaves and branches, oval open mouthings, brown green cucumber slug, and red-blooded worm.

Nibbling, at sea-lettuce and cabbage, bladderwort, mustard broccoli and cauliflower. Opening leaf seed flower and lower nut casing in water; beaded and flowing off, over waxy smooth cuticle. Feeding from leaf white and more colour reflective plant, seed pollinated and budded. After brief recovery, resealed, reformed, rested, tested and searching again, winding and un-winding off, re-verse-ways through the vegetation, coral forest, tiny crustacean washed-off, to fall and float, snapped up in droves.

Carapaced; slug crustacean, tactile tentacled mollusk, stuck to and crawling imperceptibly, assuredly along the protective sides. Scallop shelled limpet, slow and slippery clamfish. Water beetle resting, from potential assault, hiding in the watery slime mould and sand.

Tiny lampshell clam, armoured giant sea-scorpion; dragging four pairs of legs and long tail. Surviving, in-cidentally, over-camouflaged nest, and pit-trap lair.

Un-suspecting other, lured accidentally into capture. ex-huming the crabmeat, with toe nail clawed-pincer moving-on to and unable to crack resin shellaced barnacle, limpid limpet occupant, left alone.

Ignoring, the hidden colourless background periwinkle,
creeping along:
        -The-Edge of The Universe...
        -EarthCentre!
        -Earthcentrings...
        -Us!

The attempting scavenger predator prey.
Giving to compound pitted and pinhole photosensitive; tri-pointed, cubed, and multilateral shaped, multiple dimensional, stringing clustering light sensitive pigment of violet-red, yellow-grey and blue-green...
Taking-in, and flashing out, a danger-signal, for or against, homing-in on lighter, or more shaded parts; that could propitiously be-food, that could be-fed.

Small insect-crustacean, starfish brittle-feather sea-cucumber, sea-lilies, sea-squirt, starfish scaly feathery-flesh, surviving-mussel, filter feeding through rudimentary dentine, pulp hardened enamel ringed-teeth, sieving water, the chambered fleshed clam shell hinge, snapped tight-shut.

Closing, snapping shut, the interred, newly budding forms entombed, en-wombed. Flapping pentagonal furry ciliate starfish limbic extension points, floating and rising, muscle fat and bone beaked, pouched venomous stinging speared; muscle fibred starfish assault, defended against by laired rock caverned shell shrimp and crab claw crawling, ambushed.

In coral stony-fortress sheltered, cleaned, picked on by butterfly winged fish-finned, biting through rock, sandy tropical-beach, exhausted, and deposited.

Lamprey, grasping rasping blood sucking tube, sea to freshwater dying, after-spawning, digging holes for watery larvae-to-mature, to parasitic form and structure; through conductive insulating and isolating filament, electro-plated receptor and transducer, aware scanning-sensors, rapid-firing stimulators...triggering hydraulic corpuscular-flow.

Activating, conjoined-geared and ratcheted, winching and unwinching motor-activity.

Fish like lancelet, cordate proto-vertebrate side-to-side, muscle block swimming, gill's-feeding filter jawless limbless flat, eel-like, hagfish fin-tail, side-to-side cartilage-scales. Small silver and golden yellow fish, cleaning off the rocky edges. Vast darting and herded droves, curious and afraid, hid amongst immense rock-pillar; growing mineral-microbial Built-coral shell-reef, water break, breakwaters...

Near-distant, virtually blind-shark snouted-gill, lower jaw-teeth non-skeletal, to skeletal freed front-facing:
       -Calcium bony plate, sonar-capturing capsule.
Upper tail-fin sharp-knifed through the waters.

Paddling paw-fins, positioning, with mechanical bone-rattle, attenuating, over sensitive cilia mat, smelled, and tasted orientation, towards satisfying re-energising meal, dorsal-pectoral fin on the head, near the gills, semi-permeable, calcifer-calibrating...gating and sodium pressure-exchange, across muscle-nervous blood-brain membrane and inter-face.

Mucal-saliva trickling from mouth to stomach to brain bloodied-circuits Gastrul sensing tongue muscling, tasting, smelling, toothed-jawed extended skeleton, swimming side to side *thrashing*-tail, and fin-*sharp*... shell rock hard, and oily-scaly, and pourous, flesh-plastid underbelly, deep-chambered cavernous gape, drawing into sieving, crunching-tooth, rattling-bone; jaw-dislocated, wide-mouthing swallowing-cavity.

As a night moonlit sky, into daylight.

Each navigation, away and toward, in-contact and capture, to escape other sucking tube; and biting jaw, into the future, to live and reproduce again.

Snapping-up, consuming, and repeating, continuing; return Mouthing-gurney balance-operating, and extending fibred-limbs, gelatinous-wrapping tentacle-moving, from capture-to-mouth internally-warmed, cooked, cooled, chewed, digested, and warmed blue to red-veined, colours-vibrating, in bursts and waves, of renewed-energy.

Extended and contracted separately articulating food and jaw grip, controlling intake with taste and odour, sized-movement; of the mouth and gut, with instinctual-movement, reinforced retaining-record, of what is good to eat, and what it is good to leave-alone.

Triggering and conserving morphological bodily-change.
Re-producing-swelling, fattening, hardening, sensing. thwarting larger-predator, more-cunning despite size, with exaggerated swollen shape, hidden daylight poly-chrome multi-colour; mopping-up nightblind sightless-prey, before even knowing there is a scavenging-predator there.

Jellyfish, soft beaked octopus, sharp beaked feeding intelligent squid, hood-headed mantle eight ganglia legged, paddled through warm waters, specialized segmented octopus, charged and gored.

Waiting, sitting haunched, hunched tension sprung and suddenly pouncing horn toothed. Mineral calcite depositing around articular tissue connected parts' protein needing protein. Load and shear stress built layer, cementing tidelines...

Diametric building rods, layering fine thread lacunae matrix-pourous...

Spongy bony interstices attached to gulping mouth and letting, feathery jaw-boned hinged, mouth opening body. Feeding, foundational each droplet supporting each one and other grouped together; floating up-wards towards the apparent source of light.

Turned over to feed from the surface algic and plankton mite, massed ridden plains, above the wrack. Between towering branching bladder wrack, remaining tiny vesicules, twitched and flitted, phototrophic light eating bugs, numeric-algorithm genetic-mutation, slowly-exercising hovering on the ˙ under-water waves. *Threaded*: carburetor-fuelled storing and tran-sport-ing, pro-pelling reciprocating engine-muscle axial drive-shaft. Translucent oily golden-jade pellucid oceanic emulsion, pocketing and releasing, exhaustive rapid and explosive energy, charge and exchange.

Periscopic fish frog-eye, opening out, into clear ocean sky light shading glistening, facing open-mouthed, back-swimming along.

On the open Pelagic Sea, spare flesh flapping, above the surface, as a sail. *Floating*: fins running along the surface, blown with the tail wind, headed, boating across the depths. Jellyfish root tentacle feeding below, consuming morsels on sticky tentacle, pushing-out of-the-waves, taking from the breeze, above. Moving-fast, into the *air*...

Surfing the Over-wave and diving-back down into the depths.
Under the surface, bloated ball pumping up, like a balloon.
Floating back-upwards, toward the surface. emptying, to feed, to dip under
again, and flipping over, before flippering away into now *hidden*-depths.

Waterproof, heat and light-trapped head to tail bony resilin iridescent-scales,
counter-shading texture and colour, grey and blue and brown shadow,
and blended retained deposited, calcite back-rodded and ribbed-over
protective chest-cavity; surviving over ridged crusted head carapace skull-
case. Fleshed and teress dressed, locks and curls, mangy mane coat, fur wool
and pelt, follicled-over; flat fisheye, rolling over, travelling across the soft-
skulled head from side to side...

Ossified, flexible rodded cartilage, down to the balancing flicking and flapping
tail. Spiny-ray finned flatfish, ray-fin mudskipper, gulper paddle bow-fin;
angler-minnow piranha-seahorse, rivering freshwater salmon trout boned, fin
braced skeletal fish, skidding and skating through the ground-water.

Dorso-ventrally undulating forward-motions, compressed into: The-Do-Main.

Spreading, pectoral-fins, gliding in the concave watery rear-margins...
Walking-surreptitiously on extended lobe-fins through underwater sunken
cave; crossing-along canorous-canyon valley-floor.
In the still flickering darkened-*depths*, features and movement apportioned,
apportioning dim-images back-linked and coincidental projection,
proximal in time and space, corresponding, congruent, attenuating retained.
Channeled, indexical-codex light-image:
    -Copy, and checking, repeat-reflex *re-sponse*....

Re-turned, through fibred cortex, to and from blood swelling, bulging,
enclosed and front-facing *ambergris*...

Enjoined, whole transmitting and receiving, unctuous, plastid saponaceous
waxy glucose proteinous brilliantine-lobed, internal-mapping, and re-
mapping screen. Drafting and re-drafting, connected to each inwardly
attached; projected-component part, gathering-news, and building-materials
from the inner-most surrounding, to the outermost. Fed, from the exterior
waters, poisoning exiting, repeat pattern-mutating, changing and altering
Ecological-space. Nature: In-response, to sunfed photosynthetic fungal algic
bloom, *tacky*-scummy pastural plankton-feeding. Opening, in distended
dilation, fragmenting-fission; and fusing-together, sponging network-
connectivity; messaging neural-signalling extending-across crusty inter-
stical-surface. Breathing-in tractor and extractor grill-grating.

Sucking-in through light and mineral water, filtering-plates, flicking hinged grill-bars, controlled-consumed separated-gasses jet squirt propelled, buoyancy sac. Opened and closed, to sink and rise. Light-spotting, piecing together points, directed through optic electric nerve Large-blurry and stationary-object; fast-moving rock and plant-feeding...

Filtering-out, draughts of mineral and metallic water, crystal rock seasonal plankton, and algic bloom. Along the food chain, adrift with the swirling current, taking in, and powering locomotoring, grazing on algae, snipping at green and purple plant-leaf, im-bibing bubbling and tanning Solar-*rays*...

Secured under an alluring, reflective underwater surface, through sectioned opening pore, ciliate feathered shellaced fur, shifting and sifting gilled-vessel nibbling, and drawing-in, sweet-savouring, gulping crunching, drinking and feeding, quick seeing, deliberately searching-out...

Through coloured light and movement, caught in a lighted shaft,
Rising on the current, as if tranquilised in-*amazement.* Rotating spiracle-wheeling spidery-legged rock and leaf mite, tremulous in disbelief. Caught, trapped on the wave, part bitten or snapped off. Snapped-off, in collision with a rock, or larger gaping gap, prey or rival predator, attempting, competitive intentional, to-harm, to-injure, to maim; to-kill; or snagged-on, ragged-rock edge, clumsily, accidentally released, escaped the wound sealed-over already jellied, regenerating-somatic already re-growing scar-tissue. Chancing of varying-sequence, regenerated, anew from the original, or lived without.

Blindly, amputated, flippering away, deaf boneless toothless jawless mouthing-sucker, brittle-arm, bony, and toothed with such rapidity...

Once-accustomed, with rhythmic, phonic-chromatic-controlling input and output, with timing and tactics, skill, un-lucky as *lucky*-chance.

3.2.4. The Vibrant-Stage.

The vibrant stage-set, directed and redirecting...
changing unknowing chance and known choice.

To dart toward, or hide away from, known treat or suspected threat. Pattern-recognition resistant-cell surface, blood carrying pathogen antigenetic body consumed protection of the whole, skin flora non stick coating, outer and inner repelling potentially harmful bacteria, chemical signal response immunity trapped, and transporting-phage engulfed, red blood-iron removing, *vampirous*-piercing, and sucked-out the contents.

Digesting re-product-excreted, removing or procreating neutered, flicked and jumped.

Large spiky and blotched mass, attached and moving fast flared.
Like a comets tail, magic arrow fighting-off intrusion.
Between the warming, and hidden-rocks, fish-globular clusters farming growing-moulded, in-waterproof respiring shelless ovulated...

Consuming, bundled soft-fibrous specked creamy-white light-reflecting, and retaining-container. Pith-clear, speckled-brown glaireous-innards, linked-chains twisting and curling together; yellow food-ball wrapped, and sucked-into proto-stomach, to-feed, the growing embryonic larvae, to feed and pupate butterfly fin-winged.

Warming, sticky tangled networks; emulsified-fats moving coagulating-fluid, through swelling fibrous strands *spiral*-threaded.
Collected, gathering and joining up ligament twitching, soft-framed structure enclosing imbibed. Silver white and golden-brown. Dried-round, yolk-milky egg-seed, cracked-opening feathery, spread fan-tail, light-striking sensory nervous-impression. In the meager-light, poisonously engorged, roamed amongst slitted wriggling, air chambered-bell, jellied-sac, enclosed, swollen un-wrapping...

Greater variating and larger speckled and stretched striped pulsating form. Completing cyclic feeding energetic neural net charged across high-temperature, molten, amorphous cooled-strand, carbonate dioxide-atmospheric.

Substrate-*breathing* feeding nutritioning energy. With increased-energy, controlling, increased dividing split population. For growth and mobility, dissolving, renewing, to muscle powering along, reaping the benefit, into the next spawning.

Disappearing, flat and lifeless, running along the bottom; to take off glide and to swim, upwards-again,into, and toward the light. In shallow clear-water's... and dense tangled weed, provoked and retaliating as one, minnows in swarm, zig-zagging away; from snappering sharp teeth, frenzied feeding on massed smaller shoal, turning rapidly, to vortex; three-dimensional four-directional chance-reducing capture, moving into and out of the center the larger and older at the perimeter, smaller and younger in the centre; any missing, un-chancing, abandoned.

Spiraling-upwards, and along the social chase, into the darkened-depths. Flashing glinting in the envisioning light, unable to avoid the sudden jaw snapped, and snapping end; left-behind the tired and injured, picked out of the edges.

To breath and feed again. Ex-punge, seek and find, to reproduce and feed and grow, continue on, not taking the risk, taking-the-risk, that offspring may not turn-out, to model the successful pattern of the previous.

Before replicating attack or defence again; or not.

Before being consumed, sinking back down, to the sticky vegetable and de-composting depths; in paddled wake.

Over crystalline clay and shale layer, between suspended-thin veiled-vein clear atomic tissue-seam layered. Over iron red rusty shallows, elongating globules, separated out, in the surrounding water. Breast plate heart pumping, skeletal linked bony limbs, separated ribbed stanchion, Bonded backbone vertebrae, fin and gill, girdle and limbs, and skulled head, braced and conjoined. Layering sonar radar and visual mapped, correlating, including, and spun on operating ribbon fibre muscle, pushing-rod and drawn-back limbs.

Flexed-contracted and inflected, prior nervous-uncertainties, replaced more confident-probability building, shared-correlations... between sibling and species, syntactic-synaptic shared-recognition.

Faint hearts' beat: between outer and inner four-chambered muscle-wall; in-voluntary contraction of striated, blood-saturated pumping fearful-excitement, pulsating fits and starts; for good, or ill through living-tissue and muscle criss-crossed distributaries; lined pumping non-return valve, to flow along thick walled high pressure artery, to be closed-off.

Power-pressure vein and capillary-delta draining.
Surging branching-estuaried, into muscle, and crystalline fingerbone, spreading-toe delivery system tissue-depositing cellular, galvanizing *potential*-action.

Each-breath circulating-energy, to where it is called for, released and needed, to breath, feed, and reproduce.
To rest and sleep safely, in ever-ready partial aware-state, through the response of the rest of body, repetitively re-building the-mechanism, amongst floating sac scaffold protective and constructed skull bone, jawless snapped up, and snappering tentacled cyclid *electric*-fish.

Along muscle line cartilage, skeletal ethanol lubricated-tendon, loosely-strung together muscle and bone traversed, live-electric spark; fueled, and waste exhausting, reproducing form from flesh-compounded, fluorescence persisting, over-layered, muscle shelled and scaly rod and calcite-cone funneling re-ceptor.

Relaying, stem-touch, torched onto light sensitive-stalk.
Erupting, pourous-pored skin-membrane.
Mouthing-antennae, radar and independently brain -linked.
Opening and closing, inflorescent opening-feeler light-seeking, hub-tipped,
threaded webbed crystaline-horn, on muscular-pad vein-fed whirring-seated,
swiveling-calcite, zinc and cuprous-oxidal, phosphate lensed *fish-eye* muscle
squeezed into focus.

Receiving sticky light spray, shadow compounding and selecting-out.
Relaying through skin slime bony, phosphatic light pressure sensitive,
substrate lipid membrane layer. Rising-out of the depths, incrementally
folding reforming repeating, repairing and variating combination, bound and
rebound size and shape. Stirred out of sea Rock-Cavern.

Walled and sand and mud carpeted floor covering,
pushed out limbic ends, popped out, symmetrical radial vascular tubed feet,
tipped with useful suckers.

Holding-onto, to slide along the hard edges. Congealing-pointed and
sharpened tail-fin, tooth and claw, tacking muscle mouthing jaws and lips.
With the gums drawn back, lined with single and double and triple rooted,
calcium enamelled ring. Flat cobbled, and filed down fiercely toothed razor
sharpened-rows.

Wrap-around shadows' top-hardening, layering membranous plate.
Swimming turtle shell-section, fish scales falling from the eyes from the
golden-red and yellow, grey-blue sand, newly opened turtle-fin flapping, and
immediately darting into the water in their droves...

Moving along internally assembling rodded, threaded connectively built;
funneling vortexing through the water, single sharp raised shark fin.
In-water ebbing and flowing in and out and flowing around at the edges.
Swelling static crackling heard through the elongated and subsuming space.

Turning rapidly spinning helical filament hollow-filling simultaneous
exploding, imploding again, and exploding...processing and open-fast spun,
neural-reset...*memorific*-EarthCentres.

Pointing the way, splitting the subtle but shared difference.

Individual action chooses, choices, incomings and outgoings
To leave finally, perhaps to never return.

Pheromonal and geographical lessons, imbued each fulfilling halveling, to
find-our-way...creating new *pathways...*

New-*connections* with functional-help or hindrance...

Eventually to survive at All.
And the open Oceanic vast-aquaria,
the wonder of being adrift passed,
in confident passive rolling, touching,
and turning-in unveiling *luminescence*.

As if gently exercising, gliding past and touching accidentally, vaguely
unnoticing, attracting and alarming
Moving-*toward or away* carefully-brushing past and effortlessly away.

Sensing-urging, consuming and life-saving movement,
nurturing to preserve the few, leaving the many to fend for themselves
with the chance that some will survive, to their *next*-regeneration.

Glinting through a haze of liquid effervescence. Being drawn upwards,
towards the light, each swimmer needed to be aware; avoiding-collision, with
Other; by-accident, by-miscued degree, of perceived mathematical or logical,
intentional-movement, anticipatory associative, reflex and memory-
generating, guessing-at reactive-feedback, and learned-behaviour, aggressive
and passive, submissive, or attacking, in successful, or unsuccessful trial and
error, survival; living value, to trail, and to trial again.

Unable to dive deeper, or float higher.

Unable to experience the surface, or the deepest depths.
Existing in the water surrounding, ranging thermostatic pressure pumping,
in-depth ranging, nothing else existing, beyond, except it would seem;
mystery and oblivion, everything-else, stretching endlessly-away.
A surface tension looming, through floating bulbous weed and wrack;
seething algae and grey-brown moving-mass...reflecting the colours of the
deepest-depth. Beyond and above,
in the distant gloom, the blazing vestiges of original luminous,
reflecting, sparklings through the finally retreating water's...

A multitude of stars continued to shine,
emblazoned incandescent blazing tail's,
like glittering tadpoles, soared,
and fell.

Light crashed-through continuous damp-spray cooled nightime-air,
convecting with a conserved solar-heated circulate *temperately*...the murky-
surface lurked, loomed over by green brown turned purple above;
a harsh fading unfiltered orange yellow red sky *brightened*...

As the remote half-disc of Moon*light* dipped, remained...persisting glinting on as in the waters. On land, separated split-drifting continental into cloud and rain, organic Oceanic-waters, in the roughly-hubristic periodic, turning seasonal-changes, of the surrounding sun and moon and star filled Universe *shimmering* through:

-The Upper-Surface:

=The-Existence...*un-denying*; dominant sharing-offspring, ever seeking to re-con-join with another feeding and raising, the better to *continue...*

Stilled and raging waters, beyond and between.

Across stretched patched panel, continuously moving sunlit colouring pieces Not-waiting for the final un-changing, dispelling erasing wipe out, reactive, responsive gameplay; defending the accumulated moves, with intentions, of self, and other, predicting, planning, risking the next.

With slower and longer predictable Solar and lunar,
Oblong triangulating circularities.

Each of us, now, gently surface-treading water; surfing-against sandy-dry landmass, underwater, a torrential warming-wave *slipped*-through the caverned stalagmite and stalactite dripping waters...a-Cargo carrying passenger riding ridge, risen newly-rising sunlit plateau-plate, soared audience galleried, out of the depths...

Risen, rocky stage-plate consuming continuously, and impulsively centrifuging, accumulating capturing and re-capturing other smaller active carrying mineral microspore flagellum-attached gearing, and directional-steering... motor-motion...Each-of-Us: driving heat-compression:

Cellular-return-flows cyclonic cylindrical-vortex; pointed at one end, the other-rounded-out...nucleate radiating energetic, split-water molecular, hydrogen-oxiditive, carbon-nitrogen-fixing metabolism; tailing-fibrillose-mineral-microbe, gusting in the shifting waters' nightime, permanently-darkly dissipated, dissolving the watery surround.

Soaking-up, mineral water soluble lunar-Solar heat and light; Earth-*centring*, polar-Planetary, positive and negative-turning, or stilled; fielding, slaking off, hydro-electric oily phospholipid-microbial, meteoric debris, mineral-studded, muddied-sliding over the Pacific-Oceanic: Earth-Atalntis!: *algic* matted-layering the early *archaic*-EarthCentre.

In: Oblique eccentric orbital-axial pre-cession; tilting wobbling top closing and opening luni-Solar apparent...upper-watery boundary thundered trapped-strands strapped, loaded, transporting-platform, attached to swarming surface-walls.

Holding inwardly and outwardly faced, strung together; amoebic-domed, metal and mineral grey brown stained, and dark shadow studied-outer shell; foaming, inundated in the immediate circumstance; attacked, attacking, devouring dying exhumed and *exhausted.*

Each of us now, faintly-*glowing* in the darkened nighttime-waters...

Light bearing, ambient flickering spun-out from the deep dark ocean floor, light storing and emitting, seeing twitching thermal imaging stimulating and responsive, soft-gel vibrating cilia ventricular, desperately breathing in water; energetic, fighting for continuing existence. Consuming, and consummated opportunistically, dominating infectious and infecting, transforming the-living, re-set, and re-settling stage.

Leaving behind, skeletal planetary chalkstone granite-riven, risen-solitary:
  -Southern-Polar...
  -Continental-plates...

Baked to the icy frozen-Northern-Oceanic Planet; tipped, receding scorching equatorial, drying out, dying-out, died-out, leaving behind:
  -*Another* Great-Dying.

Shifting the allegiance, from Oneself to the next. Each to their Own, uniquely-altering and altering-again. In the regularity and alteration, niche and cleft of the rocks and shifting sands...

Forever changing the en-*compassing* Planet: the same and ever-changing Ocean...

***

Like monkeys at typewriters, mostly junk, sometimes useful and transcribing scripting reproducing proteins factorising, boosting, or blocking copies and binding decisive successful further amino acid preferentially clustering around forming protein production, specific triplet cyclic nucleotides spontaneously chemical bonding template messenging RNA held, hypervalue DNA in silicon plasma cell-sequencing chemical-markers continued on, colours, regulating catalysing complementaries, protoplasmic formaldehyde biotic, sulphide phosphate aerobic protist, chemoluminescent, phosphorent, halogenic fluorescent.

Dedicated to Elaine Morgan: biologist, writer, and extraordinary person.

How enduring the works of mortal man

Having-been, lasting-forever.

If no-one asks, I know.

If I am asked, I do not know.

Gone into the next moment of thinking,

knowing, or not-knowing,

where something-is,

believing, what, how, and-not, where, or who, or *why*?

What then is time?

If no one asks me, I know what it is.

If I wish to explain it to him who asks,

I do not know.

Saint Augustine (345-430 ME)

"How dangerous is the acquirement of knowledge and how much happier that man is who believes his native town to be the world, than he who aspires to be greater than his nature will allow"

Mary Shelley, *Frankenstein* tags: *life*

"No man chooses evil because it is evil; he only mistakes it for happiness, the good he seeks." tags: **inspirational**

"The beginning is always today." tags: **beginning, fresh-start, start-over, today**..."

"It is a strange fact, but incontestable, that the philanthropist, who ardent in his desire to do good, who patient, reasonable and gentle, yet disdains to use other argument than truth, has less influence over men's minds than he who, grasping and selfish, refuses not to adopt any means, nor awaken any passion, nor diffuse any falsehood, for the advancement of his cause."
— Mary Shelley, *The Last Man*

"Her countenance was all expression; her eyes were not dark but impenetrably deep; you seemed to discover space after space in their intellectual glance."
— Mary Shelley, *The Last Man*

Mary Shelley, from the historical novels *Valperga* (1823) and *Perkin Warbeck* (1830), the **apocalyptic** novel *The Last Man* (1826), and her final two novels, *Lodore* (1835) and *Falkner* (1837).

Studies of her lesser-known works such as the travel book *Rambles in Germany and Italy* (1844) and the biographical articles for **Dionysius Lardner's** *Cabinet Cyclopaedia* (1829–46)

The End of the Universe: Universal Verses4: Life on Earth.

4.1.Breathing in Air. Sunrise overland continents drifting shellfish scaly fins and gills insect and birds battles grown to dinosaur carnivorous epochs apocalypse.

4.2. Slow-Motion. underground blind earless toothless skullbone small skeletal insect and birds reptiles and mammal armadillo surviving.

4.3.Platypus. We night awakening dreaming language battles communicating groups.

4.4.Action. emergent day tools learning

4.5.Savannah. as from water return or continue climbing monkey hunt discussion

4.6.After the Hunt. Family tribe and culture

Nietzsche's ideas about ethics are far less well known than some of his striking coinages: immoralist, overman, master morality, slave morality, beyond good and evil, will to power, revaluation of all values, and philosophizing with a hammer...

Source: Walter Kaufmann, *From Shakespeare to Existentialism: An Original Study* (Princeton: Princeton University Press, 1959), pp. 207-8.

EarthCentre: The End of the Universe: Universal Verses4: Life on Earth.

4.1.Breathing in Air.

With the appearance of frozen ice-capped landed Southern-polar, frozen glacial Northern-polar, mountainous-volcanic landmass erupting, washed-up; from East to West tidal-flapped flopped lung-fish, uncontrollably on the reeded receding shoreline.

Frog and water-toad, amphibious, fertile, fertilising, birthing from egg, spawned, amongst the stones and sand at the bottom of the waters, from pouches in the mouth, skin, buried to thriving, and surviving journeys across land in the ground, ground waters' remaining, newting-salamander, beached, and climbed onto the land.

Like *any*-Other inhabited Planet, vertebrate-fish, reptilian-terrapin turtle-tortoise and Archo-sauris; iguana spiny-lizard, dragged themselves sprawled, on feet, legs and seeking wetland to-flourish climbing away from the flooded EarthCentre. Floated-off equatorial tropical-fern fen-forest, single whole-earth equatorial-Pangea Antarctic and Arctic-cap pure-iceburg continental-islanded...whole-Oceanic Pacific Panthallassa.

Pulled-apart, with the encompassing turn-of-the-planet whole Earth equatorial split east and west colliding northern movement attached mountain ranges soaring the roofs of the world giant insects and birds taking the temperature of alternately freezing and ultra-hot atmospheric volcanic burns flaming washed with the flow of waters fresh from the un-*cloud*ed skies.

From Australia, and to the Americas broken away from Europe Asia and Africa hanging onto the equatorial floated westward with the-Sun...*scorched* golden-turning, ice-covered plains, uncovering massive-forest, green and brown falling autumnal turned-leaves:

-EarthCentre!; the ground layered, deep granite-gripped, dipped gravel and chalkstone slid the solar and lunar-turnings warming bare granite, heating and scorching the seas and *frozen* ground muddy boiling-waters cooled into-streams...streaming great rivers and lakes; the five Great-Oceans and continents...

Hot-Pangea wipeout hard-shell and scaly skin protecting...from land came gaping water-snake, alligator and crocodile. Seeking safe-egg laying, burying and guarding, in-desperation, or over-productive habitat, over-populating, feeding of their own. From the South, moving polar-magnetically-Northward, the *forested*-continent of Gondwana spread...in the arid-monsoonal zone, polar ice-and-snow, shifted, moving Eastward; the Australasian-continent, front-pouched marsupial, unique, not-rare; insectivore mole-snouted carefully out of the unfrozen ground. Moving-Westward with the Sun chased, the African Cape, elephant-shrew, stepped-out; and with its underground-trunk proceeded to snuffle around, out of the hot dry ground, unearthing the insects of its' diet swelling, progressively to small-brained, pig-like priggish, but Elephantine-proportion.

From the Northern-continent of Laurasia, to the North also Westward breaking off from the African-continent; pouch-carrying South-American sloth, once-more stranded, armoured-armadillo and slug-like sloth floated Westward, and monkey-like shrew, furry, warm-blooded nighttime stereoscopic vision, thriving, developing, diversifying, and passing-on stayed African and South-American, others island hopping forest-canopy, raptor-birds, two to three colour-vision beyond the tropical-forests of Gondwana, and mangrove of Laur-Asia.

At the desert-fringes of great forest edged plains, overlooked from mountainous ledged-promontory seated: Great-megasaur appeared, raised from the ground on huge-truncated snout, running-legs, some running, some lumbering along. Separated-landmass, volcanic eruption, shocked-quartz, microspherules of splattered-rock, extinct-Archosaur-scales, plates and feathery fur.

Winged-hollow bones, no teeth, but bony bird-beak. Egg-roosting, and brooding. Settling a roosting-hole, and urinating shelless-egg, through burying-duct. Over the plains and jungle forests, from unfrozen tropical lower-pole, standing-Gargantua, duel-ultraviolet visioning large scary eyes. Light-boned, and footed, herbivorous-Megasaur, egg-laying Megapodal, moved-in, with snake and lizard, Pterosaur, Crocodylomorph, Iichyosaur and Plesiosaur competing-for-space.

Along and beneath, which mysterious intricate-clicking, and booming, unseen, unexpected echoes. Engaging, detecting response, through and between effortless movement. To seek-out, to meet up with, blunt nosed-porpoise, and smiling deadly dolphin. To-attack, assassinate, with merciless hungry-force. Scuba-cylindered agile blubbery rounded, and fin-sharpened whale-shark, emerging on the wide-horizon.

From the shadowy watery depths, snapping closing-jaw, cusped-folding, scooping at surprised live-prey...in the water, inhaling aquatic-swarms below, to float above;
discharging great-spiracle fountain of filtered sea-water, through spurting-blowhole, into the atmosphere beyond, the crashing-subsurface. Some standing on back legs, to grasp at leaf, and prey, or in combat; with some-other; some-flying, some swimming out of the waters, and onto to land to breath-in.

Through sharp-toothed mouthings, soundings-out, Other's, and seeing all the other-beast's apart from them; quick-moving, similarly large and small insect, hiding and in-hiding, disappearing, again, below-ground the wild-cat and dog; to the extremes, extending-gestation, for the young to develop shaggy-warm fur:

-The woolly-mammoth, and sabre tooth tiger...

Learn-ed: roamed the cold-wild North, while the Dinosaurs co-occupied the equatorial-zones. Southern-Kangaroo, Eastern-Bull, Chinese bamboo-loving panda-Bear. Northern Polar-bear, and penguin untroubled, except by the heat, and cold emergent; and re-emergent, internal and ridden surface act-*i*-vity.

Half-in, and half-out of the water to support weight grown larger in water, on land lolloping along. Beyond the lapping-waters edge landed, sand grasses spread, variating, opening-leaved, moss-feathery Giant-fern, drawing in cleansing the opaque-poisonous upper-atmosphere, fruited, swarming through *the* freshening-misty moisture moistened-air; moseyed, and damply,and rain-damp soil, seeding, let-loose above, blown on warm *pleasant*-wind.

Over continental islanded dry land...over sunken sea and rained-over incessantly, it seemed fresh-watered pool, and stream, raging river dug-in. Reproducing, leaf-wrapped vegative-bulb and tuber, water and air-plant, stolen-mangrove, paper-thin layered thin-fabricate, point pourous leaf and stem. Photo-synthesising filament, poured-over, and out, opening and closing...to the rhythm's of *The-*Sun and Moon. Unlimited accessed source-of-power, moving across and over, always present energy-replicating, seeding and shooting; dividing expansion gradually-warming, rising basalt-basin sea-levels, granite-land flooded; rippling-ore and limestone layering, several-times, with the rapidly changing days and year's...centuries and millennia, flooded, and dried, and flooded, and *frozen*-over.

Smaller herbivorous larger suddenly carnivorous out of necessity chosen building the fatty reserves needed to survive the cold in hibernation a cornucopia of tree leaf and bark, plant flower and bud, insect tiny brained pinhead great massively larger bodies and bone structure.

Sedimentary-feeding plant and fish, in fear and anger, by virtue of lifting the surface-sand, floundering-on paired-pelvic blades, in permanent training squat-haunches, and extended shoulder-extension. Spidery short and strong tripod legs and tail, running side to side, to disappear suddenly, coated and feeding, hidden in cloudy solute of agate, at the shallows of an abating retreating-tide, wave-patterned ocean-sea's, muddy and red-sandy plains below, soaring gas and mineral spuming, volcanic-plateau.

At the now distant lapping waters' edge, on the outward tide, distant sea-locked, open-facing and precipitous rock-ledge, overlooking wetland mudflat, the tide-crashed back, to lap around volcanic clouded peak, tumbling torrent crashing on the incoming tide.

Leaving stranded seaweed tide pools, and rivulet islets, over a morass. Withdrawing miasma glazed swamp, over lapping and leaching, torrid-undergrowth of water-grass and fern. Sheltering in the damp-shadows, and burrows of cool-wet mudded, shady-warmed, and sheltered, moist poking out of soft mud, amongst crenellated leaf, aphid-mound clinging to stem. Airborn agaric-springboarding, lightweight long-tailed dragonfly. Giantine taking-off along delicate-leaf fed, as well as other, along the rivered waters'-edge.

Floating off and between, sand glassy young eel slipped through remaining grounded rotting sea-cordgrass reed-bed. Large segmented armoured louse slug slithered, leaving wave-like curls in the sand. Glittering lamp-shelled snail mollusk-slimed, away from slurping and snapping others'-jaws. Retreating back-into, and below the receding waters.

Over damp clay muddy banks of limy substrate-ground, immersed plant-roots, wormed through the-ground. Slithered, snaked-over and reached cooling, burying,warming arid powdery red-rock, yellow-shale, and white-sand.

With ritual distribution amongst adherents, followers, a-feared of poverty and death, of self and others, of acquisition, power and control, approved, and approval of, with, and from, mystical, messianic and millenarian cargo-cult...delivered of fresh food, modern goods, and expectation of spiritual return in re-birth...ritual-programming, colonising colonial networks, social stress, ego-breaking heirarchy and individual and familial social structure, abundance and continuation, myth dreamed of the past, and future survival...magical artifact and fetish, promised return golden age of ancestral-potency, in exile, or exiled...military insignia and designs, anymore than pay for fighting, work, and leisure, grave-markers, with goods and food for the afterlife. With shaking fits and belly don't know dizziness, utterance of meaningless meaningful-madness, snake-hissing new-tongues emerging, speaking, new ways of seeing...steamer ghost-train smoky dance, mirroring life, and death.

From the waters edges, side stepping horseshoe clawed-crab, climbing up the beach, laying and burying eggs, vented breathing the oxygenated air, in and out. The shell, replenishing, gaseous-liquid organic fooded, for safety-surviving from grasping, and sucked-out predator. Deserted, beneath the lapping beaching seas, buried on sandy mudded scrub reeded-marsh. Surviving the apocalyptic global-warming, dust greenhouse-heat, and dying-destruction, diet, and distribution.

Smaller-leaves and animals, birds more easily cooled, in daytime, drying-heated, and frozen-nighttime cold-desert eaten quickly or hibernating moving-South, thousands of clicks, fluttered, between branch and steppe methane-trap, fissure, gas-leaking smouldering flame-forest, coal-marsh over the surface of algal-bacterial bubbling- bog.

Below the surface of stagnant swarming swimming-pool. Off-continental land slope and shelf, from stranded-pool, to exhausted-well, weed-pool, to matted uprooted-mass, green-mossy liver and horn-worts, flourished. Stayed-fast, steadfast, to bare-rock. On tangled once seaweed-bed, ammonitic black-grape clustered, cuttle-fish eggs-swelled, attached, feeding, bursting, ejecting inky-fluid.

Exploding, onto the land, embryonic and spawning tadpole, newt-swimming, gulping and croaking tiny-jowl, nostrilled-jumping, frog-eyed, head-perched up on angular-neck. Super-*sensory* pebble-lense twitching, breathing-nostrils, eyes-flicking, blinking-in raised-sockets focussing, silently, and catching tiny airborn-flies, stinging, eating, and breathing, on rolled, unrolled in a flash, sticky tongue, swallowing whole. Riding a leaf and bracken mat, with tentative fore-legged front-crawl, brown-terrapin, and green long-necked shell-arched.

Finches beaked, parrot-hooked, short-necked, broad-ridged flat spiral turtle-shell...rode out, extended out longer-leg free-diving reflex, below harvesting seaweed-fishing; long-cold dive, at cleaning-stations, cleaning off rock, and others' spacious shell, specious-climbing onto the sand, to drop eggs'-safely, into pre-dug hole.

To return to the sea, as fast as the cool darkness would allow.

Of off-tropical shores, to await the return. On the way, tiny reef fish grabbing fallen fruits in the water, conveniently sucking algic and bacterial contamination. Through, and of the water-breathing carapace, along slippery mud-banks, swum bladder lunged-fish, large and slow, moving through sand. Squeezed fresh fish-air, into fleshy-membrane sac, separating-body, and water and air.

As tropical-damp nighttime atmosphere, haze cleared, stranded-crayfish, flapped muscle lobed elbow and wrist-fin, extended bony fingers and toes. Silverfish skipping over the mud, gasping through sealing skin-pore. Opened gape and exhausting rigid twin-gills.

Giant gorging millipede, ran on multiple-legs, or arms, along the ground. Spread, along stem and rockwall, sectioning fish-scale armour-plated, water-retaining, breathing-air, through the damp skin. Worming blood sucking mosquito gadfly and leech, gorging on-grasping, gasping, given-up, suffocated, and starved. Rotting fish-corpse, with spiked-undercarriage, flying water-insect, seeking the warm-flesh. Suppuration, to gorge on festering meat. Cleaning off dry-bone, soggy-incubating, larvae-oozing milky-grubbing maggot.

From coiled waterfly pupae-cocooned, nest-flickering butterfly, breaking-out, spiraling into new-life winged...rapidly, unfolding halter-hinged, razor-sharp flaps of skin, lifted off. Faltered, and caught by the breeze, gyroscopically, stabilising-balanced, as if hanging beneath the once watery-surface...

On air-current, turned and lifted, dropped-over the seaweed-strewn ground. Where half buried hopper-mites, festooned, shifting the mud and drying sands, in-waves with their multitude...

Out of a puddle of floating pods, bugs, breathing vessels, that had swum-below, with fin-tail, arms and legs, emerging from the deep. Crawling sodden, tremulous and uncertain, into low-bush, shrub pampas-grass....uprooted-kelp and breathing air-plant hanging-mangrove, stilt-podded, under the moonlight *nervous* sub-marinal bugs that swam and flapped, in and over the remaining silted muddy waters, climbed-out and breathed air.

Slid-down slopes of drying rock and earth, exploring, crawling over beds of milk-white weed...worm-infested entangled fungal-colony, building and growing, with fertile and fragile brown-humus, light-speckled decay buried and dug-in.

Feeding on the lush and swarming undergrowth. Returning to the water to reproduce and spawn, and, seeded-anew, and deposited strings of encrusted shell, cocooned eggs' nested, settled, feeding from inside and out, incubated, attended-below, and above, the warming drifting-sands. Hatched, fully-formed, moved over the drying dusty and rocky-rusty Earth.

At the rim, the yellow moon began to wane, and a new light of day appeared, dawning over an opalescent sky. Warm rains swept over and cleared, the landward reaches, in river and lake and in stranded pond, and branch and leaf wrapped pool nymph bridled imago-bug's, in their trillions, and quadrillion pentatarsel emergent, from oddly golden-podded chrysalide, en-closed egg-larvae spawning, an old life-cycle completed, a new-one Only-just started.

Emergent, from beneath loose- dislodged, heated and cooled, and resettled amongst-stone and mulch. Prolonged, immersed just underwater, floated on leaf-mould, brackish-waters, water-spider, and spotted-beetle hopped.

Skating waterfly skipped, fleeting lacewinged dayfly, and mosquito-gnat flitted and hovered. Buzzard, buzzed, into humid-draughts, striding over the surface flung-out over the shoreline...splash-zone on the receding tide, leaving speckled glairous-trails, strings of clustered broken eggs, stuck to rocks, buried into the earth...un-earthed, now, loosened, eaten, and hatched, drying and warming, and calling-out in to the risen reflected sunlight crescent presenting cooling-air...running, and walking tracks and passages. Routed-through marked out network, collecting and eating, and dropping green and red foliate-leaf.

Cone cusped-tipped spore-covered and absorbing-water, and giving-air. Transporting, rock grain-nutrient detritus of the-Earth and *Other* living things, as food. Creeping, through waxy-spines, and unfolding furry feather-fronded...Giant club ferns, from underground, and the oversky puddle and droplet pool...seeping-through subterranean swamp, lily-pad and inedible lotus-leaf, swimming-across to enter and pass-through, spread sprouting unfolding, drawing opening-out, in spiracle-anew.

Clustered, clove thin-paper foil flesh-layered bulb, and stolen-shoot. Stilt buttress root-reaching down into the waters, clamping-hold, onto dry-yellow soil, reflecting, purple in the dark interior, absorbing, all the range of coloured light, ubiquitous-reflected purple brown and green, stem and foliage soaking-up, and shadowing the now rising *blazing*-Sun.

Along the verges and dark flickering-shadows moving, in deep damp dark grotto cave and cove tipped and spotted mushroom stool-mould. Of the Earth, blossomed in the gloom, glowworms spun, and fireflies flicked, came together and parted, flickered like rising and falling-stars. Shelled carapace and scaly skin, registering and monitoring heat and cold, moving-fast, now, under the rising Suns' rays.

For-shadow-ings frozen-still, in the night.
Semi-marinal holding wet skin and eyes, periscopic angler fish.
Hopper kangaroo-fish, mudskipper flapping and crawling, exercising press-ups and pull-ups, outstretched, to awake-again, to a *new* day amongst horsetail ferns and conifer, gingko and beach-palm.
Familial tribes of worker-termites, wasp-ants, and cockroach-cricket, chirruping, and chirping single-wing cover-encased scarab-beetle.
Marching through the landscape, taking everything in their path.
Arachnid-mandible, abdomen-sack proboscis, steely silk-secreting, excreting, reconsuming, remaking, facturing delicate strong-web, girdered strand-structured suspension-bridge, to lie in wait.

Mulching the soil, building vast-earthworks recycling, furry-wasp, and bees-buzzed, entrapping into resin syrup comb. Buried into branches, roots and tubers. Gnawed and carved into, torn and shredded, for-food, and nesting. Armies' of leaf-cutter ants, communicating clicks and chemical-signals, in Good or deadly-Bad taste, and smell, of fear, and rapid to-ing and fro-ing, organising · patrol and task.

Meteor-*logical*, eco-logical-diet, and prevention of predator and disease. Foraging-reconnoiters, leading back, to food, no entry signing, blocking, unrewarding-routes. Turned-back home. Spreading poisoning-herbicides fertilizer compost-farming, cultivate aphid-herds' edible fungi-farmed, supplies stored below ground. In the dark, lost-eyesight, and fur-dimmed pigment, strengthened olfactory's, moving-earth. Tasting and sifting, leaving piled-aggregate gradient, and turning-roomed spaces, along diverging labyrinthine-routes.

Pathed-maze of trampled-passageways, and ratting roomed-chamber. Leading out again, to beaten-tracks, city stone tower-block, and streeted termite mound castellated-town, tree-houses, and leafy acres. Raining syrupy honeydew sugar-water, nectar, harvested and fermented, sandy-seed, nutritious plant-juices. Scuttled and wiggly-wormed, through the subsoil, mounded mud, and excrement fertile fertilizers.

Super-structures, rose, with the sun, open-sheltered, along the peaks…Sun-galleries, below-ground, inside air-conditioned corridors of activity, tunnel-bridge, road and pathway, built between the birthing and feeding, and birthing again. Growing-pupation, growing-fatter, at the expense of the rest, battle-Royal, for the birthing nested.

The fertile few related, sibling and cousin, sterile-workers, subjugated to the whole. Assisting in the reproduction of the part, of each other, and the tribe. And when the time is up, moonlit-mutiny, *traitor*ous-sunrise.

Against the birthing-Queen, nectar pollen-perfumed daughters, raising and rousing new male progeny, to collapse in-attack, or over-extension...armies' scouting identifying and attacking, rival camp.

From some calamitous-war. Taking-off, the fighting-back group, and guards, from *their*-building, and repairing, the food collecting, and preparing duties.

Other insect, and same species-hunter, insect and bird, drawing sap. Drinking at pollen nectar, to digest, and transform in hidden chambered-nest, and comb, eating seedhead. Boring into and cracking open fruit, and nut-stones, longer-beaked birds grubbing at termite-mound.

Returning to settle over, or share the sea romp for food, checking, nested, and waited-on call. The new-breed, broody in the subsurface-warmth, determining their gender, consuming their packaged eggs cracking out into the open, digging, chipping and cheeping their way out.

Over-receding, warmed slopes, venturing out, disguised snouting sponge and jellyfish, plankton shrimp and fish, balloon speckled mangrove vegetarian-dugong and manatee sea elephant patched black and white dolphin, and black and grey white hippopotamus whale-calf, frolicked up and down, forward-limbic galloping, paddling, swimming in-safety, returned to sea's, and Ocean.

Returning to settle over, or share the sea romp for food, checking, nested, and waited-on call. The new-breed, broody in the sub-surface-warmth, determining their gender, consuming their packaged eggs cracking out into the open, digging, chipping and cheeping their way out.

Over-receding, warmed slopes, venturing out, disguised snouting sponge and jellyfish, plankton shrimp and fish, balloon speckled mangrove vegetarian-dugong and manatee sea elephant patched black and white dolphin, and black and grey white hippopotamus whale-calf, frolicked up and down, forward-limbic galloping, paddling, swimming in-safety, returned to sea's, and Ocean.

Short-beaked breaking-off, and-wielding, twigs to extrude, insect grubs. Built-nests, and fly-islanded, inter-continental termite-hunting, ant-raid, termite-defenders, overpowered, and eaten. Casualties-dumped, with food-stations on both-sides, leaving-those for the ready-foodstore, to-continue into the next season.

To mate-once, and die.

The daughters, left to struggle-again, over the most fertilised, to continue-conceiving with the love and complete-attention, of the-other's, and the whole. Afterwards, or until the drug wears-off, mutinous and misogynistic gender role specific-attack reoccurs.

The male allowed to breed again another female, or male, female, to take the Royal-place. The other, buried, eaten and excreted, into the leaf mould-ground. Digesting cellulose woody bark, chewing the cud. The wood-ant marches. In moss bed and fern, a-*hidden* marriage, long-stemmed and branching-foliation.

Axil axial- unfolding, separating downy-catkin, spiked-sepal leaf-bud. Wind-flower woodland-plant, white and coloured leaf-flower, wood-anemone, seed pollinated by-wave and wind...massing: The-EarthCentre: The Great Age of Ocean and Sea and River mountain and hill-valley lake; Tree-Plant, Fish, Crustacean, Insects, Birds, and Saurus.

And as massively-sized as never before or again, oversized beyond their efficient-survival, overstretched, to some-limit, to climb amongst the roots and branches, of arrayed wing-leaf petal-flowering *fila*-ment.

Reproducing, watery nectar and powder sacs, pollen-grain, and receptive oval-spiracle basin plughole as Universal Galaxy Star and PlanetaryMoon.

Holding-out, developing fruiting seed-pod, sweet-perfume, of rotting flesh, attracting the corpse-fly. Flying-ants and honeybee. Hatching in-hived water-evaporated, waxen flaxen honey-pots. To alight upon and carry off, and afford to each the opportunity, to consume and continue, without opportunistic attractor, and replicator, rapidly extinct, before even the next round.

Not made for each other, but used by each other, to mutual benefit. Insect, and feathered bird, burying insulating egg. To birth, hibernating and nesting and incubating, again, and again sucking-in…super-charging gas, and to buzz and land, and take off again.

Floated and run on the thicketed-water, through the heavy supporting atmosphere. Running and climbing and taking off.

Released, on spread winged bony-fingers, on gusting temperamental-wind. Surprised, taken to the air, almost, as by accident, into the blue. From curled up buried, hidden away, and ever higher places, perched amongst leaves, in open territory, hovering, suspending-briefly, as if stilled on water.

Moments of respite, snatched between chance of being caught, becoming prey, suddenly predated, by un-suspected rival. Unsuspecting predatory larger sorted-out, at the particular moment of possible over-extension.

Crustacean and fish, strong armoured-insect, picked up by the pincers, claws and beak, smashed onto a stream stone, river rock, tree. Trunk, branch, or prickle-thorn impaled through the middle, on horn spiked-insect. Sucking-out, the fluid bodily juices, the carcass left to be rotted, marinaded to a saliva-softness. Torn to small shreds, liquefied tissue regurgitated, to feed to the young, and swallowed to keep the adults alive long enough, to tend the young again into the next season.

Gradually, unnoticed except by generations, the air and land became dryer and dryer…the *arid*-land turned rapidly to dust, as beasts and plants alike, choked from the sky meteoric-collision dust-clouded darkened, the suns rays and the moons reflective edge shut-out the catastrophe, from view. Within a sheltering jungle canopy risen and spread upward. Great-rock mounts raised their peaks anew from cataclysm and de-*vastat*-ion.

Through lighted underground concourse, dripping chalky crystalline sedimentary salting fossil-mounds, and peak-pinnacle, hanging-precariously taking-off again, swooping and diving nightime cave-bat's sweet-nectar drink, feeding in the moon*lit*-outside.

In the infrared black light airless chamber, in the shared darkness, lost-eyesight and pigment, sonar-sound, sought-out, by cave boa-constrictor, reaching-out into mid-space, seeking to strangle...and consume in one swift-movement, retreated, into the lair, beneath the rock, and into slowed digestive-moves.

Lightning continued to crash-down, from an erratic electrified sky. Onto, and through the water's, crashing far-out, crackling across the waters. On-land, burning and blackening, flaming bush-brushwood, forest-wildfire's, over the ground damped-down, drying.

Wreaking destruction burning-out, destroying animal, plant and fungi, gene, and pathogene-alike dusting up the broad plains, crashing down, as if without sound, in slow-motion. The language of engagement, attraction and repulsion, aggression and pacification.

Difference raising barbs, spitting poison, spitting-feathers similarity yielding fear, and familiarity, furtive romantic-rival, decorative-fervour, dancing singing ultrasonic flirtive-tuning, melodious-in-*lax*; luminous flux-knowing when-full, and toluxuriate, in dust or water bathing voluptuate, sumptuously, revealing...indulgent, enjoying, excessively extravagantly pleasuring-together, flourishing-profusely, satisfying urgent-need to spawn again, by the light of the *silvery*-Moon.

From the sky, opened-up, a meteor, one of many cometary commentary cemetery *shooting-stars* in a random event from space roared-through the atmosphere, ripped and torn-open. Crash-landed, and erupted, with a roar, deafening, burning and sucking-out the air; filling the lacuna, with instantaneous-fire, and dust.

For a moment all was *stilled*.

Catastrophic, instant-astronomical, and gradual-geological alteration, and catastrophic energetic-change dark-energy lighted darkened matter to ash and dust again. The skies seemed to come crashing-back down-below, everything buried, subdued, and deadened, into the instant-night sky. No-stars or galaxies glistened beyond.

As comet remnants, sped-past, in-further circuit, and meteorites, in distant-orbit caught-in the-ionosphere, atmosphere, continued to crash-through, to-flare transported transporting carried-burst and burning turning hurtling to: The EarthCentre *exploded* in *flame*. Suffocating, wind-shock, and heat-shock shook the ground.

A gigantic boulder of flaming rock, driven diving from a Huge-Sky:

plummeted in collision course, the skies, exposed, exploded, again in dust and fire, spread quickly through re-forming forests, and crashed-down, in *furious*-flame. Rock-tumbled, and lifted, buried-avalanche, landslide, mud-slide massive flooding, rift-ripped fault-line, opened up and entrenched-pitched valley-plain.

From below the floored mid-ocean ridge, water and magma-cracking and-splitting, spitting heat convecting-outwards avenuing and releasing steaming-upward vented and grilling, ribbed course filiament, and around, rolling with interior-externalising EarthCentred wave-upon-wave...*echo*-sounding...pluming back inwards, dropping-back inwards, petrified in place tough skinned shifted swathes of land.

Back into the waters, over-flooded, sunken back into the mantle. Moved-apart, drifting around, over-steaming liquid-rock, flowed-beneath, and over the erupted undersea basalt, and limestone-layered raised, shell and skeleton flash-rotted mountainous granite sheet, rock-pillar glazed and glistening, through dull-flinty laminate, strip layered land sunk, and rose-up once-again. Upended out of the sea, to soar and plateau. Tsunami-seas, over erupted, sucked upwards into the sky, in one massive roar.

Capsized the raging erupting and evaporating subterranean-wave, lifted the dense cold sea dragging mud stormed backwards, in apparent slow-motion. Lifting-compacted sediment, and dropping-back over the land, back-down below, over and into the Universal-height's...to depths of the rearranging, slower-turning skies-darkened, as sheet cloud, dust snow and ice gathered, over the distant remaining heights.

In crater and valley, sea and superheated cooking desert, large amphibious reptile lizard and bird, small-bird and hidden-rodent, insect-lava, ambergris tree-say glazed, perished there. Sunk into the burned, drained, dried out, drowned, once more burnt-out and frozen-out EarthCentre.

Tucked-in beneath a raining-blanket of volcanic gas, water-cloud and dust, blanked and blotted-out; into the eradicated-light, of a newly rising-Sun. From beyond, another stray meteor, cometary bolide collided, crash-landed, shattered and splashed-down. Interrupted, ceased and blanked out the future, caved underground and below sheltering ledge, in-planning, in-spray and ice and dust; pent-up volcano-erupting ground-hydrated methane-gas leaked...exploded Overland and Ocean-basin.

Continental-ridged from plateau, overlooking, flooded and dry dusted, cleared of every visible large and small beast, visible every other disappeared, into gulf and gully, secluded sheltered, hibernating, waiting their new-opportunistic, chance.

4.2. Slow-Motion.

No-animal stirred, no-animal lit, it seemed what was left.
In the squall at sea, out in the storm, to hear, or be startled.
To-emit...*deadened*-cry.

Already dead, disappeared, hidden invisibly and *silently-*away...*lightning*-crashed down, as thunder-cracked, echoing along the valley teeming-rains' weathering-rocks and washing away altering the landscape...

Opening another new-scene, over which *new* life moved, snapped and chased. On re-emerging grassy foreground, at each passing catastrophic storm, fresh vegetation glistened all around, embedded into valley and earth, mountain and rock-face, the *blazing*-Sun, dried out earth, and straw yellow-grasses, bleached and baked soaked shell pimpled and made rough dry hair and hide, and feathered, out-of dry scaly-skin.

Below over the grasses, broad back-bodied cicada, membraneous-wings, high-pitched droning, vibrating-abdomen. Above, at branch, sleek bright colour patch-phoenix-fire and light-hollow-boned kingfisher humming-bird, *hovered.*

Drawing resin-sap, from leaf-petals opened out, along a melted-freshwater-riverside, meeting the-Sea. Oily-feathered bright fisherbird, swooped for fish and fly. Glinting red and blue, emerald and jade green, in the light, small fluttering four-wing, soaring-forms, flew, and extended their range. Spread pectoral-flap, of boned-skin, directed; directing, migrating-sunward, starward, silver-shoal, leapt, and flew in droves...through the *breezy*-air.

Over the water, splashed, squelched, thudded, pooped, landed, swam and landed, took-off again. Swallowing-air, and water, insect and fish, away from the grabbing-jaws, snapped-back, into the restraining-depths beneath.

From brown to green, grounded on underwater leaf and branch, sticky prehensile-tongue pad flicked-out, balancing boneless and grown bony-tail. Each the length again of reptilian lizard-body, in shallow-water and upper beach salt air, light gill-projecting winged-insect, catching fluttering water-fly. Dun-brown and black and greyskin and furred, barbs whiskery sharp-toothed, keeping-warm hursute-waddled and rolled in-water, and in mud. Short legged smoothed blubbery dripping flesh shuffled, on fin flippered leathery-limbs. In the swirling ventilating and vapourous atmosphere, drying fin and febra. Taking-in and expelling, hopping along, skipping and running on wet and dry-land.

With coordinated symmetrical or alternate side as if swimming in the air. Sprung-grounded movement, supported-sideways, forward and back. Pulling and pushing the body. On spindly extended-limb, fanning feeble-pads, and claw-toed feet. Tottering-forward, screaming and howling, turning broad shoulder bladed, and conjoined girdle. Sitting up, on dropped haunches, standing-up to the settled rockfall, and the hardening-earth.

From an exuberant gaping bubbling underwater world, a cacophony of crackling, sniffling, screeching and roaring, crawling, running and standing, pervaded the encapsulated scene. From pooled hollows, in branch and rock, striped snakes and frilled iguana hissed, and crawled, swelled and changed chamelion like, sought seaweed leaf, to eat and shade. From the depths, ejecting salt water through non-pourous skin spitting mouth, out of the water, ready to in-digest and digest land-grasses, rhino-sauros stamped and small rodent rummaged-through, the heights of a spiky leafed jungle.

Below, the forest canopy, towering pilons of weather-hardened, cracked and split infested, stem seed-cone reaching-down to treeless pampas grasses. Through rising woody bark of redwood conifer pine forest, split-leaf gingko, and acacia tree'd-plains.

Over stale crusted rocks, hip legged lizard jaw snouted, snorted, and scampered through the undergrowth. Looking-for heat and shade. Slug-slothed, below smudgy pudgy *puffed*-cloud over estuary delta-distributaries...along straying-streamlet and rivered pool, conjoined on crumbling-ragged, islanded-lake, fjorded-inlet and loch separated continental-shelf coastline, to rugged mountain-range, colliding with the sea, edged and haven, *hellish:* heavenly-landed. Breathing into the atmospheric thin-air, to dive, and disappear once more.

Far-below and wide horizons...nestling-alongside, reappearing near underwater surface, in protective guarding of live-miniature progeny. Emerging, from within the bowels of one swimming close-by, heaved and spilt-out through swollen and stretched leathery-wall.

Encased, membrane-anchored inside. Swelling-outwards, the extension of the placental lining, lathering, pushing-out the offspringing, from its spumy-bath. The puny new-born, live-birth gasping in seawater, to-spew glaireous-yolky albumen-amniotic liquid, back into the brine.

The linked-placental food and growth, medicinal chain-bitten broken, snapped-off and eaten by the mother. For-sustenance, her-own, and the dis-attached form, snuggled-alongside.

Suckling-on the watery salt-sweaty projecting milky-strip, the fatty-dripping outer maternal teat. Drawing on the food provided, taken-directly down through open gasping-gape. Staying, heldfast, gripped onto, then to float off, into the surrounding water's...to be nudged-off, unlooking, blindly out of the way, into the slipstream hydrodynamic flow, of the re-grouped adult-herd. Distant and close, echoing sounds, between and through the deeper, and shallow-water's...diving dolphin and sleek-shaped hammerheads, in regard of the other, attracted to follow, and copy.

Tricked traced fatal-distraction, to avoid, or collide. To be consumed, or to rejoin the recognised sized group, breaking the waves, spouting, swimming away from, and in toward the shifting shore-line. On the Southern-continents, stranded-marsupial, small tree-trunk kangaroo, furry-bear versions, climbed-trees.

Out of sight, and safe from the heat and drifting scorched ground. Below, the over-viewing peaked-ledges, from the dust and water, submerged, and dried-out burning-ground. Crawled small safely pouched-marsupial. All and each opportunistically picking out rare-leaf, and bark amongst scarce resources, growing desert-eucalyptus, flowering-watery fruit-tree, and tasty cactus-insect.

Toward, the mid-temperate, lush tropical-wet and forested-foreground...sharp toothed shark fin, re-surfaced. Small silver flitting and brightly coloured corralled-fish, escaped and swarmed off, toward shallow sundrenched palmtree islanded-shore. Northern-hemisphere, continental-plate, de-islanded on remaining ice-floe, ice, granite-grounded, stranded hairy-mammoth, and woolly-rhino and sabre-toothed tiger. Bison, caribou, auroch hippo-mastodon, musk oxen halved shafted, fur and fire, bringing-down, and cooking.

In: Mangrove-Swamp. Ice-age receding with warm-periods of polar-capped melting, sinking Southwards, retreating into the Oceanic-circulate...

Along the equatorial-tropics Elephant ponderous raised-foot of indecision, thinking long-necked body shortened tall-legged small-brained-giraffe bingeing, sampling carefully, or leaving alone. To-drop, rotten and fermenting fruit, piled high and deeply on the ground. To-await the chance to intoxicate, and knowing, to mulch, to compost spiral build, to renew-coned vortex-cored peaked-point; nuzzled nutted-pickled, picked-at and eaten muzzled; with spread out leaves, and branches.

Large and small feline wolf-dogs, canine-cats, apocalyptic sensitively-whiskered King-rat. Porcine short and long snouted, snuffling ground sloth, great long tooth tusked and hairy elephantine foot stomping, exercised, arraigned alongside mouse, and sleek-tiger, and lying-lamb: Lion, and Lioness.

Separating out the surrounding, with slower and more rapid movement, to weight and lumbering size. Creeping-creatures, hissing-through, and along the ground. Peering, Giantesimal-rodent mouse, eventually-appearing into the light of day. Peeling back the lid's to take in the micro-cosmic, and macro-scopic vast-*pantry*... Each went where the rains and water holes, and seasonal rivers-led. Moved-on, by hunger and thirst, and an incontainable need, amongst-many, to subject the self to risk, to continue or die.

To-return, to the green Great-plains, that bring and sustain life to the whole. Those extinguished, individually, and as a whole, to be consumed into dust. Demolishing-trees, and brush for food and shelter. Rhino, camel and horse, long-legged tiptoeing hooves, galloping up and down, giraffe spinal-gait, front-limbs stabilising, moving forward, steering back-legs and tail buffalo and zebra-striped strayed stayed roamed, searching: The Rain-Harvest.

Along the browse of the woods, insects-swarmed, massed in droves. Settled on warm fecal-caked hide, of roaming and ruminating brood. Broad leaf-forest edge herd *hidden* away...at the higher spots, condensed rain cloud gathered, in air-pressurized below, a sudden-shower, seasonally-monsooning, over the forest lake, marshes and sea swift and swallow skimming over a glassy sea unable to land-on, or take-off from the ground.

Where there was no draught to lift them away again. Blown by force winds, drawn along cliff-edges in flurries, over-water pouring and splashing, over sand beached-lake.

Overflowing, over the sandy-marshes, emptying, pouring back into the sea. Washing-away, the sand of times tides, leaving limy and salt trails, built ridges along the edging levels. The *bright* sun now steaming, the respiring land and rock, into the air, evaporating from the rivers and lake pools; transpiring off shiny-clean leaves. Swallowing, open-mouthfuls of plankton, shrimp in shoals, unable to avoid. Twisting back and forth, down and up, escaping along ancestral-route.

To and from mating and warm spawning fields. To feeding fields, fixed on unchanging return. To-unavoidably be met-again by moonlight, or Sun; and-both, by-surviving, the rest eaten and dropped, wasted to layer the surface below, beneath the Oceanic star-sprinkled sky. With each generation-fading, or ever more resilient and flourishing. Bi-pedal standing raising plant: flower-eaters' colourfilled retina: and fearsome four-footed, small toothed-Dinosaur, ripping at, gulping chunks of air, and food.

Warm-blooded, oily-feathered forelimb, triple-toed beast, opposable clawed-hand and flat-footed, holding-on devouring prey-*alive*...dead. Moving over the land, across land corridor, out through the forest edges.

Encrusted, egg-emerged, nested well-fed hatchlings cracking increasingly-larger sized,

and slowed-metabolism, out of the edges, swollen, herbivorous, and carnivorous-reptilian. Consuming-voraciously, mainly plants with a side of meat when available and increasing in body size, at each egg layering and cracked opening.

Warmed and grazed, in fields of variegated herb leaf, petal and fruit flower. Water fed cascading from pool to pool. Following seasonal-rains, from extremes of cold and heat. Large threatening and foreboding, long necked and shortlegged, scaly and spiked and furred lizard.

Remaining Megadon browsed, thin necked giraffe foraged and marauded, with digging claw, cutting and slashing, gripping-onto and ripping-out. Through, the leaved-forest roof, attacked, ferociously, voracious over the plains. Running, awkwardly, but fast, stamina-sapping, long-neck snapping, and grabbing, with grinding and sharp biting-teeth.

Opened, blood-filled sail-absorbing sunlight, pivotal internal blood-streamed warmth smaller large and massed-insect, small-reptile and rodent, amphibian and fish-prey. Followed, and snared. Chased and caught.

Through Mangrove-Swamp: from Jungle-Wooded and pine-Forested: over dry-patrolled savannah-plains, along waterways...habitually returned to, to spawn, and pasture.

Stayed-on land, snakes and lizards, iguana, and great flying-beasts. Spade-serrated edged and shaped teeth, long legged, bear like, thick tailed lion, and sail-backed low-slung, heavy-ankled, small-headed and armoured, car-sized armadillo.

4.3. Platypus.

Mammal-like: Over the sea and land, vast-cyclonic clouds, swept and showered rain, across peaks-of-Land. Drifting, into the opened great chasms and gorges. Ex-tinguishing, down-pouring rains, renewing-anew, seed and spore buried nutrition, to revive-stronger, and smaller than before. Fixed onto the damp, energetic land, thunder-thudded again, and boomed near-to, and, after a distance pause far off through mountain-pass, through the air where dust-storms raged, distant sea rose and dropped, many times.

Volcanic drowned islands, consumed and re-appeared, erupting fiercely into the open skies. Between the Southern hot tropical centre, and slush Arctic melting ice floats towered and sunk, into a warmed and washing ocean, and split continental plate.

Across the face of the slowed spinning, lunar-orbited, and Solar-orbiting: Solar-System: Galactic: Universal: *moving*-Planet. As: The-Sun: re-appeared: continued *shining* over the planet below skies once more cleared, precipitating raining tropical-humidity, opportunistic-recovery fungi-thriving, feeding-on dried-out massively:

-…of the remaining less than a quarter of all life. On-Earth, a few smaller insects, gilled four-winged breathing, by-direct diffusion into the body, plasma-energising less-demanding, taking-off, again, on the wind, ranged between plant flowering-stem re-arranging the eco-system, from hidden-damp sheltering-caves, and parched once more rapidly seasonal growing.

Monsoon-watered flooded-plains, amphibious reptile crawled. Leviathan-landed invader, and as yet small-invertebrate-insect, terrestrial-vertebrate, amphibian and reptilian, water retained skeletal-shell. Case-bulging, carrying, out the rear of the bony calcirous skull, neo-cortex, swollen brain, skeletal framed four strong-legged, spinal-tap first cause and effect, together walking-upright, standing, with sharp dilated-eyed, surround-vision, moving-over temperate, tempered to the-terrain.

Dramatic-Universe persona-Hyperarchic…Ultimate-Fate: *spatially* de-fined: finite and in-*finitesimal*…so:

-Event-Horizon…

-O-point, *only*…

Infinite-*information*…as constantly-changing:

-Possibilities…

-Probability…

-Facts?

-Now?

-Then?

-No-longer…

-Shortened *snapped-off*…Only one piece if information is

True:

-I-Exist?

-We-*exist*…

-*Now*…

-*Then…at-least*…

Asymptomatic, approach-point, asymmetric, Ultimately-continuing and changing, anew:

-Laws of Accelerated-*returns*...

-Proves True of The-Universe and Galactic and non- or larger more dispersed Stars Planets and Moons...*predictive*:

-Galactic-wall runaway positive-*feedback*...

-Negating-neutral...

-High-level *computation* surpassing Human-Understanding: Knowledge, or belief.

-All, of course, course-set...cosmically...*comically* neck-raised and turning-face, watching-out sentience, owning, engulfing, and controlling. Pushing and pulling, away and towards, with, and against:

-Maximal/minimal...*complexity*...

-Like Arch-a(i)c-*bacteria* in-soap...
Volcano-ing from pointed pores cannot hang-on:

-In: *blissful*-Heaven...
Ex-changing any *electrons...appropriating...stealing land and other*...

-Supreme-point...

-First cause and effect...

-Death.

-Same. Light from...

-Light?

-From Darkness cent-ring: galaxies, planets and moons...stars and asteroids and cometary-meteors...*electrons*....something-else?

-Probably...

-Of course…*tran-scendent*…

-Exists?

-Exactly. All of us autonomous, irreversible…

-…cannot *not*-be…

-Or *not* have been?

-Or-be…copy of same?

-Ever?

-Why not?

All-around, ear-twitching three middle ear bones selective-hearing listening-out, connected powerful jaws and variegated-teeth. To snip-at, chew, shear and puncture almost anything, for-food. Mammal-like nostrils opening, porcine dog teeth. Allow, chewing and breathing at the same time. And, moving-about slowly, and quick of turn, of speed, and with purpose, in the nocturnal cold safe-hunting food, and breathed-oxygen energy-extracted, through mixing aerating four-chambered heart. Into hibernating warm red-cellular blood system, re-newing, the cueing of the blood-brain barrier, nervous-sensing, to-trigger, muscle-cartilage skeletal-movement. Wary and concerted action potential retaining, bristling chromosomal-cellular, hydro-carbon chitinous, retaining-proteinous keratin-growing horns. Moulting and regrowing, black to brown melanin-pigmented-hair, eyes and skin. From sunlight tanning soaked on land: proto-mammalian laying watery-eggs flesh white. With milky-yellow yolk-feeding the young, to a-hatching.

   With familial-filial show of loyalty, love and friendship.

Webbed trapped in the mouth of predator spinning suffocating drowning in water as air. As Hag-fish slid through our own womb-like extended sac transmitting, transposing, and expressing in: The-Sun-*light*. Since the conceiving of-day, feeding, the the chromosomal cellular proteinous ropes, to learn how-to, and use the advantageous passed-on. Multiple and multiplying, intra- and inter-cellular proteinous, stranded nucleic organelle organising-potential to best-advantage, and to pass-on to the next-generation.

Over-receding, warmed slopes, venturing out, disguised snouting sponge and jellyfish, plankton shrimp and fish, balloon speckled mangrove vegetarian-dugong and manatee sea elephant patched black and white dolphin, and black and grey white hippopotamus, whale-calf, frolicked up and down, forward-limbic galloping, paddling, swimming in-safety, returned to sea's, and Ocean. Splashed and plunged.

Grotesque baby-blubbery skin-toughened, slow-moving sea cow, hippopotamus, floundered and flippered over land, and separated, back into the sea, into safety, unpredated, and to remain to modernity...

As the skies and land cleared Dragonous feet-flapping sprawled, crocodile and alligator-nosed, and snapped out of the edges, of river and lake; nearby, four-winged insect-like, on-scaled encrusted, and feathered, lighweight hollow bones, multi-lobed-shell armoured. Fur-clad walking and winged, amphibian overflying and landing, diving reptilian-birds, landed and quickly flew-off.

Breathed, into multiple air-sacs, rested, at a distance from each other. Crawled-out, into, and droned, through the air. Buried, hived and swarmed onland, and airless fed-smaller but in large numbers, hovering sapping mites, in the air, landed on plant stem and branched-trunk. Weedy-sapling, springing-up, lower-leaves and branches-growing, rapidly-away, from nibbling-destroyers.

The-destroyers, growing too, branching-off along different trails, up and along, between the branches and ground.
Flying, and landing in-safety, above the canopy, tree-trunk growth, ring-turned with each accumulated-annuity. With acuity avidity lascivious laborious lusciousness...

Each-re-newing: Age: The Tree-orbited around the now, more slowly-circulated tepid-Sun, the-mulch, and new-shoots of flowering-bushes and Giant-tree...a Tornado-Typhoon stormed unfolding at Oceanic-Sea, connate-circular, and sequential-formation.

Re-vealing spore-dusted lobe, pocketed inner-stalk, the petal-leaf, uncurling unfurling from outside layer encased, tubular assemblage the revealed-floret, and centred-drooping seedhead, dropping dried germinated-pip. Pooping, enclosed in pulpy fleshy-mush, passed-into the receptive ground, or eaten, and passed-through.

Falling, catapulting out, and reseeding beneath overhanging dry pine-cone husk. Scattering-off, flowering-fruiting berry and swollen milky, kernal seed-nut, prickly hard-shelled, ready to be cracked open to feed, to renew passing-creature. Tiny worm-crawled, and ran on multitude segmented-legs, caterpillar-spun, fed, nested and cocooned.

Amongst the end-budded twigs, and branches. Hidden in protective silken lacy-spun chrysalis, amethyst, breaking down body and reforming liquid, to tissue once more, but differently. Floating over the opening seas and distant ocean opening land. To plant palms and flower, in near distant tropical bay, to lay dormant on distant frozen and rocky-shore. Occasional flaring solar radiated electric-spikes, engulfing blasting atmospheric wind, burst over the surface as if sucking the breathing-out, and burying erupting volcano and opening great rift in the Earth. Shook and sent down, whole forested mountainside.

Front *headed*-antenna eyes pushing out, tooth horns, breaking out sleek trim lined body of maggot-fly, or butterfly-moth. Grubbing caterpillar and wrapped pupae, waiting for the light of day. Scales fallen from its eyes, along its outer edges, fuzzy-*shrouding*... Shouldering filigree blue-tinged wings, from the mouth to anus, and outstretched-legs to run and hide. Dried-out, gulping pumped-up, and expanded opened-rotary, helicoptering-overlapping wings, into the air.

Thorax back-pack, looking for a mate, taken together to good place. For egg-mating making as laying. Sperm-chamber opened and inserted. Injected, into ovary-depositor, a leaf where no other male roamed, orchid monkey-spider, amongst orchid-flower. Dangling, attached, leguminous enclosing pod, popped open along the sweated-join, sutured sweet pea-seed, flung-out in the swelling damp heat.

Split over the ground-stones, soaking up the heat. Spread, and mixed with the ground, buried from the light, seeking opening-slot, and curling outwards below, deep roots into the dry deep damp-earth. Vegetative creeper, leaf stem and bush flower, towards, and into the light sky; to stem leaf petal flower, and seed again. Shoots binding tightly together, strangling in its bid to regain height and advantage; ivy hungover, and spread across the ground, and along branches, over-walls. Entwining prickly barbed purple thistle, yellow gorse-heather and broom, brushwood, forest and heathland.

Yellow-daisy and orange dandelion-bank, opening-out atop, flowering into the sunshine. Over awing, waving and wafting acid green tender-tall, drawing straw-stalk flat round green and orange marigold. Lagoon-lily and lotus-leaves, air breathing plants, floated over the flowering pond, water-anemone, cicada-crackled, and clicked-rubbing leg-wing...humming-bird fluttered, nectar-feeding bats, in infrared-blackened anoxic-chamber.

Cave boa-constrictor edged along the upper surfaces. Hagfish-slime slimed out from between rock crack and crevice...snapped into midair, into the swarm, and captured, swallowed-whole, gradually-poisoned, and broken-down. Energy-sapped, bony hollow-pieces, dropped out beneath the still teeming-mass, animal-zoo, and circus.

Along the forest borders, magnolia and rhododendron bush, in the edge-fields, of grasses, poppy and sunflower. Dropped-cracked split-cone, from overhanging branch, acorn from scrub oak, juniper poisonous berry and prickly fruits, water meadow vetch, around aquamarine pool. Fruit-flies rapidly breeding, on sweet orange and pineapple intoxicating, attracting and depositing, wooed to ingested dissolution, imbibing into waiting mouthpiece. Snipped and munched leaf, petal and seed, tucked into evacuating pouch.

Alighting and discharging, spreading and newly pollinated, seed-grain, and crop. Blown on the wind, in what direction and distance the wind blow insects, and sealife, porpoise marine reptile, long neck, short tail dorsal and tail fins, paddle like limbs.

Warm feather fur-hide, storing strained gas in fatty-muscle. Returning acidy blood-streaming...re-heating and returning. Beyong Good and Evil, to the surface, below again, playing learning to fetch-food.

With rockball and shell sea-lion playing, with an empty-clamshell. Staying-under for breathless-period, and resurfacing, with a gulp of water, separated bladdered balancing, for long periods shifting pressure-support within, for-land, or water. At the far-reaches, floating drifting snow iced mountain-tops, way out in the frozen ocean distance, ungainly pelican and puffin.

Waddled, awkwardly, unthreatened, before dropping back into the water. Seal and polar bear, fishing and snatching with great paws from the water, suckling their young, not daring to leave the children...sacrificed to the hunger of another male, to the starvation forced-on an *unforgiving*-place.

In the seaways, between continents, around the uppermost frozen arctic pole, tern and gannet swooped, sea-seal camera, headed cracking open framing crab-shell and crustacean water screen light net captured. In its' landed-lap, standing Arctic-bear snatching pilchard-fish out of the water, and stranded waddling pink bright white underbelly black oily sheen water, back-furred Antarctic-penguin.

Squabbled and fought, starved and diseased, walked and marched, swapped and courted.

Clumsily awkward on land, caressing and communicated with partners, with honking, losing countless cracked-eggs swooped and preyed-on, by inland-crow, eagle and magpie, high in the trees, and safely away from the ground.

Then, eventually dropped and birthed young, to deep frozen-death or swooping *rapturous*-large Great-Bird. Diving-in from the sky, to its grounded-pantry. Plunged into melting warm flowing waters, torpedo swimming along, scooping plankton and shrimp into opened mouths...

Free-diving, breathed energy holding in blood and blubbery muscle. Overland, bald-rhinoceros, over-heating, in-danger-of. Moving even-toed *Hippopotamus*-like Whale. Creatures' smooth-skinned splashed-back down, taken to the waters again, mammalian Whale-like *Hippopotamus*' pelvic hipped and open mouth and nose large-lunged, coming-up for air. Tooth horned breathing through nasal cavity-plate palate.

Separated mammalian molar-chewing sona sounding and listening through the lower jawed middle-ear, rattling-vibration from beyond and across endless drifts of ocean. Bone-billed fur feathery mottled snuffling billed platypus, emerged from the water.

Over the sands *reptilian*-mammalian Otter-Seal: born at once hung-onto and carried on sweaty milk patch-glands, over bleak and empty landscape. Scrub-vegetation along *flowing*-streams and Great Rivers' eating away at the land as Canyon and Delta over and again.

Giant-platypus and spiny-anteater, surviving, bearlike short legged carnivorous lion tiger cat, wild forest-boar and plains-hyena dog. Multi-tuberculate *amniotic*-fluid:

-Calcium-carbonate and phosphate…chitinous.

-Shell-skin and long-hair manes dissolving placental-attached…

-By-blood and bone milk-producing outside-feeding stomach…

-Cooking-belly skeletal calcium-rich sweat-gland suckling…

-Slower-gestation attached live birth neo-natal born.

To-grow to-*maturity* with level of esoteric knowledge, before reproducing again with *another* and having re-produced, surviving mature-offspring to recognise, through-sickness, and *fear*ful of viral-bacterial unseen seen mosquito and twitches defining on or off:

-We To the largest-predator, and eventually, the Planet-itself.

To recognize relative security, to be licked-clean, leaving excretion, to mark acceptable self, small wiry and quick tricks, wily bio-geographical diverse niche limits...wised-up, to run and jump and climb, limited mixing increased niche safe environment, playing, and *working* for-a-living.

Flower and nut seeking scaly tailed squirrel shrew and lemur prosimian, and sweet-flower, berry and leaves seeking tree-monkey chimp, chased around the tree, and along the forest-floor, amongst wood-shrimp long bodied, narrow jaw, nostrils at the tips of their noses, in front of their eyes.

Fast glancing-looks, building pictures' in mind, of long-legged and armed-predators, with long finger and nails, tails crouching-down, with free-hands, rounding open and closing arm extension, long second-finger and growing finger-nails, instead of claws, over generations stretched to prod and poke, and dig-out tree and ground-insects.

Long coiled pre-hensile tail and thumbs' holding onto branches, and thumb to grip, clap, cling onto safe adult, clutching infants assessing, and consistently reckoning distance, and width, and depth, sidereal vertical and horizontal range.

Orbital-convergence, three dimensional eyesight, and hearing identifying, through arboreal forested cliff-edge surroundings, and across open plain. Sleeping above ground falling sensation alerting monstrous woodland predator, inquisitive food-search, imagery reflective, sharing co-opting shelter and security in case of future-need. Leader ganging-up. Sub-lieutenants, the troops, colliding clashing with another, with body twisted, grabbing, twisting neck, leg, arm, tearing-at-the-throat, the stomach, the lungs, the heart; exploding outwards, imploding emptying-body.

Neither One, or the-Other but Only-ever both, eventually, *perhaps...*

Both one or the other, incessantly friction smelted algic-diatom sky. By a hair's breadth between:

-One and The Other…

-And We Of The-Many!

Donkey-train, colluding joining-partnership, making anew. Violently, with *passion*, emotion softly, with love, language-communicating colliding airwaves, between ourselves, sounding-out, seeing, and copying retinal-shapes, lips, ears, eyes, and tongue…

Rude-red sedimentary, leaf and pollen footprints and fossil marks planted…sectioned in size coiled-shells. Landed deposit's fragmentary, and spread unevenly.

Shocked golden-quartz and splattered jade-rock and gold *ex-propriated*…

The whole new cyclorama met with the newly cleared skies

Rising at the edges. Returning and becalmed turquoise blue ocean, warm lush-lands, interspersed with arid desert, fine sandy yellow and white beached, with smooth cobbled and grit-sand skirt streaking icy sirrus clouds hung across, in opening-Sunlight volcanic flares erupted, from below, hot springs soared fountain, and cloud of steam.

Circadian-awareness, leading to the yearly harvest, the escape of just enough each year, to return to the same breeding grounds, to repeat the endurance of bleakly triumphant-tragedy.

4.4. Action: within ribbed and lined chest-cavity, constricting blood-flow to the outer-limits; in-fear drawing back-inward. The heart-filling, and charging the bloodstream, muscle-energising stretch and contraction, straining, double de-clutching, and extracting-energised, and re-energising, two-fold and more, hunt-heading, tailing-off...

Aware of internal self and external others, posing a threat, and reproductive opportunity...

Each-chain-globular passing-creature

Self -selecting, place and time, secluded protective germinating and birthing. Buried under rocks and ground. Hidden amongst leaf foliate and split-branch. Protecting the renewal of-other, into the next generation.

To re--generate, before being captured, consumed, expunged.

At the far distance, below on baking dry sandy rainforested-island, large cool-pouched cats, roamed, permanently-pregnant, neotate-in-uterine, snouted and flat tailed standing black brown and white bears.

On tough-muscled back-legs, large versions sprung along the ground. Beyond, and over calm enclosed-lagoon, and trapped lake, and crashing breaking sea-wave.

Oily-turquoise and ruddy-brown feathered ducks, inland bobbed and skimmed over the waters. Sea bourne birds, on short flight wings, to escape, to be captured and carried back under.

Sea-steamer, plumage-ruffled stiff tail, dabbling and diving. Diving, and rising, to expel, and sink, and rise again. Spur-winged, footed freckled, mane-cresting comb hooded, flat-bill, flat-feet, running on the water, whooping, trumpeting, whistling, mute pool to pool, nomadic-seasonal migratory-fluttered; out of protected rock-face crack and crevice, as if amazed, to still be around.

From stilled nocturnal, in the darkness, as the sun rose over plains and filtered, flickering through regrown forest-clearance, and jungled-edges.

Along beach, through rock cave and seaward cliff-stack. In the damp mud grounded, and burnt remains of once vast jungle forest. For-aging through burnt ground and crusted mould, on the safer shadowed-edges. From secured-cocoon and nest, rapidly-emerging sluggish-insects, warmed, opened and swarmed.

Alongside inland watersheds and watercourse, forest and plain shrubby jungle-bush, and woodland-grasses. Buried powerful rodent-rat, and shrew, small eyes peeking and peering out. Long-whiskery snout, urgently-snuffling, searching out food, and other to pair-up, and to mate-with.

From the ground, star-nosed mole, sniffed, touch-sensitive electric-pinprick eyes, dimensional colour wave-lengthening world. Couched in the darkness. Bald, hairless and warm blooded, pink live-births. Climbing-along their mothers furry drawn drawl tracks, to the feeding teat soft-tissue gland. To feed and be nurtured, holding-on in desperation against-others, determinedly-threatening, threatened, to eat the young in the scarce deadened surround.

Eating-earth and new leaf-bud, and other-young, to be preserved. The emboldened-few, or lucky, skill to go-on. Bear: cat dog large bone armoured, rolled and cooled, in the drying wet mud. Monstrous smooth-fleshed black and yellow blotched amphibian reptilian salamander, meandering sideways, breathed-*fire*.

Legged and legless crustacean and horny lizard, swooping wingless duck web-footed cormorant, flaming coloured flamingo lumbering Giant warm-feathered, but flightless useless-winged ostrich, pecked and grubbed, with its head in the ground; and chased horned-porcine warthog snuffled and truffled, in the mouldy undergrowth.

Swooping: Dragonic! blue white and grey crane nested on high, bouncing dancing-along to lift-off at the last, with seed and insect, away from chasing snapping wolverine-jaws.

Below, shelled giant tortoise, prickly marsh hedgehog, and unprotected twitching nervous dry-landed tree-grubbing shrew. Through plains grass and conifer woods, bobbing tufted rabbit, fat storing-tail, and long eared listening hare, foxes offence and rabbits run faster de-fence, run, multiplying in vast-numbers across the plains.

Gnawing front incisor teeth, burrowing through tree root and earth. Teamed up, in tandem kicking back the earth into mounds, appearing at the surface. Below, blindly furrowing the undersoil. Burrowing through tunnels, passageways and chambers. Furnished with straw, spittle, fungi and dung, worm and beetle smooth suede and bald patch blind-vole, appeared through hillocks of *dug*-earth.

The Forest trees and bushes, the marshland herb scrub and bright petal, in the blazing almost midday sun, unvisionable...cooling slowly, eclipsed by an out of place daytime-Moon. Escaped from the night, to perform the rare and foreboding ritual: Darkness at Noon.

Overlapping coronal looping all around. The blanketting shadow of the confrontational-Moon, a deep dense gap, peaked all around of the Suns' flare.

The-World: EarthCentre: gone *quiet*.

Birds no longer sang. Even the wind appeared to still. Nothing moved, no-one spoke. As the fascination and wonder held all in its awe.

For a few moments, the Earth, the sun and moon in direct alignment, seemed to rest there. Stand-alone, and still. Before inevitably moving-on.

With the Solar-plexus, re-appearance, sliding out from the captivating grip gradually the-moon, once more absolved. Consumed, back into the Suns' glare.

To re-appear, that night, it was well expected; the moons'-pendent, slowly blinking retreat, narrowed crescent opening and wide-eyed wild and reverent return.

To be reflected-out on the rolling-out waves, faded silver ribbons swelling below rainbow spray, rotated away from the Earth, from the blazing Suns'-heat, into another night...

Returning, to the land and air, through which every living and non-living thing moved, in continuous-cycles of appearance-and-disappearance, resting in sought out safety, between recurrence, and altered state:

-To eat, or be eaten. Simple...

-To sleep, to be eaten…fight or flight…

And to reproduce, in the newly warmed and chilling rhythm retaining peripheral awareness, and prowess.

In low body function, as in aroused sleep and unlikely dream From reality released, checking and clearing-blockages, between restoring-circuit's, re-navigating by temporal fixed-Sun, and Lunar-stare; pole-stars, and terrestrial condition, to particular solution, success or tragedy. The not inevitable consequence, of repetitive and compounded events. Each one levered and nurtured, themselves, and each other, into the next generations' close up Forest-edge.

Caterpillar munching its way out, and turning through cocoon. Into multi-faceted and winged, dull hued elephant hawk moth, *bright*-kaleidoscopic butterfly.

Growing out of the habitat, resembling and merging with the surround, buffer bluffer prominent eyespots, unknowlingly blinking, with each slowed down flick of the wings. The consequences of their-Being, a larger moving consummate creature, too dire to take the risk. The harmless butterfly survives, to cocoon again.

Fluttering off, disrupting the beady owlish eyed surround, and tricking deceptive staring-eyes. Landing onto harmless-petal. Copying and repeating the same feat, time and again. Surviving throughout the habitat, flapping or not flapping wings. Thereby, and by this chance, surviving, to lavae and pupate, into caterpillar again. Fluttering, resting amongst fissured broad leaves, dripping silver black and grey and orange brown towering bark, smooth and cracked, flower and insect infested Tree-trunk.

Hanging-branches and bushy undergrowth, riddled with solitary plant lice, and monstrous grounded and winged, scurrying black and yellow, red and spotted, crusted-beetle hoarded. Clearing the land of leaf litter and the dung of other animals, in another in: Giant World.

Forest-Trees and bushes, stung strung-across with glistening morning filigree sticky net radial orb spun from many different spider's abdomen, and substance, bridged between swung-out and caught points.

Radiated into and from the hub waiting, for the unsuspecting fly. Bladed, stung, pierced. Dead still, in the center of the webbed trap. For any passing flying or crawling meal glued, stuck, broken and sucked into proboscis feeding tube, before placing in the mouth. Carefully and completely wrapped.

Starved and suffocated, from the outside, the innards left to rot to cook. Eventually, with clasper-eating tube, sucked out from the center of the dried and toughened shellac encasement at the end of a patient, and rested wait.

Worm, mollusk, aardvark, elephant, shrew and monkey, snouting trunk fifth limb, to smell, trunking mouthing, snorting, hissing and popping sounds. Each leavening, birthing, and *leaving*: The EarthCentre: *different*, better or worse, as to how *they* … We. Found... ingested and imbibed; through toughened mucous flesh, the messy unco-ordinated outcomes, of difference, pulling-in different directions. Selecting and branching, changing and altering, environment, and species.

Inertia-holding back in delayed momentum, defending against competition, stagnating, extinguished, or extinguishing. Developing tolerance, and exchange, before moving on. Each producing and consuming, consuming and expunging, and being expunged, in the rarefied shared made milieu. As the sky lifted and lightened once again, from a warmed position between the ice capped poles, a frozen waste melted, across the valley floor.

From the base of overlooking precipe, ice snow and mountainous ice-burg, vast tracts of vaulted folded sheered and compressed glacial sheet accumulated in polished-striation, and strand line, tilted, pitched, and pulled massively apart.

Onto oblique liquid rock-floe, where clear flood-waters ran, and flowed downhill across glassy black rock and sandstone, crumbled into the sea.

Glacial and rainwater cascading, riverine, through towering gorges, leaving impossibly pivoted glistening pools and lake. In the gouged-out heights, the lapping waters and seaward horizon, giving a steadying plane to the re-arranging vista.

Down through rocky moraine, the regained heights of the mountain ranges transported boulders processed, down the hillsides embedded and merged with the mud brown flats; yellow sandy rivered and pooled, low lying tree forest-fallen, into brackish marsh, giant fern and moss, plant and tree deadwood, compressed and released coalite explosive-fires, burned and exhausted, over now saturated and dried-out wild heathlands.

Purple-heathers and brazen red-firewort.

Flowering *cream* buddleia, from brown-green blue bindweed
Sprung up from the *dead*-ground. Creeping-vine and sprouting open
yellow petal-cups, purple primroses, white and tallow daisies,
and bluebells playing over the forest floor, in meadow grasses.

Over succulent plains, wooded climbing honeysuckle flower,
and foliage, again to flourish and spread across the Openland.
Where now large and small wild-cat's prowled and preyed, kept
watchful gaze, sleeping in guarded groups. Scrawny clawed-hyena
howled and scavenged. Split-hooved ungulate padded herds,
camel….roamed and crossbred over the plain.

Un-aware, disinterested, tentatively peering out of the forest shadows. Stepped-over fallen-boulders, and onto the river fed grass and parsley, spiky flowering sedge-fenland, and clear-*flowing* river part forming a lake, filled from the snow and ice- capped mountains and rain-soaked, freezing over-stilled, and still-cascading forest gully.

Climbing amongst the dripping rock-faces, and along the river banks, rough grasses and clumps of low *flowering*-buds. Dangling shrubs and dry rush and hollow growth jointed bamboo cane, swayed high in the fresh breeze, along the undergrowth and rising through the river-banks. Through the trees, and above, lingering small brown and green and yellow twittering gaggles of red and yellow and green and blue brightly coloured ruffled-feathers, watching through beady-eye's cackling, and calling the hooked worm tongued open beak silenced.

The forest-borders, imbued with chromatic-colouration, Patchwork-pelts and flared-fans, feathered and furred, variegated and emblazoned florid pigment. Amongst fruit and petal, grown out of disturbed earth and leaf-shadows, *merging* with the surrounding under-storey bush and bracken below overarching canopy roof. Wild-turkey, chickens... pheasant large body, fan shaped tail and waddled.

Scaled legs and neck, brightly pink flamingo, rising over safe mudflat nested, flying off in flock, to feed, and return. Flightless birds, ostrich and penguin, using wings to swim, remains of wing downy feather. Pea-fowl, Dragon bird plumage, green, blue, red opened sperm vent, one sided, left-sided ovary active, eggs descend from ovary, while pecking at sand ground grains, triple stomachs, stone swallowed, to grind down, wet, mold, and kiln.

Water fowl, over the plains, and in the low trees, climbing flightless squawking-birds, ranged over-layered stalls. Inside, hanging branches, on the ground, in the long grass, and out of the leaves.

Rival fighting-rival, showing off, posturing, moulting feathers and preening, dancing with flapped wings and cackle. Attracting the attention, going of, chasing, and relenting. Busily mating in pairs, fucking and fighting-freely. Food-bribing, into protective nest, squatting, sitting and keeping eggs warm, in hidden pockets of picked at dried-straw.

Pecking-over the starchy corn-seeded ground, cockerels fighting hens and each other, snapping and squawking with shrill alarm. At the egg consuming snake, crawling through the undergrowth, clawing, and flapping, a screeching from the skies, warning those in the branches above.

Climbing on agile-limbs, dropping on-aerofoil, drifting and rising, flying between branches. As if gliding-underwater, scrambled amongst the shadows below, stereoscopic bright beams staring-out, frightened for the-eggs, between branches fluffy tailed shrew, squirreling amongst and around, in the dusk, a huge colony of large-eared furry fruit bats, took off in tandem.

Opened-skin spread limbic wings, massed and rose from the tops of the trees. Echoing screeches against the walls, and unheard, toward unseen insects. Converging, to scoop up and gulp down. To decorate the cave and ground with fermenting waste, a leathery bat-eared monkey-parroted screeching and squawking, grunting, howling, barking through the foggy etiolated forest gloom. In the stressed environment little room now for niceties, purring and grooming, now running, shouting, scared, and alive.

Scampering chattering big and scared-eyed bush-babies, carrying their suckling infants. Trailed on through the leaves of the leaf bedded forest nursery playground, and they secured themselves to branches, just like the others did. Napping briefly with rigid frame, standing upright on the branches. A *woolly* squirrel-Monkey, supported on flicked tail wrapped around and balanced on branch. Bony flat hollow nasal raised hooting note. Looking downward, short sightedly and sideways.

Varying voiced soundbox call, unseen tympanic retort copied, then others appeared, less furry, with remaining crested furrowed brow.

In the *dawn* from across the plains, trooped, standing and rolling along on two legs, leaping across and down rock-ledge, and swinging through high-branches. Looking back with big wide-eyes, and almost falling. Grasping with long fingered big hands, aware of the risk, from the falling, to the ground below; the talon and claws, from the air, above and beyond, and from all around.

Testing, reassuring, checking out, if being watched. Leaping to another place, filling the gap. Before moving on ahead. Checking the infants running up a tree and leaping-off with wild abandon, watched over on the tree-stump of a royal-throne. In the shaded and warmer woods, from the cooler outer woods, dark pigmentation hidden and protected by the *shadow*.

At the top looking-up, interested, at a low silent gliding daytime-eagle, taken-over from hooting nighttime owling, amongst the forest leaf-litter, through a rift valley path.

Toward the sea, splashed-beaches, and between the high cliff and mountain walls, squat-feeding, cracking nuts, timid-monkey pointing, with low pitched staccato grunts and high pitched squawks, mimicked in warning before darting-back to cover. Stopping startled-still, at moving leaf-shadows, ever ready and set-to run, and hide, from a larger wide cheek-boned standing ape-monkey, climbed up from the seashore, sitting in a tree branch nearby, making a soft-*hiccup* sound: Ape-Army...

The young-monkeys in mimicking imitation, steadying the gaze, ready to lash out. In angry fear and defiance, if approached, before departing backwards, to nearby-*safety*. Lower-down, at the tips of branches, picking at ripe fruits, and brightly Sun-coloured flowers, and nibbling at leaves. Spitting out, chewing, storing in bagged cheeks.

In-toxicated on fermented fruit, hallucinogenic nut, juice and leaf, a short dwarf elephant hunting, the marauding, circling ape troupe, suddenly ran at the small troop of female and young monkey, on the lower-branches, and ground.

Leaping down the branches, lashed out at an intervening defending adult, grabbed a young one too frightened to move. Knocked it off the branch, crashing onto the ground below.

Others of the Great-Ape Army: assault-party, rushed down the branches crashing through, to pursue the initiated attack, caught by the tail, and to finish-off the screeching monkey-cub, clubbed to the ground. The-Hunters sat squatted around, tearing the limp body apart, limb from limb. The largest, and initiate attacker, taking the best reward, sucking the juicy brains out of the smashed-skull. The remaining adults, squatted on the ground, resumed picking, at each-other and children's bloody hair and skin. With grooming short-thumb, and finger nail's tending sores, and wounds with leaf and spittle.

Intimate caressing and comforting, accepted willingly, in gratitude, and servitude. The parents to feed, provide warmth and shelter, the offspring to play on, in pretend, and real conflicting-fun. Comp-e-ting with their peers for food and mates, copying to advance, and prolong in *their*-future, conjoining cause…. Finding ground nested egg, holding up the carefully pierced and cracked open-shell. To hold up, and drink and drain out the content. Pushing long bony-finger, selected and snapped-off twig, into insect nest comb. To lick-off scampering stuck insect, as well as syrup, honeyed to the stick.

Gathering and swallowed un-stung, before any more the live meal could live into another. To attempt to poisonously sting the assailant in the mouth, the unaware-bee slurped with sharp-drawn in-breath, and swallowed with saliva into dissolving and energising *stomaching*-juices.

Others sitting around, watching on. Waiting their turn to try. Youngsters watching acutely, then practicing with mud and sticks, learning along the chain and throwing-stones, chasing, and chasing-off. Regaining-the-branches, gnawing-at and banging branches against the tree trunks, to declare their presence, in protective numbers flinging themselves through the branches swinging through with tails' balancing and gripping-hands.

On an exposed trunk, a larger-male stood, and presented himself. Flaccid, then erect with excitement, recognizing a young adult female flirting-openly nearby.

Turning and looking-back over her shoulder.

Colouful-display, expressing-desire.

Purposefully-directed, surreptitiously in case of anothers jealous intervention.

Looking around, prepared for surprise-attack.

Before together secretively singling out, eye contacting, and with a directive-nod together, scuttling off to find a secluded nesting-bower. To present presents of different opened fig and orchid to show, appealing, obsessing-over. Beckoning the male, opening inward-plunging together-coupling, swelling and contracting. Together heart and lungs breathing fast and shallow, gripping and curling the toes and hands, with a shudder, and momentarily vacant-*look*, laying holding still for the moment.

Opening the eyes, blissfully gazing and relaxed, taking in the change. Before becoming suddenly revived and alert to the risk all-around, once more. Watching out now, and protective of the forming-pairings' yield, returning to check the rest of the brood.

Squat on fragile branch, gazing into the trees, stretching deep into the impenetrable shaded forest. In the open, infants copying their elders, chasing playfully up and down, leaping from branch to branch, to ground.

Looking on, the adult parent perched on an open mound, overseeing the scene, intervening when the play becomes too rough. Watching-carefully. Others' running up and down, branches swinging, and hooting through trumpeted hand. Hanging on with distinctively marked-palm's, reversed-back to front-gripping fingers.

With confident-stare, baring canine-teeth. Ready to bite first, and fist's-clenched, as another appeared. Threatening to encroach a favored-ones position, companion-mate, and brood. The encroaching other, averting the eyes. Hanging the sideways head, in submission, without a fight. Moving carefully away, in case any movement, might be misunderstood.

Avoiding butting in, twitching uncertain, avoiding any misread facial-signal. Sensitive, not to perform any misconceived, disdaining, disrespecting behavior. To avoid any misunderstood heavy-handed persuasion, to keep-off. Staring seeming blank look on the face, ear's-back, for any sound trigger and any movement, the uncertain *superior*-Hierarchical, made a threatening noise, wanting to make sure.

By any means necessary and chosen. Communicating air exploded, expelled, and then quickly changing the call, looking down, hissing with mouth open at the ground nearby.

As a Python snake-*slithered* over the dry ground. Instantly looking up, and whinnying barking, and howling, as a speckled feline leopard, neural-scaffold sculpted for recognition and vocalisation, and language; depicted transferable fixed formulaic interrelation, of leopard spotted in the dissipating light, appeared, paired as stalking through the undergrowth.

A herd of hooved and horned beasts, tore at leaf and branch, nibbled grasses, scratched and nibbled, on insects on theirs, and others hides, staying close together at the forest-edge.

Moving-out slowly over the grassy and small tree scrub, and shrubby watered plains, and then further, in the flickering shadow moved out of the low grass, invisible yet in the green-stalk's and yellow-flecked sand.

Nothing of the silent stealthy predator moved. Except towards its prey. Expressing no emotion, no-part moving, but twitching, but for fur-shadow spots, tremulous striped tail-tip, cooling lapping-tongue, silently panting with low gasps, almost un-breathing, ears pricked and sharpened eyes-fixed, with sheer-concentration on the intended prey; sensing, looking up, snorting the air, for trace of enemy scent or food, and down again into the grass.

The leopard began crawling, pushing forward, standing on all fours, launching forward, and hit the ground, forward and running fast. The lowest chimpanzee let up a cry.

A *changed*-call, a scared high-pitched chuttering, as it realized the immediate threat, and its' own *fear*. Short barking mimicked calls, echoed through the dense bush.

As each-monkey knowing now the leopard threat was real, turned and fled, disappeared higher up and deeper still into the trees and bush. The leopard leapt at, lunged and missed the last escaping monkey. Who turned, and kicked back, turning, and ran after the rest of the pack.

Through the branches, the troop eventually at the call of one of them stopped, arraigned in the branches above. To look down fearsomely, and equally fearfully, from the top of the high forest-canopy. Wide eyed, and still braced in heightened fear; for renewed attack, despite the successfully defensive retreat away from unequal ground-fight, in fright and flight, more than equal chances in escape. The leopard stopped, in futility realized, and sensed the Other.

A small gazelle-lie animal standing, stood watching, stilled, fixated, forgotten, at the edge of a herd of patchwork antelope, mingling striped horse zebra, grazing together at a short distance on the plain.

The newly intended prey failed to predict, even from the recent past. Far away enough to not comprehend, a possible future, the animal failed to counter or avoid, the renewed, and *impending-*attack.

A larger antelope grazing animal nearby, turned at that moment, and saw the slinking-leopard, held momentarily in view; then as if in slow motion, saw the threatened offspring standing, looking ponderously, out-of the trees. With the monkey retreat, noisy screeching and squawking, into the high tree branches, from a distance the older ruminating-adult, sent up a baying warning, distracting the now charging predator.

Scattering the rest of the startled herd in all directions, and all turning immediately without looking, rapidly, in pounding timing, running side-by-side, eyes flooded blood red and wide, in horror and *fear...again.* Steering away and neck ahead, rounding-up and corralling smaller ones into the midst, of a sudden headlong rushing stampede the galloping-horde, rounding, veering off at the last moment, after the leading head and body, as the leopard overran, The-Predator losing speed and direction, the mass of pounding hooves, kicked up a fine grey dust storming.

Moving on through the fringes, into the center, the largest of the herd sharing the vulnerable flanks, shifting through the disappearing-rampage.

Changing-direction, and confusing the attackers and herd, escaping the planned onslaught, the stampede, without looking back, twisted over the dusty scrub and shrubland, over the distance, and away. Another leopard appeared, and ran suddenly, at a struggling older and weaker animal, lumbering along deserted unsecured, sacrificed at the back of the departed pounding-confusion.

Traded-off with the surprised new prey stumbling, turning and roaring loudly into the retreating melee. In ambush, reacting frozen in fear, completely turning to face the oncoming muscle and bone: to:

-The Kudos of Escape...*lost*: The-Beast: attempting to turn-around, again, and at the last second, to attack, to defend against the predatory fang, incisor tooth, and ripping clawing-assault. Attacked from both sides, now, as the leopards together regained ground, and picked up the action; joined-forces, to share the assault.

The de-fending-off: animal could only now turn again and stand its ground. Knowingly-sacrificing for the rest, the others, its' back and hooves and sides flanked to the onslaught, its final-fall, on weakened front legs, its terrified eyes wide open and unblinking.

As if knowing its ultimate fate, feebly kicking, bucking in vain. Collapsing, as a sharp stone, atooth stabbed in the flank, frightened moaning subdued, weakly and to no avail. Paralysed through gashes on its side, back and legs, side and neck. The desperate defensive hoof -kicks, avoided easily this time, the leopard's had the creature by the throat, fallen, rolling eyes and body given up. The victim fell, and was dead.

The resting remains of the herd, herded stampede zig zagged splashed-on in blind-dusty monochrome panic. Brown, white, and black. Stricken across the marshy-edges, to the safety of the river, flowing down from waterfall, and in full flood over the grassy-plains.

The Others' fruitless chase given-up, at the site of kill, at the slope into the water the rest of the herd pulled-up. At a shallow distance, turned as one, and looked short-sightedly back.

Listening, appearing to watch the slaughter momentarily. Then gradually, one by one, following, returned to the plains, continued impassively to tear at the short grasses and low branches of scattered trees, a little further way, they knew that one kill was enough for two.

But what about the others in the lair waiting?

The leopards lay-*exhausted*, paws held clamped over their kill. Held, cradled the animal on the ground, they tore hungrily at the flesh. Through sinew and bone, the lungs flooded and collapsed, the blood gushed out, and drained away.

With a low grumbling growling, warding off any potential scavenger, until they had finished; then dragging and dropping and recovering pieces of the torn and broken carcass, they ate all they could of the meat, and picked-up the pieces of most of what was left, as they left the scene.

Carried what they could of the kill toward waiting-cubs',on mounds, and high-up into the lower-rock ledges; turning, looking-back, then without looking back, left the scene-below…

4.5. Savannah

On The-Savannah, circling grey hyena dog packs, howled at a distance, assembled. Kept at bay, as a lone lean boned and hungry tigress growled. Now moved in, to tear at remaining flesh meat and muscle, with claw and tooth. Monkeys, still alarmed and frightened, occasionally calling out to each other is comfort or alarm, left leafy beds and resting places tore through the trees high running through leaves and across branches.

Remembering, and not returning, re-imaging the scene of their escape, and the other animal sacrificed in their stead. Along forest pathways and highways, hanging on and swinging to the next, not too-high, into the trees and disappeared above and below, deep into the rivering-jungle.

As: The *Savannah*-Plains'-died and only rarely another animal seen, diving, plummeting and rising, crossing as flying-over, settled in for The-Journey. Around an oasis, over the riverbank meadows, a group of flying forest monkeys re-appeared.

Bat-like to suck marrow from the remaining splintered-bones. As vultures-circled unable to land or get near, before being chased off. Swooped-on and threatening, aiming to peck-at the staring scared eyes, until the ground-forces retired.

The remaining-morsels ripped-apart and pecked-*clean* on the ground, with pincer beak and talon, leaving the rest to flies, carnivorous-ants and beetles and invisible-mites and microbes, to gnash and gnaw-at. Dung-beetle, iridescent-shell horned-head, the carcass decimated, dissipated, until nothing remained; but-dried, bleached and crumbled flesh and bone, transformed, vanished and returned, into stone, dust, and: EarthCentre.

As rain clouds swept over and gradually lifted, drifted beyond the horizon a blazing sun broke through, animals large and small came to drink at lake and river, pool and puddle water hole before they dried-up, under the sub-tropical sunny-Sun and *mindful*-Moon.

Gazelle and antelope massed-again in protective shelter of each other at the Forest, and Savannah-edges. In the heat foraging tough hairless and short tusked elephant, stomped, and furiously roared its dominating size.

Sweated and dusted-off mites, that clung and sucked on the warm blood. Long-legged and broad framed camel wandered along *invisible*-road. Through empty-desert, lowered their slurping mouths into rare waters there, tall-necked shrunken-bodies slimline giraffe, tore at the highest sweet leaves, the forest drawing-in tumultuous shower, then, moving-over, drenching the scene, sprinkle filled monsooned: Landscape. The *distant*-Mountains broke into a grassy veiled clearing, along the cracked valley floor, up to a *sheer* drop Precipe-Edge.

Life-moving into and re-appearing from forest, sky and water in ever changing sequence of group Entrance and Exit signs *shadows* moved amongst the rocks and trees. In directions from along the waterfront beaches, into hills and over mountains, following The-Sun and Moon: daytime and nighttime and seasonal transits, around The-Horizon returning, the-Same as-Different: *changing* and Different-Groups: mixing and separating-off filtering from as *through…*

From the damaging extremes of blazing hot and freezing cold, in temperate sunny and rainy and clouding climate. Shielded squinting eyes peering out in the shadowy edges, skin-pigmented, body-bone and fat-deposited shapes, moulded to the surround swept back skull and wide facial features slanted back, pinched-in receding-chins.

With self-contained speed, strength and nasal breathing stamina. Sleek-hiding and outwitting qualities, hair and facial muscle-features, through generational upon generational alteration and change; sensory attitude and response, each one-unique, one to another, and Each to All- Else.

Eyes ears mouth and nose, the only real difference between, little compared to the difference-amongst. The *continuing*-separation:

-Of Species…

-All with varying degrees of Free-Will to the outside inside…

-Eventually to branch into speciation…

-Integration to mould the special features into Survival…

Shared Love-children: born-destinies, Fates and Graces amongst multitudinous cross-familial cousining, sibling, half sibling, and step-sibling, halveling brother and sister, sister and brother. The largest Brain-to-Body (inclusive-exclusive) count, smiling, laughing at the falls and antics of others, in security playing the fool, emphasing what not to do, stumbling and falling over, farting and flashing inflamed sexual parts, guarding against mockery and seeming mis-fortune.

Parents, step-parents, foster-parents, half parents, aunts and uncles, cousins. Becoming prey and preyed upon. Continually food-seeking, in amongst reliable-stocks. Seemingly casual sexual-touching and feeling fun-ful; activity. Friendly and dependencies; between mothers and sons, daughter's protected until the mate comes-along, sympathetic social looking-after, tolerance to a point, son looking after himself, lazy and sensitive.

Brokered-*peace*, divided, segregated, split, greed and hunger driving to battle, escaping into the Forest, the braver risking all to rise stronger out of the fray.

To: Kill: to carry, and return to time and again.

Over the marshy river on the other side, where the stampede had briefly continued over the plains, stood grazing and then disappeared, renewed shouts and cries were heard. Baying and plaintiff calls, indicating one, and yet another, of a herd, fallen. Loud cries of triumph newly rang out. Large short and stocky barrel chested Ape-like tailess-chimpanzee flat nosed: Simian: adults and open-faced juveniles could be seen. Manouvring, creeping-up on, and leaping-at, dragging gouging-at their falling prey with bloodied-stones and flints, attached and tied with tightened dried reed and tendon muscle, fibre entwined conjoined to long-flexible rigid-bamboo.

Sharpened-rod, spear-end incisor-sharp antelope tooth, stolen and retrieved, with wooden handled axes swung and carried, the Hunting-pack waded waist-deep along the river-bed. On two legs shambling through the fast flowing rivered stream. Carrying on their shoulder's, above the rushing waters the corpses of hoofed animals, recently *slaughtered*.

Ahead, one larger than the rest extending a length of stick in front to test, and lead through the *wading*-depth fording and a-ffording the flooded-shallow and sometime deceptively deep riverbed. The route clearly a regular one. With seasonal-herded food-supply, after pummeling determinedly and frantically with bare hand, and made tool's, there was a yelping, the *silent* still-kill piled-up and surrounded, except for bare-chests and fierce-faces, blood-soaked coarse hair covered most of the body; blood ran-off as they carried the limp-carcass' through the *standing*-waters.

Onto earth trodden paths, washed, onto the plains. A ceremonial marching, grunting chanting ensued. The Hunter Group moved towards the lower-hill and *hidden* mountain-ledges, carrying their trophies with them.

Along the shoreline edges, through the Forest-edge came some others unnoticed, naked, but for lank dripping hair, only in patches, on oily beaded smooth and fatty muscled, rippling water repelling, bare skin.

They, and We, walked determinedly upright, freed hand swatting flying and stinging insect, settling and itching. Scratching off in swift movement, off dark tan protected and sweating flesh, out of the water and shaded edges *whole family groups* traipsed along the beaches and riverbank, where apart from the seed fruited forest and open plains edges, only desert stretched-out.

From the corner of hilly mountainous and gorged sea locked valley, on the sandy dune grassy riverbanks' edge blocking the way inland, the new arrivals stopping; by some rocks lain bare there, by the outgoing tide, kneeling to crack open crustacean, snail and crab found there, held trapped, and rhythmically beaten with a larger stone into worn rock hollow, the meat picked out with nail, clasped stone or twig.

The opened shell, lifted to the mouth, the contents bitten, sucked and slurped out, the case discarded, festooned with others eaten or escaped along the beachcombed strand; on rocks and stones, along the shoreline, split-open. Oystershells empty all along the jungle edges, using sticks to gather weed ants, climbing and falling from the seaweed rack and sea grass, climbing again, buried in the sand, infested fishbone and crustacean shell refuse *scattered*-shore.

Dis-attached un-legged crab, and emptied egg store. All *feasted* on the move, along the rounded line of the beach. From the seaward side…another, similar group appeared. Led by a standing bearded male, looking gesticulating long arms aloft, as if sharing off-springing spreading Food, Children, and Home.

Un-noticed until then, moving out over the plain accompanying groups of wide-hipped and *pregnant*-females stood at the water fringes, and stared; gathering babies and children to them.

Holding their breath, and letting out with a controlled hollering, frightening ululating wave upon wave of warbling, switching on and off, louder and softer, announcing, something. Some of the People; standing-upright in the waters, looking to retreat, back off, to stand and stare; dripping, and distantly safe from the fray, others, of the Males and Females stood and turned and of the watchers, stood on the sidelines, verged edged into the forest edge, hidden, and from where they could see, and knew uncertainly, unwillingly, and some willingly, to what would ensue.

Brink-border boundary-margins speaking as watching with their parturated offspring safely at a distance. Looking, appealing perhaps for a rapid and peaceful and safe in The End to the impending foray; or *bringing IT on*. Over the Forest-plain, burned landed into seaside sanded reaches, the perceived opponents, beckoning toward the Plains hunter-troupe along a valley floor from the interior.

Appearing hairy and heavy, the tall thin non-Hirsute Tribe would not be able to reach them in the water. The new arrivals emerged from the seaward beaches, wading silently through the waters, inland and onto the land. Through the tall reed grasses, standing, looking around, and around, at The Hunter pack ahead of them, treading carefully, watchfully, relaxed, and aware.

4.6. After the Hunt.

At a shout, the newcomers, running full pelt, fanatically, as if addicted, *gambling*-on empowered long-legs, onto the open plain with open un-frowning high furrow browed brown faces and eyes with flaring nostrils, high cheekbones, bared gritted tooth and open mouthed, revealing incisor fang, large heads rocking from side to side, for balance.

Brandishing large fishbone and tooth and flint wooded-weapon spears and azes, shoulders back, arms raised up, swinging, pumping silently pounding the water and dry dust raising smeared EarthCentre, water splashed off from the glaring wide-eyed, the adult males and some younger females ran forward first, the younger males followed less silently behind whooping and crying out.

A *display* of roaring and chest thumping, shouting and waving of fists ensued, in the centre of the scene: The Hunter Group: moving toward the lower rock ledges, looking alarmed toward the shallows of the freshwater river ocean-let. Un-sure of the intrusion, or the intruders. Looking confused, up and sideways, each side, and down, they dropped the carcasses onto the dusty ground.

The-Visitors corralled their dead weighted loads, surrounded and delaying their prepared feast, in anticipation of loss picked up and placed stones in a pile over and around. As if to hide their bounty; and picking up the stones, weighing them in their large hands for weight and shape, leaving the youngest children and females behind, one of the older male hunters, grunting louder and leaping higher than the others as moved forward as one.

As The Scavenging Group joined and advanced from river, lake and sea, The Hunters moved toward the forested mountains reaches, before circling around. The rest of them standing-off roaring and projecting small rocks from the ground-Plain, randomly *almost* with poor distant eyesight aimed toward and hitting enemy targets, easily warded-off and ducked out-of-the –way; a well-flung if *lucky* missile striking with a yelping, and only minor blood letting injury.

The approaching Attacking Troops, the leaders ahead of the marauding spread-out aquatic bands of tall and agile: Hu-Men: and some of the Olders *flashed*-looks between Each Other.

At a call and waving of arms, the scavengers, rounded and stopped, came no nearer-to. The guarded pot, and the protecting Defenders: The-Hunters with their dead prey as the bounty. Watching, staring at each other, and the hunter group in front of them, mumbling together.

Occasional, timed directional-movements, and with a nod of the head sounded-out. Along the ranks, as the main Scavenging-Group began to retreat, back towards the forest and Ocean.

The largest of The Hunting Band raised himself to pound and roar yet more *fiercely*...into the apparent retreat. As in-*pain* moving-forward, confident and unwary, hurtling more small stones and rocks, raising the dust with their hands, in admonishment, and disdain.

The Invading-Tribes, with a *shared*-disdain and *timing* complementary-cue clued-in. Variously modulated and understood in advance, made as if to withdraw into The Forest. At the same time, gradually began counter-encircling encountering no understanding or organization amongst The Hunters at this point checking the disordered flanks of their rivals guard, for weaknesses, then checking with Each-Other.

Making sounds between themselves, checking-back continuously for re-assurance, less invincible feeling, as invincible without realizing this, carefully and in the moment *pointing*-forward and to Each Other. Moving-away also, and around; they began waving long-arms and legs astride striding-out. Bellowing from One and *following*-on taking up The Chant. Turning suddenly, around and ahead.

On command, synchronised co-ordinated cries and screams, and waving of arms, a group of younger males and females broke off, and began further encircling the larger hunter group, which halted in noisy confusion.

The Hunter-Pack became quickly entrenched and encircled away from their un-guarded Home-Base on *hidden* rocky Ledge, their loot launched in large-hands. Realizing the tactical deception, halting.

As the roaring and yelling increased in volume, in the impasse between frozen fright, fight and flight; the scavengers at one enormous roar from the ranks, suddenly fell silent.

Unaware of bluff or double-bluff; unable to countenance the situation. Turning only in outright-*terror*, to attempt to retreat in regret unregarded; and to protect and to retrieve their meal, the children and female-family group standing with commissioned-guard over the rock pile of carcasses still laying on the dry Plains. With a final command and flourish, of revived noise and active display, the Scavenging-pack advanced fiercely, desperately, into the fray.

The defending mainly adult-male Hunting-Troop, into desperate fight, or now to retreat. Scrawny hairy backs turned, dangerously to their attackers, and looking around, in terror realized the weight of numbers and tactics against them, too late. Almost surrounded, they made to move off, into their only Escape-Route. Back the way they had arrived, and towards the lower-Ledges, where they camped, below and in caves beneath.
Unable to countenance *their* situation and planned departure into the lower ledges, having to adjust their plans.
Backing-off, looking fiercely, bravely but unmistakably afraid into the faces of the surrounding advancing armies. The Hunters scrambling and scampering back for snatched and dropped pieces of their *slaughtered*-bounty; forced to leave the rest behind, already requisitioned by The Scavengers who had attained their goal.

The Olders *yelp*-ed and screamed and over excited ran-off with what they could take. The young rear-guard beckoned and called to retreat, or left to fight-off *ritual* humiliation.

The sharks' toothbone axe, snapping and biting, the blood-letting of the assuming-Victors from the: Seas Rivers and Trees.

Symbolic defense and revenge of the defeated in retreat, frightened and scampering-off, the largest of The Hunting Band turned, raised himself to pound and roar yet more fiercely out of the unceremonial retreat; empty handed, back along the riverbank and into the hills, grabbing a last piece, of the abandoned hunted dead-prey.

Humiliated, attempting a show, not to show. To indicate readiness to fight another day. In final empty gesture waving a piece of *bloody*-carcass in the air. To indicate some kind of *glorious*-withdrawal, a small-victory in Defeat-winning too:

- Food to the Victorious!

-All!

-Winners All!

And The-Defeated. Moving ahead of The Re-treating Tribe; moving upwards into the dry hills, to squat, back turned at safe distance, amongst the slopes. Ripping at, warding off others and sharing out carefully, small pieces of rescued fresh raw meat:

-No Losers!

-Except…

Looking back, anxiously up and down; and through those remaining Mountain and River Tribe. Those not *limping*-back, or left *writhing*-injured, or laying-dead on The Plain; or carried-off as slave servant master or mistress.

Roaring a defiant, but distraught plea, into the bright sky. Awaiting an inevitable overpowering threat from within, and succumbed to exile, leaving by another route, at a safe distance, from the victorious foe. With pastoral-power, slave hunt illegal immigrants, primitive accumulation, the *dialectic:*

-Master-Slave! Heroic!

-Never!

Fabulous Mystic risked-life and lives...

-Dead.

-As any Other…

-As Other: *that's about it…*

and standing, scorned-Own and Other's Only Other's put-down. Conscious as *dominator* playing exclusively with others'-lives...

-Games...

-Master and Mistress of the Predator-Prey.

-In the eyes of The Prey and The Wolf…*wolves*…as Society!

-As Death. To the Dogs! As Life itself as Death! Cats, are different. Many-lives! Many-Universes!

-Elevation of Master to Absolute…

-We are Absolute!

-In Ourselves and Other are in their Otherness The Otherness of All! Outside:

- The-Law!

-Lawless-zone: The-Future:

-Our-Law! All-of-Us! Sex-p-loitation of *almost* All…

-And the *Really* Have-*not*'s: almost or Nothing…

Until:

-I want what you've got!

-I want what they've got!

One, or the other, or other other...

-I will take some of what I do not have…

-For yours...

In the wilderness. Political-economy pastoral Communist-Capitalist-power's:

-Animal Political-economy…

-Separation of The means-of-production…

-Unfairly. Of course. No-one would start-out if they did not blindly unhearing alarm or alert deaf to entreaty believe they could win overall strength fairly…or *unfairly peeferably*…

-To One or Other.

-Exactly. Fairly, almost, always...but the *precarious* consumer, ever wanting more, to
be safe:The Middle-Ground.

-Not necessarily…see: illegal…reasonable-*manhunt…invaders…*immigrant…

-Persecution?

-Market predation and Sovereignty-*exclusively*…

-Exclusiveness of The-Celebrity! We! Can! All! Be!

-Easy. Murder, kill, for Success!

-Happiness after *necessity*...

Both at the left and right, up and down, the same:

-Central-Command.

-Indigenous indignant pluralism, love, and hate.

-Free-Market *economy*...

Anthro-po-centric and humanist genealogical bio-politics religion and *none:*

-Political-theory and *philosophical*-anthropology says....

-Cruel, and lawless piracy on the high seas...

-Socrates' says: *...hunting is not simply tracking the animal to be killed, but killing too.*

-Cynergy: The Art of Hunting...

-But what of Piracy? Slavery? Man-stealing…Women-stealing…

-Tyranny...Theft? *Murder threat...Murder?*

-The *whole Martial*-Art?

-Legitimate: Art of Acquisition...

-Robbery or Theft?

-The Exclusion that Proves The-Rule…

-If you like *submitting* To-War...

-To War?! As *wild*-beasts?

-As-Nature...

-In-Time: War *and* Peace!

-What should Masters do but to Be (masters)?

-On what Laws, procedures, do they operate?

-Does *their* Power *depend* on Nature?

-Or in-Nature?

-Contain, control, and eradicate...for conservancy...

-Mega-Kill? Poisoning, and burning. Potentially?

-Opposed...to bad-Kings and Queens, of their siblings together, or not, taking care of...

-Presidential-Right: to-Hunt and *bear* Arms against *Your*-Government…

-Denounced?

-Denouncing! For *betraying* Their-*task*! Designated Bad-*shepherds* for leaving their flock to The wolfs and hounds?

-Failed-*pastoral* and *domestic*-Power *defective...*

-Field pastoral Domestic-values…Power! Shared

-As Nimrod! Hunter of Men...and of Women:

-Antitheses: *foil* to the sub-ordinate Shepherd...

To flock, with and conquering an Empire instead, enslaving, and condemning to death, both:

-Imminence, only ever, seemingly..

-Ever Transcendence of the Divine...

-Law...as the foundation of political authority?

-For *All* of *US*? (See CriticalAnimal.com)

-As then not necessarily fatefully gracefully (often, except in dance and literature and music…Art.)

Furiously the defeated troop, the assembled females and younger males, ready to fight again; and to now choose their selected prodigy, or else to quickly starve and potentially, ever to *die-out.*

To remain, return another day; seek another food niche in which to continue. The carcasses stolen from their relinquished rock laden piles, along with those of the bodies of the slaughtered dead-foe on blood soaked deserted-Plain. The-Dead *pierced* and raised-up on bloody spiked-poles and along with those of The Hunter Pack *selected:*

-For-*survival and self-protection...pro-generation and Other-protection...*

-Life!

And those too-injured to walk spear pole-stretchered

From the Final-melee. Moving-back toward The Mother's and Children waiting-out of: The Forest cover the others of The Youngers roaring, Shouting and making arm and hand signals, in recognition, responded to. Into The-Retreat, and picking out each other, gesturing the signals of *shared*:

-Victory!

-Both! All?!

Turning-back toward the forest and waters edges, the largest of The Scavenging-Group of slender, manipulative, and victorious males, gesturing to the females and offspring of The Other Troupe. Assessing the spoils, and Each Other: *courtships* Traded-for and ready to be celebrated on the Sacrificial alter of food, fought and killed for. The re-birthing power, of shared fertility, victorious whoops and voices broke into noisy-*chittering*.

Excitedly, loudly without fear of arousing any return assault, the victorious group, returning to the low bushes and trees, rummaged through on the way.

Back-to: and spearing in the low water, raising fish and crustacean on sharpened bone points, hastily gathering fruits and berries, leaves, bark, twigs and boughs through The Forest.

The Allied-Groups from: The-Forest and: The-Mangrove *Swamp*: laden down with food and materials, disappeared back along the rounded beach and cliff face path, and into The Forest depths. The Scene-below, immersed in falling misty clouded foreground. Evening-haze spreading over the town, clearing:

-Iron-Diamond Star! The-Sun…

-The-Moon.

Flintstone graphite spark, struck under dry brush, lit-up fires carried along, in torchlit procession from One setting-place to Another. Soon a thin plume of smoke rose in *drifts* from high in the hills above below The Mountain Peaks. Below The Precipice-Ledge.

Along the tidal-flooding *meadow* and beaches, and the ledges opposite and below low arched caverns could be seen *disappearing* deep into the sheltered hillsides camped out, in protection of light and heat, cooking and social fulcrum.

Along inhabited rock cave path and clearing, overlooking the Forest Plain, River stream and Lake; Sea and Ocean beyond the swirling of shouts, chanting, laughter, and singing in-tune interlaced with airy notes of fluted bone and stretched skin rhythm, repeated, resounding through the air, imitated airborn echoing, across The Valley-Passes…Sounds as *visions*: as felt improvised as spontaneous. Deep sea-booming echo drummed, sonic higher and lower pitched birdlike screeched, threatening a warning call, song bird singing: Lament of Love. Of Other; of Place, and Space.

Attracting attention, the copied voiced and repeated song, the fearful, and then for its own sake, joyful effect, mimicking, telling the story that they all by now knew; in howling, hissing, humming and calling, pounding drummed herd hoof beats chasing, following and stopped. Faster and faster, telling the story, notes changing up and down, clarion call, replaced with dancing hypnotic, racing and then quieted, in worded chanted song and tuneful lullaby.

In communion, sounding out into the night, filling the vacant air, feeding the iron night encompassing darkness; the sounds and images drifted upwards, echoed against the overlooking-precipice.

The *gradually* sinking-Sun *faded* into a newly star-filled night. As the world turned upside down and inwards as outwards through-out the night.

In: Constellation: A Lone-Star: You! *perhaps* with another binary other nearby, stilled by a silent lunar beam beneath which the world was encapsulated.

Shadowy-silhouetted *movements* was all that could be made out. Reflected eerily against the rockfaces and walls down to the raging river and along the valley floor, drifting with the sounds of revelry, over the rivering-land and Oceanic-seas.

Whilst a real or unreal sleepiness and dream pervaded the spectating senses, the funereality and festivities of the witnessed scene, it seemed, would go on all night. As full moon rose over river and mountain, land and sea; clear un-*cloud*ed nighttime full moonlit, starlit sky *darkened*-lit studded with familiar: *Stellar*-Galactic: as: EarthCentre: Universal: *configuration*…****

For David Attenborough.

EarthCentre: The End of the Universe: Universal Verses 5:War!

Copyright M.Stow15

Trapped.

They looked across, from the escarpment, a Girl and a Boy, sprawled out on their bellies gazed-across the rift, from the top of the terraced ravine, to the *edge* of a river, as a Sun*lighted*-scene of devastating beauty opened before them. In the foreground valley life dug, crawled, scuttled, and ran. In the panorama climbed, flew and swam again. They looked over the broad teeming-forests and plains, and Southern Ocean; turned to watch eastward, as the pitched edge of the Earth on which they now stood, appeared to turn slowly, shifted toward a newly rising-Sun.

Lifted once more over the rocky ledge, as if drawing them in, faltering hesitating, and then tipping themselves, and the whole of The EarthCentre into its' Golden-rays...

They stood, riding the Earth, seemingly passing into the orb, rising with shimmering motion over-tilting, the revolving Earth sought, it seemed, for the sun to engulf them with not only the promise of light and warmth, in abundance; but also the perturbing presentation: of fiery devastation, daunting, un-retaliable, both vengeful, and revenging; in un-exhaustible fire.

A portent to be propitiated, it seemed, only, and immediately, in fear, and in hope by prudential penance, some kind of symbolic sacrifice, demanding tribute, taxing as some indebted, humbling dues, slowly standing, in Sun-*salutation*, salvation, to be saved. Once more from the flames, to secure a lasting, through to the next rising. That this was not the day that the sun may not have appeared at all, or yet still, may gather them, and their EarthCentre, The Visitors *trembled*; as The Sun heralded The End inevitably as The Start, of the Earth; they held life, Themselves, and everything else, in The Sun's overarching dominion. They remained in awe of the spectacle, entranced, waiting to be engulfed in the solar archipelago, that now hung over them.

As the heat intensified, they made to move away, and the new sun moved away too, hung-up in the sky; consuming, and giving flight, instead, to a waning yellow moon settled facing, counter stilled and slightly turned, nearside periodically, interrupting and reflecting, as a faintly beaming disc, a Walking-Man, carrying a bundle of twigs, passed amongst-them.

The light began to lift, below drifting cumulus cloud they looked out and over The Plateau-*edge*, as drops of morning dew sprung with The Sun; from the air over the plateau on which they stood amongst trees and clumped grass shoots, waters trickling over the *precipice*-edge. Down, and along a rolling river valley, up to a swollen overlooked lake, the pale gold orb now absorbed, into sky blue over the calm sea beyond. Melded into the opposite face of the sky, mountains and hills arose around, in drifting rising silver and pink tinged valley mist. Rising, awakening into a vast open bright amber blue sky, stretching over them, the huge sun, as they turned away now, behind and beside them, shifted slowly over and turning toward its time memorial-zenith.

Lightening the waters of the river, following its flow, towards the lake, and the westward sea; The Visitors turned and with the warmth at their back, following Guides ahead of the *risen*-Sun; onto a pathway around the overhanging headland. The heat began to drop to a pleasant, temperate clime. A cool wind gusted, and as out of a trance, they found themselves meandering, down a sharply turning track from the precipice parapet edge over which they had earlier gazed. Following Local-Guides *emergent*; along a well worn track, bordered by high lush meadow, and solid layered plummeting rock, towards the valley; and outwards towards The Aquatic Sea.

As The Sun rose further, and dipped to linger, flesh and senses were touched and sensitized, with the sight, and slight subtle scent, of damp deep brown fertile earth andsalt-water. Above, on Land, amongst wild flowering plant, low tree and bush, but for The Visitors and Guides, chattering amongst themselves, or passed in silence.

Down the rocky path scattered with broken stones as pebbles picked up, looked at as if imbued with some ancient, but long lost significance. Drop-kicked and rolled aimlessly, and discarded, insignificantly over the steep edge. As the visitors stumbled over them, stones bounced downwards, indicating only roughly, the height from which they trod downwards,
and the depths to which they would descend.

The Guide was dressed in rough-loose smock-wrapping, and simple footwear of leather sandal, or wooden clog, and changed into the new clothes provided for The Visitors; *sacking*-cloth over usual outdoor wear, where uncovered rough on the skin. The Visitors all talked together, and at once, about that which was seen, heard, felt, and experienced. What seemed to be, or what they thought they *knew* something about.

Picking at low trees and bushes, pointing to and identifying the leaves and fruits, footprints of creatures, that had previously passed. The Guide, showing The Visitors how to crack open a protein rich nut, with blunt and onto hollowed stones, plucking unusual ripened berries and fruits, the Visitors savoring the unusual taste, reminding pleasing; or spitting out in undisguised disgust. Chatting simply, and being shown how to tread, and to maintain interest and sustenance on the way down. *Sparkling* on the cool ferrous-flint spark, feeding the fire, fanning so it does not go out completely, taken and shared with others, the oxygen of life burned; kept dry un-dampened, heating stone and metal pans and pots, captured and tended hearth, varying colours of *earth*.

Stopping at a camp just below the peak, crude decorated caves and animal skin shelters,
Stood in a clearing, on a great ledge of mountainside forest, overlooking The Sea and Valleys inland. Amongst strangely shaped windswept trees, that dotted the otherwise barren and dry arid edge; to one side on a flat stone set with ornate vessel, water splashed out, and grain spilled around, animals, long haired woolly sheep and goat, tied to a heavy stone, stone bloodied like a sunrise, or sunset.

The fleece of a sacrificed and slaughtered sheep hung up. The creature fed its last meal on the dry ground, precious water spilled onto its brow. Seeing, looked up, accepting, knowing, or *unknowing*, blood flowed, streaked out over the apparently sacred stone. Cut throated carcass divided, fat wrapped around bone, to burn in the fire, The Visitors were told. The Fire fuming skyward to the seen, and unseen deity above: They were all absolved.

The slaughtering and feasting from the night before...

Crustacean shell and fish, monkey and antelope bones and carcasses, now strewn around The Encampment in caves on the valley floor and along mountain-ledges and Ocean-edges. Starchy and sugary tubers and bamboo,
chewed and drunk the cud spat out; into the fire, sizzling the remains. Swelling the stomach only slightly, but energizing the whole, otherwise a once drunken, hunger drunken-*delirium* took over, they were told.

Energetic dancing and singing from the night before had taken its toll, and people started appearing, rolling out of makeshift bedding on the ground around the fires inside the caverning shelters. In the early morning now, people, the first they had recognizably seen, sat around cleaning and picking their teeth with sharpened twigs and earth. Men and women sat with rolled wrapped, started repairing, fishing, bird and insect net, they were told, sharpened spear and venom blowpipe dart tube stood nearby. Bow and arrow attached in carrying container, and laying on the ground at their sides, as they had slept, and slowly awoke to the day.

The Camp Dwellers rose, with bone, flint and stone, scraped scale, fur and feather hide, cleaned pelt and carcass, cleaved at giblet and entrails; strips of meat hung over branches and wooden framed structure, set in the ground. Blood stained red and drained white meat hung raw, cured, dried and preserved. Smoky cooked over the ready fire, that still crackled and sparked. Around the last of the fire, the camp dwellers dressed sparsely, in animal fleece and pelt, lay stretched out on the dry ground. Reed-matting spread out, amongst the rock caves, amid dying, burnt charred bone, reddened and fire cracked-rock.

From the flying embers and still glowing flames, smelt pitted globules glistening copper green malactite, silvered tin bronzed mirror stone and charcoal-*heated* melted out-of –the-Rock *metal* ran, opportunistically collected. Risen to the close to the surface, from:

-Molten-Iron! Nickel and Jade Diamonds silver and Gold and every flashing colour between...

-The *very*-Centre of The EarthCentre!
Ready to be smelted out, alloyed tools, as manufactured limb extensions, with handled sharpened tooth blades.

Taught to children in use learned and adapted with purposeful energy, hard wearing, worked, shaped and pointed tipped, long faultlines iron seam flowed pillars and lumps, ferrous-crystalline rock non-pourous clay layers wetted and wound into cups, pots, and plates. The TribesPeople, continued their working, and with others who stood around, talked, and touched as they exchanged polished stone metal and bejeweled objects, shell bead jewelry, and they did they made connected variegated sounds to each other, and to The Visitors, only vaguely comprehensible.

From deep in the throat rumbled, with high pitched nasal guffaw, indicating apparent disagreement, or approval, disgust, concern, pleasure or displeasure. With the early morning mist lifting, The Sightseers watched on; ignored by the camp dwellers, or approached to purchase gifts, with what they had, and as if returning, coming out of a dream.

At The Centre of The Group; a story of instruction was being gently told around them. In conjoined sounds and simple phrases, overlapping and louder and softer, and exaggerated speech. Comprehension assisted through finger and stick pointing, at burnt ochre crimson and dried blood scarlet, woodash white and charcoal black, binding plant and fish oily, inked and painted images.

The Story-Tellers' moving roughly moulded and carved figurines, amongst line and colour-shape drawn. Within scored circle, puffed cloudy watery and wind circular wave pattern; *stars* in moving graphic pattern, picked out of the chaos, timely and seasonal markers, drawn with dry bone and twig brush on the ground, and with words, in the air. Stories told, apparently of animals and ancestors. Of seasons turning and times of this and that.

Of animals speaking, talking to people, and people talking to animals. Animals becoming people, and people becoming animals. Half animals and half-people, demi-gods in storm-*stressed* pacts and treaties; Troll-like sky Ogre, *earth* pixie-mischief; and them not liking human-noise.

Eating, sitting and standing around, girls and boys, women and children, and men, and Giants.

Stealing sheep, and cows, and horses, dogs and cats; industrious goblin moling salt rock-mining underground, with mandrake and cinnabar, garlic and ginger-root to eat.

From the smell on their claws, One or *not*-one of Ours? Returning spirits, conjugating historic mythologies. A present, of remembered existence and seemingly recalled life, chewed over, ripped-at, cut with knife made of teeth, thrown into the fire into the pot, to cook, tenuous and casual, and causal relationship, with All of Existence.

The Audiodrome: camp culture stories of: The animals, plants and trees, dust and earth, sun and moon, clouds and star changing altering sky intertwined around them. In pictorial image, expressionful features and mimed action; the stories spread, wide-armed scene surrounding and embracing.

In a tented cave, a shadow of movement across the wall. In front, a changing and straggled-out group of people, sat cross-legged. From within, the sound, the screams and curses, soft murmurings, and cry of a mother giving birth. Young and Old either watching the story, or the birth, or ignoring both; sitting around coddling infants, picking at and stroking each other, staring into each others eyes, for confirmation.

Moving shadows painted on the cave wall, on flat the stone floor, like re-spirited *ghostly* Holo-gram *pixelated*: Homo-gram reflected in the tree as a Green Man and mixed in with the dust on the ground abstracted expression and mark. To one side, and only able to be glimsed and be explained in whispers, a closed stone piled burial mound. Inside, the body of a former elder, died of old age, and those perished in the previous day's battle; under piles of stone as battlements, and left out to carrion and maggot, with gold and silver and coloured objects, to carry with them back into the ground into the *air*:

-EarthCentre! Out-of-Africa to: Arabia Indo- China Australian Pacific America's Euro-Russian...

-Neanderthal-Mountains to Black Forest Alps rivering Danube Rhine and Rhone to Middle-Ocean...

-Handy upright hominid wisely worked flaked flintstone obsidian anvil cave school of *magic: drawing* blood-berry juice zinc-oxide pigment *grunting* approval in language and disapproval angrily lost-control in violence against Each Other and All. Warm-fur clothing replacing hair and colouring-nails red and black. Hieroglyph pictures, ideograph and word, animal half-human hunting image with planetary stars at sunset and moonrise movement over land and sea and sky. Birth and burial burning-ritual slow or fast ended and with them: *new beginnings...*

Anytime everytime wider birth-canal and hipped-female
Menstrually delaying-heat and energetic male, consistent partnering
through child-rearing Larger brain right handed perspectual reaching
left-clutching at straws in a storm at sea.

Apeman ponging smelly sea mountain-living ManApe Warrior-
Hunter...
Amongst The Group and shared around a concoction was passed.
From steaming wooden cups and bowls, from cupped hand to hand.
Soon various of the group stood up and started to dance,
intoxicated interacting co-ordinated rhythm around the middle of the
fire,
ember circling; as it must have been the evening before,
in the morning The Dancers faces were beguiling, painted and shaman
masked.

Representing and displaying entangled patterns of related being.
Acted out death and non-being. Being between living things.
Bright patterned and symbolic colours adorned the decorated
garments, hair and skin worn made amulets and talisman of polished
shell bone, and gemstone; supposedly and apparently to ward off the
banality of evil, and deadly disease; as heroic charm, mark of received
beauty, of mystery, of belief, and quite clearly, of status.
When several of the most highly decorated,
The Inner-Group to the fire,
were dancing together, and chanting.

In the remaining night caved darkness within shadowed ghoulish and ghostly silhouettes,

who danced-*also.*

As The Stories drifted off, with the lingering smoke of the fire,

there was a mute roaring sound, that in the ensuing melee no-one else seemed to hear,

except one of The Dancing Group; who quickly and abruptly, separated from the dance,

and looked up, arms held open.

A man, dressed in extravagant leopard skin hide with iridescent luminous feathers on his head began a mesmeric, intoxicating, ritualistic dance, around the fire.

Arms aloft, feet pounding the trammeled earth, chanting repetitive sound and word.

He appeared to be identifying with a huge winged bird, flying and searching, and finding.

Throwing off the winged feather cloak, he clasped his hands together, open and unclasped, parted, and aloft towards the top of the precipice the visitors had just recently descended.

with voices delivering accusation and threat, fear and loathing felt, oddly *weirdly?* Mottled seaweed-strung turtle-shell half of an opening golden egg, diver fish far out At Sea. The Earth fair-grounded and funfair trees as if on fire, lighting the watery heavens in their own reflected image.

The Young Men and Women charging changing as they moved and stayed at Each-Other

together and moved again and stayed, flat noses and dark skin protecting against the rays of the sun, lighter skin selected to soak in the rays in the northern darker lands where lack of sunlight became damaging, eastward wider jawbone squinting against the reflected harmful sunlight, westward pinched long noses, wide eyed against the frosty air; sweat cooling losing body hair, retained where the body was covered, for pace and stamina and clothed for warmth, oily skin acned, bulging veins, bipedal, furless sweating, fatty heavy brain carrying, carrying live children, otherwise burying their dead, Old and young. Talking, tearful, shouting, singing and dancing.

Pair bonded, coupled, making out on on the quiter darker secretive edges. As if through water prophecy-divination soothseer *saying*-sage. Astronomically born; in the sky, above the cliff face, the early morning sun shone blindingly, against a green-lichen stained rockface.
From a high glacial field frost flowered beads dropped,
A waterfall trickled smoothly, one drop at a time, and then at once, cascaded. Branched through, over and down through the rocks and caves and sheltered camp.
Through a dried out gully, and onward...
Where The Sea Level had receded to the far distance,
and lush marsh and drained land, spread out and beckoned,
a route around, once impassable desert and sea,
they stood, from there warmed-rock:
    -Cave-Habitat.

Hunted tooled and fertility artifact, mapped the earth and rock.
The whole cliff-edge and the camp itself appeared to drift majestically
upwards, into the sky; falling from the sky, rising with the smoke and
steam of the fire, as water, reflecting, tumbled downwards, along the
watercourse, and into the valley below, many, most, leapt up, and fell
down prostrating themselves.

In dry mouthed, wet headed, beguilling in reverence, and awe, in what
seemed to be exaggerated emotional release; to the waterfall, to the
sky, and to the feathered now un-feathered Man. As a chicken *goosed*.
Allied, reinforced by the miraculous relief, by the co-incidence: The
Bird and The Man, the man and the fire; and *air and water-miracle*.
The Men and Women and Children of The Tribe, bonded in their
mutual need for water and food,
and Each-Other To: gather hunt and cook.

Reposed in simple correlated belief. The Bird-Feathered Man turned, and made clawing, stabbing motions, towards some the other Older Males of the group, and others, who had determinedly *not* stood up. As if he were distributing the power of life and death, most of the other males and females and children of the group gathered around him, or were forcefully and threateningly brought in, sat in groups, herded together. Those singled out of The Tribe joined by few of the females and some of the children, signaled together with their eyes, and shared conjoined sounds. In fear and resignation, stood, shrugged shoulders, and began to slink off into the shrubland and forest around. Mumbling, gesturing, and glancing protectively backwards. To the rear of the departing families, the remainder of the tribe mimicking now in collective mockery of the sounds and actions of those removing themselves, into reluctant and *uncertain*-exile.

Small-stones and rocks thrown after them. Hitting their targets, they did not retaliate, but
looked back with resentful, scared and leering looks, from a safe distance. Related some of them,
others clearly not. Not for the many *past* generations anyway! The Bird Feathered Man turned
to survey the rest of his remaining tribe. With decorated axe in hand, as if to threaten anyone
else who wished to leave, others shared in the reflected glory of power by grinning *stupidly*,
baring their teeth and looking fiercely around. The closest to the leader, the Alpha male,

the rest of the newly bounded and bonded clan, clapping hands, chanting and gathered together, The Bird Feathered Man, and others similarly but not quite so elaborately dressed, directed first one, with a low referenced sound, and then another; with a different linked sound, and gesture, pointing to one, and then to another, and to each an item to be carried.

Each of the conscripted recruits were assigned, knowing their task immediately.

They collected and filled dry hollowed gourd and calabash and empty bladderskin from the now gushing fresh waterfall and gathering pool. They efficiently and quickly rolled up mats and collected together all their carriable items into fibre net and bone needle sewn sacks, portable baggage bundled onto rod and hide stretchers.

Those more finely dressed, dusted over the burnt patch of ground, carried and carried the ritual smoldering cooking-fire remains with them on: The-Path...

Metal-melted decorated decorated spear-point or sword. Crucible
bowl, incense leaves smoking and wafting through the departing air.
The burial mound, left behind, the nursing mother led out with
suckling child, the aged parents, grandparents, the wounded and sick,
on stretcher together and with all their possessions, lifted onto patient,
uncomplaining small-tamed warm hide feral tamed forest-pony. Forest
small sturdy and heavy set donkey-mules were brought up to the
camp from below, along pathways unnoticed until now. Fed and
watered, kept clean and dry, untied from trees on the downward path.
The whole remaining troupe of thirty or more people, adults and
children, now moved off together, they left the clearing behind,
walking and riding with leaf woven pannier jogging at the side,
ignoring now all the while, The Sightseers, and Their Guides.

Map horn blasted carving shell necklace round sharp cutting edge and
narrow arrow head, flint cut skin and dried leather. A storm shadow
snake coiled thunderbird-Dragon, rampant lion, a gently nodding
rabbit. A bucking buffalo, a standing bear, a spider tree monkey,
telling tales.

The eyes, and nose and mouth, of a kindly craggy *watching* face.
Only the marked and painted cave walls, the fire pits and over-
mounded ground remained behind. The Bird Feathered Man, with his
close entourage of men and women and children,
and others in preference, allied, left the site toward the rivered green-
pastures below;

the spectacular waterfall and pool now dropping beside a planted tree-lined trodden path. From the rockface precipice edge, the water falling from a silver and golden sky, along the line of the river, and with the newly rising sun.

2.

Beyond the now receding waning ice and snow capped mountain-range:

Heights, at the edge of the whole panorama, of less forgiving climes.

Viewed at the extremes of distance and curvature,

through the line of the rising sun vast desert haze, to the limits of sand, and ice

And rock broken-down

Over dry duned desert plain led Camel-train *meandered...*

As a mirage, along invisible roads. Against a blazing sun, in turbulent twisting skywards, from open-Oasis and Beach encampments... between glinting waters, moving through smoke funneled wafting and drifting. Beyond, tropical ocean island, in snowfields driven sleighs chased white lumbering bear, on ice floes and cut ice holes fur clad folk, clubbed helpless elephantine and tusked walrus and whiskered seal for meat and fat and fur. Between round snow cave huts, smoke and steam rising from ice chimney, on the ice tundra toward blinding bright snow peaks, floating floes, and: EarthCentre SnowBall Perma-Frosted Planetary Ice-Cap(s).

Where Sun warmed and *ice*-cold oceans met across a clouded great-Cape of southern-Storms. People seen closer, moving amongst sand dugouts and brush screens, fishing with rod and line and lifted crustacean and fish trap. Baskets drained of water stacked alongside stilted river and lake cabin, raised against flooding river tides. Donkeys, small horses and camels pulled-along these built canals . Across the plains they stretched, and as they ran their forelocks racing forward, back legs kicking back extended taut tensed foot and ankle compacted hooved, vertebrate spine stretched and head raised nosing ahead, eyes alert and staring, forward facing, rigid unyielding. Until, from one extent to another, the smaller more unusual beasts, trapped and slaughtered, leapt on, clawed at and torn apart, butchered. At the specialised border-*edges* hid and held their ground, beneath rock and beaten bush, retired back underground to pursue a solitary, blind and nighttime life.

Whilst below in the now rising Sun-*light*, fleeting herds, spring heeling, in safety congregating in numbers. To distract, to form a larger and social being, more protected against Lone-Hunters and Groups; packs of cats and dogs, that with cunning and wily exterminator effort together survived and reproduced, in abundance over the plains. Off onto broken island, from south to north, snowbirds and storm birds nested on *craggy* outcrops.

Rap-torious flyers, through falcon eagling telescopic vision. Slow glutinous buzzard-circling, waiting the moment of death. Phero-monal, the sweet smell of death, degrading carbohydrate on the breath living capped de-capped de-centring cells degrading, dying, replacing, no longer re-placing, dying-off.

Strategies to stay alive, within species variant and specific world shared, experienced differently, radio wavelength radiating between everything, reality in felt sonar, solar, pheromonal, phenol-typical genetic sex cell memory received adapting throughout the growth of the child, to be passed on, with added value, and random unused alteration passed on endogenous, with the need to adapt and survive, daily, second by second, world mapped in sound and vision, grey, or colour odour, felt radiation waves, passed through the air, and water, to provide the backdrop to everything, and every activity, gauged to be received, responded, and replied to with hawking-talons, freshly bloodied. Heat sensitive reference frame, dropped into warmer air currents, lifting high up on the cliff rock edges.

Picking-out smaller-birds out of the air, performing aeriel challenges, over marsh and uneven coastal-landscape. Pivotal centred-gaze eye-muscles flicking integral steadying, trained and focusing. Landing and taking off on the wind, into complex manouvre.

For food, and sport against their smaller rivals. Riding, waiting for the wind wave, eyeing the ground based prey. Wheeling around, high above. Taking to a secluded spot. Away from thieves to plunder and steal, to pluck the feather, and prepare the morsels, for chicks hidden tucked away. Fed and silenced, from giving their bedded twig and straw hiding spot away. On land, sparrow and morning lark, following flocks and trampeling herd, over spilt seed trail over the plains.

Rooks and craning storks, laid nest of straw and twig, on ground and heightened branch, flat roof or crag.

At the shrubby edges people could be seen picking and cropping, In muted and burning smoke filled sunlight ahead, communal seasonal bonfire, burning the dried leaves, felled and fallen stalk fields, ready for renewal. Others pulled rope and dragged water container from the *freshwater-* river.

Through forest felled jungle and across log cleared open ground and meadow elephant and horses, mule saddled with large leaf and animal fibre, leather roped and ridden. Through rugged tree-lined rocky mountainous terrain, guided and following, the visiting group continued downwards. Rounded a turn in the path, below pine and gorse forest covering looked out over an overlooking rocky outcrop, over hilly expanse of beech and birch, broad-leaved oak and sycamore maple woodland.

Untended rough-haired wild sheep and goat munched and grazed wild grasses and leaves. Roamed along grassy outcrops lower down snorting bush hogs rustled and snuffled amongst tree brush and forest. Looking over low open plains and pastures, horses, lean and agile, hot bloodied and hard ridden.

Outriders yelling, leather booted sharp spurs digging the bare and saddled galloping and turning sweating equine flanks of wild horses. Tamed snorting nostrils and flared eyes, directed to herding, cattle and cows, a bullock and bull separately fenced. At the snowy edges reindeer reined in, below, goaded in controlled stampede of cows towards a huddle of nearby wooden and brush *fenced*-enclosures.

Eastern-plains, desert, arctic, rivers, isolated buildings, stag, bear, dogs, fields and cattle, seaweed fertilized, village, lake, sea docks, wooden galleon armada, massive forest, city walls, kings and sultan, general and religious head, library et., market and war. Flat-faces short noses narrow eyes ice desert sunlight separate Branches of Humanity.

Bamboo-spears reluctant-Warrior Peaceful-Warrior *suffering* flesh-beaten punctured fatal- injury from Challenging-*authority* why? How did we let it happen? Battle, destruction of forests to build ships, steel coal charcoal steam driven electromag. lights, controls, and motorized wheels. Crops and mineral technology. Industry and Transport, Shopping-Mall, Train-Car Café, Center of The EarthCentre Café: The End of The Earth: at The End of the Earth.

Agro-Business Forests-felled for Homes and Furniture. The re-mainder burnt-out accidentally from the ever-closer-Sun and wind-fanned Planet. Behind, arriving with a clashing of hooves, kicking up a fine white dust which stayed in the hot air, running dogs alongside recruited to the task, sharing in the spoils.

Cleaning off the rejected entrails of caught game, as the nomadic Herders and Hunters arrived back to the evergreen dense thicket fenced Chapala Chaparral, Stockyard rounding up, lumps of small game hunted meat thrown unceremoniously to the *obedient*-hounds. The riders, ignoring the inquisitive passing group watching them, appeared from the otherwise plains desert, through forest trail, below they dismounted and tied their roped horses to gatepost fence. Unsaddled, blanketed to keep warm, the horses to drink at trough, and tear at prairie hay-grass. Dry balled tumbleweed, rolled along the ground, on the light wind, to the fringes of lowland steppe, facing soaring snow capped mountain range. Leather Clad-Riders disappeared from view, into windowed buildings, log piled and mud and stone built building below where shouts of laughter, and snatches of tuneful song emanated on their arrival.

Amongst clattering and chinking of wooden clunking and tinny metal and clinked pottery-plate and cup, seen through the windows, moving around furniture, tables and chairs, constructed out of branch and stump; a smoking-stove inside. In the corner, cooking and filtering out from chimney and door as it opened and closed, the smell og cooking, meats and vegetables, brothing and oven roasting, beyond the ranch house, at a distance the tourists gazed out, over open tended pasture.

A covering of acrid-smoke lay over the arid valley forest clearings, in low cloud and risen morning mist. Around them from the hilltop and mountainside edges, tumbling cascades rivered and watered newly, furrowed and planted fields, irrigated from hill stream cascaded, from pool to pool, and reservoired through redirected rocky gully, filled tunnel pipeline and still settled sky *reflecting*-lank and made tanks and wells for water and oil, devastated across plains and dug-out mountainsides de-nuded.

3.
Around the clearings at the edge of the forests,
cave-like shelters, tents of hide, leaf or hair woven cloth,
the skeletal frame of a house, covered with skin draped over branch awnings.
Alongside tent-like sheds and huts built of mud and bracken,
Hemp-thatch tied over raw-timbers cut-down and re-stood and lain-down in place, before hurdle enclosed, framed field paddock.
Within a circular palisade, squared off along the sides,
to the deep forest flank, people brightly dressed, mingled around, chatted amongst themselves.
In low tones, roaring and light cackling laughter.
On swept field breeze they cleared land, broadcast seed, and news.
As they worked, chatted in low and loud voice,
and picked at neat rows of plants, fenced in from the ragged forest edge.
As The Sun continued to rise in the sky, in the open pools,
Women and Men washed clothes, themselves, and small Children,

while youngsters splashed and played. Waterfall sprung and coursed, over base rock pooled, and soaked into the ground, running into streaming brooks, narrow-channels irrigating the fields.

Dammed reservoir and filling sunken well and tank, tapping underground water pump tipping hollow bamboo reed; gathered around by people chatting, drawing up splashing water filled leaf and leather skin tied rope-handled bucket.

Ignoring, unnoticed, occasionally looking up and waving, shouting to the visitors and their guides, or to each other.

Alongside fenced in grazing pens, peering over stream watered hedgerow, animals, not unlike animals the visitors knew, but with some subtle, some stark, *differences.*

An elongated head, longer snout, or longer tail, that made them different animals, and eventually different species, left roaming in the given space, shorn and shaggy, rough-haired and sleek coated, decided by who they were allowed To Mate with. They stood, unaware of themselves except when one of The Villagers greeted them.

The farmed animals, chomping at grasses, munching leaves and petals from trees, nuzzling and attempting loped-off, to wander away, or gallop off, to climb on the back or be mounted, in the heat of excitement, and necessity.

To in-seminate to have to have-been
In-seminated. Grouped sheep and goats,
milking cows stood around calves, changeling cattle and mule,
and a single fearsome and agitated looking Bull, penned and tied
against escape, or theft.

The-Visitors descended the steep path, from the precipice ledges,
following guided through forest path and clearings, to ground level.
Past encampment and ranch, grazed and planted field,
reaching the cattle droveway and apparently public roadway,
poplar and willow trees now lined the river bank path they walked
along, as so many before them, they felt, had walked and ridden,
the hoof stamped studded ground.
Along by the edge of a deep rain and river filled ditch,
where beaver built from habit every season,
piled river dam house for trapping food and sheltering.
Past rugged patches of woodland, on the other side along the lower
valley, the trammeled bridle-path led.
Over a wooden wicker trellis fenced bridge. Toward the last of the
hills, the mountains, and desert, along where the river valley rounded,
to a now still, and only gently wind brushed distant inland freshwater
lake, and beyond a promontory, salt and sand seashore.

Back around to the now hidden base of the precipice, from where they had descended. Over the fields now passed alongside, farmhands spraying arable crops with water and waste over the stubble cleared ground, sludge drawn from ground pits where ants and beetles, in the ant and beetle 'scape, flies buzzed and dug in, composting dungpiles in a mud caked yard.

Around the built Farmyard, cats and dogs roamed freely, chasing plump tailed rat and mouse, in the fields wild rabbit and stalking fox; in garden and field and yard chasing-off parasite carrying vermin, feral wild untamed.

Birds, and insects, seed and crop snatching; all the while the roaming small cats and larger dogs,
each tormenting each other, mostly ignoring each,
individually, and pack, master and servant,
livelihood and occupation; work for food, sport, and play.
In stable pens and barnyard, the grunts and snuffles and smells and movements, of tethered sheep, goats and pigs, snuffling and feeding, mated readied with care to give birth.
Readied for sheering, sheered, for slaughter, skinning butchery knife and cooking skewer. Laid out on cold marble rock slab, bloody running out into filled ground gullies and draining pot, next door stood calmly by, a Farmhand, another sat beneath pulling and squeezing on the giving teats of the cow, filling a jug with warm and creamy white milk.

On higher dryer ground, cockerel pecked, clucked and strutted, while soft downed chicken scampered alongside, watching and copying the scramble for seed, cooped and fluttering, following the tracks through layered constructed henhouse, a startled late rooster, morning sunrise crowing, in the foreground the farmers children perhaps, collecting hen eggs into woven basket.

As the shadowing low sunlit precipice moved behind them along the valley they could make out people more clearly now. Adults and children, working in the fields, at the near distance, digging and weeding, standing and talking, deliberating over the dibbing and sowing of seed and seedling, swinging sharpened sheering scythe to clear the ground. Posts lined quartered and sectioned spacing points between plantings, to give maximum viable population, fallow earth and variating crop rotations turned through cyclical-=harvest.
Set-out
between shared and
unshared land, drawing through the nutritious and well watered ground rooted spiralled upward and outwards growth, to absorb the ground and air, to let out leaf and flower and catch the rising Sunlight.

People tending the fields, cultivated plots by hand with hooked hoe and sharpened adze. Wooden yoke shouldered pails poured out, drag steered ploughed land, turn into and over the earth, and into eventual crop. Clearing, streaming, brooking retaining watering flows, between raised seed beds, cropping, harvesting, and carrying bundles of root vegetable, ground nut, leaf and dried grass, onto store drying stacks. Laid out to dry and ripen, boxed in covered retaining dry darkness. In the open, with flailing action, separating wind flung chaff, and piling hulled grains, into woven twig, bamboo, leaf and rattan grass-baskets.

Over broader planted-plain, bullock and donkey mule dragging furrowing sword plough, rotating blade and seeding wheel with oxen, and carted transom braced horse, the crops, and people to be carried off, along the lanes and onto the road, and raft barge boated waterways between. People appearing now on the road, and passing by dressed in worked hides and woolen cloth cloaks. Riding a saddled and bridled horse, at a loaded cantering trot or freed fast gallop. Walking, leading a roped-cow, carrying shovel and pitchfork, bales and bundles, over the shoulders, loads pushed and pulled on rolled rigid log rounded wheel and freewheeling axled hand-cart.

Beginning to migrate along the road, throwing uncertain looks, as they drew alongside, uncertain puzzled looks, not unlike those on The Visitors faces themselves. Small children bound tightly to their guardians backs, older children running alongside,
chasing each other, or with the older adults, holding hands, un-conjoined *wearily* trailing-along...

They passed by with suspicious look, or with greetings, in apparently un-recognizable, or only *vaguely* re-cognisable tongue.

These strangers could be seen, talked to returned greetings, brought a smile or laugh as they moved by politely,
clapping hands together, their own and others in friendly manner, and talking amongst themselves.

Not apparently regarding the visitors any differently from themselves. The Visitors touching or gripping hands if proffered, just as the people from the fields and farms did, eye contacting or simply nodding with passers by, calling out:
>   -Hello!

With open embracing arms, followed with:
>   -How are you?

With grinning, questioning expression. The other walking on by, or stopped to reply. Smiling,
>   - Good! Well! Thank you!

Gesturing, nodding, bowing almost, and following up, asking,
>   - What's that?

pointing to the crop in the field. Replied to, pointing likewise,
>   - Rabbit?

as two, four and eight sets of animal ears appeared amongst the grassy edges, within shared visioned range across the maize corn field.
Questioning-*again*:
>   - Good?,

and replied to, smiling still,

   - Good! Yes! Good!

with fingers and thumb closed together in a point with one hand, held
up and tapped to the lips, exaggerated chewing, then rubbing the
stomach, followed with a broad grin of edible satisfaction:

   - Good! To Eat!

Articles of information passed on, rapidly repeating the related words
between them.

Pointing upwards towards The Sun, and then indicating with a hole in
the opened hand, the seed sown, when the sun is low. With the hand
opening upwards, growing with the sun, rising in The Sky with the
other hand. Then the opened fingers sowing and reaping, the indicated
sun was to sink again, in a different part of the sky, pointed signified
opposite half horizon, the hand then cupped elsewhere in the sky, a
sleeping yellow harvest moon; pointed out rusted stone red colour,
rounded and opened to full setting, and crescented, before rising with
both hands together, to a full moon, and then again to the sun almost
above now, the cupped hand corn seed cast once again,

   - Ah! Seed? Sun? Sun-Seed?!

Understood, in demonstration and sounded word, the language spoken
and attached was pidgin between the visitors, and the guide and the
villagers and others on the road.

Strange, spontaneous and rapid, but almost comprehensible, with intentional assistance, words shared were pronounced differently, but not so at variance with the visitors own tongue, for them not to comprehend the meanings, associated actions and indications, and in return be understood.

They walked and watched, signed and talked. Yelling a greeting to an austere group passing
along the track, looking not unlike the people met at the hillside forest camp, on the fields and road before. The visitors now separated the others and from their guides, in the gathering throng of field workers, carts and carriages, coming and going on: The Road.

Led in The General Crowd, along a River-Valley, sometimes forgetting, and talking to others as if they were the lost guides, or part of the same visiting group. Nearing a Village Boundary, buildings bustled up against and amongst and along, unwittingly the visitors themselves become field hands, farmers, and villagers, traveling along the road, wandering past and alongside the river, trailing up toward a village of wood, stone, and EarthCentre-mudded.

3.

Passing now tall, peculiarly architectured storage silo, drying granary, stored, charcoal smouldering. Roasting oats and barley odours wafting in vapourous smoke, grain and dust, burning their eyes and nostrils. Churning windmill and flowing watermill river, turbine wheeled gearings, cogged and connected, to curdling churning milk-butter cheese-barrel paddle.

Propelling fixed heaving, wooden beamed and cast hubbed grinding stones, grain pouring down from the attic store, through measured gaps, crushed and poured-out. Through arching gates and along other roads.

A small-horse haltered lowering rope, and metal cast linked chain, over turning winding capsule and winding wheel. The lifting crane frame, pulley and platform, locked off, for cornflour filled sacks to be loaded, tied and stacked alongside wooden strutted and lashed sealed drum barrels of fermenting grain, powdered crackling charcoal, heaved by several sweating and gnarled-hands.

The Machinery: strain-released, the drop-resisted, goods-lifted…swiftly onto weight bearing brake cart, to be free wheeled away. The space prepared, for the next load appearing with hand and horse drawn cart. With the straggling queues of friendly and smiling chattering folk the dusty track now led between more wooden framed barns and sheds. Stone and fired kiln brick built cottage houses, with smoke of domestic fires, billowing from windows and chimneys, into still-air.

They stopped at a river and roadside site, where generations of men, women and children were busy climbing wooden tied ladders lifting materials by hand and roped over structured frame, onto the roof of a new building. Tying shaped wooden beams together, to form an open drying loft, below, shoveling clay and mud bonding into stacked dividing walls, laying heavy wall stones, chequered and pattern tile floor, with platform pulley and lever.

The Visitors called up to them, watched and discussed their activities with interest. Asked about the building decorations, consecrations painted across the scaffolded post and lintel porch and wall, the upper transverse supporting beam, and upper floorboarded rail carved and fretwork stair banisters, like the rock and tree trunk steps on the path. The ornate woodwork gum enamel lacquered, the stone flagstones laid.

With shell patterned circles and lines, chimney and floor space symbolic plaque and pattern, on shaped and formed walls inside and out, filigree of tree root and branch, leaf and petal, animal facial features fearsome and overly happy; fertile arching phallus and enticing curved female form, abstracted and transferred.

Bringing out a ceremonial kettle and cup set, to celebrate, raising filled cups,

      - For family,

they were told,

      - For the Good Life!

The spacy-sparce buildings spread out over the hinterlands, huddled up to and along the rivers edge. The occasional outhouse and barn, peat and dung, logs and charcoals, piled alongside.

What became an untidy conurbation of walls and wafting hearth, at the perimeter of the stone enclosed village led over bridged culvert, ditched excrement, ordure and detritus, river washed midden and *muck* moat. Past the stench wreaking entrance, vaulted sewer below the low stone Arch-bridge. Entering The Village amongst a further huddle of buildings, and along a village street, the tourists peered inside open doored cottages where people sat at mealtime or busy with some task.

Minding-children, or door closed against intrusion. Past a walled vineyard and sheep grazed around pruned and pollarded orchard tree, where children, and visitors stretched for them, for grape, prickly pear, plum, and apple, just out of reach, to pluck the juicy fruit. Dropped fell from leaves wet it seemed from an earlier rain shower where each drop had puddled into pools, and fruit scattered picked fed to the animals, or rotted back into the ground.

The Visitors passed on, across a central grass green with horse trough, and sundial water clock filled and emptied with pendular regularity. Set to the turn of the sun and the Earth, adorned with tumbling vine, image of fruits and flowers, and bales of cereal and drying hay. Realistic and imagined, allegorical and life *critical*-Beasts, with implied entreaty, to revere, or to beware.
Of milk-cow and raging-bull, grazing goat and snarling wolf, diving fish, and treacherous overwhelming spouting giant sea serpent. Above patterned smooth leafed and spiked plant, gargoyle serpentine griffin fish, winding around standing, and inverted

Tree; reflection cast in wave-*patterned* water.

From the Earthen, deadly and yet more fearsome seas, guarded underwater, underworld. At the top, a naked pair, much giggled at, in rapture of bare passion. Spouting monumental golden bearded sea god, wild creatured devilish winds and rains, blowing over the Earthly and underworldly shores.

Great-Chariot, drawn by hippopotamus, whale and horse *galloping-waves*...Protean servants, changlings, changing shape, siren calling. Naked mermaid and merman nymphs with cherubic babes, sun, moon and stars arraigned.

Black, and white swans beaked the fountain spray of the clouded celestial realm. Fresh water gushed, for drinking and watering. The river, brooked and streamed on through the village, and splashing down the middle of the cobbled village High-Street.

From the bridged river sewer and drain below, as if water-Demonic Devilish: spouting-Fire, wizard and witch, phantom and phantasamagorical-Paths outwards-leading...

Toward messy and muddy farmyard lanes, the main village street with provisions and General Provisions stores, and cottage houses with tended vegetable, herb and flower garden. Alongside trodden earth and now paved pathway, of the garden itself, made and laid out, to access the neat and tidied cultivated patchwork, walled in against the road and field, around the Village Green well and Church; shops and houses, houses as shops where children played loudly, mimicking and Pant-o-miming.

Ran around, pushing and shoving each other.

Jumping marked out squares and hoops, without touching the edges.

rolling hoops and balls, spinning tops, tossing sticks and casting

stones. Boys bouncing a ball, against a wall and floor, knocked back

with bat and ball. A group of Girls, feeding and cuddling crude carved

dolls, all singing songs, making up stories, rocking them to sleep.

The two coming together in sportive, self organizing, shouting, tactic

challenging, elaborately pre-arranged rules. Laying down a complex

arrangement of fair game play, starting a fight, status and servitude:

who is to do what, and who is not.

Who agrees and who does not.

Watched over, by Mothers and Fathers and elderly working and

wandering around, and between sitting and chatting, passing on

rumour and news, with the time of day. Babies swaddled, and cradled

against the world, held up high in the air, aloft, as though a good luck

charm.

By several large hive shaped stone and mud baked ovens, sacks of

emptied ground flour, jugs of warm water,

bean and milk urn and pots of cream, pats of butter and trays of eggs,

taken from, broken and mixed and kneaded together.

Yeasted-*fermentation*, kneeded into long lengths and rounded mounds,

on long wooden pallets fed into the fiery open stone and clay,

steaming flat breads, leaven loaves and cakes being brought out of long

ovens. Dressed and decorated, laid out onto trestle tables.

Cut portions and whole carcass of meat being turned on a roasting

spit,

Fish-grilled and frying in pans, bowls of vegetable steaming,

raw salad and ripe fruits, piled in bowls.

Barreled and bottled wine and beer,

and more intoxicating fermented and distilled spirit,

jugged, corked and capped, in preparation for a celebration feast.

From an upstairs window, a cloaked and shrouded women gazed-out

briefly. Returned inside, attending the joyous or awful cry of a

newborn or teething infant heard, piercing-the-*air*.

Between the low mumbling beseeching, and screeched plaintive cries;

Others outside, arguing and squabbling, laughing and crying in the

hubbub below.

They passed through The Village scene, and arrived at the far corner of

the village, where colourful banner and flag pole bunting, draped

across the tunneled roadway.

Through bowed wood and stone arch cusped doors, in polished light

letting glass. Framed in stone and metal, to shut out, and let in.

Mediating between the seen and unseen worlds, sunlight let in,

through arched ocule illumination, to sparkle, the light and essence.

Images and icons, of plants and animals, and people working trades

and tasks, Ancestral and Astral, Zodiacal, Celestial-lives entombed, laid

out inside, or with just their carved image remaining, beyond the

immediately extant, beyond the terrestrial grand building, labyrinthine

to walk amongst and around, boxed relic bone, magical hatted mask, of

wood, or cloth, and ritual vessels for eating and drinking, washing and

dressing.

Paying their dues accordingly, for entrance, walking amongst candles lit, amongst goblet chalice and plate, ciborium and monstrance showing, cupping seed vessel lotus flower and collection bowl, for the poor, passed around by their hosts.

As interested and *invited*-Guests, The Visitors were clearly supposed to stand on the fringes.

As the families and friends moved into the main part of the hall, a solemn ceremony was begun.

The pair, to be coupled, were led to the front. To ceremoniously *re*-cite the given words. In communion, to exchange vows, marks and rings, and to pass the given bequests. Securing their futures, sharing their legacies, the brief ceremony was over.

4.

As the adherents thronged and paraded, The Families moved further inside the great building, to socialize the merging of families, securing the accession as soon to be succession. Affirming and denying incantation. Sentimental worship and prayer, read and repeated, from lectern copied sacrosanct *compendious*-book. Opened to a page, read out, and carried forward in reverence, and to be *revered*:

     -Metal-riveted...

     -Tree or sand-Paper...

     -All! Digitalised!

     -Anachronistic-analogue...

Taken time-out from the everyday, a ceremony that would, the intention was clear, last the coupling the rest of their days together.

That would bear them, their children, and their forebears children, comfort into old-age.

The Older members of the congregation smiled, and grinned with happiness and joy, some with tears, as they crept and maneuvered carefully, into their place in the congregation. An overwhelming reflex, swelled amongst the gathered families and peoples...rose from the gathered choired throng, music lulling and lilting, with passionate, mellifluous chanted and sung words uttered. In communal awe, in necessity and belief.

In a kind of perpetuity, pungent incense burned into the air, beaten gong and melodious carillon bells rung out. Affirmation, rites, ritual, and denial.

Outside now, from behind a large public house, Village Hall Social Club, on the edge of the green.

Outside of which a decorated pole stood the garlanded man on horseback, and women bedecked with flowers and leaf, and crops of the field. On horseback, being led by a plainly dressed man walking in front, appearing to a noisome welcome, the horse carriaged pair moved-off.

In ritual and ceremony. Ribbons held aloft, alongside the youngest, and then the eldest of the girls and women of the village, following joined and entreated, serenaded alongside by garlanded boys and single men, and taking up the last group the married couples, youngest, and finally with the eldest, before the visitors all enjoined, the party continued dancing and singing, laughing, and looking smilingly, appealingly, and warily toward each other, the gathered suitors, and suited, along-The-Way.

A whistle fluted, and polished brass band, marched and played ahead from side streets, shouts and laughter, as the entourage was followed, and more villagers and visitors joined.

The Visitors became part of a planned but seemingly spontaneous wedding party, carried along in the street, by the families and friends, presumably of the bride and groom, riding on horseback ahead. The whole party talking, singing and dancing, shouting best wishes, and lurid laughing yells. The marrying pair turned along a side path, entered into a large hall set back from the road, decorated, and austere.

Dressed in their best, off the peg shopped or brought-with.
Congregated and aspiring, to ally with the top table, the celestial
sphere. Mediated by the place, and the ceremony, they awaited. Like
minded, or to become like minded, they and their children to follow
them through these doors, in the safety of their number. The Visitors
were offered of The Wedding Party. Meaded and fermented and
distilled drinks, and strange tasting foods, laid out on the long tables in
The Wedding Hall, for all to savour. They ate, or politely refused.
Accepted a drink to toast The Newly Weds in whatever tradition, the-
same. As charcoal sparked and fizzing fireworks were let off, sparkling
and exploding into the air outside, The Visitors were shown their way.
Led on their way, touched gently on the arm to leave, as custom
seemed to dictate.

The music continued to play, and faded behind closed doors. Amongst
the joyous celebrating throng, along the proceeding way, oil and reed
rush lamps lit in readiness for evening and nightfall, around tables laid
outside, for a feast, for an evening of fun and laughter, joyous
merrymaking, games, and fond farewells.

Overlooking the fields around and sea beyond, leaving the ancient
stone castlement village walls, that meandered now on up a hill, past
windows, a school classroom, empty rows of desks, and board left
blank except with with numbers, letters and words written scrawled
on.

Shelves and cupboards of books, allowed out, to be read, and returned for others to read. Read- out, feeding the air with verse and rhyme discussion thick with intellectual questioning; searching for knowledge, and understanding, repetitive rote belief, walls daubed with childrens' paintings, models constructed and instructional picture painted posters and words.

The windows blank, the village school wall ended, the wall separating the road from field, now rising upward toward a dominating hill fortress of stone, piled and wooden, mortar and tar, iron strapped and bolted planks over solid-rock: City-Walls. Along the wall toward the Castle-Capital. Troops of Foot-Soldiers lay resting. Set up tent and fire, flags fluttered in the wind. As if separating one part of the landscape from another. By their uniform, and presence. As if standing between a Feuding Vendetta, jealous or Revengeful-ruler, One against another; and their people, whoever they were, all-together now, the nearest people they would fight and possibly die for.

The Visitors greeted The Soldiers well enough, and Each marched-on, past frosted windows neither looking in nor out, of a stark dour bastion, blankly squat, behind gate and wall. Antiseptic smell burned inside, wafted outside of a grey foreboding Convent Monastery, a Hospice, Orphanage and Workhouse providing 'sanctuary for the poor, the ill, and the dying.

A cowled black robed figure, spoke to a small group of gathered, bedraggled, penurious elderly, sick and injured, attending the outer wood-and-metal gate. A child, scrawny and plague ridden, eyes hollow and wormed through, held out pitiful *filthy* and prematurely aged *gnarled and blistered*-hands. The pleading sorrowful eyes turned-away, and the awful-figure rejoined a lonely crowd, converged at the entrance path:

-To *die* in battle, so what?

-For what?! Bread ...

-... and guns!

-To die anyway, by accident, rotting, eaten away from the inside? Brain worms on

-To Battle!

-For what? For right or wrong?! Left, or correct, the right thing to do? For food, and a child's chance in This World!?

-This Ship of Fools?!

Parting from the road, making way to let The Travellers pass-by, without touching, without solid greeting. Through a slotted opening in the chiseled tied leaf knotted carved doorway fearsome faced *demonic* figures showed the fear of what contagion lay within; and in the mounded laid out unmarked graves to one side.

The Visitors hurried on now, reaching a branching in the open road. Over a graveyard high stone wall, by the branching roadway, the scent of jade and jasmine wafted over another ceremony being carried out. A funereal cortege stood down from a horse drawn cart, lowered a cloth covered casket before an open new grave outside, the village cemetery, outside the village.

Solemn words and chanting between tearful weeping howling ululation, silent holding thought. Attended by worshipful grieving pleadings, amongst familial and communal relationships rituals and obligations, votives and offerings.

Scenes of great doubt, and decision. Sadness for missed opportunities, missing of place, the finality of the departure, thinking of others', ones own, and loved ones passing death.

Celebrating in gladness for the release of another, known and affectionately loved, from worldly struggles and cares. Left behind, all this, to those continuing on, in earthly torment.

Each mourning their own death, and the loved ones, looking like ghosts themselves, one of the mourners wailing, pleading through the mystery of death, lifting the veil from the face and eyes, declared:

-Why?! Why, so much harder, for those they leave behind?

Near the gate, on an untended overgrown stone cask, at each corner, an archangel, holding an empty hourglass poured grains of shifting sand, or salt.

Named inscription, and dates, beneath, the visitors could now pick out the places, high in the hills, where ancient burial and urn field mounded flat topped barrow lay, pyramidal and rectangulate Temple stood, new trees and bushes grew in places where the distant ancestral deceased were laid out. To worm and carrion and putrefaction, burial pit and cave tomb, dry ghostly charnel bone house sarcophagus, and *funeral*-pyre. At Once! sending risen reels of spirited smoke and dust rings, funneled into the opened skies, sprinkled, decomposed and dusted into the ground, gone.

These places, to be visited, on occasion, by the living, and by those destroyed, but not forgotten, and otherwise passed by as these visitors did, in and on their way. They imagined these places, revered, made and placed by those they had been with earlier. Predecessor, forebears, ancestors, actors, to those departed, and those to arrive.

In their turn,

to be buried in the dark earth, to decay, to be carried off,

to blow in the wind.

To remain amongst the green overgrown undergrowth,

of those ancient places,

on the hillsides above, dotted with standing stones,

piled cairns, and fallen shaped carved rocks,

from the very mountain peaks,

that stood around.

Great granite chipped and stone menhir, sacred memorial rock stone pillar, set out to catch the rising suns rays, onto alter to be laid out, left out

remains to carrion,

hewn and strewn scattered around the disrupted remains.

In altered celestial cosmological alignment.

Clearly-placed, seasonal and geographical shrine, to the dead, and for

the living. Beyond: The-Fortress village and monastic castle outskirts;

on raised and shaped plaque on a field wall, carved and cradled by a

placid harvest moon, in triangulatory transit, with a point on the Earth,

where a ocean wind sailed and river rowed boat, ferried along a

gloomy river; towards a risen and *fiery*-fabling *noonday*-Sun.

Cradle to Grave *tributes* flowers, everlasting metals, gold and silver,

and needs for afterlife food animals, to protect, nets' *ensnaring traps...*

*

Universal Verses6:War! Again...

1.Castle and Battleground.

2.FairGround.

3.Parade.

4.Capital Battle Captured.

5.Limbo...

Universal Verses6:War!

1.Castle and Battleground.

As they passed,
they felt as if they moved through the same epicyclic times,
of people they had seen and met, who had lived, and now gone.

Along with those who now lived, and would live, with them,
through into the next times, and pass along the roads they also trod.

The opposite fork in the road,
Where the roads parted and the next one,
led them further down the valley track.

Through a cobblestone built and raised shallow ford,
across one of the many river tributaries,
flowing down from the hills and mountains around them.
Removing the rough footwear they had been given to start the path
downwards…

They paddled in the refreshing cool clear running waters.
Floating leaves and dropped flower, and keel ridged petal,
washed along, like tiny boats. Stepping out of the other side of the
multitude same-streamed waters.

Flowing-on through riverine marsh estuary, to rise over the seas, and to rain soaked into and over the land, washed on down to pile riverbed and mountain slopes,

to drain and sieve out, iron, gold and lead silver filings, trees to

…paper, to fill freshwater lake, rivered out to the surging open flat sea, where kelp farmers toured the shore.

Flowing over rocks and through grazed pastures,

towards the wide lake glimpsed earlier from the high wooded path. From the top of the precipice they had descended, over and on the river and multitude streams and rivulets, turning into river and sea estuary, taking the routes of least resistance, over fertile, temperate and once inhabited ground.

Risking being lost in isolated stagnant pool, or washed flowing down toward sea level, blown up and over open plain and clouded misty mountain-top.

Sand wave patterned dry parched desert sand, meeting from hillside, and grassy dune rivered fed-Oasis.

With: Emerald Forest-Roof: leading down to a quagmire swamp, of quaking marsh reed, swayed and rustling, wafted wafting in waves, guided back and forth in the breezing wind.

Like children in a nighttime forest, holding onto hands, walking in the woods, in a direction, listening out, for fallen trees, looking for a path out. The path now led on down, through a coppiced wood, alongside the deeper and widening: River-Bank.

Over wood and rock pebble laid pathways, and routes through.

Peopled groups and separated individuals,

wandered and searched, bent and crouched,

shadowed and reflected over the sands and dried flat-watery and oily

marshland.

Lifting driftwood and shore-weed, to find and winkle out filled

cockle-shell and mussel.

Sustenance out of the marshy estuary waters, and wave patterned

beach,

left by the receding tide.

Rushing outwards and to return, again and again, in timely fashion,

lapping habitually along the deserted *beach*-Littoral.

Gulls and tiny plovers, sandpipers, settled on tiny hillock island, dug

nesting hollowand pecked at the saturated banked sand. Skein of

black and white grey primordial heron, goose and swan, flew and

landed, with fluffy cygnet and gosling, floated and paddled.

Ducked below, in a flash of oily green and blue feather, and came up

with a wriggling fish, or other swan male and female, male and

male, decoying, into the fray, forced collusion, self-defence, defense

of the brood, and the mothering broody. Clasped between sharp

toothed beak. The fish swallowed whole, to be re-gurgitated for

nestlings, hidden in the bushes and rush-weed beds.

Over the sheltered windbreak poplar and ash tree-lined fields,

buntings and linnet, canary yellow and variegated short beaked-

-finches fluttered, flocked, and chased-off. Cloudy string centred circular sweep of Sky. The Sun-*shone* implacably, over rock strewn marsh clearing where small songbird warblers, hidden and jittery, perched and fluttered in tree tops, twittering singing loudly and repetitively, flinching, surveying every movement around, swooping to intersect a swarm of fly, over mosquito infested malarial-swamp.

Over the fields beyond, a hissing hurtling rush of winged grasshopper flew, scoured and scourged, through fresh water cereal crop, across open sun baked and droughted fields, a great grey mass of thrashing wing locust, massacring the crop, taking everything in its hurtling flock combined and singular-path.

Great rafts of thin stranded nets, strung out to catch migrating birds for feathering and feasting at one season, now trying to arrest the destructing devastation. Swooping through, at least some of the deadly killer insect force trapped, to be ceremoniously and ritually burned, hung out to dry and die, the smoke attempting to warn off others of the barrage.

Getting away, to disperse and disappear into the surround. To continue, to threaten, to vanish elsewhere, the most part of the fields saved for the harvest.

Watched at the edges, away from the live and living rushing furore, beyond the marshland, on rivers and streams, from hollow reed and rush matted coracle, and wooden flat hulled boat projecting rod and hooked line, into the depths punted along the inland and laked waterway-canals.

On one side of a built floodwater levy erected against the encroaching rising waterline, opened and let onto the marshlands, regulating against the battering returning sea-tide.

The Visitors passed along a raised surfaced path past fertile silt fields, alongside and towards the freshwater lake wind waved and choppy, lapping against breakwater wall, whitewash painted house-lined harbour front and wooden-jetty.

As The Visitors arrived, small fishing dinghies being tied, ropes thrown out to wrap around the quayside moorings. Rowing and ruddered boats bobbed, laden with crustacean and fish from the lake. Nets folded, lake, river, seaward wind sails taken down, keel hulled shells, built and lived on, to float and drift on the incoming-current.

The Tourists nodded toward and greeted returning Boat-crews, and dockside-Anglers sitting at the edge throwing-lines into the *deep-waters*. Greetings returned, with a lifted wriggling fish, added squirming for breath, on to a dead lifeless pile on the stone paved banks. A flotilla of painted vessels lay roped against the side, the trawler crews on board, busy mending torn nets, on: The-Keyside: Families with small children running around, older ones playing diving and swimming in the clear water in the risen midday heat; or sat on low stools along the sidewalk, talking or thinking quietly, helping out the adults.

Piles of crustacean, mollusk, large grown brown eel and various smaller and larger fish from the mornings catches, sorted into stacked woven basket and nailed wooden crate. To be carried off, piled precariously, on rattling wheel barrows handcarts. Taken and offloaded, sealed into racked sealed ice tray or smoke-filled salting and drying-sheds, *preserving*-Storehouses.

Along streets and paths leading away from the fields and lake, the woods and hills all around, they moved on, carrying with them offered and accepted fresh shellfish, eaten live, raw, and whole, as shown by their newly found *friends.*

Followed-on, wandered along and up steep steps behind the harbour, where loaded fixed axle donkey carts and hub-less horse and camel drawn wagons, trundled the rutted and bustling alleyways. Along the lanes, winding inwards, leather and cloth over-alled and aproned men
and women sat outside warehouses on steps and stools, hammering metal spiked nails into wooden crate slats. Weaving straw for baskets, wood and leather, clog and sandal, shoe and
boot cobblers, cloth sails and clothes makers. Stirring and dipping threads hung out to dry, fixed onto frame, woven through, led back and forth, and through and between, in emerging patterned and intricate embroidered, interlocking material-Design.

Artisans mixing and fixing pungent acid alkali bone ashes, metallic and vegetable salt crystal colours, In vast closed tubs and vats, dug into the ground. Throwing wet clay onto turning flat wheel, hand moulding, pitted and lumpy, based and cored, smoothed, crenellated and embellished, attaching handle and moulded spout, to pots and basins, incised and left out to dry. Finished polychrome painted marking and decoration. With thumbprint, finger combed, wavy curved line, string whip scored and tooled motif. The sound of hammers beating metal against stone anvil, and a smelter glow emanated from the door of one of the open sheds. Along a side alleyway, low buildings of brick and earth ranged, where rhythmic ringing sounds, shouting and talking, singing and a sweating haze of smoke and leaked cylinder pressured steam pervaded. Towards the wide and windswept inland lake, in the woodside and woodland, cauldron pits dug into the Earth EarthCentre. Heated flamed funneling steamed and smouldering, thick grey and thinning transparent blue waves and wafers, into the breezing pleasantly *cool*-air, as Home. Grass and earthen sod mounds, closed off, dampening down. Smothered, starved and deprived of air, denied an ashen burial. Uncovered burnt charcoal alum, potash remains, to fertilize the ground, to fuel the stoves and ore iron furnaces. From open forge fired, running green silvered copper and tin from the melting rock. glowing smelter red hot collected, to dip into water filled vats. Separated through heat and weight and size, pulverized amalgam, of mineral and metal rock, brought down from the heights. Out of caves and caverns, and purposefully dug potholes, passageways and cavernous mineshafts. Smelted and mixed worked ores poured from mined and pummeled rock, salt and cement-quarry.

Brought in by Horse-Cart and Hand-Barrow from: the hills and colliery pits dug, and sprung out, from all around, wood-fossil charcoal, fuelling smelt and forge, pouring steady clouds of smoke chimneyed into the air.

Turning out cast iron, copper and zinc bronze alloy, and lead, panned *silver* and golden nugget; amazing and mysterious objects, crafted and drawn from the compressed skein of a fiery-*underworld as Over Each Sky The Moon and constellations...*stars and galaxies...

Melted and melded, kneaded and knocked out, die cast moulded, leapt-*steaming*, clattering on

the stone floor, hammered and impression stamped pots and pans, knives and swords.

Buckles and buttons, medallions and coinage, minted to adorn and exchange.

Tinkling on the carefully swept work-surfaces, where smiths and craft workers polished and assembled, the final-piece(s). Signed and displayed in cabinets, for public impression and show. Finely crafted metallurgy, sculpted clay and blown sand crystal glass, for social, personal and domestic decoration, functional and ornamental, ceremonial and military. Returning to The-Streets now, peering into and entering other doorways and buildings, more at ease now.

Following the initial encounters passed workshops, and where loud hammering and rattling machinery could be heard and seen. Furniture and cabinet-Makers cut and planed, jointed and varnished planks from forest trees cut down, brought in , trimmed and cut. Through sawmill machines, operated by taut belt and rattling chain, on ratcheted winching wheels, wedged peg and screw threaded, bolt and hexagonal sided nut, turned and twisted.

Tightened, framed and held in place. Machinery, measured, gauged and designed, balanced and returned, to emulate and enhance the tasks of many hands. Water wheeled and steam pressure current, released to bend softened ash and willow, to cut and drill and shape, hard rose and teak mahogany, carved and plain chairs, tables and cabinets, clothed in milled-material.

Spun and combed and brushed, weaved in and over, through and across, in homely disorder, stacked outside for display, advertised to passers by. Past a window with rows of carcasses hanging from hooks, blood dripping entrails, stripped from torn flesh. Shouting to an overalled and bloodied figure, the reply to the shouted,

     - Who are you? What are you doing?

An instant smile and *laughing*:

     - The Butcher, the Baker, and the Candlestick maker!

Rising fumes and air of preserved and fermenting fruits and herbs, wildflowers and tree-sap drawn out into vacuum tube piped, bottling store-cellars and kitchens. Mingling once again, with the aroma of food and cooking outside, provided by the benevolence and exchange, of the butcher, the baker, and the brewer.

On open stalls, and through windows opened wide, rallying and enticing customers with mouth watering cries, entreaty to quench, perhaps until now unthought of, thirst and hunger. Receiving, in return for the victuals asked for and handed over, embossed impression stamped and rattling copper and tin, silver and brass and gold coin, paper painted and printed notes, from opened folded wallets and string-pulled purses.

Entering: one of the low, dimly lit café houses, they were given beverage, infused and decocted in waxed gourds, terracotta cup and bowl. Still and sparkling, intoxicating and refreshing, with food, meats and breads and cakes. With fruits and vegetable, raw and roasted, steamed and boiled-*sustenance*.

They returned what they might have supposed, from the en-dorsed be-figured *rattling*-lucre given previously, to be carried in pockets and purses, and to be recognized, in exchange.

Laughter and noise rattled on all around them, shouting and hubbub, singing and music played with drummed and noted reed and string. Someone spoke loudly at them:

-This is great, isn't it?!,

and they did not know if they recognised them or not. From the characters they moved amongst, from The Party they had arrived with.

From this time or that, as they mingled and exchanged, relieved and revived and enlivened themselves within. Replete and encouraged, they stepped out through the low wooden framed door, over a stone-kerb. From the packed rowdy house, through the last of the earthen and stone village and Harbour-Town outskirts. Onto a burgeoning paved street. Villagers and TownsPeople mixed along the ways, over dressed in fashionable styles, allied with a vocation, aspiring class, and with cheaper copied versions of the going echelon and modern trend. Mimicking toward, or rebelling against, the aristocratic hierarchical Alpha type, Beta or Gamma what did it matter? It did. Adult/Child Male/Female Owner/Slave Rich/the rest of Us. Simply-*steeped* in the necessary workaday garment, to hide and to emphasise animal nakedness beneath.

Leather sandaled and booted, dressed in simple cloth tied and wrapped, others showing off their assumed or aspiring-*wealth*. Clothed in *lustrous*-velveteen suited, caped and cloaked. Elaborately decorated with individually ornate rare metal, beaded glass and exceptional polished mineral stone, green jade and blue sapphire. Purple ruby garnet, yellow opal and silver pearl, plain gold and silver, with airs and graces worn. Set in ornament finger ring, wrist and ankle bangle and bracelet, dress brooch, necklace linked-chain.

Shaped cast symbol medallion, brushed and braided hair, lip plug and ear spool, marked and flayed skin, dressed, so it seemed, to charm and impress, even to jinx, curse and hex, and put a spell on. To intimidate those without such protection, without such feigned finery, in false bravado, in confident step, and snarling *unfriendly-* voice.

Riding-fast trap carried sedan, and calling from enclosed carriage saloon, along busy pavemented thoroughfare. With flower and sweet smelling herb, perfumed and adorned with rank, familial- significance and marriage-status. As The Visitors copied, walked, or hailed transport which stopped for them, or not, dependent on their appearance and the taxis' availability. People walked on the pavements, carried goods and chattels in bags and sacks piled on trundling carts and vans. Stepped onto vehicles, bussed and coached, stood and chatted, as others, giving brief accounts of the comings and goings on, as they traversed the various areas and routes. Pointing out the ornate signs and guilded letters, in windows, specialized container, bottle, and carrier-bags.

Over the doors of workshop factories and craft houses, the houses and offices of townsfolk and gentry, simple criss-cross or figurative- -picture, phonetic, monogrammatic, in clay and bitumen designed lock, stamp and seal.

For each jealously guarded trade and craft, belief and creed, each distinctive for a specialised skill or arcane knowledge, for deference and *privilege*.

The TownsFolk bustled along, ignoring the visitors more now, busy in their various tasks, amongst towering stone and brickwork edifice. Three, four and more corridor interconnecting pagoda style storeys, that lined the way. Mysterious overhanging attic rooms and roadway arches, halved circles like a rising overarching, or sinking-Sun. Out of the paved Earth, pillared in rough stone, through a snarl maze of backstreets, old town shanty slum and urban sprawl. Alongside new city spread tenements and high rise, the stench of manufacture and sweaty unwashed bodies, waste bins, and sewer ragged shacks, beneath small gardened houses, grand villa's above, overlooking, set into the hillside from where the visitors had earlier left.

Barbers' Shop, Hair-Dressers and Beauty-Parlour.

Sports' Arena, Circus Horse Track, Time and Motion Activity gambled-on for deferred-challenge and self-satisfied delusional shared-gratification and dis-appointment.

Overlooking below, a wretched air of sordid menace pervaded, defiled, trapped, augering it seemed hate, and felony. Haunted with *potential* and actual peculation, of theft and embezzlement, vice, extortion and exploitation, risked and agreed for the price-of-Survival. Alongside moral-preaching and prayer-room, casino and bordello, nightclub bar, cheap hotel and mission *doss*-House. Police-notices, intimidating, deterring and joined in hypocrisy, shared in collusion through the layers, rife in the thick air, fissile competitive tensions.

Faith Houses, Doctors and Lawyers, Astrologers and Healers, Hospital and Poor-Houses.

Discreet and more obvious Game and Gambling-Den, inside, fenced and walled leisure-Arena…line-ruled sports fields and pitches. Hippo-Drome and DogTrack, for Races to be Run. Teams and *numbers*, matched against each other, supported vociferously, by groups of loud colour and badge attired Patron or patronee.

On their way, calling their bets, cheering their side, swapping displacing banter, and intimidating-*insult* to Each Other.

Passing *noisily* past, harmless to any but each other, if the arguing got too intense, the excuse of allegiance, to pick-a-fight.

Passed and along rough looking alleyways, and inviting doorways, dusty hallways, dustpan and broom-brush swept out, as if ridding the home of evil or unwanted-spirit(s).

The Visitors followed each other through the low wooden doors of a window-fronted shop with a window loom, and advertising cloth and garment, examples hung around the walls. At one side, the other a counter with sacks, pots and jars, of grains, herbs and spices, roots and leaves, barrels and bottles of oils, beverages, teas and juices, alimentaries and cures, potions and pills, antibiotic and emetic, sedative and fermented stimulant. For all kinds of illness and wound healing wound, victuals and foods from the surrounding fields.

It was dark inside compared to the street filtered sunlight outside. They smelled unfamiliar scents burning the eyes slightly, their eyes took a moment to adjust. In the backroom a family group gathered. Cooking and sewing, weaving on wooden frame, a family dog laying down in front of a warm fire, asleep.

The new customers bowed and clasped and shook hands with the shopkeeper, sitting behind an ancient time-stained wooden counter. The shopkeeper, an elderly woman in shawl and wearing long clothes hanging down to the dusty floor. She had come out from the backroom, smiling a yellow toothy grin, and pointing to the rear lounge, as if offering them inside. A child by her side pointed, copying, hanging onto the long clothes, saying,

- Ma. GaGa. Pa. KaKa. Baba. Dada. TaTa. Ah?

Both Women and child carried on smiling, with a laughing friendly contentment, of assumed understanding. The Shopkeeper pointing again to the back room, indicating in faltering tone, what she knew the child to be indicating, with finger and head nodded look,

- Mother, father, aunt and uncle, brothers and sisters. Cousins … and …

and pointing to herself proudly:

- Gran'Mother!

In the back room there was banter and laughing, friendly competition over the co-operative kitchen and laundry taking place in an inner courtyard. Stone rubbed and cleaned cloths hung out to dry, food cut and readied for the pots boiled and steamed on closed: fire-chimney cooking-stove.

Satisfied for the urge for land. Rooms, buildings, in chambers, high rise flats and bungalows. Occupied by one and the other. One another, family. One in one room, many in one room. One in many rooms. Many, in many rooms, in many housing projects and estates, condominium and gated park. A place that felt like home. That they would want to return home to. A fire roared in the grate, a boiling kettle, on a stone and metal stove. Chimney funneled out, into the outside air, inside clearing the bugs from the walls, that might bite and scratch in the morning.

The Visitors waved and smiled, unsure if they might be invited further inside. They went to look at and touch the goods, and to go into the backroom as if to encroach, or even threaten the family and child, as if they were museum pieces. The shopkeeper reacted as anyone incurred upon, stepping back behind the counter, the family in the back room watching protectively, ready to intervene any transgression. The grandmother pointing to one of their purse wallets and a string beaded counting frame on the counter. The social introductions completed, now expecting a coin or note of transaction.

They responded, embarrassed at their misunderstanding and lack of politeness. Faintly blushing unexpectedly fearing, uncertain, awkward, apologizing. Stepping back through the low outside door. The ordinary social censorial protocols refused them the right to wander any further inside, but just, on departing, to peer into the back room, where a dog barked at them. They returned into the street again, feeling socially inept, and without-purchase.

The ShopDog ran out with them, passed them along the road, turned, barked at them again.

As others mingled into view, and into their path, the dog ran back into the shop. They laughed simultaneously to each other, and at the dog, putting on its act more for its return to its owners, than for them, strangers in town. Walking amongst buildings, lining and overhanging the streets, *bristling* with people. Wending their way through winding alleyways and streets, passing ways and courtyards. Couples chatted and laughed, touching each other faintly and relaxed, holding hands, kissing and smiling.

Others stood together in groups, chatting, discussing, exchanging information, discussing or arguing with low or loud tone, laughing and smiling in-*mockery* or agreement.

FunFair ground Others hurried alone, looking straight ahead, or turning to acknowledge one here or there, hurrying on. Through a cleft in the valley and hills, leading out beyond into the forests and mountains and abated ocean, of now distant memory, between buildings that led back down towards and down to the sea. A wide seaward docking deep water basin trading port opened out before them.

Along the broadening navigable river inland, past the lake harbour and town and village, from between the ranging waterfall mountain passes, and all the way to the sea. Great wooden and metal hulled vessels bobbed on the water, carrying and discharging people and cargoes, from over the seas, and beyond, inland on river boats carried inward. Along the warehouse wharves great wood rigged and masted and metal hulled ships steamed engine fumes burning and leaking charcoal tar and oil pumping, propellers pounding foreward or stern, or tug towed out into the water, on the tide and into the gusting sea-air.

Lined and moored haphazardly against a bustling key-side drifting large and lazy on the water, painted lead white, bitumen black and copper orange, indigo blue and silver yellow reflecting earth and the sea and the sky, glinting across the water.

Washed and weathered grey stone and redbrick built taverns and chandlers shops crammed into and embanked the cut, into cliff and stone wood lapped waterfront docks. At the walled gated archway entrance to a shipwrights yard a single sun dial, set over ship and sea. Set into the brickwork and braced onto solid earth foundation wall, stone carved, a single ship figured, guided in passage by the sun and moon, the fixed global position of the first seen lunar star, and of the northern, and southern most stars. In maelstrom thunderous lightning windstorm, mountainous seas, typhoon monsooning rain cloud, through earthquake and volcano, with time drifting precession tilted below, compassing metal magnetic lodestone rock, carved out in triumph over the equinox seasonal tides, otherwise overwhelming the Earth.

Taking-off cliff-top and sea-edge *breezing* through which they roamed and from which they breathed; at the Portside, cargoes from all parts of the globe. Unloaded with hundreds of hands, and bodies in tattered overall. Yelling to each other, in what appeared, in strange and foreign languages, to be utterances and curses. At and to each other and to the loads being handled and hauled, from the decks of the ships to the ground, loaded onto rows of pallets and onto carts and wagons. Large scaffoldings rolled on wheels, incessantly from key-side to vast warehouses. From warehouses, on to carts and wagons, carried to and from the countryside around,

towards and over a *vast* River-Bridge that now stood before them.

A magnificent Granite and Stone Pillared and twisted steel roped, wide spanning suspended over the shimmering river rolling wide and tidal towards the sea, lit up by seawall end blazing and turning lighthouse-beacon.

Lighting-up, beyond the field of even-time vision, over seas and distant ocean, to desert tropical island and coast. Where the sea lay mirror flat, below haze of mist and sea fog. Billowing *racing*-clouds; The Wind picked-up; The-Sun began to sink beyond the horizon. Glowing early evening pink and purple, as the first flames, dropped over the Ccean distance. Ringlets of icy high cirrus passed cleared over the clear Mountain-Tops, misted into a brazen sky, through mountain pass, past ice-capped towering peaks, toward pitched snow and ice-flow melting-edges.

Under embankment lamplights lit up with the gradually setting sun, towards yachting and boating marina, advertising river trips, Riverside Hotel, *leisure*-parks to wander through to restaurants, musical pantomime shows and theatre, clubs and alcohol and smoke-bars. More people spilled-out onto the paved terraces and roadways, leading down toward the public ways, bridged across the river, toward the main city center ahead.

On the opposite bank, on the largest hill above, a great and impressive colonnaded Capitol stood-out. Built scaffolded and platform lifted, upwards from below, the capped tower roofed, flagpole standard fluttering in the pleasant evening sea and river breeze. Towering over the scene an ancient bulging pregnant cupola; bulb-shaped onion steel and glass plastic-panelling box:

Planted-gardens and walled-foundations rooted open balcony floors, with soaring pyramidal phallic tower steepled minaret; the last of The-Sun *glinting*-off; a Golden-fired crescent-moon and single star at the nipple peaks of brick-built and volcanic-*ash* concrete-mixed and poured milky polychromatic dome; simmering, glowing like a sinking or rising sun, over the open atrium. The roof resting on marbled stone colonnaded portico arches.

Tension chained held brick piled outside walls, dressed with door and window wood lattice and frame, plant patterned tile ribboned around. Bestiary figures in sorrow and joy, around the gated doorways. Windows of stained colour panel, set in glass engraved, solemn and triumphant word and symbol.

The whole appeared from below as crumbling remains. Dilapidated ziggurat, sepulchral monument, over looking and over seeing a city, facing both toward the sinking orange sunlight, facing also the reflective pale yellow moon now rising.

The temple basilica, pantheon, castle royal, ancient vaulted mausoleum, or palace of justice, possibly once formal seat of government and rule, rising from times past, even to the lives of:

-The Present Day.

Now only guessed at, the monuments' use and prestige, style and concept apparently changed many times, over receding time, its current usage, historical:

- It is now a museum, a public library, concert hall and art gallery, shops of course...
-On: The Market-Place, now...

Name-plated in a consequent-language a passerby re-marked, noticing the visitors puzzled gazing look of interest. Opened palms and slightly hunched shoulders indicating readiness to receive, to continue. The Stranger continuing, responding to their unspoken question, with a smiling, pleased to help response:
- Otherwise a Necropolis, you might say ...they are all open to visit and see, the procession starts soon ...
- ... Thanks,
they replied, waving, in unison.
Smiling back in re-ciprocated *alliance*.
Acknowledging the intuition, the intervention shown to their enquiring look, the final reply. Moving off and away, smiling, just glancing at the retreating responding figure,
- Anytime!
At once, over The Capitol Hill, explosions, aerobic fireworks let off in overarching display, filling the sky.
The sound first heard at the beginning, a thudding, booming, roaring and sizzling, beating beats and rolls, marching drums and trumpets sounded, military, celebratory. Exhilarating, oversung with whistling fluted tune and deep rubbling trumpeting , as the expectant crowds gathered, to watch the colourfully flagged and lighted processional Parade.

Choirs-chanting, The Orchestra *quieted*, solo voice carefully expounding sounds and words, along with the reverent ringing of bells from The Capital Building, *soaring* country tune and sea shanty, and the a firing of galactic fireworks. A mingled presentation reproduction clothed Figure-Headed, in ceremony, made their way from The Capital Building: in en-tourage.

Singing along to hearty tune, brassy village band booming, tuneful strings lamenting, or jigging hysterically, chaotically, accompanied by whistling and heraldic trumpeting. Fiery cones lit and lined The Processional Way. From the top of The Capital Hill out-rider body-guard exited The Capital, bearing weapons of threat and protection, honour and social standing. Armed men, and seemingly haremed women, charioted at the head of The Cavalcade; only after following half froglike human, half scaly fish carrying bone daggered spear, shell shielded scallop bedded mermaid, and Throned Sea-Gods and Goddess'; *hairy* with dripping wrack, turned horn and trident fork, coiled shell held to the lips, calling and blasting the animalistic introduction.

To a following band of fur cloaked hunters, bundled rod and pitchfork, bow and arrow, branch armed and leaven forest green folk, children with flowers, basketed and scattered through the air, over the procession and down amongst the watching throng.

Next along, determined and with smiling faces, arms held aloft in salutation, fingers clasped to the heart, bayonet and blowpipe gun outstretched, to the obedient and submissive onlooker.

To the strength of mistrusting and contradictory diplomatic alliance. Forge fired sword and pistol, to resurrect, rebuild the aims of even more beneficent and vainglorious rulers. Bribed to the envy of rival actors, money thrown in the air, to be actually and *symbolically* destroyed. Acted out, through the ages, putting off any threat in absolute rule, the inevitable and finally *fatal*-error.

A Show Trial of men and women, and their offspring, of genius and brilliance, lost in the lust for power and glory. Spectacular influential flaunted opulence and indulgence, exaggerated insecure untrusting avarice. Sophisticated-pirate, *techno*-thief, cyber-crime and media whores cynical and manipulative machination, seeking public patronage, religious, political theatrical media patriotic and self-publicing platform.

For: Power: given out to protective fall guy, and leering girl, to secure the succession. The-Dynasty, the place into the history book, the ancestral tree, the road, branching-off. The gaining of power, to change, to hold onto, overwhelmingly not to lose. To take over the vacant crown, the unoccupied niche, the empire. Expropriating anything, and everything, in the path of limitless desire. Banqueting and bathing, carried on glorious float, down the hillside. Desperate to show off a semblance of public and popular support. Feigning and fawning, forced and false-Hero *worshipping*.

Sycophantic-selfish entourage drawing the crowd into scenes by association, by adulation, of fear in bloodbath, and ultimate destruction. Taking place at a removed behest, havering and handwringing. Through fixed election, at the waving parade. Throngs in splendid attire and common dress, through the times, descended.

One onlooker ventured,

- How the mighty have fallen!

Another:

-How they rise again!

-Why is there War?

-Why is there peace?!

-Both a common Other-power to keep us in awe!

-There but for Fortune!

The final stand arrived drawn forward: A Warrior, and Arch-*Angel* of Peace; *fountaining* showered over rainbow spray of water cannon, smoke poured like teargas, blasts of deafening noise and electric pulses of laser light showing beams, flashed over the fountaining water wall reflected, of over surrounding buildings. Along the rivers and seas lapping, and into The Sky, over the gathered onlooking and cheering and screaming crowd, intimidating as well as *Triumphant!* a dull beaten gong chimed and the bright caste bell from The Capitol peak-broke into triumphant cracked crackling peal. Over the final lightning and fireworks din, as the parade vanished from sight, then a single bell-tolled…three-times, and ended, echoing across valley and hillside Mountain beyond The-Capital.

As drum-beats and thunder-claps continued to echo across the distant reaches, into the night sky, they seemed to rend the skies, shattering light scattered over gathering and silencing parted-clouded, deep starlit reflective darkness, with neither Sun, nor Moon. As All *quieted* gradually into solemn and enveloping evening's Empire; *dampening* and sprayed clear water; through the glittering light heated parade, the *dreamlike* unreal HuMan-Wo-Man Statue; of The Peaceful Warrior, the *reluctant*-warriors descended finally and out of view.

The Parade over, families with young children and old folk no longer able to keep up the pace broke-off, to wander along the riverside promenade. Along toward the lighthouse pier, with restaurant and party boat trailing back towards the town, through linear river park and pleasure garden, streets winding up through the old town and Harbour Hills.

With applause petering out, with due warnings and exultations, the younger and fitter, headed over the near proximate bridge, and inward. Ready for action. As if on migration, to escape the past. For fresh-experience, determined and resolute. Stopping to peer over the *precipitous*-bridge; below, where lighted boat's engines chugged and yacht wind-sailed. Turning to look back, along the constructed gridded canal and causeway, curving over to the now other brink, from the pitch, overarching river prominence. Looking back towards the marshland harbour and town, the village dotted fields and hillsides stretching to the Mountain peaks.

Along the precipitous-valley below, the sparkling lake, sea and wide river, looking once more along the road they had trod that day, leading to and towards the narrow rustic river bridge in the far-distance.

Moonlight, cutting through the darkening eventide fields, leading upwards toward the overhanging-Precipice, from which they had at first descended. Stars sparkling as *flickering*-lights flamed through windows. Along the still busy thoroughfares, gazing back over the rooftop buildings, houses and workshops, back along roads and paths and tracks, through forest and field, village harbour port town, and city, they had walked. Disappearing into the dusk, amongst outlaying villages and hamlets, stately villa's and castle-Houses, Landed-Estates in sweeping-grounds, reached along winding tracks and paths, through remaining forest and openland.

Rows of dwellings, in progressive crammed in and cramped size and separation, below clearings in ever narrowing terraced steppe. The bustling provincial suburb, wholesale industrial operation of urban life, leading up to, and now crossing, the ornate badge bedecked bridge, busy with carts, vans and trucks. Carriageways and riverside gardens lined the riverbanks, on either side, further inward toward boulevard percolated with movement, from bustling side street crossings and interchanges, through the grand buildings of the shimmering central city, that lay ahead. From the village and town, river and solemn flaunted bridge, leading into the dazzling city, towering before them. The riverside walks gradually faded, as others moved away into the evening. Together they crossed the built river isthmus, into a wide avenue stretching as stretchered before them. There were even more people than before.

As if they were drawn, brooking and streaming, into a population vacuum, taking in tides of humanity. Each as just one, with a held onto, immediate-proximity, of self, in a Crowd.

They brushed by and crossed in front of the hustle and bustle of strangers, who ignored them *completely;* or looked at them, passed by without greeting, and walked on ahead. Passers-by busy with trade, business and Social-*expedition*. Returning their tentative greetings, and if not ignoring them spoke to them and returned answers to questions they asked, or comments they made. Moved past and in front of them, as they inspected them, and they became startlingly aware of themselves. Their safety, as Only part of their immediate and swarming surroundings, not to get *hopelessly* lost:

- Where are we now?,

One of the visitors asked.

- The Greatest City on Earth!

-When?

A passing-strangers' reply:

- The Land of Opportunity! That's Everywhere!

Another walking in the other direction mocked.

- … For some!

Another retorted, completing the shared joke, and moved on.

In and out of doorways, shopkeepers, customers and browsers, artisans, engineers and mechanics, entrepreneurs and technocrats, with monied expertise changing and exchanging, lending and safe depositing, through legal and commercial advisors, scrivener and notary, script and letter writers offices. Papers stacked in bundles on shelves and stored, filed and racked in cupboards.

Cloth stitched parchment, portfolio ordered and tied with coloured ribbon, sealed with wax, and encased in leather, stamp rolled and printed out, in oily black and blue dried ink, on mulched wood bark and leaf fibre cut and pasted paper bound in hard and soft covers, declaring their contents to the literate.

Passed leisurely Gymnasia, for active and artistically accomplished performance, described on marble tiling. Taking the physical body to extreme tests of endurance, stamina and dexterous merit and self-attainment.

In recentring of self, lost in concentration and meditation, or in the challenge of argument, debated in café bar, or wrestling and boxed pummeling of another in the ring. Cool pool, for swimming races, and idle relaxation, Mineral spa and bathhouse, to laze-in, cold shower-in, washed and massaged in preparation and partaking, of intimacy.

Plunging-out from hot steam bath, toweled and cleansed, massaged and ready to face up to The-World again.! More People and Buildings…as they walked a little further along a torch and sparkling lamp lit evening pavement. Railing and walled, zoned and fortified residential and office areas, and shop windows displaying wanted and tempting wares, affordable or unaffordable price specified, number and fraction worked out and listed; or left blank, perhaps for barter, haggling or no limit.

Passing before perpendicular parallel buildings and other squared off, large seemingly public, but guarded and *protected*-buildings. Police posts and palace of justice, secular centers of administration and accounting, overseen by shadowy interior and stark-frontispiece. Buildings high and daunting, threatening, intimidating, with entrances and decoration, or lack of, toward simple Earthly and supreme extra-terrestrial confluence and seeming attainment. They passed a barred windowed stone courthouse and jail lock up shed. A notice signed, pinned over the prison cell gate, enscribed 'The Cage', and read:

       -For miscreants, misfits and wrongdoers.

       -Repentance, prayer and charity, remove the evil of his decree…

-Beware of the Dog!

-Waiting for Joe

And another, where someone had scrawled,

-Only God may Judge.

And one of the visitors commented,

-Well, how come they, mere humans, judge, then? Do they think they are God?

-Why wait for judgment day, when heaven and hell can be wrought right here, right now?

-At times different and contrary viewpoint? Man worships gods, but man worships only man. We consider ourselves, willing and able, benevolent, omnipotent, Godlike … Not just willing or able, or objectively legalistic, like a spiritual giving up? Willing and not able; not willing but able, what's the difference. Maybe God is just a judge. Justly watching, and wondering? Just like us …

- … so what's the point of God?

- Humans are the most fallible judges, justice is made up of more human parts than any other system. We think we are gods, or doing gods will, so maybe, therefore we are?!

-Just how many just, or unjust, gods are there?!

-Just how many there are? We are what we eat, and what we eat is just what we

started with.

-And what we think about what we started with, our
conscience…

-Do the right thing…Do the wrong thing .,.

-… and caput.

-Who says?!

And drawing a finger across the throat, looking up at the decorated
ugly spouting gargoyles:

-Sex and death.

Ma-liciously ma-lingering *luscious-ly*:

-From Paradise to Slaughterhouse!

-Well God Help Us then!

-To Judge is only to *demonise.*

-What Good, is Good?

-What Evil, is Evil?

On the Crest of a Wave: white whale and grey blue shark, surface finned, and peaked overclouded mountain top. With The Stormcloud Army-billowing a Great Ship sailing across The Universal Sky. Riderless galloping wild horses, elephants in circus ring, flanked by running crazed, snarling dogs. Lion tamer, ringmaster! A tied snarling dog barred the way inside, presaging terror. Menacing, a cold stony silence, but for occasional wimpering cries, calls and pleadings. A set of vilefying stocks and shackles, a public whipping post, torture chamber, let out onto Execution-Wall. The tapping of a sentry guards pencil bored, inside the open posted gatehouse, The Barricade was as far as The Visitors could see, or go. Fear; of losing authority, dutiful inquisition, withholding information, the rituals of denial, of torture and death. As the sign of being at One. Guilt, repentance, and conformity. Tamed unicorn, the *fierce*, free and innocent lioness, the scales of balance, held by the sword, by the angel of glory, and the angel of fear. They could have if they wished enter an imposing courtroom, presided by a judge. At each side representatives of the people, the police, and of the church. To swear allegiance, an oath, a promise, a belief, couched in the truth, true justice, beauty and love. The more easily disbelieved the more power over and of the *believers*.

On the wall a list of crimes against society, sins against heaven: Murder, rape and pillage. In the first, second and third degrees. Crime of passion, manslaughter, rape or sexual assault, infanticide (including abortion). Felony and grand felony, larceny, arson, and conspiracy.

Incitement, perjury, insult and slander. Blasphemy, and common
assault.

The list accompanied by scenarios' against which evidence and
prosecution

Seeking *punishment* of guilt and compensation to be brought.

A bedraggled group of shackled prisoners, listening to the testimony
against them, arguing or having argued the case, for their innocence,
or mitigation.

From the stalls, family and friends, huddled, begged for justice, or
for mercy.

From the tables and chairs, and front bench, judgment to be made.

In the case described, the flash of a knife in the dark, the firing off of
a gun.

Removing the harmless knife on its own from its holder, laying it on
the table:

> -It takes a deliberate act to turn a simple kitchen knife,
> into a murder weapon
> -They made me do
> -But it was your decision, your personal allegiance, group
> identity, commitment,

you who wore the mask of ordinary innocence, to cover your Evil
Act! Diminished responsibility within the group, making the
commitment, not wanting to be seen to back down, wanting even to
be found out, so the glory and the shame could become one? Yes
there is group psychology at work.

-But within that, there is the cowardice of individual responsibility. Under threat

perhaps, to friend or family, what would you do?

A wound, a bullet buried in the back of the head, of a stabbed and robbed victim.

Now as much on trial as anyone The Judge summed-up:

- Was it accident, or deliberate violence? Had the killing, saved the lives of many others, from the direct or indirect impersonal exploitation by the rich, responsibility for this unhappiness. Was this a selfless emotional act of pity, or revenge for others sake? Accidental even, mistaken, or deliberate? Who pulled the trigger, what individual? What collective responsibility? The Visiting-Group were split, split-Jury of Masters and Mistresses:

- Had it been a selfish act of deliberate and immediate *self-defence*; or an *unjustified* act of unprovoked robbery and brutality. Had the murderer, or murderers, been insane, and therefore not directly responsible? Or had they just been Hopeless Social Desperados? Does this mitigate, or worsen The Act? Was The Action, The Event, done out of *pardonable*- Reflex…

-Rather than un-pardonable Rational-deliberation? Did this mitigate or worsen the act for those of the victims family that were left to resent, to hate, even to forgive? For their own, and for the victims sake? Is there a reasonable doubt?

The Jury, The Visitors were out.

They had a brief moment to consider and decide. To press a button that would convict or release, that would free, or render shut away. In the punishing regime of the prison courtyard; or in a hospital prison for the insane; or death by simple immediate, or drawn out and cruel means:

-...Out of Harm's Way, no-longer...

- A menace...

-Except as a *warning* to others.

-Perhaps as a role-model!

With the possibility of pleaded innocence, or mitigation, remaining, hanging, over.

-...You take a view. Then you decide.

The Judge continued later, after the verdict was read-out:

-Innocent,,,

-Until proven guilty...beyond *reasonable*

doubt...unemotional...death.

-Victim...over-rules...

-The wisdom of repugnance, aversion, indignation, emotional response...

-The longer you take, the more the reason takes over, compounds, *confuses*...

-What if there is more evidence unheard? What if there is an Unfairness, a Miscarriage of Justice?

-...What about The Victim?

-What about The-Judge? Is it the Revenge of the *innocent*?

-Or the safety of the remainder?

-What about ..?...

-Is there a Natural-Justice?

-Simply a Law of The Jungle? For food. Emotionless..

-Children born of Nature ...

-... love-child, born of fateful, accidental even, destiny?

-And Time. Everyday we make and have to accept or deny moral decisions. Now, you must decide. Do you release the button, or press it? Which button do you push? Switch relay. Do you see the victim, or the accused. Or do you close your eyes?

The decision made.

-Now you must live with yourself.

-Allow the room, the chance, to take on the next.

-Game!

As the next case was about to commence, The Accused left the dock, to a fate, rung up on the list. Taken from the collected, objective and anonymous decision made. Outside of the Everyday World. Almost, like a God. Safe and Secure. All betsThe people, the peoples representatives. Provenders of justice. The visitors moved off to allow another case, another group to decide. Perhaps differently. They moved along, down stone steps, along a paved path, within garden square, soldiered garrison and security guarded-*blank:* Administration-Block.

Amongst the crescent and grid-planned City moving westwards with the sinking Sun; further in towards the City Center, apparently opening out the street-corners became sharper-angled; where Boulevard and narrow-roads and alleyways spun-off in radial-spoke and turn, closing towards The Center. Older and *ancient* buildings, remains of established Monastery-College and Secular-University, walled and gated oasis of calm and reverence. Places of tutelage, learning and rectitude, study seemingly objectively removed, subjected to the rigours of religious, and political confirmation. Resistant to change.

Distracted by the prestige and careers established within and without. In socially-bonding perspicuity and perspective, led by the maintenance of shared values, and risk of academic, religious and political-exile.

In want of nothing else, without need of anything else, but food and drink and shelter; and protection, to study and philosophise, about Everything-Else. Power. Everything...

Spun-into homely wise pedantry, for consumption and discussion of the masses, cohorted and cohered, beyond the emboldened ivory bedecked tower, modern brick and glass buildings for Engineers and Scientists, Machine-shops and Laboratories. Further along, past grand shops and stores, wide streets leading inwards, towards an open round plaza, in which the touring visitors now found themselves.

Within an enclave, that may have once been an Ancient-Village or Town-Square, originated anew in praise of an earlier conquest, subsequently taken and retaken, renamed and decored, marked out as a suitable stopping place. Stuccoed stone and marbled monuments stood, in walled and dappled white and grey sanctorum, on the façade of imposing frontage of commercial and financial exchange. City-Hall, Church, Theatre, and Grand Opera House, taking up the whole of one side. A frontispiece of shops and covered market stalls, over which a monumental mechanical time piece chimed; to indicate a further fraction of the turning dial. With calendrical and seasonal reference: of seven-sister stars, set around a harvest bale, and horned bull, in cowfield. The Sun's face moving across the field-full Solar and Lunar Planetary Solar-System:

    -Astrolabe.

Across a sky chasing a crescent to full-Moon
With its seemingly fixed Solar-Star,
Moved around a passive central spindled and ratcheted rotating: Tellurian.
Geared solar and lunar marinal chronometric cycles, from some roughly specific point, date timing the circum-navigations of - passage.
On a plaque with runic alphabetic, to be secretly divined, or pictographic fresco image relief, hieroglyphic and cuneiform tablet carvings, marking out quantified-dates, names and honorarium. Description of name and year and event, each building facade marked out around the square, from another.

Ancient and modern stone and granite and marble images, idealized mythological and naturalised figure, timid animal and monstrous creature in histrionic chippings and mouldings. Full length standing statues, of chiefs, kings and queens, emperors and empresses, princes and princesses, presidents and prime ministers, generals of armies of empire, state and religious leaders, all powerful, for their own, and others vanity, and record, stories of love and war. In the centre of the piazza, a large and daunting statue entitled and Guide-directed as spoken:

-The Warrior and Archangel of Peace.

Over spectacular, soaring and tumbling droplets, on rippling pooled fountain, dominating the square. Wagons and carts continued winding over the bridge, along the boulevard, carried on through narrow alleyways. Into stone paved and tiled courtyards, along the carriageways and alleyways from the bridge side, more carts trundled in, and began unloading.

All around the square, overflowing loaded carts brought in from the woods and fields, workshops and warehouse and portside. From up river and over the ocean, brought in from near and far, a festive carnival market scene took over, stalls and regalia strung up. Amongst the hoardings and pillars, amongst the gating arches, colourful bunting, balloons and streamers the visitors moved on into a now crowded market square. Where wares stood in teetering stacks, and hung up, in embellishment, piled high on carts and trailers.

In every available corner, the sale of food and drink, cloths and clothing materials, foodstuffs and household goods, children's toys and ornamental novelty took over.

On display stalls festooned heads of maize, cereal grasses and pulses, pea beans and peppers, heads of maize, root and leaf vegetables and fruits, with winesacks and beer barrels. Flat and round breads, stick bread and doughnuts, pancakes and sweetbread and flavoured cakes. Sacks of wheat, potatoes and corn flour, paddy wild grasses, long and short grain rice and manufactured flour pasta. Wood and charcoals, and oil in sealed drums.

The sale of fresh and jarred, bottled and tinned and wrapped, foodstuffs preserved in starched aspic and sour acid vinegar pickling jars, preserving salt and sugar treacle syrup and honey.

Live-caged, hanging, cured and freshly butchered meats, scaled ice packed filleted and shell-fish.

Carrying containers, holding and storing, water and fatty milk, butter and cheese and sweet and sour yoghurts, fruit squashes and fermented-crop. All for immediate, or later consumption. Crated and set out, bought and wrapped in terracota, ceramic and porcelain glassware crockery, with cutlery haft knife, fork and spoon set, pots and pans, plates and dishes, for cooking, and for drinking and eating-from. The visitors mixed with village, town and city folk, dressed in fancy clothes and drab outfits, wearing and purchasing cloth, to cut out themselves, and sew.

Woven flax linen, rough jute hessian, woven cotton and silk threads, damask fabric embroidered, wave lined and circular pattern, worked and brushed wool. Stranded, twisted and twilled threads, cleansed and fabricated skins and hides, covering closeting cloths and curtains.

On rickety-stalls and stands, on wheeled temporary tables and platform stage, spoken pleadings, diatribe and printed leaflet handed out. Tableaux theatrical and re-enacted historical mythology, personal, comical and tragic deeds, satirically and mordantally played around them. Fairground dances and acrobatics, without safety net, entertainers and hawkers, heckling and chuckling crowds at InnHouse and Comedia del Arte: Three friends and crossed lovers, wicked witch/kind old women wine loving cobbler peddlar woodman carpenter silkweaver puppeteer:

-Pierrot *grinning, bashful sad clownfacing indecision…*

-Quasar ringing star-crossed lovers on screen…

-She the East risen bright new star, garish all seeing-Sun…

-She teaches the-Sun to burn *bright*!

-But He, to the morrow, the sinking moon…

-A comet defying the stars…

-Tragically in love with another, it seems, boy or girl, chased away by The Sun and its' servant The-Moon…

- Columbine, she loves *rogue*-lover Harlequin…

-Her Father Cassander's servant…

-Chasing Leader King Heracles of the Hearthlings…and…

-She with furious wizard devilish chased to Hell, from
Heaven on Earth meets with…

-Dwarf-King goats hooves red-bearded Elven hirsute: astute
wily living sentient divine or semi-divine herders, hunters with horse
and wolfhound, initiates in a warrior band, *ghosts* on the back of
Bulls as six and eight-legged Beasts in Nether-World Battle!
Skirmishing Scaramouche clown/gallant friend beaten by the forces
that be for boasting and cowardice; never-mind successful hunted
feast and gifts, returning back-to:

-EarthCentre!
Un-realised tragedy only comedy yet derision hurts. If You prick Me
I bleed. Punch, to th-chin, nose, hat. Professor's swizzle stick
struggle with Supernatural-Law (policeman, clown monkey,
crocodile, doctor, himself as ghost, hangman executioner, Pretty
Polly screeching bird, blindman beggar) and Judy (and baby), ill-
treats wife children and animals and police are after him; he still
expects a happy ending, yet tragic still. Victim of his/her own cruelty
and daring (killings, a washer women/old man peddler for clothes,
garmented to court).
Cassander is *skewered* with Own-sword by the *wraithlike*-ghost
luring to a Wedding-Feast and Party. Old shepherd old-news of
Queen C's tricked into betrayal with The Dwarf-King (searching for
the-Servant), disappeared into rocks, chained at The Sea.
All *alighting* now We! Into-*dust* of Warrior and Lover's otherwise
eternal-wanderings…

Wraith-like *Ghost-survivors* with useless gifts, or hunting-dog or burden of guilt, shame, anger, fear, without alighting into the *lighted*-World: rid of these experiences and emotions: Fairground rides, dancing and acrobatic clowning troupes, beauty pageant and strong man competition.

Everyone's attention turned to the pleasure and enjoining of others, and the sale and exchange of everything. Amongst the Traders, exchanging gold sun and silver moon marked pieces, signed printed notes, handed back and forth with the food and goods and artifacts. The Visitors queued and exchanged the tokens placed in their pockets, and in bags distributed in the course of their journey, purchased packaged and wrapped foods and goods, as they mixed and mingled. Families and groups of young people running through, young children being carried or holding hands tight for safety.

Old-*folk* holding onto arms, and walking with supporting sticks and crutches, grouped together, huddled and chatting. Outside tavern and eating house, young men, hanging around, watching, chasing with their eyes, girls bunched in a corner, or briskly walking along, arm in arm together. Couples *passionately* embracing, hanging onto each other. Giving valuable and valued gifts of food and trinket, bought and received. Prerequisite to bonding, the value dependent on value given. The need of the receiver to receive, for commitment. Daffodils and diamonds, for the lover, for the wife, from the husband. Rare rose and cornflower, glinting onyx pearl, gold and silk cornelian. In the swarming microbial mass, there was gregarious song and laughter, argument and anger, from the various places where people lived, and from where trade took place, and where life was lived. Family groups, the old and young, single solitary unattached, at the edge of groups, of girls and boys, laughing and chatting, flirting with flashing sparkling eyes and actions. Competitively between and amongst themselves, defiant and dismissive, shuffling a newly dealt pack of internal sensations. The Build-Up, and sudden outbreak of terrifying, life threatening injurious shameless and shameful drunken violence. Mock fighting, wrestling, jabbing and poking with controlled sudden violence, running and chasing with the pack. Instigating, starting a fight. Enormous risk and chance taken, for the chance, to be conceived, to eventually conceive, and bring up, out of the underlying tension, to have another brought up, to be brought up in the image of other.

The fight getting serious. Girls squabbling, in fighting and watching, seeing who would win out in the verbal and physical joust. Who would step in and take over, crank the wind up, or loking, laughing, calming down. Who was reliable, kind and strong, to be serious about life, as well as light hearted and funny. To be gifted, of the emotional as well as physical care, of the next generation. Not wanting to get the selection too wrong. Not wanting to let any opportunity go by. Girls and boys, flirting and showing themselves off, in practice, just in case. As if this was right, the right time, the right one, this time. To be nurtured, for the fantastic future, for the next generation.

Looking around across the market square, The Visitors were disappeared into the crowd.As the crowds became more dense, there was hardly room to move. People pushed and pulled against each other. Yelled wisecracks, and minor arguments ensued, all and each, bargaining, arguing in regulated manner.

The toss of the coin, for fair chance and exchange. Not to be cheated, not to be seen to be unfair, not to be caught.

At each stall and stand, an excited bargaining, to satisfy-each.

Pick-pockets and thieves flourished, and what appeared to be criminal gang marauded, thieving, robbing, and running, shouted pleadings after. Gambling, for thrills and spills, victim and victor, victim and villain, for the richer to get richer, and the poor to get richer. For the one to survive, for other to lose house and home, and family. The House always Wins! Gamblers, in the lottery of life. With outrageous-odds against, filling The Banker, Book-maker and toting with *glee*.

The Chance for Glory: the spilling of blood, the cause of poverty, affecting vast and few. Not far between the commonwealth, the borders clearly drawn. Wandering entertainers. Fire swallowing, consuming The Sun. At stalls, pleasant exchange and agreeable clap of hands, supplanted by angry allegation of confidence trickery, accusation and argument broke out:

- What are you talking about?

-What Language is that because it's not one I recognize!

- I can tell what you mean, just by the look on your face, the way your standing ...!

Unclenching the fists,

-Wolf-child!

- It's just an organised extortion racket!

- Pirate!

- Robber! Gangster!

- Imposter!

-Trickster!!

Magistrates and Arbiters of The Peace: tax-collectors for the social security and protection walk amongst Us.

Allowing and overlooking certain infringements for the maintaining of livelihoods. That may otherwise threaten the status quo in lack of livlihood, in poverty, in potentially riotous assembly and uprising. Crime more deadly, more subversive, more overwhelming, less easy to ignore, with more cruelty and violence than could be tolerated, without response in kind.

On a square street corner, a group stood around cursing and discussing loudly.

Shuffling together, some crouching on the pavement. Arguing still, as all life, all existence, depended on the roll of the four times six-sided dice, the amount resting on the spin of a coin, the critical number placed. Shouting and laughing, gesticulating to each other, and into the air:

> - OK! My Win! Are You even playing?!

> - All or nothing! I'll kill you next time!

Expectantly watching the decorated marked card sharks three card trick. Missing again the sleight of hand. The illusion, focusing on the winning card, that turns out to be the losing one. To win at any cost, at any others expense.

Others holding their hands out in despair, of trickery, with looks and begging pleas. Suspicious, unsure, the visitors looked at each other, and laughed a puzzled, wondering kind of laugh. Watching and waiting, for something else to happen.

From: The Market Square: vantage point, onto: The street(s) below, it seemed more arguments raged.

Shoutings out, supporting this or that, selling this or that. For want and need. In separate niche markets, selling sunshades in the sun, umbrellas in the rain, religious and political, economic and academic points, made and argued with.

While, down roads, not too distant, towards river bridged boulevard, dipping over and across downtown. Across the marshes and through village and hamlet fields, distant hordes of invading martialled troops appeared. Led by one in bright red, blue and white striped cloak, marching battle-hungry, and desperate from over The Borderlines.

What seemed like a Frontier Dispute, became a sudden outbreak of violence within.

A riot bubbling though and erupting, cutting through the tension within the enclave, the safe boundaries between people torn down. The gentle and continued exercise of self and other in immediate personal and territorial space, smashed through. Erased, split into faction, schism, arguing dissent, separating out division.

It was unclear, at first, what for. The burning of fields below, perhaps to clear and replenish the harvested ground. Unclear if the flanking skirmishes being fought below were exaggerated inter family feuding, was internal revolt, civil war, a roughshod rising up of some popularised replacing, displacing of some perceived belief, some idealised hierarchy from within.

Creating chaos, high risk strategy, in order to assert and re-engineer social-control. The seeming spilling of consanguineous blood, to the honouring of some felt only ever tacit-agreement.

To destroy, in order to survive. To continue together, in alliance, in comradeship. For some kind of bravado survival, out of control, through conquest, in the imagination, to impress. To suspect the actions and machinations of others.

The necessity to continue, to mix into the fray, into the fury, rippling through, the shockwaves locked on, to the iconic city center above, and below. War(s) of Foreign Invasion, decimating pillage or controlled colonization, from fields, battalions marched, ahead of them horses fiercely ridden, towards The Bridge, and The-City Center.

Encampments rapidly set up across the whole of the plains they had passed through earlier, flag tented, banner standard carried, troops ranged and infested over the hills.

Amongst farms and fields, orchard and vineyards taken, around the remains of the village walls below, steadily encroaching, along the riverway, toward the castellated fortified hill. Stealing crops and livestock, ransacking and looting as they went, the portable spoils ceremoniously and unceremoniously gifted. Taken, and the rest destroyed, to no other, assaulted and razed to the ground. Ambushed troops, dead sacrificial prisoner and hostage, slave taking raiding parties could be seen, set out and returning with rustled horses and sheep, captive recruited and allianced troops, forced to fight for their freedom and their lives.

The continuation of Familial-Homeland; the protection of this principle or that, this rule or that. Increasing battalions in numbers swarming the plains, overrunning farms and through the village, onward toward The Capitol and City-Bridge. Villagers and people from the fields, fleeing in advance, carrying what they could.

Staked out tribal parceled out land. Demolished in hit and run raids and skirmishes, striking with surprise and terror from dense foggy forest edge, escaping alongside snaking river, toward the sealine of the seemingly encircling-Ocean: The Edge of The World.

Minor irritations, demands, dependences, begging pleas and claims, polite requests, ignored, pointless, or dealt with abruptly, quashed in the ensuing melee. In the marketplace, people grabbing what they could, running, dragging children and goods with them. As much as they could, dropping and leaving to fate. The next-meal, the next roof over their head, the next chance at survival. For them and their families, in the here and now, risking everything for the immediate and perceived necessity of escape, of honour and glory.
An echoing voice heard over trumpeting rally, over the mayhem below, orders given out, heard above the rising storm:

    -Live by the Sword, and Die by The Sword!!

    -Victory or death!

    -Death or Glory!

    -Armed or Unarmed!

    -No surrender!!

-Surrender!!

-Live and let Die!

-Live by The Book! The Word!

-Live to *let*-Live!

-Die to let-live!

-Payback!

-What for?!

-Time!

Smouldering, burning huts and houses, unclear now, if burnt earth
from invaded or invaders, from defenders, collaborators, for sheer
demonstration, leaving nothing of value behind.
Toward The City carts and vehicles lined and blocked the roads out,
as The Insurgent-Armies moved along and through.
The Defenders and Countryside Populations *melted-away*…to
shelter, taking up positions behind ancient castellated walled fort,
along the hillside rugged rocky vantage.
Delaying, harrying, holding the last road block checkpoint, at the
        bridged-entrance to The
City.

From the hill and fields and forests, refugees fleeing over the bridge, into the streets and courtyards below, to escape the rushing fear and threat of violence, cutting through the air. Carrying out small scale defensive assaults on the way, retreating back to The City. Along the roads, the insurgents, and the fleeing defenders, moving closer. From over the distant plains, close knit phalanx, platoon and legion, regiment and brigade, marching over and through, taking everything in their path. Threatened and intimidated, intimidating and threatening, in advance, and retreat. Beyond, into the edges of the fenced and embattled clearings and foothills, people running, evacuating, and leaving behind, with little thought, of hope or chance of return held onto. Attacked, invaded, overtaken, colonized, the taking of looted land, livestock stolen, driven, the death or servitude of people by force.

Territorial-rights seized territory; as a block against some greater fear, some greater enemy.

Embattled in destruction and death, for survival and continuation into the present. Infantry appeared suddenly from side-streets, charged, whooping loudly, wielding long handled swords and staves, slashing at the air, and at people below.

Unseen in their advance, or in retreat changed even from the plains folk, farmers and fieldworkers, gentle and rowdy village and townsfolk, soldiers and city people, they mingled with.

In The Market-Place, people came running out of buildings, shops and houses, or bolted
themselves inside. Barricading the doors and windows, stalls abandoned to The Invaders.

Men, women and children fled, were plucked up or chopped-down, as the young soldiers, led on by men on horseback, rampaged. From The City and Castle clifftop. Embattlement's arrows flew down, like a stream of tracer fire, in one direction unfaltering, onto The Invading Horde.From beyond the crowded marketplace, a pounding and splashing, over the fields, across the breakwater and marshes, and along the river banks. From beyond the bridge, saddled and stirruped horses came, fiercely ridden. An onlooking visitor remarked to another, taking flashed scenes pictured, burnt into their consciousness One of the Observers *shouted* over the din:

   - Sticks and stones may break my bones...*laughing*, and as suddenly as this reminder of the protective and temporal nature of their visit was uttered, death and destruction was visited upon and in and of the scene.

Alongside them, Horses and Riders pounded, towards and into the marketplace, in terrifying display. Charging through, wielding fearsome weaponry, soldiers, body-armoured and breastplated, fought hand to hand with bayonet and gun, in the Town-City Square.

Banners held aloft, bearing contesting dynastic images, coiled snake, snapping stabbing scorpion, clawing snarling dog, griffin rampant lion and swooping eagle, flying tigress and fearsome dragon. Chasing fiery pearl, glittering-Gold. *Silver*-horses, clashing antlers, crossed and crowned swords, a rising or sinking Sun, full and eclipsed crescent-Moon,full-darkened Gunpowder-Moon; in-Confederacy row and star stripes and circles emblazoned amongst flashes of colour. In flame and freshly bloodied ground, beneath darkening nightime Sky. As if spectating, yet immediately trying to tell which side they might be on, The Visitors victors or victimized conquerors or conquered, invaders or invaded, they, We, had to decide. To Run and Hide, with instinctive self-protecting and *protection* of others…Other. Cast into the brooding anger and frustration, felt jealousy and revenge, felt and exploded into panicked shouting:

- Whose side are you on anyway?!

Trying to identify the enemy, the threat. To identify family and friend in the crowd. In the melee easily ignored, lost, or felled. Each treated each other like a breed apart, even old friends and neighbours, the unbred and ill bred, it seemed, of the *supposed-*Enemy:

- The Survival of The-Fittest!
- Decided by the Fittest!
-In-Advance…

Advanced-Guard checking all-around, moving-off…

Back-turned on the unfolding atrocity, looking back, checking forward, and then fleeing, in concentrated seeking of shelter and safety, from the intense battle engaged. Shields, decorated, clattered on swords, unsheathed and lashing. Flashed metal blades slashed through the air. Stabbing pains felt, yet unfelt in the adrenaline fed fear and panic. From a severed limb, dark curdling blood spurted from a glancing-blow. From unprotected bodies, silver glistening and unctuous innards fell. From a sideways swipe, a body was sliced open, gushed out, with only shocked staring eyes, head rolled amongst bodies, fallen to the ground, as yet another was severed through.

Dis-em-boweled: shattered apart, over the ground, paving floors and against brick and stone piled-walls. Body parts strewn, spiked, and hung onto erected poles and gatepost, for all to see. Limbs left to stumble over, ripped muscle tendon and jutting splintered white bone, still oozing in pool of blood. Along the boulevard, piles of corpses, beginning even now to smell of rotting flesh, thrown over the bridge parapet, dead and drowned. Like the vermin left to fed from them, floated and polluted the river, with their waste. Shocked and frightened cries and yells echoed throughout the terrible slaughter, trapped beneath the cavernous and cadaverous, fire and smoke *fume*-filled sky.

It became impossible to tell who was who, and whose side they might be on. Who were enemies, and who were allies. From each side they came, slaughtering, herding and carrying off. The old and decrepit, those no longer capable of escape or fighting back, sheltered cowering. The sacrificed military aged young men and child bearing women, lost in ritualistic slaughter and atrocity. The Young risking-All, in the interregnum, with no real-Power to stop it. War! For the vainglory of continuation, of personal and tribal, *fundamental* Terrorist-territorial imperative given.

As their chances seemed to run out, until only apparently with a lifes' own preserving interest and intent, there would be only One, or none left, for anyone else to kill.

Denying, disallowing, the chance to continue, like some awful game, the last to remain the winner.

Frightened and suddenly each alone, they looked up into the sky against the *set*-Sun,

disappeared and consumed into the outer-distance. Siege worked ditch-and-wall mound-fortification, machines racked-up and projected burning-fireballs into the midst of The City, besieged and attacked.

The deadlock broken, along The Castle and cliff tops, more Warriors arraigned, swinging chain handled mace and pointed sworded-blade. Heads crushed and cracked open bodies fallen trodden into the ground:

      -War *legitimized*-by…

      -Or not…

Get away with it demonstrate to other clashing armour-plating, *terrifying*-Trumpets siren- sounded, clarion-called walls of as if cross-bow flung virtual indiscriminate points rained through the air. Another tirade, in quick succession, poured down, on the invaders from the fields, burning oil spilled over the ramparts, setting the wooden houses of the old town, on fire.

Out at sea, against the distant horizon and flat *glassy* calm-sea Galleon siren-calling, A Great Fleet appeared, flagships bearing cannon, heading towards The City Port. Cloud armies, from the seaward-side billowing emblem bannered nearer, and from the deck, cannon flamed, boomed and searing projectiles, crashed. Thudding in the water, and against: The-City-Walls.

Closer volley of shot and shell, bombarding the enclosed City from Abroad. Ambushed and besieged, bomb-shelled with overwhelming force. Pounded and pierced the seaward perimeter defenses of the city, and then quelled. Unclear if banners of this side or that, rescue, or further assault. Civil protection, or war, of even more remote invader, or closer to Home.

At the demolished bridged entrance to The City, pontoon slung across, over which none could cross or depart without leave. Suspended on steel girder and rope, lead pointed toward the avenue, the marketplace square, and the hilltop enthroned castellated-Capital.

The Visitors watched on, frozen in place, at the market place raised kerbstep. From vantage point looking down over the river, over town roofs and village fields. Ablaze, the distant lands, the buildings aflame, the nearest ripped through with incendiary device. As the walls onto the marketplace were taken, the city seemed to explode, bodies fell out of the sky, someone shouted,

- This way!,

and The Visitors filed back along a street, into a courtyard. Standing back, going up another level, seeking escape, way out, seeking solution:

- If it is a Revolution, then it is War!

-It's confusion!

- And 'where there is confusion …

-'A man who knows what he wants, has a better chance of getting it'!..

- The HomeLand, the Territory, the Money-Banks, The Dreams of Wealth …

-The People!

-The Power to overcome hardship, pain and poverty. The power not to be overcome, … not to become enslaved?! To exchange fairly, to leave alone, freely?

A crackling hail of arrow headed ball bearings, as if flung in colossal acceleration. Rattled and sprayed all in one direction, hurtled down upon The Market-Square. Below, rebounding off walls, penetrating flesh. Bodies fell, like ninepins bowled out. The dead and injured left behind. By those fled from the town and village and fields, to the city for safety, now fleeing The City.

No entreaty, no plea taken, not even to negotiate from position of strength. A dreadful and terrible commotion heard over the distance, and then abruptly from all around. Yelled panicked warnings and orders, and fighting struggle. Hand to hand combat with the invaders, and the invaders with the people and soldiers left to fight. Erupted before them, horses and riders, nostrils flared and steaming, leapt and thudded on the ground.

The Invading Forces crossed the pontoon bridge, and entered the city. Pounded on ahead, toward the clifftop battlements. The Centre attacked now from beyond, and from the battlements inside The City Walls. The inner-defences fallen. On the seaward side, life rescue boats and ships waiting off-shore loading with those willing and able, leaving to escape.

From the landward side, amidst now burning cordite and ballistic, thudding cannonball space-missile laden   and:

-Unfire! from dog tagged troopers crossing the City-Bridge, along the Main Street and invading The central square. Firing into the air, crackling hand grenade and booming mortar, exploding along the ground, over and inside the buildings. Civilian defenders hid and ducked and dived, lay exhausted and bleeding, over blood stained stone. Vehicles stormed in, like ancient chariots, motored rocketing mortar artillery, and tanks rolled over the remains of The Bridge, and pushed through to The Center. Roared in through the boulevard and streets.

Battery gunners atop in protective flak jackets, grinning skull marked metal helmet. Firing manically, intensely in all directions. To preserve their own life, against anything possible left to end it. Battling, mopping up, around ambushing sniper traps, and deserted market stall barricade. There was minimal return fire now, from the soon deserted Market Square. Through crosshair sighted, target triggered shrapnel shards, flew through the air. From the sills and frames of remaining shattered windows and doors, explosions. Burning fuse, sizzling tubed mortar, and rifled bullet, whistling turning, through the air. Repetitive, one after another, sniper single bullet, one at a time, targeted, shot. Rapid fire returned. Defenders, with determined retribution, in a final defiant, or entrapped reluctant, act of resistance. Firing-back, holed up in upper floors and basements, collapsed and buried alive. Amongst jagged metal and heavy concrete pieces. Bullet and bomb smoked out of hiding holes. Into the open, through the fog of war, as the air cleared from the onslaught, voices heard yelling:

- Kill, or be killed!!

Answered swiftly:

- Kill, and be killed!

-Live and let live!

-Live and let die!

-With God on our side!

-Our place in History!

- To Live to see another Day!

- Ours is not to wonder why.

- Ours is just to do …

- … and Die!,

The voice halted.

Another heard out of the silence, pointing to the surrendering soldiers and huddled civilian groups remaining in the square:

- Seize them!

They had been warned, but forgetting the warning, had gone on. The pre-warning of horror-rated experience, forgotten, in the instantly accustomed haze of fear and loathing.

Despite pre-training, in Play ands Skill at cover and attack, the wish of a Homecoming fit for Heroes, the chances of being hit, killed, or injured, or if lucky, captured, seemed more likely.

Ultimately unavoidable in the chaos, apparent friend or foe fell around them, and were slaughtered. The Carnage went on and on, in sheer terror reigning through side-streets.

Militia rampaged through the streets and down the alleyways, escaping, attacking, defending, or fleeing. Taking building by building, small arms and rocket fire, explosives fused and lit, destroying and altering the flattened City-Landscape.

The Visitors, with an uncertain protection of neutrality, stood back with the remaining panicked crowds, in fear and anguish, moving with the throng. Stampeding, running amok from the wrecked market place. Not knowing where or why. From the melee, an aged women stood out, standing over a dead child, still protecting, beating her breast, and crying:

> - What have they done? Oh God! What have we done to deserve this? Oh God! Where

are you now?

Another yelled:

> - Does it always have to be this way?! Does it always have to be?! For what?!

Another:

> - Why you?
>
> -Why me?!!
>
> -Why Us?!

The Child lain down,

> - I only pray that The Great God in Heaven takes care of you!

The wounded, old and young and infirm, nursing and faint hearted, trapped, pinned down, lost in grief. Shielding with arms over the chest and head, ducking and diving behind stalls and remaining walls, doors blown in, *smashed*-down.

Shrapnel-shards, like a shoal of frightened fish, a flurry of suddenly startled starlings, leaving the feathery ghosts of grey doves and brown hawks, all blown up, and flown high in the sky. Dropped pieces to the vultures circling overhead, ready to reap the fooded reward. Laying splayed and splattered over the corpse spread and rat infested ground, in dust, and blood, and flies. The escaped, injured, rounded up, and shackled prisoners of war, identified-by-failure. All consuming grievance and grief, the bonds of the victim, the victim of the bonds. Hopeless, demoralized, and ready to be held hostage to fortune. Exchanged, expelled, taken into slavery, dutifully tortured, or summarily-*executed*. In systematic-Genocide, rape, pillage, random and suicidal or murderous-death.

The wealth, stolen, the prisoners marched out, between lines of victorious troops, pushed and shoved, kicked and punched, pleading, bargaining for their lives.

Trooped through, brutalised with mechanical violence, *beaten*. Picking out those easiest to target, and exacting the worst atrocity. Selecting at random those most fitting to the zealous stereotype, with prejudiced victim detestation, and self revulsion with what else is left, beyond the banality and non-entity of everyday existence.

The fit and healthy taken-off, to slave, for no reward except extended life and some kind of future, and hope of a release. Into a resentful and possibly bitter freedom, one day. Like animals in a zoo, infesting parasites in a petri dish, inspected, stared at, and then bought and sold at market, to work, or entertain. Led toward the city arena, lined up to be recruited, enslaved or shot.

Resisting retaliating, to perhaps save themselves and others, men, women and children; not knowing what was happening to them, shocked and scared into submission, to the seemingly inevitable. The dead and injured and captured, in dilemma no less or more heroic, than the whooping bands of easily comradely-Victors.

Survivors, left only, in the eventuality of disillusioned anticlimax, disappointment, themselves to be ignored, disdained, outwardly unscathed, in the continued and constant hope of continuously avoiding defeat, the claiming of some kind of group, but personally hollow, victory. The dead, and injured laid out to die. Disposed of extinguished, wasted, rubbished, expunged to anonymous historic existence, dissolved, rotting into dust and water.

The remaining Prisoner-captives assembled, to be transported to some infested burnt-out hospital, some forsaken gulag, prisoner exchange, enslavement, or genocidal-grave. The victors and survivors, to live the nightmare. In ritual remembrance, in ceremonial grief, in lived continuance, before a walled plaque, down the years. Until, like others, left to the pages of blurred events belonging to The History of the Victorious; The Survivors. Living, to live another day, perhaps. Without water, food or medical supplies, now sharing out what they had left, bartering, swapping and giving, snatching from those who would not give water, to the desperate child, elders, just living. Living only in the kudos of shared hope, of rescue, together now, into the *uncertain*-Future.

In the pleading, the treacherous paradox of human benevolence so much more stark. Deciding to keep quiet, head down, gaining or losing, more or less, by going along, pretending to go along, or not go along at all. Dependent on the moves of others, others controlling the situation.

The Trooping Guards ever watchful, for any chance of escape, of safe-collusion, of selfish and greedy collusion, tat for tat, personal and group ownership. Stay with the crowd, even if in mass murder, or make a personal: break-for-freedom.

To trust in some foundation of virtue. Left looking for self, looking for a leader, someone willing to have their head put over the parapet. Brave enough to lead the resistance to all this hatred and brutality, left looking for someone to blame, someone else to accuse, of the worst excesses. Revenge the death of family or comrade.

The relief of which, could be to change allegiance. Deny the existence of another formerly sworn friend, now sworn enemy. Denying the existence, or benevolence even of a once praised god; ot to reveal the traitorous snipering ratholes of others. Colluding with the captors, in the hope of saving, owning ones own life, perhaps, at the expense of an unknown Other. As another might possibly, at the expense of theirs. Prisoner-hostages, now separated, lined up against a wall, the guards as if in total-control. Dictating the terms, in fear and panic, holding the ultimate power of life and death:

       -You, were only following Orders?!

       -On the Lives of my Children! I was only a pawn in this
       game. Who wants to outlive
their children?! Take me, and let them be!

       -You can always make more children! Or may be not! Who
       is your commander, who led you into this? Where are your
       leaders?!

The-Guard(s): menacing, tried terror tactics, threatened death and maiming, despite the anonymity of those already killed and injured. The Prisoners with no-bargaining counters, except their own lives, and any useful information they may have about who did what, when and how, and even why, and now where. If anyone knew anything, to assist the conquerors, to betray their own:

- Tell us, or it will be worse for you!

The guards tried to exchange limited freedom, for information. But still, even though the guards had the strongest and ultimate hand, there was mistrust in the information given:

-I'll tell you! Just let my Children live!

-How do we know you are telling The Truth? How do we know that you know

anything at all?!

-We don't, why would we ..?

-I don't believe you, you're hiding them ... you're lying!

Over finely tuned suspicion, antennae radio crackling positions and advance on the Capital. Comparing information from other parts, cheat detection ready to exact lying guilt, shame and brutal revenge,

- They have escaped!

- You are lying!

The pistol whip, the recipient caught, at the wrong place, at the wrong time, bad luck, the risk taken. The bluff countered by bluff, instant uncertain revenge, another attempted resolution, consensus with the heard report:

-They are in The Capital ..

An-Other: concurred, seeking distraction from the bristling assault
on all assembled and afraid:

      -They fled and abandoned us here!

      -You told them to go, where are they?

      -They are at the Capital!

      -They have escaped in ships, they are free from you, and us!

      They are holding your

Generals captive up there! Seeking to converge the stampeding
dazed and confused moment. Only responded with:

      -Traitor! You are only looking to save your own skin! Don't

      try giving us useless

information, leading us into a trap, tricking us. Cheating will get you
found out, there will be a *brutal* revenge …

Neither had reason to suppose that information they did have was of
any use, or was not a deliberate trick, a trap.

Each side like a nested den of mistrusting thieves, threatening to kill
each other or be killed, for the ultimate prize. To lead each other to
be annihilated in mutual ending zero, no-one gains, everyone loses
completely:

      -If you're lying …

      -I'm telling the truth, we've never done anything to hurt you,

      it's *Them* …

Neither side, none knew who was telling the truth, if any knew or believed they knew, what would be The Final Truth. Giving perhaps *false*-Promise, of Revenge, or Hope. To Bargain, as to what they thought the other would accept, as fair enough, as against the chance of being treated more unfairly, more or less cruelly. In immediate future-bargain and indebtedness, optimum positions held, for now.

The Prisoners, and the Guards, both dictating their own terms, trading favours instead of blows, between real or imagined enemies, careful not to be trapped. Without pre-emptive potential self destruction, holding the race to arms, awaiting the accountants answer. Standing back, going up a level, leaving loose open ends... To achieve, to impress enemy and friends, to show a kind and gentle side, a sense of self with morality, justice and community, to include some element of mutual fairness:

-Non Zero-Sum...

Winners and losers, living to see another: Day.

Each to try to *guarantee* the Exchange, lest they should be condemned themselves. Feeling willing to commit atrocity in malicious and vindictive revenge, through a regime brutalized by fear, and to be protected. Moved into a world not of their making, cautious:

- How can we know what you are really thinking, what you really intend to do with

us..!

The Guards, faced with such dilemma as well as the hostages, the distraction of possibly misleading innocence, into revengeful fear misguided, each only seeking of relief, of escape.

Residual doubt and fear, dependent still on the paradox of benevolence, weighing up the gain or loss of co-operating. Pretending to co-operate, or not co-operating, the risk of certain, and uncertain outcome, dependent on the strategies of others, prisoners, or guards, those reprieved or ignored, onlookers ignoring or looking on anxiously. To be Selfish and Greedy, selfless and trusting, nice or nasty, exploited or exploiting, the others strategy unknown, start by being nice, co-operative, generous looking for equal-*reciprocation*. Only. Tit for tat, trusting and kind, looking to avoid high risk strategy, or high risk for its own sake, with escape clause if it all goes wrong. One, crying, into the dying wind:

> - Look! They've dessimated de-seminated! Our Lands and Resources!
>
> -Our People! No-longer belongs to anyone in particular, or even everyone in general, any of Us. We've had ownership and trade, built trust, and trust builds virtue, and

society allows for division of labour, synergy between specialists, well connected, co-operative, social and trustworthy, evolutionary advantage to thrive, now we're annihilating and accumulating, a people, property and land.

By the contagion of belief, with the aiming of overwhelming force, echelons of guided and misguided command, exchange of prisoners, of membership, the domination of one group
over another established. To share membership in a shared destiny, redistributed dominance
hierarchy. Bureaucratic administration of empire, to be fair to whom, and how much.

Virtuous circle, become vicious, become, in brigandage, exerting persecution for tribute and self protection, guided, by rule and ruled, by force, troops threatened and threatening, with punishment torturing, that's not the way is it? Finally, everyone moved out, in chains, in field Hospital ambulance, to *safe* area; to slave in fields, or to genocidal funeral-pyre; or freed into evacuation and exile. Incantations, and fireworks, first heard at The City Bridge, propaganda banners fluttered torn, burnt but victorious alone, leaflets and posters torn and flapped in the silent wind.

From where procession had emanated, and trod down the hilltop fortress, the palace, the head, the nerve center. From the funeral pyres and evacuation, buildings collapsed and pulled down, cleared from the citadel piazza destroyed in flame, as a huge sun began to rise, from the eastern flank, to challenge the gradual re-appearance of day.

Led through the town and city, out of houses and buildings burned out, a ghost town people, moved slowly, carefully, intently aware that any moment could still be their last. Not knowing from where, or when, or really why. Unaware of what had happened, to others, stripped of possession, in reverted ownership, the dragging off of goods, women and children, and remaining men. Not knowing what fate might befall them, whether they wanted any longer to live with this, or to die.

Guarded, ignored, and taunted, in chains. Given up, spitting, throwing insults, making to escape, baiting the guard to do something, if only to relieve the tension of being half dead. One occasionally furiously fighting back. Singularly, alone, afraid, and without anymore fear, to resist and live, or die trying. In the belief that others might be saved.

Attempting to ascertain the relative value of such selfish hopeless betrayal. Facing final suicidal martyrdom, given up, leaving others behind, bringing an End to it All.

Or to succumb to continuing Hope, staying on to fight, to live another day, another micro-second. Taken away, and off, the dead and dying, and injured left moaning alive movement amongst the pyre of arms and legs, turned over staring face, finished-off. One more missing out, on the parturation of the future. No longer taking in the light of day, the heat from the flames, and nighttimes fall. Prisoners and Guards moved off together, toward a new dawn, a Brave New World. Perhaps. Definitely. The *remaining*-Onlookers, scared, confused and amazed, found themselves beneath an imposing turreted building, pillars and columnar arches, austere and daunting. Above, The Capital Hill and edifice that loomed over them, hemmed in against a walled façade, atop of which, from the tallest bell-tower, the tolling of caste metal rang out.

There was a collective shock and amazement, agape and aghast with what they did not know. A fear not to be feared, an amusement to be laughed at.

A fear to be feared. An amusement not to be *laughed*-at.

The Visitors led now, mute, amazed, unsure of what to do next.

Through an empty courtyard, in pitched night, lit dimly…

From the now seemingly distant lustre of the flaming town and city, sea and countryside around.

From a dissipating and gradually extinguishing furnace,

Beacons of stars and Galaxies *shimmered* above.

Through a swirling odourous acid-fog of burnt-saltpeter and gunpowder, *lamentation* over pyres of putrid and burning flesh.

The marketplace and city buildings, flickered, rolled and stilled.
The lights come down suddenly, like an instantaneous nightfall.
A baying moon, and atmospheric twinkling of seemingly
unchanging stars, surrounded-them. Cannon thudded and crackled,
continued staccato volley over hills and valley, peppered amongst
crowds beyond, who wailed and cried out, faded gradually, into the
night; as trumpets and the pealing and tolling of bells from the
burning City-Centre, the sounds of battle died away, the flames
faded, archway merged, over the light of a new ever distantly rising-
Sun. Within the entrance and hallway of a concrete pillared and
buttressed, screened glass and steel partitioned edifice, someone
shouted:

      -Would you believe that!

and The Visitors, and the last to *witness*, laughed an awkward,
frightened, anticipatory *laugh*, in the limbo.

The End of the Universe:

Universal Verses7: Life From Earth.

1.Business-Centre.

2.Theatre.

3.Library.

4.Engine-room.

5.Bio-Tech Journey.

6.The Museum of Life. Capital Plazza.

7. Pastoral Industrial post-Capital…T.V.

Universal Verses7: Life From Earth.

1.Business-Centre.

From the shattered and burnt remains,
buildings half standing
With windows blown out through teetering walls and roofs,
collapsed.

Smoke still rose, and hung like a pall,
and cries still emanated from the metal twisted rubble.
Drenched and put-out, the last remaining flames,
Lights set-up, and *wired-in radio*-communications *broken.*

Posters and banners hung from buildings, aged and of Now!
Warning to join The Fight, or Die! Bird-soiled statue of Past-Heroes;
around the collapsed and demolished: Peaceful-Warrior fountain.

In the midst of The Enclave: Water-tankers and food aid vehicles,
power-cables, tents and stretchers were gradually moved-in.

Even now, grasses and trees began growing, out of collapsed flint
and felt, porcelain-roof, of Jade and Gold.
Dust brick and lime, and granite cliff rock face,
As the remains of The Buildings...

A Field-Hospital and Feeding-Station: ambulance and fire-crew moved out, amongst the rubble, demolition squads, and rebuilders, moving in: Army and Police took control, the Reign of Terror *over*, or only just again beginning…Again.

Turning away, and inward from the courtyard gateway, up stone steps, through great arched doors, to the inside, The Visitors, We, were entered-into a wide polished wood and marble clad Ancient Hall. Statues and Heraldic plaques, wax and stone and metal death-masks portrait in Familial-tree erstwhile ruling elite and returning Elite. Around the walls. Pandemic, of Plague and War enscripted in tapestry pictured along Remembrance Wall: amongst more Monumental-edifice, and full-length standing statues, of Chiefs, Kings and Queens, princes and princesses, Emperor and Empress. Descriptive-plaque, worn and unintelligible, just the remnants of a crest or badge, an honour stained, or deleted.

Only vaguely remaining, in faded relief, decried, discredited, forgotten in deliberate dereliction. The stark reality emerged, of The Worlds We had traveled through. Depicted truly, or otherwise, in selfish short shrift, brutal glorious greed. Envy, moral collapse, disliking making evil suitor, debasement, diminishment, thinning, chaos and death. Self serving and suicidal, continuing on, in a history of memory and golden age mythological-fantasy. Dented-breastplates, and empty armour, hung uniformly across the walls. Spear and flat-sword, cut-throat cutlery, strapped to ploughshare; battered armed tank and aircraft, on tractor wheels and planed wing, displayed across the stone paved ground. As in amongst realized computer console images, battle and closed-battle scene.

2. Theatre.

At the end of The Courtyard Hall, the small group of *Survivors* gathered. Looking down over The Hall below; through arrow slit windows alongside. Below could now be seen the courtyard arched-Gate, and The Square once more beyond. Re-built, similar but different, a glittering example of earlier and later Architecture, taking some of the old, little of the ancient remains; and some of The New now Old: The Peaceful-Warrior *once* more arraigned in its central podium place. Above them, inside of the raised angular pillared and dome topped capitol building, columnar architrave and cornice frieze imageries, stucco moulded, carved and engraved. Once in seeming destruction, de-lapidation and decay. Now transformed, and transforming the flamelight of the *new*-Sun; Through *stained*-glass. Once shattered mosaic patterned window, pictured in depiction, after a now historical, made mythical, and then made mystical, stilled historical event. Inside and elevating through the remaining hillside, the hilltop Capital-Monument.

They were moved on through hung carpet and wide hinged doors, and onto a wide enclosed balcony, overlooking a long wide-chamber.

A spaciously seated, circular Room: white walled and blank benches of mahogany and plush, faced inwards towards a central platform. In the circular stalls below, gowned and suited figures moved around, stood purposefully and in turn, and *spoke*.

Each a Figure re-cognisable from history, more recent, and from the more *ancient*-Past. Standing, breathing in and raising a finger to speak, to attract attention. To make prepared quotation and speech, announcing some Great-Event: a *declaration* of War or Peace; or enslavement, or freedom, of some people a statement of cause and belief; Buddha inwardly discursing from beneath an imaginary Banyan tree, part of a Confucian speech to the Chinese people, a crowned King and head of state, followed summary announcement as if to the Athenian, Egyptian, and then Roman assemblies, as a toga wearing Cicero standing purposely and quoting *himself*, rose persuasively, and added: Audiodrome: camp-culture village-religion town-buildings permanent-port/City Capitol Hill:

    -In: This Mime Show of Life!

    -In traditional-*ideals* and Self-Interest:

    -Immortal Gods!

    -And Goddess's!!

    -What do such *trivialities* matter to Me?

    -I go with sublime-*indifference*…

    - Oh!, just to die peacefully in bed!

An ear-ringed and fop-haired bard stood, waited and then addressed the newly arrived visitors directly, rather than the assembled great figures, quoted and added:

-'In this exercise and experience of life, you will, feel want, taste grief; and need friends'.

-Oh! 'The Vanity of Our Human Hopes!!' with that thought copied, repeated, and passed on, extant and in continuation, We now move-on: One of The Visitors interrupted and as a joking *aside*:

- Adieu!

Another:

-Enter-stage left…I mean: To Be Or Not To Be?

The Scots poet, Robert Burns, stood and *lamented*:

-'That Man was made to *mourn* …

-Mans *inhumanity* to Man…'

-Make's countless thousands more to *mourn!*

-Time's *ritual*…

-Nature's Law's *made*…

-*War does not determine who is right…only who is left…*[*]

Others now stood in-turn, or amongst themselves, leaning-forward, discussing and debated and argued issues of their day, to this particular day. A loudspeaker hailed to:

-*Those* who carry on Wars! Build and defend fortresses, and in *their* Royal-diversions make those great expenditures which neither I nor Other Private Person may?

-'Mankind must put an End to War before War puts an End to Man-Kind.'[*]

-In Peace Fathers bury their Sons; in War Sons bury their
Fathers...*

And appeared Galileo, brandishing telescope and reading quoting:

-From 'The Starry Messenger.':

As of *notoriety* and *apparent*-virtue, dressed in various attired
design, fashionable or unnoticing, solitary and dominating-figures,
from the battlefield and the conservatoire philosophical and political
theatre, a great trench-coated be-medaled General:

- An Army *marches* on it's *Stomach*...*

A field-*poet* addressing Virtue, Love and *beauty*, and with a
scowling, puzzled voice:

-... So what, in time, finally, eventually, becomes of this, and
us all?

Amongst themselves, gesticulating, talking heads and hands, arms
and shoulders, mumbling, muttering and raised voices occasionally
amongst the pews.

Aristotle Avicenna Al-Gabra and Al-Kwari Ulugh Beg stood.
Thomas Paine and Mary Woolstencraft briefly declared the Rights of
Man and Women, and responsibilities: Darwin, the Descent of Man,
Elaine Morgan the descent of woman and the child, Newton
declared, and Albert Einstein replied, with reverence and peaceful
intention:

- Every force has an opposite and equal force ...

- I think that a particle must have a separate reality
independent of the measurements. That is, an *electron* has spin,
location and so forth, even when it is not being measured. I like to

think, that The Moon is there, even if I am *not* looking at it …

 -Adjusted his frockcoat, and sat.

Looking a-round: peering at the assembled celebrity, others' now stood, from various times and places.

Recounted in phrase, and praise Golden Ages of Creation Myth: purposeful, presented briefly, for account and succour. Stood and declared quoting, each others' disciplined and supplicant, prophet and priest, raising and moving themselves, over mountains and seas. A light flashed brilliantly, in anger, accident, or *sheer* boredom …

 -… and out of mud and clay …

 -A *molded* Golden-Egg opened.

The fiery Sun and Moon and stars rose in one half of the sky:

 -Over the earth, the singing waters flooded …

 -Amongst shoots of hollow reed grass and seed herb seed, sprung out of the *moulding*-Earth …

 -The Diver-Fish swam below. A muddied turtle, rose out of the water, carrying the world on its back …

 -… creeping creatures crawled, moved hissing over the land …

 -… numberless beings, separated into groups …

 -… aligned with The Stars *named*: The Dragon Thunderbird flew…

 -Risen into a wind-driven cloud, over misty mountain, …

 -The Elephantine-trumpeted!

-The *sleeping* Tiger and Great Lion roared.

-Liger! Rose out of the dust …

-Whilst in the *magic* dark wood, an enchanted spider spun its spindled-woven web …

-By the carrying the rivers lapping edge …

-… the *story-telling* Monkey *distracting* with tales …

-… from The Tree of Knowledge,

-… of Good and Evil …

-Plucked, the stolen fire,

-… *lightening* The Day.

-Separating Man, from the *unfortunate* Beasts…'

-'….and in the beginning, God created the heaven and the Earth. And the Earth was without form, and void … and the word was with God…

-God made all Creations according to their Kind … and Man in his image. …

-World without end ...

-Without beginning?

From a cradled book, a gown wrapped and sandaled Socrates stood, and read out, repeated from the words of his pupil:

- 'You do wrong to think that a man, of any use at all, is to weigh the   risk of life or death, and not to consider one thing only. Whether when he acts, he does the right thing or the wrong, performs the deeds of a good man or bad...',
and concluded with:

-The hour of departure has arrived, and we go our ways - I to

die, and you to live. Which is better? God only knows',

As following Democritus, Lucretius stood,

-Many Atoms! Jumbled in many ways … come together and

try all combinations.!

Thoughtful and discursive, they moved on.

Around the cell, the chamber, leaving space for the next group of

Visitors:

- Well; what if We do return and remain?

-… and still as part of everything else?

-Bone dust, and water vapour into rock and air, a fungus, a

plant, another animal, another person, the air, another breath?

-What of that?

3. Library

From stairs, leading onto another floor into a ceiling and wall
paneled library gallery, lined with moving video screens of talking
heads, with headphone access to their spoken-word.

Vast virtual library constantly updated, access on request, screened
and sounded booths beyond, translation and interpretation services,
extant examples stored in climate controlled glass cases in safe
storage, original manuscripts on papyrus paper preserved.

Over -entrance screens of pedant and literary characters quoting as
id discussing and debating: Socrates, Lao Tzu, Burns, Ghandi,
Mandela, Obama. Shelley, Mary. Escalator to Art-Music : live

theatres and cinema, as night drew over The-Square Shopps and restaurants and food-stalls at: The End of: The World.

Another part of the world at noon, another time language. Live theatres and cinema: as night drew open-air: over: The-Square:shops and restaurants at: The End of: The-World.

Another part of the world at noon, another time. From hieroglyphs to picto-gram idea-gram: and: The Written-Word: and:lists of dotted and number figured accounts, rowed and repeated object symbols, an insect, perhaps an ear of corn, an elaborate furniture-seated.

Stamps of thronal patronage and bureaucratic officialdom, repeating poetic pairings, couplets in rhythm and rhyme, passages of imaginative flight of fancy, loosely tied to the standing held with *white*-gloverd hand: Gold and black, red and green leather and board bound manuscript, and painted book tied runic pictogram and ideogram, iconography and brain teaser patterned puzzles, with intricate religious and secular philosophies.

All of which, at one glance, were clearly all of immense and historic significance. Vast and various, encyclopedic reference library, linguistic phrase book, dictionary and thesaurus, antonym and synonym, name and etymology, profound parable, proverb and prophecy, recorded speech, quotation, religious and Civic Legal-Code.

Biography and autobiography, non-fiction, fact and fiction, written and recorded music, play scripts and film. Competitive team and solo-individual and entertaining board and card games. Surprising, contradictory, fanciful and telling books and stories of comic-*humour*. Amusing-*musings*, thoughts and passions, sorcery and science, inventory and diary, of domesticity and voyage.

Almanac and calendar, books of days, time-framed prediction and recollection, maps and tribute lists, of tax returns and bureaucratic record. Family history and family tree, genealogical database from ancient and modern record, of births, deaths and marriages. Beneath the bookshelves, rectangular squared-screens could Commend and Command reference to any part or whole of the Libraried-Store.

Where quietly spoken, silently mouthed word and written learning, picked up from copying, taught, and taken up, distracted, extracted and distilled, in the historic memory reflex, and immediate *experience* of Everyday-Life: As if in a *medieval* arched-cloister, watching, and glancing over the shoulders of scholars and students, studiously moving images, on 2 and 3D to 4D moving sono-vision screens. They moved amongst this curriculum, through this conservatoire of remaining cultural reference, at once aware, that this, and everything else, as far as they knew, still existed. From this point initiates for what remained of discarded worlds, revisited and revised, renewed in another. Where driven by ethics, austere and familiar, open animal-Sex covered by a cloak, biting like a dog. Amongst spoken diatribe and dialogue, satirical playlet star-born and lunatic fringe-speech. Filmic and theatrical, they mixed and mingled, in their group and other groups. As if time, now, had been forgotten, in passive collective chemical memory and perception, studded with sealed and past events, *smoothed* into: The-*Present.*

At the End of The Library; The Visiting Students stepped-up the wide banister sculpted staircase. Into a wide enclosed echoing corridor, green and red painted, silver and gold leaf gilt. Gilded along the walls, framed motif of cherubic and archangelic, fantastic creature and imaginary unicorn, with re-growing horn antler, seaweed green plant red with blood. Dripping-off. Every beastly and human foible and pleasure depicted, over and below flowing river and full cloud, tree and field, flower and plant, sea and pale blue sky. In embroidered filigree and wood and metal fretwork. Grid and grille panel, along warmed and cooling airway and stairway-railing. The Visitors, moved onto a decorous carpeted, wide travertine wooden staircase.

Stepped-up, turned winding root and stem banister and rail, led upwards, onto an embellished balcony of angular, curvilinear undulating, and free-flowing, metal banded wrought-work banded. With spaces between, along the walls and into galleries along each side. Vast halls and rooms off, tapestry stories, furniture, carpets, tiles and papers.

Posters and photographic pictures. Exhibitions of paintings, artifactual made objects, lined the walls and floors.

Iconography, self-celebrating, political and religious authority, stilled images of people and places, peasants and austere farmers, village and townfolk, city fathers and media celebrities. Supermodels with rare proportion, ordinary-people.

Stone-carved voluptuous female and exaggerated male phallic and muscular build, roughly and with time with ore sophisticated and explicit fertility erotic and pornographic depiction, moving on to portraits of covered-angels and naked-cherubins and seraphins, to doting parents and children; aunts and uncles, grandparents and great- grandparents, cousins and friends, animal wild and livestock and *domestic*-pet.

Still and life reaffirming fruit-flower, death-*reasserting* eyeless-Skull. Lovescenes and sexual fantasy. Family groups, sea, sky and landscape, high days and holidays, with records of ordinary days, of the landscape. In countryside fields and village, in Town and City, on the beach at the seaside, at Home. Figures copied intricately, and fantastically, all shapes and sizes imaged. Stern belief, in the delicate and subtle. Dust and planted-ground pasted poster painted-markings. In familiar and bizarre and strange, functional and symbolic design,or re-design. Informative, expressionistic and impressionistic. Delicately idealistically perfectable symmetries. Trenchant tooled, geometrically defined symmetric motifs, a-symmetric: natural-realism.

Defining relations, prestige and association. Impasto layers of pigment, giving the impression of high relief, and solidity. Illusory, magically realistic, naturalistic and psychedelically surreal mural, objects oddly-set and counter-poised.

Codified, commodified, in abstract decoration, of leaf and stem, wave and body. In line and surface, field border and piece, galleried framed picture. Real, or mythological, disgusting and fearful images. Creating dis-association.

Dynamic dislocated pattern, on intricately decorated walls and ceilings. Diversion, distraction and reflection, on Everyday-*cares*. Each of Us related, each telling a story. In colour, line and composition. Trop d'oeuil, contradictory impossible images and symbols. Of what it is to be real, in presented and installed realities. Background un-seen played music flowed in the Spaces. Dependent on apposite historical and cultural context. Or otherwise, appropriate tone of the presented subject. In Time and Space: *purposeful*, and for its own sake around the final corridor gateway, carved into the wood:

- 'Art is limitation. The essence of every picture is the frame' (G.K. Chesterton).

One Visitor read, and remarked, as they moved on through:

-You might as well say, life is limitation. The essence of every person, is the body.

-And the *imagination*...

-Is?

-This?

-Sport is the Hunt and Sport is drama not knowing the end like war and all the battles that make a war…for food and furniture and home…

In rooms marked: For The Study of the Flight of Birds, and the Falling of the Rain. Work is for the Pleasure, of Art and Science, for Good Food and Drink. Create your own Perfect World rooms dedicated to Arts and Crafts; where Mind Music, Art Attack, Dance.

Mat and other expressive and creative games could be played, taken more or less seriously, for popular, and more esoteric, enjoyment, pleasure and pass-time.

Where buildings and landscapes, inventive machinations and processes that could be practiced and developed, practiced and assessed. On screened and projected 3D and 4D saved recordings, for entry into competitions and exhibitions, or for personal value and satisfaction. In *echoing*-Sssspace…in silence. In rooms off, now in museum halls, like moving photographic images. Memories returned, as if inherited. Felt oddly familiar with. Iconic hieroglyphic symbols, pictograms and lettered words and written numbers, from-Zero, de-coding *mysteries* horror thriller revealed to speak to: Future-Generation; a standing stone, rock-tablet, a cave-wall painted; Genus-specie taxonomy, classification de-ciphering the GGnome *barcode*… Unraveling the chemical, electromagnetic, the mechanical, the intended and the un-intended:

-Chance and Choice…

-The Building-*blocks* of The-Universe.

From an original sand drawn exemplar. Matched square on triangular squared sides.

Dreamed of *perfectibility* in The Geometric-picture.

Defined on the page, in the minds eye. Idealized line and shape, depicted transferable fixed formulaic interrelation. Circuits and connectivity's, translated in diagrammatic form. Imagined circle, cylinder and cone hemi-spherical area.

Magnitude and miniscule number, 3D square graded, comma myriad separated and decimal pointed calculus grains of sand counted, distance, breadth and depth.

Hydro-static balance nanocrystal shell shape and size-structure...

Micro-*graphic radio-active:*

 -Beam-Spectra-*graph*...

 -*Massive!* Ultimately beyond the reach, of each optimal measured con-straint.

Non-contradictory, identity, *excluded*-middle *i*maginary number; construct-marks across an un-broken and curved-Space...

Finite and non-finite calculus, identical and empty sets, conjoined conjunction of sets. Non-countable defined set, sets' multiplied-by power-sets set-selected from other-sets set...set a member of itself, otherwise, the set of all sets: Ourselves. The-Spaces between consecutive windings and over-laps.

Growing exponentially, at a fixed, any positive or negative rated number or letter, or word. They read inscription and legend, scribed amongst spikes and blocks on charts. Spheres encircled and crossed with logarithmic and algorithmic ratio. On an electronic board:

-1+1=0;-1+1=1;1+1=11;1+1=2;1+1=3;1+1=4;1+1=5;1+1=6;

-1+-1=-2;-1-(-1)=0; 2+2 = ? and a list of possible answers to select from....

-From Zero-finity to 1.3 to 1.6, to 4, to 4.1, to - 4.1, and an ever expansive-*infinity* of *possible*-Answers. As *impossible*-Questions. Impossible-answers...possible-Questions...

Beautiful-*imaginary* complex infinite number and equation. Random-prime (unpredictable, non-formulaic indivisible numbers) and (irreducible perfect ratio's, equivalents and non-equivalents, straight lines and circles, oblong and ellipsoid. Three and more dimensional numbers, gridded graph and computer simulation. There from, and there on. From sand drawn irregular shape and the written number, to solid stone and rock. Flora and fauna growing through, genus speciation and exception. Explanatory derivations and sources. From reality finding exploration and experimentation. Circumnavigational, mapped geographic, from east and west, north and south, shipped glass cased models and examples. Voyages of discovery, and re-discovery. The whole-World: landscape-hill and mountain-valley and deep-caverned rift set-out laid out to be studied at leisure. Collected together, with explanatory notes, diagrams, commentary.

Fly-through generated virtual travel simulations...*curious*-Visitors and Curators' mingled together in Rooms and Halls crammed with exhibits and artifacts. Amongst phials and vials, coloured and colouring liquids, powders and gases.

Heated and *frozen*...evaporated and condensed, molten and solidified. Changing in mixture, elemental combination and separation. Odours and tastes, of the chemistry laboratory. Light box extracting spectral comoents of sheet white light in a pitch darkened space. Glass- testing tubes connected-to boiling and freezing flask evaporation and condensation capture-tray wind-tunnel and fume-cupboard; *electric*- furnace and stone-brick forge mixing atmospheric-gases and liquids- melting and re-shaping metal-*memory*...

Extracting-ores and making alloys' transmutation of One to another: *mixture*-reaction and *purifying*-of-elements...with further-*variating* imperfection alerting changes at different-levels of fixing nucleic-bonds atomizing-atoms; with yet more level of force or matter. Radio-carbon dating-mass *spectrometry* measuring crystal-exposure to heat and light:

-*I*sotopic ratio in half lives, record or earth shifting geo-magnetic field from place to place, rock-fragments and lived-fossil metal-salt *precipitates* ice-fronded chemical-garden star-like crystalline-shards physical electro-magnetic forces, in *virtual*-vacuum.

-Attracting, repulsing and deflecting isotropic interactions, matter and anti-matter. Evenly spread throughout the room, fairly distributed.

As through a screen cover-all-ed: Scientists moved around. One stirring a cup of hot-liquid, mixing congealed butter into a cup of watery-tea coffee-cream: as the two *liquid*-mixtures merged chaotically mixed and settled into a new-consistency: interference of the whole contained reaction, the cup dropped, the mixture spilling-out; separating droplets pooling in the air and on the ground, broken chipped fragments scattering, the puzzlement at this sudden and shocking scenario relayed onto a probability outcomes screens. Silicate sand conductive electromagnetic *magnetite*-conducting:

 -Genetic-*numeric* and linguistic-algorithm computation…

 -Of all *possibilities* at any One-*state* the most-*efficient* and the *luckiest*-together will-Survive...

The most likely outcome intervention a gathering together of the atomic pieces in random lottery of cause and effect, to be abandoned to their separate fates. The medium likelihood, the pieces to be left to find their newly organized roles to disintegrate slowly, soak in become part of something else, a stain, a hastily hidden remnant for some other future to decide.

The least likely of any, the reversing of the entropic, catastrophic occurrence, to reassemble exactly as before. As if nothing at all has happened, this least likelihood becoming an impossibility, only a virtual rewind surprising the onlookers to such a degree, the laboratory technicians continued their inner tasks.

Selecting-*items* from marked elemental racks, friction sparking and watching hydrogen fuel, split nuclei fissioning helium, firing through gaps in a phonic and photonic-lattice. Cloth-covered converted covert cone of Each *watery non*-transparent super-conducting foaming, silicon and crystalline-diamond *transparency*. Chipped and emitting light, through heat field, across plated surface, jumping across from high energy to low energy. micro and Macroscopic-*array*, screen rounded and squared off, regulated and readied. To access and reshape records, in relevant and regulatory networks. Through screened atomic energy leveling cloud, projected in microwave chamber. Swirling, rising and falling under gravity, laser beam slowed and cooled, to near absolute zero. Trapped ions, recorded in electromagnetic field, as energy level *regulated*-frequency of radiation. Brooking and bridging, streaming, rivering estuaries and seas, leaves and buds, lakes and inland fresh waterways, cattle and people who come to drink, formed out of the fog.

4. The Engine-Room

Difference-*engine* iron carbon-steel wheels element and number tables, formulaic-depictions of energy-and-motion.

Spectral-map relayed-*through* passing-through

Laser-*beam electron*-microscope electro-magnet tunnel accelerator image through optical-lattice, periodic-counter clocking trapped-movement; *between*-particles. Gas-floating *nucleus*-Orbiting:

    -Neutron and Proton…

Layers of *surface-electrons*…

Spinning-off stable and unstable

Gradually and as rapidly changing-*Elementals*:

    -We!

Switching the balance of proton and neutron, fine tuning into a stability. Bombarded-intense radiated sound-and-light cannoning-off…through Vortex-holding Core! Letting out *star*-focused maser-*light*:

    -Intense-Gamma…

Ray-*burst* repairing and tearing apart, in transmutation and refinement. Fixing and *lit-up* in swirling blue-neon through grey-catalytic trace. Exciting beryllium, lithium, boron, fluorine, caustic sodium fountain un-salting. Magnesium phosphorous smoky shiny flaring aluminium residue. Conducting through silicon layer. Separating-out onto graphed-screen representation. Eggshell, and composting orange-brown and green-black manure. The concoction, burning-off yellow sulphur, clear methane and dioxide poison wafting. Deposited calcium, phosphorous and potassium. Copper, tin and zinc ore, heavy heated and melted. Through hydrogen iron core, frozen gas, into steaming liquid. Quicksilver and sulphurous, mercurial lead arsenic burning-acid. Exploded and congealed, clouded out of nuclear reactive-*Starburst!*

With increasing scale of distance, leaving laser optical after glow of *vapourous*-element:

-Carbon-*soot* and silica-dust turning liquid-and-metallic heavier and slower solid nucleic-iron rock.

Radiating invisible rays, inward and outward, with variant amplitude. Crackling and hissing, booming, and with deep dull thud, pulsed into the invisible microwave background.

Isolated faltering oscillation, timed repetitive regularity. Laser group patterned. Against: Solar-movement...pendular movement. Through shielded quartz, resonating, molecular vibrating, at high frequency. Randomly picked out next nanosecond, numerable mathematical dissection and accuracy. To a point of solid arrest.

Stopped in it rough tracks. Bound to the moment.

Reverberating, from past to future, and back again.

Atomically and astronomically, energy derived time frame.

Leap seconds apart, to make the erratic difference, one to another.

Force and matter, space and time, moving, flowing back and forth.

Beneath and above, unseen beyond and below light speed.

Smashing head on, through hot fireball squeezed to microscopic tubule.

From each blinding collision, spray tracked and identified. Microscopically slowed down, into a weighted volume. Near supersymmetrical copied partner, near identical reformations. A-symmetrical colliding.

Fractal amplified magnificent bearing off, shattering to form yet slower and more differentiated solidifying display.

Gluing glued-together into granular-specks, fused and fusing.

The potential for disastrous triangulate-navigational positioning.

Information transfer, desynchronisation apparent. When the extra-second counts. Providing consistent and inter-related, and vast Information-pack. Determined, and determinedly stored, and passed on. Silicon and metal conductive crystalline-lattice.

Liberating into an electron sea. Surfing through remaining obstacles Slowing to conductive, more certain position. Less certain momentum, actively *freely*-moving reaction.

Decaying-plasma conversion-*altering...*

Capturing and retrieving, matter and releasing vacua, as new matter, radiated outwards. Emitted, accelerating to-scan to-target, to Travel *through* Space.

Shielded, or opened to collide in fragmentation in pico-seconds *fractious* to the nth degree *firing*-continuously. Perpetually, holding together, and breaking-apart. Into quantum half-lives started, beginning and without endpoint, or return; to any beginning, any end. Recorded and read, mirror reverse oblique angle reflex, multiple lensed-image.

From clear mountain peak radar-dish Satellite Space-telescope. Through bombarding neutron proton and electron-detector. Photo multiplier laser tube, sound wave generator and light-box. Processed on electro-magnetic tape compacted onto silver disc consistency of landscape.

Spinning around, sharing the space. Locked on, gridded, counter number and picture preserving. Primitive-Earth *experiment*, recycling simulacrum, flask gas filled. Heated oceanic waters, lapping and steaming into the upper atmosphere. Organic soup, of mineral crystal-growth, amino acid and glucose sugar freely floating alteration. Fitting as befits enzyme body-cavities to catalyse cell-replicating protein chain-cell.

Synthesizing and metabolizing, cyclical linking base, cumulative pairings, twistings and shaping variants. To form more variant or catastrophically, to base molecule again. To reform again with another, repetitively, progressively combining, resistant and adaptive function. In the thickening mineral-nutrient enclosing stew separating-out moving-apart. Untwisted, split, and contained in their own, separated pulsing convulsing bubble…

To repeat the process, in rapid and uninterrupted function. Singular continuing expanding, or otherwise to collapse, sunk sublimated. The display continuing, with static and moving, bioinformatic protozoan and genomic data.

Circular, tubed and minute centrally wadding virus strains, binding onto sugary molecules parasitically infecting crossing species and retro immune body functions, in epidemic and pandemic.

Alveoli air sacs taken in and taken over influenza and pneumonia strains, straining the host to the point of death. Stroke-*strain* on rest of body multi-walled, polyhedral triangular-facings, wafting unfolding dense thicket of hair-strands.

Mimicking-host, guesting as food, binding and recentring, reproducing the quantities and most successful qualities shared and reproduced in each. Separately and autonomously, selecting deliberately and naturally seeking-out.

For overwhelming Survival of Self, and reflection of Self in *perpetuity...*

Gradually lost in the individual, with age the cell nodes wearing, tissue tearing and no longer repairing.

Life-principle in The Here and Now.

Sentient-reflexive and learned-species response. Selecting, choosing mites and mates. Viral strains and bugs, picking up and carrying and returning with fashioned and ill-fashioned style. Moving small and fast, large and slowly, perhaps finally stopped dead, in the branched path. Budding and branching again. Dispersed, scattered, held in a *relative*-velocity to another.

Long enough to image. Through binding plasmic fog, forged into container, let in and out. That from which everything else may flow. Terrestrial, historic, from composted spiral building, to coned, cored peaked-point. Picked at and eaten and grown. Spread-out leaves and branches, fin and gill, leg and arm, ankle toe and hinged finger, grown and re-grown.

Bred upon and seeding, breeding and cross breeding, to a branching point. To a point of no return. Separate, and speciated, to a point, to a limit, and then again. Changing colour and shape, in response to internal and external stimulus.

In deep-water chasm, contained and enclosed silica membrane, muscle pulsing tidal water plasma. With flagella wafting tails washing off, moving around in the warm waters. In the tiny water cellular space, undissolved passing atomic particles, and subatomic pieces. Caught, stampede herded and strung together. Exchanging magnetically charged ionic parts. Adding and altering in the heat energetic swirl. Swelling to the tensile limit, bulging and splitting the membrane. Down the middle, crosswise laterally and horizontally. Across centrifugal floating, wadded up polymerase strings. Incredibly strange and bizarre, yet familiar, recognizable, through magnifying *reflected*-image.

Known colour and shape, mediating the mystifying complexity of different worlds. Another microscopic, and macroscopic world. Yet part and parcel of this same world. Irreducible complexity. Improbable magnitude. Through multiplying frames of-reference: In *principle* un-ending.

With no beginning and no End. Purposeful Only as to the present image, experienced, retrospected over previous layers, and prospecting layers to become Planet-sized planetesimal. Dominating the immediate neighbourhood location and composition. Wild-life landscape scanned scammed empty *extreme*-Nature filmed; intricate and interesting, in amazing range of detail, unseen by the naked-eye. Time-*lapse* speeded-up and slowed-motion *ultra* close-up and distantly-viewed frames and features. The ordinary, in detail, becoming more intimidating and unfamiliarly ugly, yet more beautiful. New-*fossils* and species and genus-Taxonomy discovered all the time at every point in the continuum of life, large and small, overwhelming variety and beauty. Unimagined links and connectivity; in minute and massive view, previously smooth-surface appearing jagged and rough the *rough*-nesting and smoothed-line; taken to another resonance.

Variating between wavelength colour changes, chaotic-verges between-fronts movement where none seen or *imagined* stillness where movement held, in the grip of visioned: View-Point: Wind-*blown* scudding cloud below rapidly shifting rising and setting, waxing and waning sun and moon and starlight constellation, slow- shuttering.

In a state of nature, as strange and complex as any unfamiliar natural-landscape, cloud and coastline, estuary-basin, countryside scene, village dene; as any Town and City conurbation, distributaries and rows of parked pieces vehicles for transport of other pieces. Along and alongside tracks, flattened out through routes of convenience and expedience. Heat turbine driven, electro-magnetically and chemically powered along. Field and ragged patches, plants and trees, fanned out follicle and rooted fibre, breathing and sapping, sprouting, growing through, cyclical times. Camera with high speed framing, metabolic rate moving along with the flight or swim, running charging, attacking leopard, scared scale-blurring of escaping monkeys, and caught-*gazelle*.

Short and long beaked bird picking and snatching at periodically smaller and larger seed heads. Variously thriving at the expense of another, dying from insufficiency, or choking on oversized sufficiency. Bacterium to elephant, flea on flea. Through more than twenty, possibly as much as 27, 28, or 26 orders of magnitude…

Disrupted and restored pattern, through choroplastid plant, viral germ animalcule, and ever more complex, sophisticated and branching, living and dead ended extinct ancestral lines, through insect, reptile, avian, and mammalian description:
- In: A Great Chain of Being…
- Biogenic Tree of Life.
-As We *know* IT!

Computational apparition, set cladistics, classifying reforming the evolutionary relationships, in language formation, from the most ancient to the most modern deep structure. Geographical accidental and Trade-routed history. Flora and fauna continually and continuing to be discovered and re-discovered, altered and changing genus speciation information-exchange. Descriptive of shape and pattern, shown in leaf-vein river-estuary colour-pattern petal-print eyeball almost symmetric radial turned-shell rough proximal-diagrammatics and distance representation taken-directly linking the trunked and seeding branching-out.

Between matter and species, the smallest mere effects, of changing and interchanging recombinant material. Gradually, very slowly, accidentally, rapidly, spontaneously, and deliberately, with the will to survive and reproduce the successful. Tending and mending, copying and inheriting traits of competence, refined to the exclusion of others, with *learned* Free-Will.

Picking-up tricks, passed on, re-constructing the furnishings open to *change*, and infection; out of The Given-World, in front of their eyes.

Contemporaneous mutating patterns of microbial, plant, animal, terrestrial and galactic change, survival and death, and continuation. Human-*species* bi-pedal naked large the only latest living-Member of a Genus, alone on The Planet. Extinguishing, for food, energy and territory, the lineage a lonely, broad and stubborn, disconnected except by from the trunk, a singular and branch of spread, and still spreading Tree of Life; still a reaching toward Sunlight and re-reflected Lunar-rooted to: The Centre; and from The Center of The Earth. But with no closest-branch to rely on, no nearest offshoots to continue; should Asteroidal thunder and lightning-strike, should a minute-infestation begin and takeover. With now only ourselves and our knowledge, and our willingness to understand and protect to keep us going.

Electronic music played in the spaces, standing now on a moving floor, ahead, a fibre optic manikin model, a 3D MRI CAT spectroscopic scanned image, moved towards them.

The Visitors entered, each into their own body, like a ritual de-
fleshing, dis-emboweling, heart and brain extraction, surgical
removing, like a meditation, through X ray and functional:
Magnetic- Resonance: *imaged* snapshots. Ultrasonic tomography,
stacked 2D pixelated and scanning 3D voxel image slices, algorithm
attenuating sound waves, emitted through transducer drum, spectral
bar code, producing artificially digitally enhanced red, green, blue
and violet colour *image*.

Through the eye and ear, almost simultaneously, through the mouth
and nostrils, and through the whole of the flesh. With a shudder,
through the whole of the epidermis layer and interlayer of oily
membrane, wetted from the inside. A damp outwardly conjoined
fatty tissue inner membrane, spread out and folding in around the
expanded body. Viscous greasy grey and light pink fatty matter,
conducting carbon root hair fibre, given interior from outer
sensation, connected inner fibulating nerve tissue.

Inside the pore-membrane capillaried vessel, soaked and flooded in
red bloodied vein.

White globules, spiked yellowy packages, and mineral crystal pieces
floated, flushed through pipework, around the containered tube
pumping machine. Moving with the flow, through running viscous in
hydraulic and gas fuel propelled and propelling capsule, washing
back from offshoots, pumped back used up thinned out purple blue,
sumped return through pulsing thick lining tissue, scanned through
paper thin membraned venous wrapped around entering, swelling
and emptying shunting organ.

A foetal heartbeat, flowed through swollen and emptied chamber, along connective tissue wall bypassed, whirring through arterial tubes, around air filtering swelling and exhausting ciliated adjacent bags. Breath from outside shunted in and out, absorbing into and floated off, on the re-reddened outgoing briny-tide.

On a journey with camera obscura, as in a lensed nanoscope, air fuel driven engine, past other strangely shaped geared motor spindled bushings and fairings, paddling down the pool shute tube, faster and slower running pieces, in the swim bearing and churning out copy and revision on the way. Sticking and absorbing, snapping and wrapping around. Wrapped up and consumed in resistant corpuscular globule, in chemical endoplasm, absorbed with the liquefied gases, water and minerals, before able to cause any trouble, swelling or blocking, using up the bodies resources for themselves, rather than the greater good.

Passing now channeled outward routes, repumped with regular swelling breath, as if being saved from drowning each time. Tumbling down and through to saturated stinking, nauseating and gurgitating sac. Churning out and around and into huddled multitudinously massed, regurgitating and reproducing microbial noisy, seething bubbling and burping gut flora.

Through a clear wall, seen working on plant and animal fibres delivered along walled ultrastructure vast surface, of sweet and sweaty, acid fatty absorbant and sensitive spikes and spindles, through muscle pushing tube, from above. Squeezed down, into and out of, into a long maze of tube below, eventually squeezed out again, once the bacterial horde has done, washed through as waste.

At the rim, the invited guest, collecting simple granulated lumpy sugar particles and fatty linked chained globules, taken off and stored ringed outer layers, carried around to be energetically pumped out and burned off at the veined, muscled and sinuous tipped ends. Sieved through brown heavy sagging bag, further on, through thudding and thumping vein, and capillaries spread out. Zooming in and out, through tissue and organ, past tumbling fall, a well springing ductless gland, manufacturing and giving rise to hormonal secretion, passed directly into the plateleted blood flow, streaming, esturied brooking, into enflamed fibre.

Chemically powering and setting, development and growth in further action, motion bubbling and leaking, into tensing and untensing muscle, soaked through, filling and emptying.

Endoscoping through internal cavities, osmosis through less dense fluid. Through semi-permeable membrane, separating from denser, past circuitous veined junctions. Capilleried to moving letting and restricting tissue strung muscle jointed, calcite bone, shadowed through the sticky bloodied walls. Ham strung sensors and stimulators, rapidly firing nerve cells.

Muscle extension and contraction. Triggering and articulating grip and release. Holding and releasing waste product. Ridden through muscle, over and into, moved catacombic and marrow fat middle, and out of the opposite, bony knobbed and crusted bow capped and cupped, lubricated tipped end.

To continue through more pink pale tissue muscle, with a flash of bright red light out onto the adjoined sparking axion.

Onward through thickening cable, wrapped into a protective setting sheath, coiled along corded curvatured column, past cobbled spaced bony pieces, held up momentarily on entry, to pass through into swollen folded and contoured, cloudy grey puffed lobe. At the triangulated ended nerve, tissue along with entangled arterial vein and estuary, sutured and saturated, extending forward and back.

Connected bio-electric feedback, now detecting the inner activities of the body, passed through. With re-cognisable picture, the sized body to a quarter of the now ensconced brain mass. Waves of inflating and deflating, switching on and off messages, through intraneural circuitry, chemical gradient defining, flickering from: space-to-space.

Simple reflexes, linear and exponential, listing and linking operator, coding and decoding, attenuated through complex bargaining valence. With internal function, to interact with each internal side, and the now once more seen and heard surround. Looking out onto mirror scanned whole body image, radiating spidery rays. Electro magnetic thermal aura, through meridial and focal points, rounded budded and lobe forms over lapping, like filaments of brain coral, radiating image. Preserved on clear photographic plate.

Brainwave boogie woogie, stopwatching time, looking for the rythms, the similarities, the minute differences.From slow to delta to theta to alpha to beta to gamma fast frequency, 1, to over 30 wavelengths, through preparing to move a muscle, deep sleep, drowsy trance, relaxed and awake, activity focused anxious thinking and dream, forming chemical perception and memory, genetic remembrance and re-learning. Converted into sound, and pictures.

A dance through the conscious, and subconscious, through the will, the moral maze, the decision.

Information delivery; greetings, farewells and social dialogue; empathy; encouragement…

Through dissection of the subcutaneous layers, peeled back, through flesh and fatty conglomeration, thickened strengthening contracting and extended muscle twitches, nerve ends electro-magnetic and chemical firing. To and from the pulsing, sensing organs, to and from the pulsing brain, secured inside the skeletal and skulled frame. Continuing para-sympathetic un-thought of breathing, digestive energy system, learned movement, recording the light images and sounded echoes, sympathetic comparison of thermal chromatic graduated shape and movement, positional capture, from each side of the separated self, from the entrance through the now exiting body-shell self.

Holding the arms outstretched, internally sensed, as if standing still with eyes blind closed, not even colour. Testing the impulsive response to immediate threat, or desire, outweighing the weighing-up.

Regulating homeostasis in phased inner chemical bursts, sinking or re-energising plasma globulins, hunger and digestion stimulating, passing into tissue raising function. Across the blood-brain barrier, in mental activity and awareness, of self across the divide, of light and dark circadian rhythm and local movement, opening the eyes and constructing 3D and phase time effect picture, of the outside world. *Flash*-ing back and forth between neural clusters, the outside region, the mirrored self, now reflected into the brain regions. Given meaning to the organism, for food, shelter, and companionship. Communicating with others moving into the picture, with movement and vision, feeling the bodies' movement.

Instructing, imaging, silently lifting one finger, to make a statement.
Brain cause actions mindful only afterwards,
Genetic and historical makeup, illusion of free-will
Trust-Game: sharing co-operative, fining free will riders,
Free-loaders' regulate group-actions
The manipulation, the ready prediction, on practiced novel and
unique circumstances, and outcomes, realized after the event.

Listed in the protocols and conventions, of rationalized everyday
life. The violent confrontational impulse shot through the system,
only recognized and recorded situation afterwards. Maybe in blank
puzzle listed, the qualia in conjoined statements, that make up
everyday experience, chosen selected, from the repertoire.
Behind the opened eyes and ahead, in front, looking at self, from the
outside. Each to themselves, watching, standing stock still. At the
world around, as looking through their own bodies, hearing and
seeing themselves, in exact replica, crystal clear mirror image. The
image moved, when each one of the visitors moved. Their own, and
others bodies, moving-through.
Making the move forward, to touch, to greet, themselves, and each
other, *laughing*
Looking-out, with distorted altering image, reflected and feeling the
strange sense of self, as seen through the minds camera eye. Felt
through the reality of the moment, each watching and waiting visitor,
in temporal processing-lag.

Causing: image to re-appear in the consciousness, a fraction of a second after the flash in the eye, after the recognition event with the outside-world. Turning, the realization trailing behind, stamped into the unconscious memory, for further rapid reference. To reflex the grinning captivated re-sponse, ever reducing the trail to auto-function, referencing the choices and decisions and events made before avoiding, seeking and selecting-out.

The Resulting-Action: made conscious, in the second after the enactment. The sensed mental image of what may occur, preceding the actual occurance, the actual fact, taken place.

The result, the outcome, ever in doubt. The test, sensory and mechanical, acting out the simple-act of indicating on the screens now in front of them, which shapes matched.

Routine motor-control, sensing a miscalculation, something amiss, when there is no clear image to be had. Selecting and choosing, to form a clear mental image, and image of the outside world.

Object imaged, goal selection, overt verbal behaviour, naming pictures and association, responsive body language, deep structured reception, procrastination, and decision making, matching and comparing and relating, posting a shape through a slot.

One to one correlation, variant sharpened or blunted, clear or confused response and reflex.

On a fly through diagnostic adventure, whole body magnetically scanned, resonated cross sectional sliced images, computed tomographic screening.

Screened result, the model now taken through bio-metric measurement, biocentric, anthropocentric and ethnocentric, navigated through graphic display. Now the model image, the self, turning upwards, in reverse, and inside-out.

At the inside pointed end of one of many a floating tube chamber, rolled out from the cellular nodal tip, a single cell absorbed chain length, released moved through the ululating tube. Separated pairs, singles dis-attached, from protective double cavity wall shell against which they were apparently leaned against.

Spun released and away, singularly racing through an enclosed space, one into a flood of dark blood red, another extruding tubing tailed, let out in a creamy white plasmic seminiferous cloud.

Water and fuel dissolved, soaked into energizing, pushed and pumped and erupting out of a follicle tuber ending, falling, floating, afloat and rolling gently in viscous fluid. Curled up and waiting, or flapping the legs tailed together wildly, to stay afloat and target, holding the breath, arms wrapped around and tied along the sides, catapulted through, tearing ahead.

Through narrowing tube, to be wasted in mass-extinction, or as the one on impact to crash headlong, to be crashed headlong, into and against the cracked membrane dermis, of a waiting unfertilized human-egg.

Once inside, each, both as if in a trance. The cellular head only, unneeded tail broken off and dissolved slowed and moving forward, into the cytoplasm.

Drawing renewed energy and strength, turning around, bonded absorbed with the centred core. Both dropping down together now, settling and burying into the feeding surround. The unseparated host sapping, the newly arrived spore struggling for air fuel and food, they moved into conjoined position, to keep the foetus growing until it must be born.

Sperm fused with egg, seed primitive streak, thickened nodal band forming gastrulate nervous systemic thread, secreting, subtracting and adding, multiplying and dividing; along chemical differential concentration gradient, fading into the next and onto the next, recharged through the whole.

Locked in to remain on the same spot, reset combination, bacterium or elephant, ratcheted together, purged of previously failed part, testing out resample, bedded into the damp edges of a salty swamp pool, rapidly growing to fill the space. From the centre, doubling, triangulating and quadrupling, separating across and along the middle, cluster forming around the repeating tubing core. Switching differentiating part from the potential whole, ballooning, puffing out in controlled continuating bi-lateral cupping, folding and reverse folding back on itself, radial elongated streaked disc cylinder, hollowed and curled, hunched huddled segmented budding, funneling out mouth tube flow gut, inner feeding attached connected to outer cord, pumping into the ventral fanning capillaries and vein swelling return valve, self starting pumping tissue layer.

Feeding and forming carapace body and skeletal wired and linked brain case, head and neck, chest rib cage, to lower curving back and tail, barnacle feathery fin comb, tucking in lengthening conjoined growing muscle block and spacing bone cartlege disc. Wrapped in fatty padding, with proximal distortion, loosing an inevitable alteration, along branching, turning budding nodular arms and legs, finger and toe bones, and reformed tail, tucked in and lopped.

The whole combined form, attached and bonded in the middle, buried into the inflaming and expanding warm spongy wall around, and latched on to. Warm pumping blood and water, flowing around and into the greasy wrinkled bundle. Unwinding, and floating off, still attached, into a warm pool of gushing salty water. Cord, attached at the middle, lay outwards, attached inwards, a found way in, and out, its bloody contents sieved and circulated through swollen tissue moulded beating heart.

In unison, in competition with its nursing mother, energy feeding through retaining spongy reservoir, coiled in the sac, part bloat filled already, through closed mouth gut and anal tube, with bile and water, in held nutrient teeming froth, excreted back waste. From belly gut to blocked mouth and anus, linked transmitting cord, to fan out along blood vessels to the organs and skin, to connect the specific sensory functions of the ears and eyes, and cerebrum swelling and folding and gently folding over again. Simple gut and complex sensory blood and nerve endings in the bloat, controlling the whole now, maintaining its quarter in its fight for survival, the swelling cyst twitching life.

Awareness, and awareness of awareness. Vaguely aware of light and dark, spewing back morning sickness, powering, steadily building, cell by cell, along strands, and with strained through running chyle, passed newly wafting tubed cilia funneling, supped and exhausting back thorough the cord, and into the engulfing surround.

Linked throughout, attached in increasingly putrid water and flaky shed actin layered flesh. Expanding slowly, and now rapidly, in regular and changing fashion, stems twisting and turning outwards and inwards. Taking over the variating forms, front limb to toe, built flat tissue, plate folds of cartilage along ossifying calcifying skeleton.

Each stage forming and developing rapidly, otherwise reabsorbing to be turned into another creature, in another egg like womb, the reflections of the each potential inscribed in the unique original atavism, the intimation of leaf flowering insect, tadpole toed snake, or birdfish, bacterium or mammoth appeared and dissolved, silenced as the features ripened, reflected in the sounded reflexes present.
Themed non specific genes sprouting cells
Canine teeth
Nipples and breats, dark aureolar skin armpit to groin mammary milk lines
Hand walking
Extra webbed fingers birth defect
Hiccups, close glottis to stop water getting into lungs, pump over ridged gills/neck

In water, aquatic,
Limbed and tail budded appendage foreshortened and lost, spreading separating ligament, webbing digits and scaffolding cartilaginous noto-cord, and bony-spine.

Malleable large head-part cranium, folding tissue inside, linked to wiry sparking cable, to the rest of the membraned cavity surfaces, the exterior shape lit and scanned in fuzzy outline, solidifying fed muscled and skeletal frame.

Liquid lapped around and passed by small gill like slits in the side of the head end, hinged conjoined flaps, moving around excessively expanding moulded soft skull. Closed and sleeping, open and staring through the lapping slough bilge, moving inside, a large retinal eyes bulge outward.

Seeing ahead, now enclosed side hearing, booming thudding sound through water. Touching swelling parts, at the jawline, stretched and parted nostrils and lips, sealed into the inner integument, and at exit point drawn in. Retained inwards and rolled out of the internally insulating fatted flesh covering layer, connecting inner membrane tissue, and reflected shiny milky wax greased follicle skin, breast ribbed and pinched symmetric suckling nipples, on both girl and boy.

The new brain folding the enclosing inner membrane, the sac full
and functioning, the genitalia flowered, divided between the toe and
abdomen, between the abdomen and head. Laddered steps mixed,
and split between preserved and deeply retained germ cell, the
preserved retaining half variation, produced, and ready to produce as
many more as required in the lifetime of the whole. The half lives of
sons and daughter cells ready for the replication of either.
Waiting their time to waste, renew, and diversify.

The breathing flat lungs and heart, pumping and feeding, the firing
pattern, linking parallel sides of almost symmetrical matter,
mapping the expanding fat and muscle fibre soft boned pulsing
organ. The eyes hazily aware, to look around, at a watery reflected
sense of self, in space all around.

Follicle soft down, wafting in water, gill, fin, shell, scale, wing,
claw, gummy rowed tooth and nail could have appeared.
Moving a reflexive arm and hand, kicking a reflexive leg, and
curling the separating toes. The vision scanned, photographed
moving, as if in a dense watery hall of mirrors. Almost full, almost
sized, almost identical, almost perfect body model.

Rolling restricted around, kicking legs and pushing arms and hands feeling, smiling with some satisfaction, with vaguely recognized sounds and light shadows, grimacing and closing down to sleep. In the tightly enclosing disgusting space, the waters space swelling, pulsing, until burst, pumped, flushed out, in a sudden and terrifying rapid rushing water ride. Narrower and narrower, through the end of an only just giving tunnel. Converging in at the sides and roof and floor, squeezing and squeezed through, until exhausted. Pushed out, and turned and pulled out, in a spluttering of light, noise and surprise.

Gasping, puking fatty stopper wad, out into the air, drawing in, startled, and amazed, shocked and screaming. Bawling out, unable to gasp in, until the last desperate moment, and out again, crying eye balling, without tears yet. Warm fur shed and left behind, except for soft down all over, and a mopped large and swollen skull cap. Now in the sleepy gradual awakening of light and noise and nurtured growth, unable any longer, to return.
Washed in the sheer dimmed lighting, with crackling of liquid voices around , warm clean water and cuddled.

Coddled against familiar scent, now outside, finding the found nipple, gripping onto for dear life. Breathing through the nose, suckling, choking, nearly asphyxiating, through the mouth, warm gushing. To become a familiar warm waft, of milk, sweat and blanket.

Tight shadow coloured the surround, with slow almost silent breathing, and once more thankful airy asleep, dreamt of shuttered womb.

Awoken, a genetic molecular clock timer ticking, of lost memory and perception, pumping, pulsing, and beating time. Collected on the passage and through the air and all around, breathing and swallowing microbial bacteria to gradually, defend and over the years, take over the organism. To choose the menu and diet, for now to settle in mutually assured continuation.

Watched, continuing regenerating, and restoring, flare peaked capped packages, in polarized laser charged synergetic exchange. Infected and erasing, with each toxic exchange, mycobacteria, aggressive pathogenic disease ridden infection.

Acting within host cells, antibodies and macrophages of the cell mediated immune system. To continuously assault and destroy from within, invasion of freed parts, randomly, radically attacking and altering. Blocking and shortening at each divide, setting upper limit, reactive free element, poisoning, the junk and rubbish allowed to accumulate. Toxin cell surface receptor and suppressor, losing conductivity, shared and chaperoning, losing their shape under stress, energy used up, repaired, repeated.

Frailties and disease attacks, pustule and deformity. Fungal extracts inhibit or promote cell growth, bubble micro-pump, split to unequal parts, move through longer heavier end. Cellular motor unclogging arteries, artificial limb, sense organ, plastic remodeling surgery?

-Bio-tech can stop Bioterror!!
-Bio weapons, poisonous and corrosive drugs to counter poisonous and corrosive pathogen plague through body population, transferring trading genetic deadly material, virulent, antibodies becoming drug resistant, and more virulent, overwhelming the host in shared mutual destruction.

Uninvited party guests, raiding the stores and structures of the hosts house and home, eventually but not inevitably, destroying the base and all its contents including itself, destroying, or transformed into something else.

Hormon€al growth-fact-or, marrow bone blood damage repair. Bone marrow stem cells, surface protein blood platelets, fat and muscle, stem cells from sternum and shoulder, Achilles tendon, and , regenerating tissues in the injured cleft crevice, taking on showered bone particle.

Nerve releasing, shielding, columnar encasing. Cortex sheathed, finding reacting, altering to the replacement set. Quick recovery time, and protected with extended wear and endurance.

Through portal veins and main artery to the damaged,
malfunctioning or diseased functioning part, to replace, to r-grow, to
re-function.
Cognitive behavioural, hypnosis, association, drugs, from intrusive
memory and nightmare, panic and depression, neurosis and
psychosis
In the awakening, back to the body. The imaged self, it could be, it
could have been, a dream, a nightmare, a desire, a hope, a reality, all
together.

Bringing on the haunting spectre of death, ones own, and others,
dear and distant. Pus suppurating, arteries clogged, heart and head,
condemned in constant flux, and state of disrepair. Through the ages,
sepsis and pneumonia, leprosy and malaria, plague viral fever,
immune disfunction, tiring sapping energy. ?

Like a dead fish sagging, hanging sideways, curving downwards,
under pressure, to give way. Outside the body again, recomposed,
tackling the inflicted forensic injuries of life, and the entropy of
ageing…

Combating the poisonous by-products of life, itching and infected
necrotic oozings, osteoporosis fracture, the combating of
inflammations and infectious disease, along with the balancing of
heat and cold and blood letting pressures, waters and salts, sugar
insulin.

Freed body radicals and malignant tumor, loosed cellular energy crisis, depleted and deranged connectivity, bringing on weakness and blockage, exposure to toxins, sunlight, and errors in replication. Vaccines and retro virals, microglobule supplements and magic pills. Straightforward talking, exercise, chemical herb plant, and derived drug. The complete herbalist. Therapeutic intervention on injury and illness, re-stimulated soft polymer gel ventricles, activating and growing bone graft, plastic prosthetic limb, metal replication, manipulation and massage, stimulating acupunctural impulses and repair.

Replacement transplant and transfusion, implanted cell and stemcell derivatives and repair. Developed in body fluids and petri dish, from cord blood, fetal amniotic or adult family cell bank:
Remove: *absolute* random*ness*
Beethoven-fallacy, music makes you brighter?
Telemere length trancated capping chromosome, young old age
Predictive personal or public institutions, unintended consequences, species and culture-cloned miniscule nanopod devices, laser electrodes and magnets, to correct and add nervous and muscular response. Microscopic, biomolecular, enzyme motor propelling nickel plate blade, single molecular electro-transister nano-particle. Nanotubular sensors, detecting composition, chain linking strands inside tiny micro-globules crossing the blood brain barrier.

A determination to go on, or an inability to fight any more. Ultimately unable to turn back, or rerun the biological clock, disrupting the suicide of the body, assisted, defined, in the release of the mind, leaving others before, and behind to carry-on.

Licking wounds, disinfecting, any incident or accident that could bring an end, to it all, at any time. The healing mysteries and methods, the apothecary and physicians gentle and invasive, genuine and exploitative arts, to deter the inevitable decline.

The fragile skeletal frame curvature, assaulted with life, hands clawing, returning, collapsing, broken and wasting. From soft and resilient, to hardening and brittle, fusing and crumbling arteries, bone and tissue, diminishing movement and sensory receptivity.

No way back, no immortality, no extension of maximum life, 120 Earth years. From which the interior would not survive, even if frozen and thawed, even if radiated and irradiated, even if exactly and perfectly cloned. Would be lost in decay and decomposition, returned into water and dust, without spark.

Death shock, blood loss, draining away from the skin, brain starved of blood sugar and oxygen, dilate vessels, attempting extra supply of blood to brain, from liver and long muscles, euphoria set in, mental detachment, and flashback. Through stored memory, for perhaps the last time, in consuming bliss and transcendence, the heart stops, respiration stopped, eyes reflexes stop, clinically body and brain, dead.

The waning spirit-soul, remembered, resided in the living organs of the blood, the heart, the liver, the capilleried sensitized skin, and the live brain, weakening with the rattle of the bodies bones, dissipating with the lifeblood, the flesh and blood remaining and new blood passed on, blood run cold, in the coldcoldground.

Select Object, Display Mode, Graphic, Modify Mode,
at various angles of rotation, picture cut-off, around and across zoetrope moving magic eye picture. The simple-act of posting a shape through a slot, of indicating on the screens in front of them. Which shapes matched others. Routine motor control, and thought sensing a miscalculation. Something amiss, when there is no clear other image to be had.
Select Object, Display Mode, Graphic, Modify Mode.
At various angles of rotation, picture cut-off, around and across zoetrope moving magic eye picture.
Select linear and depth perception, illusion of concave and convex face, recognized double vision, two eyes, mouth, and nose, elongated rounded, featureless template. Recognised immediately, the features began to appear, lip and hair, eyelashes and ears.
Sounds entering, but poorly shaped for direction, looking around to see where the sound is emitted from.
Hearing the sound all around.
Within and without.
The sound of breathing, heart pumping, ears ringing quietly, drum beating, feathers, grasses-singing…

A scene, a lived in, living scene. Outside the EarthCentre,
in parklands, walking running, the beat increasing, the pitch rising,
dropping to slower, pacing trot, lower chord, vibrating the muscles
and limbs.
Holding up and moving through the landscape.
To a village, a harbour and town, and city port, stepped into and
traveling through.
On dog, or camel, or horse drawn cart, on wheels, of a bus, a coach,
a car, over the water rainbow, wing planed into the air.
Dropping, the reflex-gasp, to retain air, energy conserved into the
midpoint, let slowly into the muscles, slowly becoming aware, of
being underwater.Drifting on a tide, slowly rising, to the surface, to
swim to the shore, and walk again, naked over the sands.The group
knew each other, waved hello, as they lost body hair and wrapped
themselves in leaves, knitted together. Dressed, re-emerged into the
present. Grouped together, in a room, where tests were set out, to try
to attempt to score points; state facts, about the subject, their family
and friends.

What is your name …?
… Thank you.
What is your age?
Do you drink excess alcohol, or smoke at all?
Thank you.

Are either your parents still alive? Please state clearly whether either your, 'mother', or, 'father', or, 'mother and father', are, still alive. We offer our congratulations. If you know how many years … your mother … has at this time, please indicate her exact, or approximate age with the median-medium: counted to the nearest N-years.

If you know how many years … your father …, has at this time, please indicate … his … exact, or approximate age, with the mediun counted to the nearest 5 years.

We offer our condolences.

If you know what year … your mother … died, please indicate the exact, or approximate year to the nearest 5 years, of the year … she … died.

If you know when … your father … died, please indicate the exact, or approximate year to the nearest 5 years, when … he … died.

Selecting and choosing, forming a clear image. From the recording upside down negative plate, the untouchable emotional feeling.

From the membrane of the skin, the imaging of something that does not yet exist.

That has not yet happened, except in the imagining.

The intention, and action selected, the outcome ever uncertain.

Benign, and malignant, psychosocial profile, computer modeled, telesensory input, behavioural output.

Object imaged, goal selection, overt verbal behaviour, body language, deep-structured.

Reception, procrastination, and decision making.

Turning up-wards, in re-verse, and inside-out.

Seen structured, overlaying the reflex system, linked similarities, to the here and now.

Laughing into their own and each others eyes, stepped out of the river, and into another, the journey took them back inside.

A life flashed past. Through a tunnel of light, hyperactive brain function, random firing the visual cortex cord, trying to repair, to bring back together. To summarise, upsetting or pleasing events, life review, brought back from: Near Death Experience. !Robotic-Arm: attached to synaptic axon nanowires, chipped neural prosthetics, long transmitters, short receptors, manipulating numbers and letters, pixels, soundwaves, speech, and listening.

Gates and building blocks

Biomotors, circular silicon track,

Through: 'Medical Notes' cadavar. Background music of sequencing acids, sequenced proteins. Harmful-toxin in-fected food, alerted through inflaming abdominal bile. Ducting nausea and diarea reflex. Telemere graphed and masted messaged, testing the threat, overloading networking, error-messaging attracting streaming combatant. To fat-wrap, and render harmless, to disarm and capture. Absorb and discharge, recharged and dispatched, in the service of the larger, hydrating and re-energising whole.

Droplets flowing together, fusing layers and rings, muscle and artery forming, tubular clumping, Poisonous waste drawn from the system, thread like ducts at sensitive terminals matter destructive of its life, small intestine openiung out, increasing flows, through great sewer and drainage canal to the open sea, buried in the land.

Brain fatty mass, sheathed transmitter and receptor cells enclosed and conjoined with the rest. Ride accelerometer, measuring g-forces, pulse ECG, helmet mounted face expression camera, intra-venous, invitro fertility treatment no more pregnancy, no more sperm production. The agony, and the ecstasy. The corpsed, programmed: Life-Growth: pending accident, or natural death.

The death of everything, no minerals, no liquids, no gases, alive and made up of. Licorice for cholsterol and adrenal glands, garlic ant-viral, red hot and green chilli peppers for the heart, fruit and vegetables for the diet.

Despite continuing modification and selection, screening out and balancing the non symmetric, exchange between parts,

Gene boat rocking on a gene pool, the given sea, drifting aimlessly, raising a sail into the prevailing wind, taking the helm, tiller steering away from stormy sea, finding new waters to sail and swim-into in-pain, glued sacs, tissue holding-together. Feeding, and excreting. Keeping warm, and cosily, tucked up, sheets and blankets, folded in.

Knocked, bruised, drawing blood and distortion and pulling of the scar tissue, minutely fractured bone set in dried pourous. In rain humidity, and cold wind, stmospheric pressure around, and inside. Swelling, with air and water and vacuous gaps and spaces. Bubbling between the vertebrae and skeletal ligaments and bones. Stimulating enwrapping nerves, rapid onset of pain. Stretched to relieve, hot tub and gentle exercise. Keeping dry and warm. Sat back, in a chair against the wall, out of bed now for a few hours, then thankfully back to bed and a long sleep, why not sleep here, the eyes dropped, the rest of sleep-taken.

Electro-magnetic brainwaves low-amplitude, high frequency alertness, high amplitude, low frequency asleep. Large slow waves, deep and dreamless, with: Rapid Eye Movements in: Sleep.

To imagine, remember, and remember anew. To dream. To awake. Cerebellum controlling movement and co-ordination. Frontal and parietal lobes, reasoning and conscious control. Mathematical algebraic algorithmic symmetry: Group Theory. Reality: The Imaginary Friend(s), the-Other of: The-*I*magination: developing the theory of mind, and mindfulness. Transforming themselves into other, sharing beliefs, desires and intentions, understanding, and misunderstanding.

The illusions of free-will, and personal identity, of soul, and self. Useful fictions, of which the author, and audience, are one and the same. Machine muscles, conducting polymer dielectric metal composite, air and sugar-fueled. Healing, re-scarring, and sealing over.

Pungent smell of infected and rotting flesh, inflicted by the wrath of the gods, bad karma, evil jinxing jinn. Looking to cast out devils, poison the patient, amputate, treat patient with herbs and spices, ground animal parts, bones, teeth and claws, as corrective, revitaliser, to evade, counter pain and death, this time, enfeebling glows lowering, lights going out.

ultrasound detection

ears ill equipped to hear directional sound, limited smell receptors, radiation damaged cells broken into fragments, plastic extruding machine desktop printing out control electronics circuit board, screen and casing, knobs and buttons, ZXY drive belt motor replicating reconstituting recycling parts and spare parts, design out of trouble? DNA replication laboratory machine

Embryonic blood and stem cell

Contraceptive diapause halt to development until weather and food supply sufficient to survive, until body able to repair itself

Deep dive reflex, divert blood to central nervous system and brain, globin fatty energy storing muscle-cells

Without-sleep, drowsing, micronapping, unihemispheric sleep eye closed, limited focus, failing eyesight, photoreceptors failing…

As if revisiting the crime scene, the remains and the culprit leaving a fingerprint, biometric record, bone and drop of blood leaked from flesh.

The mystery murder weapon, the droppings from the feast beast, the attempted escape, the mystery murder. With a body, like a murder mystery, with a weapon, forensic tools, but no suspect. No body. Many suspects. All innocent, except one, or maybe two; or maybe all. Like: Detectives:... arriving-on: The Scene after: The-Event. To: piece together what might have happened, from the evidence,

- Not: *I*mmortal-Gods' then?

One of the visitors hesitantly mentioned.

    - Beyond time and space, each one of us a different take, some say Prophets, some say just each of us take responsibility for our own God.!

The Visitors: *could* ask predictable robotic questions, or ridiculous unanswerable questions, the answers to which anyone could guess, and no one could know.

    - Unbelievable!

    -Except that it is.

    -You better believe it!

It is happening around us all the time, never stops, started, believable is the first principle, of the already existing organic life of the universe. Us! You and Me! Here and now! It is obvious if you just look around with an open mind. It is simply obvious that we are unique animals with advanced technology and culture, that share characteristics with other animals, most notably monkey chimpanzees; that there may or may not be a God, that without faith there most likely is not a God; nor gods, apart from ourselves perhaps, gods the father, mother nature-bearing more child gods, and mothers, mothers, and fathers, fathers…

How come there are so many different things, atoms, grains of sand, plants, animals, so many we cannot even count them all? There seems to be continuous similarities across all things. Elemental atoms, species and speciations, that make it impossible to differentiate exactly, between one and another, rather than for the obvious differences, in naming for our own needs and purpose, and to help with research.
-How do you know this? Our knowledge, our paradigms, our belief systems are constantly changing. Like spiders webs, we trap different ideas and fit them in. We make them our world, and make worlds for ourselves out of it all.

-Then we do it all over again, once we've fed from and survived. With what we are given, the everyday, and things that just get smaller, and larger, more strange and bizarre, and yet more similar to what we know already, the more we look.

Biological scaling, the tree branching off, in animal, and to some, angelic hierarchy. To explain and dismiss it all, through the comprehension and understanding of desperate mortal reliance in self image, of the immortal ... gods. Eternal. Of: All-Time.

Who would want to live to be some immortal god anyway?

Enjoined in battle, for survival, the lion and the lamb, trapped in a great Earthbound and Universal bound cage. In a vale of laughter and of tears. Standing up to tragedy, falling under the comedy, acted out, on the: Great Stage of Life.

Through optic fibres and fields, sensitive pendules, sounding out, feeling, of attack and being attacked, fight and flight, regrouping tactic, and wild abandon. Feeling pain and emotion, guilt and betrayal,

> -To know what it is to be a bat?! ... or a speechless reed
> blown in the wind!... or a super animal ... super human!
> -And are we responsible for ourselves, and our own world!
> With free-will then?

-Of a sort, maybe. In so far as everything else has free-will.

-What rocks and stones as well?

      -Maybe it is a kind of free-will, they do what they like,

      within the limits, the constraint of everything else …

The commentary continued,

      -With drinkable water, and breathable air, and food to eat,

      regenerating ... being, becoming, here and now.

      -Not so much chicken and egg, as egg, and chicken, and egg

      and chicken and egg and … then us!

      -The vast majority of species, extinct, unable to continue.

      The remainder, with us, like us, similar pressures converging

      on similar solutions, with differing limitations, nesting and

      building earthmounds of remarkable architecture.

      Domed and arched in functional proximal proportion,

      layering and tunneling, piping with vast industrial design and

      production, mechanics and engineering, location,

      communications and transport systems.

      Swarming, industrial building, farm food production, feeding

      and waste disposal, warming and cooling, building up and

      emigrating colonies, moved and moving on. Remembering,

      plotting and planning, across vast, mapped areas.

      Using all of the complex detail, in invention, innovation,

      ingenuity and imagination.

- Complex and intelligent design, by us, or for us then?

- No-one person has ultimate rule over what developed and what did not. We all did this, together, for better or worse, for each of us, our parents, their children, and our childrens' children, with everything and everyone else.

-What is there to say, to show, to evidence, that we are not, each of us, the highest form of intelligent life in the solar system, if not, so far, the Universe. Are not we more likely, even so, to come across, and in contact with other life forms, yes similar to those on, and from: EarthCentre:

-Times' Up!

- Perhaps, variant bacteria or something,

-… and we are likely to find that close to home, from or left to die on Mars, deep below the solar systems planetary moons, regular, and mostly irregular meteor, asteroid, cometary stardust. Although we like our heroes, and villains, it took all of us, with some part to play in each others lives, and the next. What we choose to do, and choose not to do. What we can do to help, and what we cannot help doing. Still it is us, all of us, who have done these things, got this far, and we have got someway further to go yet!

- To where ..?

-To ourselves, and The End of the Universe, perhaps. With no further answer, the display continued its commentary,

- To continue, and develop, using the prevailing paradigms and conditions, adapting to the new. In theory, and in practice, adapting to the immediate environment, and with immediate necessity, the driving force, upon present matter, in space and time.

From the Museum of Life, The Visitors ascended now, on a moving staircase gauntlet studded by glass fronted and steel rope suspended display-cases. Enclosed time encapsulated, made reproduced manufactured objects, from their past. To now; from now, into their future. A stone pestle and mortar, flint tipped spear and metal axe, fired pottery shards and treated leather saddle strap. Hubbed grindstone and metal cart wheel, mechanical clock and heat engine, inert gas radiating light bulb, and electric diode-cell. Telegraphed Radio and Televised Wi-Fi: Transmission, computer links to and from a silver sheeted delicate steel and titanium, aluminium and carbon-fibre framed telescope satellite, rotating: Space-Station.

At the peak, in the stairwell of the escalator, over a protective barrier, an undisturbed pendulum hung, moving imperceptibly. Pointing downwards, indicating the Earth turning beneath them, between encircled marked points, on the ground floor from where they had risen.

Looking down into a near vacuum tube microscope, above a vast open observatory roof, staring out at a pointed, open to the sky. Where the nearest sun to the Earth glowed, in an unseen star strewn milky galaxy, static crackle hissed and spluttered, as occasional objects passed over the silvery sky.

The-Visitors ascended, moved upwards, seemingly standing still. Deliberating the moving steps easily, with automatic holding on or nearly falling backwards. To glance forward and back, at each image, and every artefact, original or otherwise. Depicted, retrieved, as real.

Each object turned in three-dimensions on its solid stand, in time continuing, each one explained, through hidden spotlight speakers to the congregated visitors, in passing, as they passed. Through an opening door at the end, one way arrowed signs pointing toward the exit.

They moved upwards into: Telescopic-Time: at each stair sub-level signs alongside arraigned, stating:

'Not to be touched', 'No photography, or food, allowed', 'Souvenir models may be purchased at the shop at the top of the moving stair'. One directional, one-way arrows indicating the way to the upward exit. Stepping outside, they entered a long brightly lit shopping mall, below looking out onto a lively piazza. The Peaceful Warrior statue spuming fountained, as earlier lit, flickered as if in sunlit flame, and in falling rubble, the steaming waters flow dampened and pool dammed. Let into a continuous running, mountain and hillside streamlet, let down to the river gently flowing, out to meet a calm sea-ward horizon.

Outside now, and before the capitol building, from the Museum of Life, looking once more onto the market square below. Inside a mall, spiraled on oblique and reverse axis, convex and concave in regular and tapered steps and stairwells, along polished wood and steel platformed framed walkways, intersectioning elevator lifts and escalator(s).

Traveling up and down, and along and between, popular piped background music, entertainments and announcements met them. As others arrived. From the museum library, from concert halls, dance halls and theatreland. people moving from the opera house to cinema and stage show, festival and celebration, up into the libraries, galleries, and back into the museum.

At various points, amongst more escalators and elevators and promenade walkways, sweeping spiral staircase fed out below. At the lower floor and top, ascending and descending, to landings at various other levels, roof and sub-basement.

At each foyer entrance, sampled sonovideo widescreens. Prospective audiences watched screens advertising performers, acting out exaggerated roles, reading and singing aloud, with various instruments producing sweet and strange and familiar themed-music. From the concert halls, theatres and cinema, club and radio performances, broadcast or recorded live. Where theatrical and dance events took place, colourful and dazzling flickered, flowed and played in the spaces, restaurant and staged circus. Amongst live and recorded sounds, from closed door clubs and open bars, they could retrace their steps. Revisit places previously passed, along the streets and boulevard, with the same repeat performance, replayed and relayed. A sound, and visiontrack, to our past, and most recent lives.

In an empty auditorium, a clock showing: current and next performance-times.

At each new filling of the seats, rewound and set forward for each following performance. Screens showing previous highlights and advertised clips from each event, screened and re-screened, re-livened, enlivened anew.

Concert music hall performer, playing from orchestrated part, staved and scored to a single conductor, director, impresario. Personally and arbitrarily timing and emoting the-whole-together.

Performers, co-ordinating and improvising, syncopating between themselves loosely tune hooked and free playing jazz, dance and lyrical choir or solo song. Playing, and singing, rhymic and rhythming talk, accompanying exquisite and tuneful freeform variations. Harmonious and discordant. Melodious and cacophonous, strumming and clatterous, philharmonic and symphonic, synthesized in a single beat. Doubled, triplicated, septuplet and octet, signaled fractioned note and beat, electro-static and technological rumblings, mixed within the aural range and sympathy of the listener.

With pleasure and displeasure, relaxing and alarming, drifting and attention seeking, for exchange of the correct concert and entrance checked and clipped ticket. For galleries, concert hall, theatre, sports park and arena, virtual-reality games and 5D cinema.

Announcement and audio visual display, posters and programmes, cinemagraphic display advertised. Screens advertised, everything and anything for sale. For browsing, window shopping, outlets for printed books, audio-visual and CDROM, posters and artifact, cultural icons. Logo-grammed: Super-Market Shop: goods shelved and aisled, piled high. Sales assistants taking orders and checking goods out. Customers crowding and crossing paths and following on, with shopping-trolley and basket, looking at rows and columns, priced and marked-goods.

The visitors stopping to purchase fashioned period clothes, trinkets and ornaments, gadgets and models, furniture and electronic and mechanical equipment, to be ordered from stock, for collection or delivery later. Iconic pleasure, fads and fancies, fashion strictures, must haves, and must have-nots.

Departmental and inter-departmental delights, with religious devotion, indulgence feasting, and relaxation. From: open-areas: on: The Upper Floor of The Shopping Mall, Courtyards below, and large Public Buildings stood, Leisure and Sports and Dance and Concert Halls. Music and conference-theatres, relaxation-rooms, restaurant and snack bars, all inter-connected. The immense store of: The Capital Museum: entertainment galleries and shopping mall, set around above the old plaza square.

Anything and everything could be bought, from salespeople marketing for want and worth, valued and priced, flaunted to taunt and tempt.

Rested and snacked, finishing their food and drink, rested and toileted, the groups of visitors went in and out of shops, restaurant and café bar as they wished. After separating again and meeting up with friends and family, agreed between them, each moved forward with the other, and others, toward indicated neon signed restaurant café bar: to visit: The End of the World.

5. The End of The World: A Bio-Tech Journey.

Moving around now circular turning view outside, hills and mountain, rivered valley and ocean sea, the old city, and inside the new, surrounded plush seating, chairs and tables.

Robotic waiters and waitresses distributed food, poured drinks, moved around on roller skates, with trays of ordered refreshments. The visitors, drinking ice cold and water cistern steaming hot ground bean, herb leaf infused and flavoured drinks, from handled cup or tall logo encrusted beakers. 'Aqua Vie', and or 'Citrus Acid' juices. Imbibing prepared food with exaggerated sounding names, 'Boulder Burger', or 'Earth Crust Cake', talking, laughing and chatting, exchanging pleasantries and shared reference.

Restless beneath them, they stood and sat over a transparent, and apparently suspended-floor.

Background music continued, customers sampled changing video picture and sculpture lined, streamlined self-service, steel and glass rest rooms and toilets.

Wide screen TV stations, live and recorded celebrity rumour and gossip, sanitised news viewpoint and another station given another.

Winning, losing, drawing combative and competitive sports results. Weather and city market reports, recipes and diet plans.

Amongst studio broadcasts, historical footage continuing with entertainment and infotainments, documentaries, film, music, soap opera and comedy with canned laughter.

Quizzes and game shows rerun, with prompted applause, song and dance. Exaggerated but seemingly normal expected everyday, but reassuringly family, home, hospital and courtroom drama.

On individuated selection, from flat screens on table tops and screens around the walls, news reports, from apparently outlying villages, towns and cities. War torn region, with threat of skeletal famine, viral and bacterial plague and other natural disaster. Zoned zoomed picture, of huddled masses.

Frightened, up against a resisting wall, cowed into submission. Dynamite exploding everything inside and out, silver, red and green and blue, flashing debris of bodies and parts, bricks and mortar. Twisted metal shells and shards, the camera dropped, film still running, still filming along the corpsed ground. The next scene, prisoners, enslaved, led away,

- To what fate …? the commentator extolled.

From the escalator, as characters drama busked below around the reformed: Pizza-Plaza Square.

The-Visitors could wander passed glass-partitioned rooms, busy with people carrying, and loading desks, with similar bundles of papers. Papers carried like firewood and food, to rows of locked cabinets, copying machines, and computer square screened, ethernet connection to every other Home and Office: Home as Office. Papers it seemed representing the energy and commodities, power and wealth, weaponry and ammunition dump, carried and reloaded, vital to the life and leisure. That of all that they had seen and been with in the previous-times.

On each level a rain washed or sea de-salinated mineral water-cooler, cool store refrigerator, photocopying machine, and telephone computer modem-terminal.

Ignoring enjoining: The Visitors, the administrators and clerks, mingled and hurried amongst each other. Shouting, talking in huddled groups, waving papers, running up and down staircase, and waiting for elevator lifts beyond.

Along enclosed air conditioned, radiator central heated concrete and broad carpeted corridor, they could see inside myriad offices. Closed off to the world outside, administrators and clerks systematically shuffling and carrying papers along a lobby, to others, wearing intricately patterned, and startlingly simply designed. Mixed brightly or plain coloured, robe, rolled up sleeved shirt, and sharply tailored-cut suit.

Walking and rushing and pushing in and out, of rows of soundless opening and closing doors, spread along other enclosed landings and corridors. As they peered into one of the rooms, one of the officials asked them what they wanted.

- What do you want?

They laughed together, and said they did not know. One visitor said,
- Nothing ..!
then,

- … the answer to life the universe and everything!

Another,

- O.K., well ... what, are you doing then?

- Well … nothing much!

- A lot for 'nothing much' then?!

Depending…on the received intonation, the reply *laughed* at together, or met with a shrug, the visitors returned to their visiting. The workers returned to their work, ignoring the visitors as they stood and watched banks of screen flash with a rhythmic blinking of coordinated pointed dots of light. As high resolution pixels danced and transformed in liquid-crystal quartz-display.

Transmitted: rows and columns and graphs docs.and pics. Emergent indices and number lists, letter-code(s).

Operators tapping frantically, or pausing, only for brief thought or comment to another, returning to keyboard. Moving blinking letters and figures on array-screen.

Buying and Selling, Hiring and Firing, *I*nvesting and Bank-rupting: tithe-and-tax-tribute and charitable-funding, gangster-mob and under the counter-pirating, protection money-and-theft: oiling-the-wheels-of: Commerce and Trade: A hubbub of publicly broadcast voices, through loud speakers and telephone headpieces.

Wall-mounted screen publicly now transmitted relayed constantly updated pictures and information, data and message, from and to, somewhere-else.

Above each-screen: digital clocks numbered the passing hours and minutes. From Cities across the northern and southern hemispheres, eastern and western zones of the globe. Gradations of earlier and later points. Counting the revolutions of the Earth, the revolutions of the planet around the sun, in dated season. Compared and contrasted, shared opening times, markets opening and closing, remaining open T.24/7. the signboard boasted.

'No sleep for the living'.

Instantaneous automated and lively trading, time adjusted to co-incide. Looking through floor to ceiling glass windows to the outside, tall and narrow steel buttressed and concrete cast buildings emerged into a light of day.

Some ancient buildings and monuments and pillars remained, recognizable from earlier times. The dried stilled fountain bowl of the Armed and Peaceful Warrior plaza square below, almost irrelevant, amongst streets and roads.

Like capillaries, veins and main arteries, busy with vehicles, cars and lorries and bicycles. Underground trains rattled and rumbled, out of and into tunnels, disappearing.

Like trailing armies of marching machine ants riding shell encased ravaging beetle, on rolling wheels, infesting, multiplying production and excursion, into the surround.

Along tried-out routes, pedaled, supping in at stored fuel dump, piped in, sapping through and firing out. Through the motion of parts, and exhaust waste, mechanically, electrically and intimately checked and monitored through its drivers, amongst which people walked and jammed the streets below.

Trams rattled and trains rumbled overhead, beyond the conurbations, wide lighted autoroutes, elevated tracks and flyovers, disappearing underpasses, dotted with lighted moving vehicles. The smell of cooking asphalt, wafts across queues of cars and lorries, flickering red and green and orange lights, through tunnels uptown and downtown, pulling into toll plaza choking braided interlocking interchanges and intersections, the screech of brakes and pending crash, smashing tinkling glass and dented metal; the continuing bass rumble and high humming, of trucks and cars along an open highway.

Stretching, stretchering away cruising away, from the skyscrapers surrounding the townside port, crammed with metal containers, forklifted on caterpillar tyre, tracking chain segmented claw crane, chain and hissing hydraulic lifted. Pallets and containers, seemingly precariously balanced, placed in staggered interlocking stacked rows, ready for transport, out to sea, or along the widened embanked clear and: Navigated-River. To: inland lake harbour, village town and city, the river artery feeding to and fro, inward and with estuarial reach outward, abroad and afar, sea gulls screech overhead, looming and veering frantically away and towards ships the size of the old city itself, anchored and drifting out at sea, carrying thick black oil and clear cooled liquid natural gas, to birth where platforms were set and floated, sunken and buried, piped and flame flared out from the seabed, and into the sky.

Vast shafts into the sea and hillside dug pits mined. On continuous piped and escalator belt from the depths.

Brought-out, loaded in a haze of dust, taken off, to smelting and cement works, gas and oil fuel plant, rolling metal and plastic sheet and mould feeding parts dropped out of and onto: Auto-Factory: production- line…or: How Robots Will Build Habitat for W./M. in: Space:…

Venting-stack wreathed tubing containered incinerator. Onto trains and trucks, waiting to pass through on/off lights, opening and closing gates, to pass on routes past neat brick shops and houses, up and down and through the hillsides. Buildings taking in goods and energy to live and carry on, with their inhabitants chosen or accepting abode, their food and fuel from the supermarkets and remaining small shops and market stalls. Piped and carried and taken in, and used up, electric light and voltaged wavelengths, bottled and piped gas, to fire the energy requirements, for warmth and cooling, food cooking and digestive-leisure.

To: power radio television aeriels and dishes and video and telephone cable points, connected in to the rest of the world. Paved paths and asphalted and concrete layered car parks, streets and gridded and endless roads covered the bare earth. Led away again passed giant metal and concrete edifices, solid rectangles and bulbous spheres, connected to complex mesh and extended pipelines. Poisonous waste drawn from the system, thread like ducts at sensitive terminals matter destructive of its life, small intestine opening out, increasing flows, through great sewer and drainage canal to the open sea, buried in the land.

To gestate, carboniferous plastic oil reserves returned, with tree paper, metals of all kinds mixed alloy, the forests cleared and stripped tree floated on log river, onto rumbling lorries trundling onto sawmills and paper-production.

The river dammed below, above flooded valley lake, slung along its length and into the hidden surround beyond encircling bare hillsides, eroded mountainsides, with hydroelectric cables piloned across, and buried alongside.

Bird song chirruped and echoed from cable wire strung across poles connecting, leading between houses and buildings, from remaining tree and shrub through the distant hills. Sea to air to road and rail freight specialists, carried water, gas, oil, and information, to every home and workplace.

Every house and hospital, every business center; to every other business center. Transported everything; to everywhere.

Every piece: of: The-Earths' *riches,* to give: from its hydrogen and iron core, to its uranium mined material, every manufactured object, every word and thought, in vast numbers, to and from vast numbers, of ordinary people, literate and switched-on?

Across and through remaining fields and forest, to beyond the otherwise barren hills. Over and through every vast distance, wires linked and massive long pipes tubed, vehicles scurried and hurried, people wandered in and out of doors and shuttered entrances, to the enclosed and opened: Organic-State.

Massive works and mounds of earth and ore, churning dust, and burning. Vast insect mounds, giant chemistry sets, connected and linked together. Storage vessels, flasked mixed and sparking through, separating and combining. Concoctions of gases and liquids, smoke and steam escaped, through tall and wide conical brick and concrete and metal cooling tower chimney.

Billowed merging into cloud, drifting and falling into river and field, over rows of uniform homes that stretched out to the line of the forest. Into the earth, drilling, and drawing upward layers of dissolved and transformed waste, rock metal and minerals, organic remains, vegetated ores, sunk and submerged into the Earths core, and below the ocean, drawn up, to fire the future.

The forest now pushed so far back that trees now only existed as narrow strips and patches, between built up area and remaining countryside, littered with houses and buildings, desert and scarred wasteland. Fields lay bleak and lifeless, drains spilled into a curdling churning river, dead woods lay rotting up to the highest bare rock and melting glacial peaks.

Small figures slurred and slurried to and from fields and buildings, down industrial town streets, and amongst the traffic blocked city buildings. Sifted through piles of discarded rubbish spoil heaps, picking at rags and scraps of food, sorting junked metal and plastic-chips.

Beyond and between, brilliantly lit intervening and interconnecting routes stretched across and through and beyond the remaining landscape, clouds of sheer white and yellow sulphorous and black carboniferous smoke from chimney stacks, waste oil and toxic chemical mixtures, stained the air and ground.

Quarry and shaft abandoned and flooded, back filled with waste taken out from the houses and homes in bins and carts, ditched and run into dug piped underground flood drain and sewer, into river and sea, and buried back into the ground. A bright moon began to wax dully in an open sky beyond: The Office-Building: they stood inside.

Through *fogged* vaguely *twinkling* stars, a sinking sun shadowing aeroplane-vapour ice-particle contrail. Moving across the overarching blue and cirrus streaked sky, above and below hung with a grey pale. Flashing-shapes, like birds in soaring silent flight, light-cruisered, glided and helicoptered, fixed beneath balancing spinning-blades. Whirring in and out, from rooftop and ground, over field and taking off from marked platform, and into the sky.

Radar-traced: from rooftops, across seas separating supercontinents, over lapping tropical island and stilled frozen arctic and antarctic, from nowhere came screaming metallic jet planes.

It was not clear if they were swooping to attack, or simply passing over to roar off into the distance. Beyond terra firma, from beyond the clouds, appeared a blinding flash. Exploded across the sky, hurtling everything upwards, exploding to Earth.

Luminous, fearsome, ballistic soaring flame; across: The Hole of The-Sphere. bursting through the layer separating the breathable atmosphereric-layer from the depths of the vacuum-universe beyond, the implosion, silent at first, rocked the room, the space, the area, the EarthCentre visitors stood in.

Air licked up the sides and across the roof, and disappeared into the sky, encompassed in sheer white, funereal and shadowy, enclosed *ghostly*-veil. Blue flashes as power sub stations detonated, exploded gas mains, streets and buildings in flame, the whole scene imploded, swept-away.

A scene of bare *utter*-devastation confronted them, cratered smouldering and smelted-rock and crumbling-mountainside, sending up clouds of steam vapours and radio-active debris into the air. Pluming firestorm, the landscape returned to sand and dust, atoms, cells and spore space bound, and then the light, blinding.

Everything was shut-off instantly, and they did not know if this was part of: The-Show. anymore; or if everything had closed down, and they had simply been stopped, a total atrophy of space, and time. The point at which it had all begun, and the point at which they now stood. The whole of space and time, absorbed into one flash of light.

Each alone, with the hopelessness, and expectation, which now enshrouded them.

Nothing.

Happened.

Others in the group, other people, unseen, apparently, began to shuffle and mumble, to themselves, and each other.

There were others still existing out there. The shadows of the buildings erased, and there was a speculation as the heat intensified, that they themselves may not have survived.

Contemplating what had happened, in the collective memory and perception, in the mere time they had encountered. Of all people and places. To the moment, it seemed they, and everything else, may no longer exist.

As one we automatically, reactively, looked at the digital computer quartz, crystal vibrating bio timepieces, strapped to our wrists, pulsing, lit and we together looked around for some indication from each other, and from the blanked out sky, devoid of sun, or moon, or stars.

Needing something else singular, solid and shared, to cling onto.

No longer clear, if it were day or night, or whether a whole day, or days, or but a few hours, had passed.

Everything had changed irrevocably. Yet nothing had changed very much.

Danger pervaded every sense. Every sense intimated individual, personal, and thus total destruction.

It was as if the sun would not rise again.

Features of everything, and every relationship between everything else, absurd and seemingly irrelevant recollection, in a flash of blue, white light, brighter than any other, dust mushroom clouded, collided the building from the outside,

And then inside and along a corridor.

A feeling of completeness, in calm, overseeing the situation.

As the light absorbed everything, back to a point of rare,

and unique originality. Everything else gone. In amazement,

surprise, and relief, a gathering together. In anticipation, we could

only just see each other, touching and holding onto shadows, moving

around in the gloom, the acrid smell of burning, and an electrostatic

buzzing stillness.

Each of us could no longer sense ourselves,

except, as ourselves with others.

Nothing surrounding, in the still void, a dull thud;

again, popping, gentle crackling, buzzing sound in the plenum

ceased.

Each fading, each into silence,

each into each other, met blankness, un-lighted, and finally…

everything, but memory, then: *Nothing* at all.

*

[Saul Williams] Act III Scene 2 (Shakespeare)

This is a call out to all the youth in the ghettos, suburbs, villages, townships
To all the kids who download this song for free, by any means
To all the kids short on loot ,but high on dreams
To all the kids watching T.V. like, "Yo, I wish that was me"
And all the kids pressing rewind on Let's Get Free, I hear you
To all the people within the sound of my voice

[Hook: Zack De La Rocha] + (Saul Williams)
Spit for the hated, the reviled, the unrefined
The no ones, the nobodies, the last in line (Shakespeare!)
Spit for the hated, the reviled, the unrefined
The no ones, the nobodies, the last in line

[Saul Williams]

I didn't vote for this state of affairs

My emotional state's got me prostrate, fearing my fears

In all reality I'm under prepared

Cause I'm ready for war, but not sure if I'm ready to care

And that's why I'm under prepared

Cause I'm ready to fight, but most fights got me fighting back tears

Cause the truth is really, I'm scared

Not scared of the truth, but just scared of the length you'll go to fight it

I tried to hold my tongue, son, I tried to bite it, not trying to start a riot or incite it

Cause Brutus is an honorable man

It's just coincidence that oil men would wage war on an oil rich land

And this one goes out to my man, taking cover in the trenches with a gun in his hand

Then gets home and no one flinches when he can't feed his fam

But Brutus is an honorable man

[Hook: Zack De La Rocha] + (Saul Williams)

Spit for the hated, the reviled, the unrefined

The no ones, the nobodies, the last in line

(Shakespeare!)
Spit for the hated, the reviled, the unrefined
The no ones, the nobodies, the last in line

[Saul Williams]
If you have tears prepare to shed them now
For you share the guilt of blood spilt in accordance with
the Dow Jones
Dow drops fresh crop skull and bones
A machete in the heady: Hutu, Tutsi, Leone
An Afghani in a shanty doodle dandy yank on!
An Iraqi in Gap khaki Coca Coma come on!
Be ye bishop or pawn, in the streets or the lawn
You should know that these example could go on and
on
And what sense does it make to keep your ears to the
street?
As long as oils in the soil, truth is never concrete
So we dare to represent those with the barest of feet
Cause the laws to which we're loyal keep the soil deplete
It's our job to not let history repeat

[Hook: Zack De La Rocha] + (Saul Williams)
Spit for the hated, the reviled, the unrefined
The no ones, the nobodies, the last in line

(Shakespeare!)
Spit for the hated, the reviled, the unrefined
The no ones, the nobodies, the last in line
(Shakespeare!)
Spit for the hated, the reviled, the unrefined
The no ones, the nobodies, the last in line
(Shakespeare!)
Spit for the hated, the reviled, the unrefined
The no ones, the nobodies, the last in line

[Saul Williams]
So here's the plan
The Ides of March are always at hand
And when the power hungry strike, they strike the
poorest of man
And if you dare put up a fight, they'll come and fight for
your land
And they'll call it liberation or salvation
A call to the youth!
Your freedom ain't so free, it's just loose
But the power of your voice could redirect every truth
Shift and shape the world you want and keep your
fears in a noose
Let them dangle from a banner star spangled I'm willing
and able

To lift my dreams up out of their cradle
Nurse and nurture my ideals 'til they're much more than a fable
I can be all I can be and do much more than I'm paid to
And I won't be a slave to what authorities say do
My desire is to live within a nation on fire
Where creative passions burn and raise the stakes ever higher
Where no person is addicted to some twisted supplier
Who promotes the sort of freedom sold to the highest buyer
We demand a truth naturally at one with the land
Not a plant that photosynthesizes bombs on demand
Or a search for any weapons we let fall from our hands
I got beats and a plan
I'm gonna do what I can
And what you do, is question everything they say do
Every goal ideal or value they keep pushing on you
If they ask you to believe it question whether it's true
If they ask you to achieve, is it for them or for you?
You're the one they're asking to go carry a gun
Warfare ain't humanitarian you're scaring me, son
Why not fight to feed the homeless, jobless, fight inflation?!
Why not fight for our own health care and our

education?!

And instead, invest in that erasable lead

Cause their twisted propaganda can't erase all the dead

And the pile of corpses pyramid on top of our heads

Or nevermind, said the shotgun to the head

Also by M. Stow

Pan Tan-Gou: Paradise Won!

ArcTol

WarFair4

Walter Mepham

EarthCentre: The End of: The Universe.

Contact

M. Stow ll@ Gmail.Com

Printed in Poland
by Amazon Fulfillment
Poland Sp. z o.o., Wrocław